The Fundamentals and Practice of Marketing

JOHN WILMSHURST
M.A., F.C.A.M., A.M.B.I.M.

ADRIAN MACKAY
B.Sc.(Hons), Dip.M., M.C.I.M., M.B.A.

Fourth edition

OXFORD AMSTERDAM BOSTON LONDON NEW YORK
PARIS SAN DIEGO SAN FRANCISCO SINGAPORE SYDNEY TOKYO

Butterworth-Heinemann
An imprint of Elsevier Science
Linacre House, Jordan Hill, Oxford OX2 8DP
225 Wildwood Avenue, Woburn, MA 01801-2041

First published 1978
Reprinted 1979, 1980, 1981, 1983 (twice)
Second edition 1984
Reprinted 1985, 1986, 1987, 1988, 1989, 1991, 1992
Third edition 1995
Reprinted 1995, 1997, 1998, 1999
Fourth edition 2002

British Library Cataloguing in Publication Data
A catalogue record for this book in available from the British Library

Library of Congress Cataloguing in Publication Data
A catalogue record for this book is available from the Library of Congress

ISBN 0 7506 5449 X

Typeset by Keyword Typesetting Services, Ltd.
Printed and bound in Great Britain by MPG Books Ltd, Bodmin

The Fundamentals and Practice of Marketing

Dedication

To Jan with love, always, and to Andrew, Jenny, Graham, Duncan and Alexander

Contents

Preface

The Fundamentals and Practice of Marketing Map

This fourth edition has taken a fresh look at one of the most popular British marketing texts. It provides the student and practitioner with a route map through the subject to enhance their understanding of both the fundamentals of marketing – to build a workable plan – and the practice of communicating with and delivering to the market. The same fine components of the third edition remain but the content has been completely revised, extended, and updated. Moreover, the structure of the book has been reworked to guide the busy practitioner, enquiring student and thoughtful tutor through the text giving easy access to the whole subject of marketing in the twenty-first century.

Part 1 deals with the fundamentals of preparing to go to market. So, since marketing starts with the customer, so does the reader! Chapter 1 gives a foundation in what marketing really is from the customer viewpoint. Recognizing that tracking the changes in the market place (Chapter 2) is essential in order that the organization makes the necessary changes (Chapter 3) to provide satisfactions to the needs, wants and desires of customers, Chapter 4 focuses on the fundamentals and practice of market research. Chapters 2, 3, and 4 are brought together into a product and service plan in Chapter 5.

Having gained an understanding of the fundamentals of getting ready to market, Part 2 deals comprehensively with the practice of marketing and is divided into two sections.

Section 'A' looks at the wide gamut of marketing communication techniques. However, rather than going slipshod over a selection of activities, the reader is first given a clear and practical guide to devising communications as part of a strategic operational plan (Chapter 6) to guide the hand of the enthusiastic practitioner. Chapters 7 through 13 cover communication techniques and have been completely updated and revised from the third edition with the addition of a new chapter on e-commerce. With recent examples to illustrate the practice, there is much to engage the reader in discovering many of the *how to's* of the business of marketing communications; and rather than leave the reader with a bundle of disparate activities, the section concludes with Chapter 14 showing how to integrate marketing communications.

Section 'B' continues the practical theme and looks at the delivery to the marketplace. Chapter 15 shows the key added value to be gained through appropriate distribution activities, which leads to a review of managing a field sales team (Chapter 16) and has been updated to review modern key account management. The changing retail scene is explored in Chapter 17 while new material has been added looking at the fast developing customer relationship management (Chapter 18).

At the end of the day, marketing is about the management process responsible for identifying, anticipating, and satisfying customer requirements profitably. Therefore, this text closes (Chapter 19) with a view of the customer being satisfied both today and tomorrow.

The material in this edition is enhanced by revised questions and examples throughout and is now supported by a dedicated resource on the Internet. While many international examples are used throughout the text, practitioners and students of international marketing are directed to a further chapter on the supporting WebPages. Those students that require a few guiding thoughts on the many questions posed in the text will also find a select commentary on those pages.

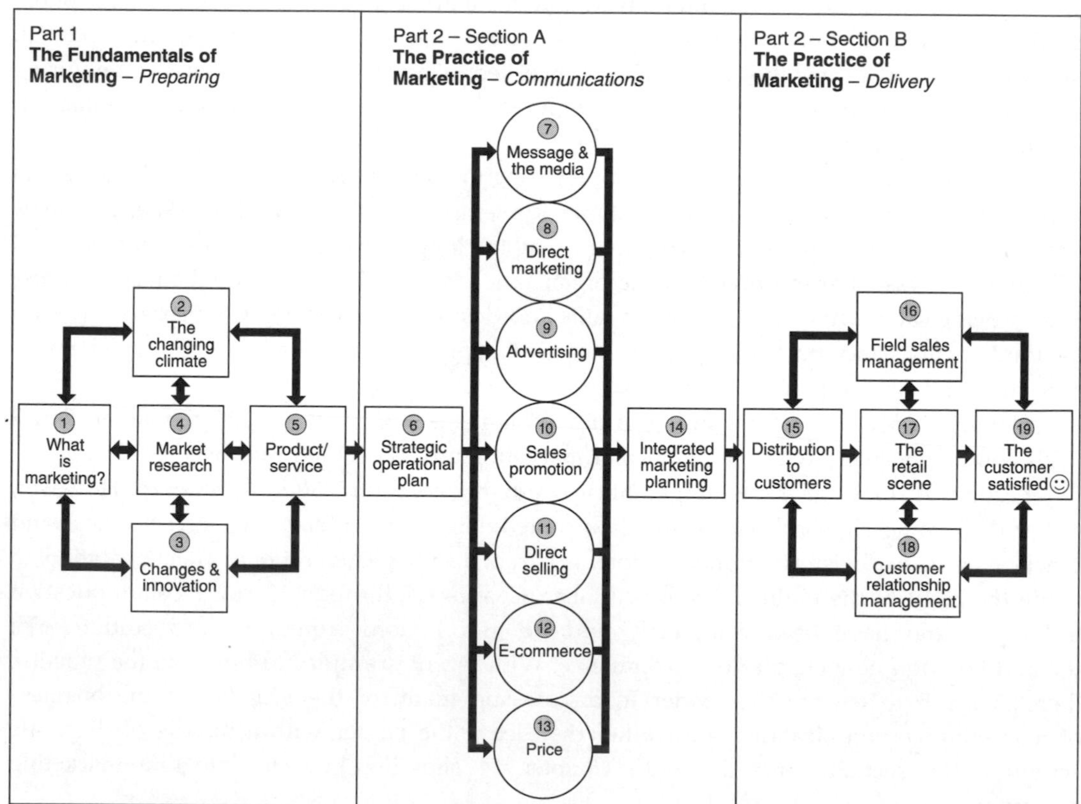

Part 1

The Fundamentals of Marketing – *Preparing*

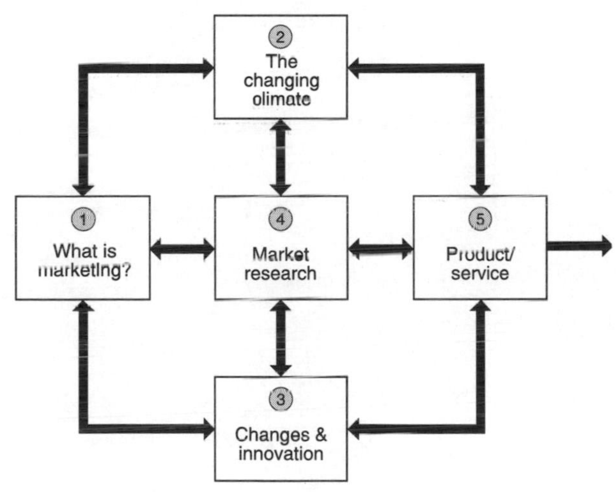

Chapter 1

What marketing is all about

Introduction

By the end of this chapter you will:

- Have reviewed the development of marketing through to the current day.
- Know the full meaning of the term 'marketing' and the reasons for its growing importance.
- Recognize that, while many organizations may not have 'customers' per se, like clubs, charities and public services, they will still benefit from adopting many of marketing's approaches and philosophies.
- Realize how widely the principles of marketing can be usefully applied.
- Be aware of some of the criticisms that have been levelled at marketing.
- Realize the need for companies to have a 'competitive differential advantage'.
- Appreciate the need for a dynamic approach to deal with constant change in the factors that affect our business.

'Marketing is the management process responsible for identifying, anticipating and satisfying customer requirements profitably.'

Chartered Institute of Marketing Definition

1.1 What Marketing Means

Before going any further, look back at the Chartered Institute of Marketing's definition of marketing at the start of this chapter. What for you is the key word in the definition?

Is it *customer*? Indeed, marketing is about customers. The whole purpose of many an organization has to do with dealing with customer requirements and making a profit.

So is it *profitably*? Certainly, one needs to profit from the interaction between customers and the organization and so much the better if both the customer and the organization are satisfied by some sort of 'profit'.

Or perhaps you feel that the key word is *satisfying*? Well, no business is going far without satisfying the needs of those with a financial stake in the business, the creditors and the employees; and these are satisfied in the long term only when customers continue to be satisfied. But how do we know what they need?

Then does *identifying* needs seem paramount? Clearly this is going to be crucial, yet so will many other organizations be aiming to identify the same needs so there may be more than just satisfying identified needs alone.

Thus *anticipating* needs suggests that, if we can do this better than our competitors, we will keep ahead. So, perhaps this is the most fundamental point. But without being able to satisfy the current need, the organization may not survive long enough to deal with those anticipated needs!

All that is left is *'management process'*. If one takes a moment to reflect, how do any of the above happen without someone making sure that they do? How can an organization identify, anticipate or satisfy any given customer requirement and make a profit without someone managing the process? Thus, the management process is the foundation for all successful marketing.

So, in the Chartered Institute of Marketing's definition, it is the *management process* that is responsible for 'identifying, anticipating and satisfying customer requirements profitably' and that enables everything else to happen. And this process is the duty of all the people in an organization whose activities make up all the stages that ultimately deliver what the customer needs. These are the marketing people to whom this book is directed.

However, the term 'marketing' is used in different ways by different people; so, to avoid talking at cross purposes, it is necessary to disentangle these differences at the outset. Commonly, there are three ways in which people use the term:

1. As a description for some part of the organization or in a person's function or job title, such as the 'marketing department' or 'marketing director'.
2. To describe certain techniques used by the organization. Such activities as advertising, market research, and sometimes sales or product development, can be conveniently described by the collective term 'marketing' to distinguish them from other activities coming under the headings 'production' or 'finance' or other similar main subdivisions of an organization. Some organizations feel that producing the brochure or launching the web page is doing the 'marketing'.
3. To indicate a particular approach to business, or a management attitude, in relation to customers and their needs. This 'business philosophy' has become known as the 'marketing concept'.

It is in this third way that the term is mainly used in this book, and the meaning and implication of the marketing concept are discussed fully later in this chapter. However, we must look briefly at the other two uses of the term in order to get them in perspective.

1.1.1 Marketing as an Organizational or Functional Term

There are fashions in management jargon as in everything else. In recent years 'marketing' has become one of the more fashionable management words. This means it is often used widely without too much attention to its true meaning. For example, many a sales or complaints department has been renamed the 'marketing department' overnight with no change in its function or attitudes. The term is often used to describe advertising and public relations activities, market research or merchandising. All this means is that it is sometimes wise to ask 'What do you understand by "marketing"?'. Are they focusing on the fundamental management processes that go on in the organization that deliver customer solutions, or are they simply classifying a certain set of techniques that are the visible manifestations or outputs of those activities?

One of the direct drawbacks of having a marketing department, or someone with that specific job title, is that they get labelled with 'doing the marketing'. This seems to absolve everyone else in the organization from any responsibility of having to worry about customers, and gives them cover if the 'marketing' should fail.

1.1.2 Marketing to Describe Certain Techniques

Many activities are particularly concerned with a company's relations with its customers – for example, market research, public relations, customer enquiries and advertising. Often these activities are grouped together under the collective term 'marketing'.

Since we all see advertising, buy products and services, or get direct mail through our letter boxes, we all 'consume' great volumes of 'marketing' and, therefore, become immediate experts. Since it appears so simple to the man (or woman) in the street, the role is often added to some poor hapless individual's task list with varying, and often poor, results.

As we shall see in the next section, marketing in its fullest sense must motivate the whole company. The managing director, production people, accountants, keyboard operators – all must be concerned with marketing. To put the marketing label on some parts of the business can be read as indicating that they and only they are concerned with marketing. This, in turn, would mean that they and only they are concerned about the customers on which the business depends. The saying *'Marketing is too important an activity to be trusted to the marketing department'* contains a great deal of truth. A fairly common solution to the problem is to label these specialist departments 'Marketing services' (see Section 1.9.1).

Be that as it may, we do commonly find within a company structure a marketing department set up something along the following lines:

> Marketing is one of the three basic areas of activity in the typical industrial business. It begins by influencing the format of the product to secure maximum acceptance in the market. It also defines the prices at which and the quantities in which the product should be offered in any given period to secure the maximum return to the business in the long term.

It normally includes:

- An evaluation of the market and estimates of sales.
- Development of the marketing approach or policy.
- The planning and operation of the marketing function overall (internal and external) for maximizing sales and for dealing with customers.
- All forms of promoting sales.
- Setting budgets for the marketing activity.
- The evaluation of results by reference to internal data and the results of market research.

This is a perfectly valid and worthwhile approach, provided it does not obscure the need for the whole company to be committed to the management process that 'identifies, anticipates and satisfies customer requirements efficiently and profitably'.

1.2 The Marketing Concept

During the 1960s there emerged what is known as the 'marketing concept'. This is how we refer to the way in which many modern businesses have come to look at the total activity of their company in a different light. William J. Stanton, Professor of Marketing at the University of Colorado, stated:

> "The marketing concept is based on two fundamental beliefs. First, all company planning, policies, and operations should be oriented toward the customer; second, profitable sales volume should be the goal of a firm."

As we can see, in its fullest sense, the marketing concept is a philosophy of business. Simply stated, it means that a customer's seeking of satisfaction becomes the economic and social justification for a company's existence. So, all company activities in production, engineering and finance, as well as in marketing, must be devoted first to determining what the customer's wants are and then to satisfying those wants while still making a reasonable profit.

A marketing executive at the General Electric Company, one of the first companies formally to recognize and implement the marketing concept, expressed the philosophy nicely when he said: 'We feel that marketing is a fundamental business philosophy. This definition recognizes marketing's functions and methods of organizational structuring as *only the implementation* of the philosophy. These things are not, in themselves, the philosophy.'

If one thinks about it, every major industry was once a growth industry. But some are very much in the shadow of decline. Others, which are thought of as seasoned growth industries, have actually stopped growing. In every case, the reason growth is threatened or has slowed or stopped is not because the market is saturated but because there has been a failure of management – at the top. The executives responsible for failure in the last analysis are those who deal with broad aims and policies.

Thus, in America particularly, the railways did not stop growing because the need for passenger and freight transportation declined. That grew. The railways are in trouble today not because others (cars, trucks, aeroplanes and even telephones) filled the need, but because the railways did not fill the need themselves. They let others take customers away because they assumed themselves to be in the railway business rather than in the transportation business. The reason they defined their industry wrong was because they were product-oriented instead of customer-oriented.

In the introduction to their article on the orientation triangle, Osing and Paliwoda wrote:

"According to a number of marketing authors, the degree to which an organization demonstrates a market orientation will determine the effectiveness with which the marketing concept is implemented by that organization, and the degree to which the results will impact on the firm's performance.[i]"

We will be looking at the measurement of marketing's effectiveness in more detail in Chapter 6.

The terms 'product-oriented' or 'product-led' and 'customer-oriented' or 'market-led' have become important in marketing and in business management generally since it is the customer who determines what a business is. Only the customers' paying for goods and services creates economic wealth. What the business thinks it does is not of first importance – especially not to the future of the business and to its success. What the customer thinks they are buying, what they consider to be of value, is decisive – it determines what a business is, what it produces and whether it will prosper. Moreover, what the customer buys and considers of value is never a product. It is always utility, that is, what a product or service *does* for them.

Peter Drucker said this of the basis of business: '. . . *its purpose is to create a customer, the business enterprise has two – and only these two – basic functions: marketing and innovation. Marketing and innovation produce results; all the rest are "costs"*'(Drucker's italics).[ii]

It is vital for every company regularly to ask the question 'what business are we in?' and to answer it in terms of what its customers buy and not in terms of what it produces.

More recently, Professor Peter Doyle has said that 'Marketing – the task of seeking to provide customers with superior value – is so central that it cannot be seen as just another function alongside production, finance or personnel. The central task of management is to find better ways of meeting the needs of customers.[iii]

VIGNETTE

The Premium Fountain Pen

Consider the premium fountain pen. What, in the mind of the buyer, is being bought? That would depend on the purchaser if it were bought for oneself. But what about the person who buys a fountain pen as a gift? Since most premium fountain pens are purchased as gifts, the competition is not a biro, a personal computer or a voice recorder. Competition is in the mind of the buyer who is buying a gift to commemorate a special event or an anniversary. For this reason, the competition is an engraved pewter tankard, a watch or a piece of jewellery. This is why premium fountain pens are to be found in good jewellers on the high street and not the office superstore alongside all the other writing implements, PCs and voice recorders. Understanding what is going on in the mind of the buyer is fundamental to understanding the key drivers in a successful marketing strategy.

Even in the 1960s there was nothing new in the idea that the entire activity of a business should be devoted to serving its customers' interests. One of the first writers on economics, and still the most famous, was the Scotsman Adam Smith. He said in 1776:

"Consumption is the sole end and purpose of all production; and the interest of the producer ought to be attended to, only so far as it may be necessary for promoting that of the consumer. The maxim is so perfectly self-evident that it would be absurd to attempt to prove it. But in the mercantile system, the interest of the consumer is almost constantly sacrificed to that of the producer; and it seems to consider production, and not consumption, as the ultimate end and object of all industry and commerce.[iv]"

So why has 'marketing' and the 'marketing concept' come into prominence only fairly recently as an important aspect of management? This is largely because the growing complexity of modern industrial nations has tended to obscure the relationship between supplier and user. Some important aspects of this relation are listed below.

1. **The chain of communication between basic producer and ultimate consumer can be very long**. The manufacturer supplies wholesalers or overseas agents who, in turn, supply retailers from whom the consumer buys. Manufacturer may never meet the consumer. The relation between Allied Bakeries or Rank Hovis McDougall's and their customers is quite different from that between the village baker of 100 years ago and his customers.
2. **The big development of the Industrial Revolution was mass production**. Many goods became available for consumption or use by ordinary people for the first time, because they could be produced in vast quantities and therefore cheaply. Production on an ever-bigger scale was often the major factor in supplying customers' needs. There was a ready market waiting for the goods that were produced.
3. **As basic needs become satisfied, people turn to more and more complex goods and services**. It is likely that this will require a more sophisticated approach from suppliers involving more investigation of customers' needs and greater communication with customers. When the car was a new wonder suddenly made available cheaply by Henry Ford's production line, turning out more cars was top priority. Henry Ford's 'you can have it any colour you like as long as it's black' has been replaced by a very wide choice for automobile users, because they do not all want the same thing. As more and more choice becomes available, as the steep increase in demand tails off or perhaps turns into a decline (as it did in the 1991 recession, and again in early 2002), then manufacturers need to consider more and more what kind of transportation their customers truly need. For example, there is

continuing research into a cheap electric car which would be quiet, non-polluting and convenient for shopping etc.

4. **As companies themselves become bigger and more complex, there is a greater tendency for objectives to become confused.** The entrepreneur running a small localized business, dealing with sales, production and finance alone, stands a much better chance of correctly divining how to turn customers' needs into profitable business. (This is not to say that the marketing concept is not applicable to small businesses, merely that it is perhaps easier for them to stay constantly aware of their customers' needs.)
5. **The need to monitor and respond to changing customer requirements on a planned basis is evermore paramount**, particularly with ever-increasing political, economic, social and technological changes.

1.2.1 The Historical Development of Marketing

Professor Philip Kotler (see Section 1.4 for reference) sees a changing emphasis in management through the decades, as follows:

1910 Emphasis on engineering.
1920 Financial restructuring, mergers etc.
1930 Accounting, 'making the books look better' throughout the depression.
1940 Production – getting more goods out faster.
1950 Sales – as production overtook demand.
1960 Marketing – to develop new products and markets.
1970 Greater emphasis on strategic planning.
1980 To ensure optimum use of resources.

From there, we have seen two further developments, namely:

1990 To treat the customer as an individual.
2000 To engineer permission to maintain the dialogue with individuals.[v]

To summarize, the marketing concept had become necessary to correct:

- The preoccupation with production as the overriding business activity.
- The communication gap that had developed between customers and their suppliers.

When you think of successful organizations, which ones come to mind? Amazon.com for their customer service, Nokia or Sony for their innovative electronics, Toyota for their reliable cars, Dell for customized PCs, Microsoft or McDonald's for their sheer ubiquity? These companies, and others that you might have named, have dominated their market segments through offering the best goods or services, or have provided you with a product or service that you think is excellent.

High-recognition firms like these are heavily marketed and constantly brought to our attention. Marketing hype alone is not enough, however, to create excellence – organizations can only be excellent with excellent operations. This is true for all organizations: those that help and protect us, such as hospitals, fire, police, ambulance and coastguard emergency services; those who provide general public services, such as schools, public utilities, transportation and universities; and those who provide goods and services to customers and other organizations. Operations are at the forefront in service delivery in every case.[vi]

1.3 Present Status of the Marketing Concept: The Difference Between Selling and Marketing

To many people, at least until recently, marketing had an important part to play in the state of the economy. A modern 'market economy' (i.e. one operated by individuals' decisions as to how they will deploy their personal spending power) depends on a high level of commercial activity to generate a high level of employment and prosperity. To quote Stanton: 'American marketing activity has the task of encouraging the consumption of the vast output of goods and services of American business and industry.'[vii]

However, as the idea that our planet's resources are finite grows, and as careful husbandry rather than ever-increasing consumption becomes for many the desirable aim, this approach could be criticized.

Some might say that mass-production industries have to produce all they can. The prospect of steeply declining unit costs as output rises is more than most companies can usually resist. The profit possibilities look spectacular. All effort focuses on production. The result is that marketing gets neglected.

However, it could be that just the opposite occurs. Output is so enormous that all effort concentrates on trying to get rid of it. Mass production does indeed generate great pressure to 'move' the product. But what usually gets emphasized is selling, not marketing. Marketing, being a more sophisticated and complex process, is ignored. The difference between marketing and selling is more than semantic. Selling focuses on the needs of the seller; marketing on the needs of the buyer. Selling is preoccupied with the seller's need to convert his product into cash; marketing with the idea of satisfying the needs of the customer by means of the product and the whole cluster of things associated with creating, delivering and finally consuming it.

In some industries the lure of full mass production has been so powerful that, for many years, top management in effect told the sales departments: 'You get rid of it; we'll worry about profits.' By contrast, a truly marketing-oriented firm tries to create value-satisfying goods and services that consumers will want to buy.

Many of the criticisms aimed supposedly at marketing are really meant for some of the excesses of hard selling – shifting the goods on to the consumer at all costs.

It is difficult to see how much criticism could be attached to marketing's aim of establishing customers' needs and setting out to satisfy them. However, there are still some criticisms. Consider the following:

- The 'limited resources' argument, that suggests that it will not prove possible in the long run to satisfy everyone's needs. There is increasing doubt whether the whole world can ever live at the average level of present-day American families.
- However well conducted most of it is, some marketing activity is bound to misfire and attract justified criticism. It is important to disentangle such situations from criticism of marketing as a whole.

- Since marketing is concerned with satisfying customers' needs, there will always be concern over to what extent it is right or desirable that those needs should be satisfied. One man's necessity is another's totally undesirable luxury. A legitimate aim for one person seems a perversion of human existence to another (e.g. hard drugs).

Add to this the fact that (in the quotation at the head of the chapter) marketing is concerned with anticipating customer requirements. This is bound to lead on occasions to the charge that marketing creates needs and in the process causes people to buy things they could be perfectly happy without. During the 1970s and 1980s vociferous minorities emerged in strong support of consuming less rather than more. The whole concept of constant large-scale development (see Chapter 2) is questioned:

- **On ethical grounds** – For example, Shell's decision to dump the Brent Spar oil platform at sea once it had no further use for it sparked Europe-wide boycotts of Shell products.
- **On environmental grounds** – For example, McDonald's has switched from styrofoam packaging for its fast-food products to paper containers, substantially reducing the amount of non-recyclable waste.

Since the 1980s there has been a growing emphasis on 'market-led' economies throughout the world and a decrease in the role of governments in providing goods and services. The outstanding example was the collapse of the old Union of Socialist Soviet Republics and the switch of Russia and the other constituent states to more market-led economies.

This being the case, it seems undoubtedly best that businesses should devise their policies and carry them out with the customers' needs, not the needs of the businesses, as their central concern. Indeed, any business that does not follow this course is likely to be unsuccessful in the long run, if not in the short term, since, ultimately, it is the customer who decides whether to buy or not to buy.

It is this crucial role of the customer, the buyer, the consumer, which is the essence of the marketing concept. While our present economic system prevails, any business ignores consumer needs at its peril.

In our present economic system, for most businesses – even many of those in the public sector – profit is the measure of their success. For those in the private sector, profit is indeed essential for long-term survival. Since profit comes only from winning sufficient revenue at a sufficient margin over costs, profit ultimately depends on support from customers. Thus, the whole future success and even continuation of the business depends on offering customers what they want at prices they will pay. This is the essence of the reasons why the marketing concept is so vital to a business. Increasingly, in the 1980s, it began to be recognized that even publicly-funded services cannot be sustained unless the investment in them produces worthwhile returns, i.e. they too have to be 'profitable' in a sense, or show 'best value'.

The British government's privatization programme and insistence on the importance of market forces was one political response to this recognition. So, by the 1992 election, all the main political parties in the UK were giving some degree of importance to market forces.

1.4 Social Marketing and the Concept of Value: A Wider View of Marketing

It is becoming increasingly recognized that the marketing concept is just as applicable in non-commercial situations, where profit (at least in the strict sense – but see above) is not one of the objectives, as in commercial situations. The term 'social marketing' is often used in this context. Government departments, the police, trade unions and trade associations, environmental groups and churches can all be said, in a sense, to have 'customers' and to be offering products and services.

However, all of these types of organization have a problem to some degree with the term 'customer'. Nonetheless, there are always individuals involved with such organizations and who have some interest in the 'output' of what they are doing and will interact with the organization to a varying degree. Since such 'customers' have a stake in what is going on, the term **stakeholder** has been used to help understand how the organization may add value to the transactional relationship for the other party.

While any organization that is legal has a right to exist, no organization has a right to the support that is required if it is to exist. Therefore, don't be skilful in making a customer suit the interest of the business ... be skilful in making the business do what suits the interests of the customer and convincing the customer of this. From this philosophy will come the concept of 'customer advocacy' – that is, the support the organization needs to prosper.

Philip Kotler, a Montgomery Ward Professor of Marketing at the Graduate School of Management, North Western University, Evanston, Illinois, has examined the wider view of marketing in depth. From it he has developed a broader concept of marketing than one that deals only with profit-making commercial organizations. The central theme of his argument runs as follows.

He asks what the disciplinary focus of marketing is. He suggests that the core concept of marketing is the transaction defined as 'the exchange of values between two parties'. The things of value need not be limited to goods, services and money: they include other resources such as time, energy and feelings. Transactions occur not only between buyers and sellers, and organizations and their customers, but also between any two parties. A transaction takes place, for example, when a person decides to watch a television programme; she is exchanging her time for entertainment. A transaction takes place when a person votes for a particular candidate; he is exchanging his time and support for expectations of better government. A transaction takes place when a person gives money to a charity; she is exchanging money for a good conscience. Marketing is specifically concerned with how transactions are created, stimulated, facilitated and valued. Kotler, therefore, has the transaction as the generic concept of marketing.

Kotler goes on to suggest that marketing is an approach to producing desired responses in another party that lies midway between coercion on the one hand and brainwashing on the other.

Therefore, we can see that the core concern of marketing is that of producing desired responses in free individuals by the careful creation and offering of values. The marketer is attempting to get value from the market through offering value to it. The problem for the marketer is to create attractive values. However, value is completely subjective and exists in the eyes of the beholding customer. Marketers must understand the market in order to be effective in creating value. This is a basic premise of the marketing concept.

Kotler suggested that marketers seek to create value in four ways: **configuration** – design the social object more attractively; **valuation** – put attractive terms on the social object; **symbolization** – add symbolic significance to the social object; and **facilitation** – make it easier for the market to obtain the social object. Marketers may use these activities in reverse if they want the social object to be avoided (as in the case of hard drugs). These four activities have a rough correspondence to more conventional statements of marketing purpose, such as the use of product, price, promotion and place to stimulate exchange (see Chapter 5).

1.4.1 Added Value

This brings us back to the commercial profit-making world again, where it is common to talk of 'added value'. Porter's (1985)[viii] value chain model, as shown in Figure 1.1, is a useful means of tracking the flow of movement from inputs to outputs. In explaining the model, Porter states that:

> "Value is the amount buyers are willing to pay for what an organization provides them ... creating value for buyers that exceeds the cost of doing so is the goal of any generic strategy. Value, instead of cost, must be used in analysing competitive position."

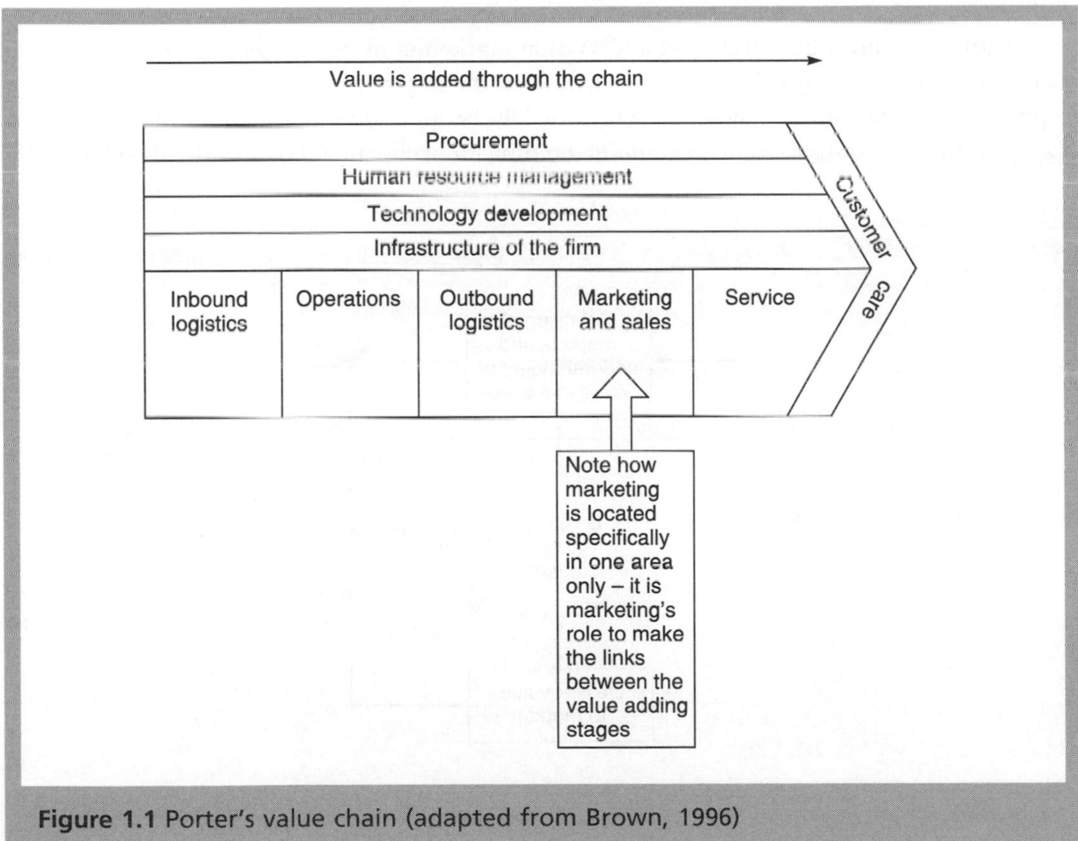

Figure 1.1 Porter's value chain (adapted from Brown, 1996)

1.4.2 A Map of Marketing

Malcolm McDonald and Dr Hugh Wilson of Cranfield School of Management suggested that a map is needed to help managers understand what kind of marketing tasks need to be supported by what kind of IT applications.[ix] They provided their own definition of marketing and suggested that, wherever the function of marketing is located in the organization, and no matter what it is called, it will be ineffective unless the whole company is market-driven from senior management downwards.

They suggested that marketing is a process for:

- Defining markets.
- Quantifying the value required by the different customer groups (segments) within these markets.
- Communicating this value to everyone in the organization responsible for delivering it.
- Communicating this value to customers and consumers.
- Measuring the value actually delivered.

They went on to say that 'marketing is not responsible for delivering customer value. This is the responsibility of everyone in the organization, but particularly those who come into contact with customers'.

Figure 1.2 shows the McDonald and Wilson marketing map. The process is cyclical, in as much as monitoring the value delivered will keep the organization informed about the value required by its customers. The cycle will probably be an annual one, with a marketing plan documenting the output from the 'understanding of value in market' and 'develop value

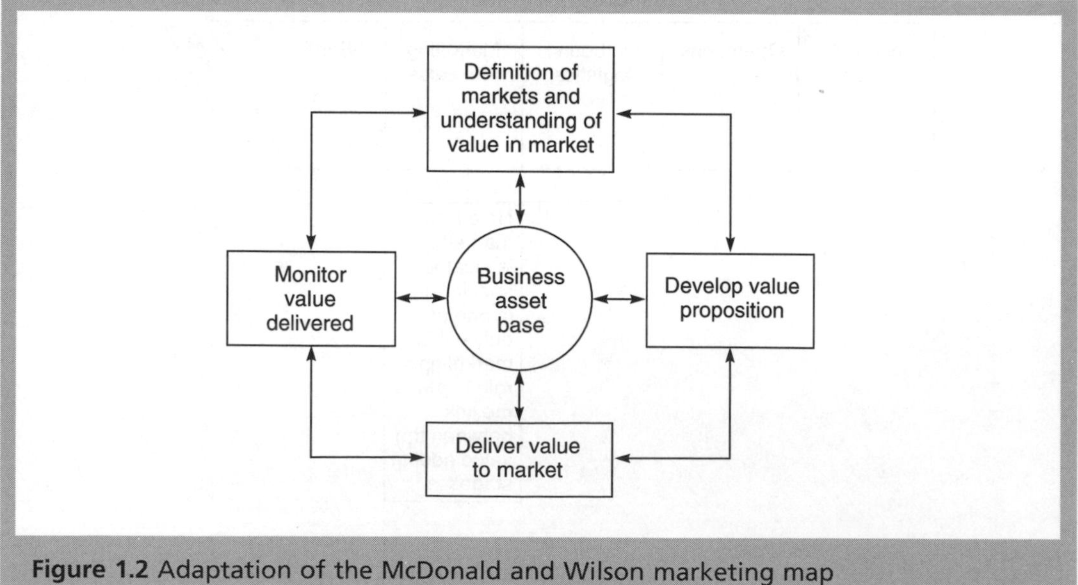

Figure 1.2 Adaptation of the McDonald and Wilson marketing map

proposition' processes. However, changes throughout the year may involve fast iterations around the cycle to respond to particular opportunities or problems.

The term 'develop value proposition' refers to the process of deciding what the offer to the customer will be – what value the customer will receive at what cost. 'Deliver value to the market' obviously refers to the process of delivering this value.

Not all of the sub-processes will be under the control of the marketing department, although it is likely to be responsible for the first two processes, i.e. 'understanding of value in market' and 'develop value proposition'. The whole company will be involved in the 'deliver value to market' process.

While marketing needs to make the links with the other value-added parts of the organization, Brown *et al.*[x] argue that operations management needs to be linked with customer requirements. They suggest that the aims of operations management include supporting the business in the marketplace, and enabling the organization to compete successfully against other players. In order to achieve this, they make the case for operations managers to be closely allied to marketing: 'By so doing, operations can help to shape future sales of existing markets and also determine the viability of entering new markets.'

Value can be added, for example, in the following ways:

- By converting raw materials into components or finished goods (e.g. steelmaking, car manufacture).
- By breaking bulk, packing or processing products (e.g. wholesaling, takeaway meals).
- By transporting goods from one place to another (e.g. importing tropical fruits).
- By making goods available at a more convenient time (e.g. canned or frozen foods).

1.5 Customers and Their Behaviour

Since the customer is the focal point of all business activity, we must be clear about how customers behave. Because marketing is concerned with satisfying people's needs, we must understand what those needs are and the ways in which people go about getting them satisfied.

Any individual has a whole range of needs that they must or would like to satisfy, from the purely physical necessity of food and drink, through the emotional wish to be loved and appreciated, to the desire to develop their personality – through education, a leisure activity or a fulfilling occupation. An American psychologist, A. L. Maslow, has expressed these varying levels of need in a way that is still useful today in the marketing context. He has written of the 'hierarchy of needs', with the following five-stage progression:[xi]

1. Basic physiological needs (food, sleep, warmth).
2. Safety needs (protection from danger).
3. The need for recognition (love, belonging).
4. Ego needs (self-esteem, respect from others).
5. Self-fulfilment (realization of one's total being, creativity).

It is clear that, as we progress through these stages, we are dealing first with needs that all people at all times have to some extent or other and have to satisfy in order to live. At the other end of the scale we have needs that few will ever satisfy, mainly because the majority of people are preoccupied with the more pressing needs at the lower levels. On the other hand, once a pressing need is satisfied, it is no longer felt. This is why people with sufficient income to keep them well fed, safe and warm become more and more aware of other, less basic, needs such as ego satisfaction. 'Keeping up with the Joneses' may or may not be laudable but it does become a strong need for many people once they are fed, housed and clothed to a reasonable level.

Thus, individuals will vary widely in the needs that at present preoccupy them. Some will be mainly concerned with acquiring the bare necessities (you will fail to interest them in fancy furnishings), whereas others will be seeking exciting leisure pursuits (no good talking to them about buying their first television – they already have four).

We also need to be aware of how people satisfy their needs. There is a multi-stage process, which can be expressed as follows:

1. **Need**. A need is felt. This may be a vague or general need (I am feeling jaded and need a bit of excitement) or specific (I want to go to the cinema today).
2. **Search**. Ways of satisfying the need are actively or passively sought. The newspapers and magazines may be scanned for offers that may satisfy the need (e.g. the lists of 'What's on' in entertainment); or I may merely keep my eyes and ears open and register more keenly than usual any possible solutions to my need.

In more complex situations the search process may be long and deliberate. The family seeking new kitchen equipment will read magazines, talk to friends, go to showrooms and exhibitions. The industrial buyer may ask for samples, demonstrations and competitive tenders, or carry out extensive cost-benefit analysis.

3. **Decision**. When sufficient information has been gathered and suitable alternatives examined, a decision will be taken and the purchase made.
4. **Post-purchase feelings**. For the customer-oriented company the process does not end when the purchase is made. The customer's need is only satisfied if the product or service does perform in the expected fashion and does indeed meet their need not only initially but, where appropriate, over a longer period. It must perform in the expected way, and after-sales service must be adequate.

The precise way in which this process works needs to be understood. It will vary from one group of consumers to another, in particular in its time-scale: for a snack bought to satisfy a sudden pang of hunger the whole process may be over in a few minutes, but for a power station or a new military aircraft it will take many years. The domestic appliance industry in the UK wasted vast sums on advertising at one stage because it did not clearly appreciate that only when people are in the 'search' stage will they be receptive to advertising of this kind of product. (See Sections 2.1–2.3 for further discussion of these aspects.)

Remember, while any organization that is legal has a right to exist, no organization has a right to the support that is required if it is to exist.

1.6 The Competitive Situation

Marketing is not carried out in a vacuum but usually in a highly competitive situation. Classical economics talks of the state of perfect competition, where the following conditions apply:

1. Many suppliers, none of whom dominates the market.
2. Many purchasers, again unable individually to exert pressure on suppliers.
3. One supplier's product or service is no different from another's.
4. There is free entry to the market.
5. There is 'perfect knowledge', i.e. everyone knows what is being offered and at what price.

In this situation the outcome is that prices and profits are pushed down to the minimum, since new suppliers will be attracted to the industry if prices rise, and the extra amount available over what is demanded by customers will force the price down. On the other hand, if prices fall too low, some suppliers will leave the industry, and the drop in quantity will make prices rise. So there is an 'equilibrium price', which anyone trading in the market has to take; firms are 'price-takers'.

This is, of course, the real-life situation in some specialized markets – commodities, fresh farm produce, the Stock Exchange. But, typically, this simple model does not fit the facts of the real world – as economists have realized in developing the concept of 'imperfect competition'.

One of the main factors in imperfect competition is that all products are not the same. Indeed, since firms generally do not wish to be price-takers, with no control over their level of profit and, hence, whether or not they can stay in business. They will do all they can to develop ways in which they can satisfy customers' needs in a better way than their competitors can.

This has given rise to the concept of 'competitive differential advantage'. Firms will try to outdo their competitors by offering customers a clear-cut difference in the products and/or services they offer, in the hope, naturally, that customers will find the difference an improvement on what competitors are offering. The difference may be created in a number of areas, as follows:

- **Product**. The product or service itself may be different. The soup may have a richer flavour or take less time to prepare; the car may have better performance or use less fuel.
- **Cost**. There may be a cost advantage to the customer, because the initial price is lower, because maintenance will cost less, because better credit terms are available.
- **Services**. As well as the basic performance the product or service gives, there can be a whole range of services offered as part of the marketing process, including:

  Pre-sale. A civil engineering company may do a free feasibility study; a television rental firm may offer a week's free trial; a car dealer a test run.

  Post-sale. Free maintenance for a period; training of operators; a supply of 'updating' material (Encyclopaedia Britannica, for example).
- **Distribution**. The sheer availability of a product may be a very attractive feature. Car hire firms will have desks to deal with customers at the station or airport; Coca Cola is available in lean-to shops in African bush villages as well as in big city centres.

- **Promotion**. The way a product is presented may enhance its appeal to the consumer. Perfume attractively packaged and exotically advertised; bakery products with an 'olde world' presentation ('like those mother made').

One of the reasons why the idea of the marketing mix is so important (see Chapter 5) is that from the elements of the mix we can develop a strong competitive differential advantage to offer to our customers. (See Section 5.3 for further development of this theme.)

Michael E. Porter[xii] in *Competitive Advantage* asserts: 'The fundamental basis of above average performance in the long term is *sustainable competitive advantage*.' This can come from a cost focus (enabling a company to offer customers unbeatable low price) or a differentiation focus (offering customers significantly different satisfactions or benefits). The differentiation can be designed to suit a wide or narrow range of customers, e.g. it may be directed at a particular segment or niche (see Figure 1.3).

The key question to ask is what are you trying to do? There can only be one cost leader – the one with the lowest costs, which usually means the one with the largest volume share. You may be operating in a niche but the question to ask is not is there a niche in the market, but is there a market in the niche? Finally, if your focus is one of being different with some form of extra added value and this is giving you a competitive advantage – is it sustainable over the long term?

So, it becomes important to analyse just who really are our competitors, both direct and indirect. For instance, a supplier of compact disc players will have as direct competitors other suppliers of similar machines. However, potential buyers of such machines include all people who want to listen to music. They have a wide range of choices. Not only can they get their music from tape players but also from compact disc players or radios. Music can also be downloaded from the Internet, and even DVDs (digital versatile discs) are potential competitors. Alternatively, potential customers can attend live concerts or even make their own music with a group of friends. All of these are indirect competitors for our compact disc player supplier. Then, if one were to look at the market in broader terms than just music listening,

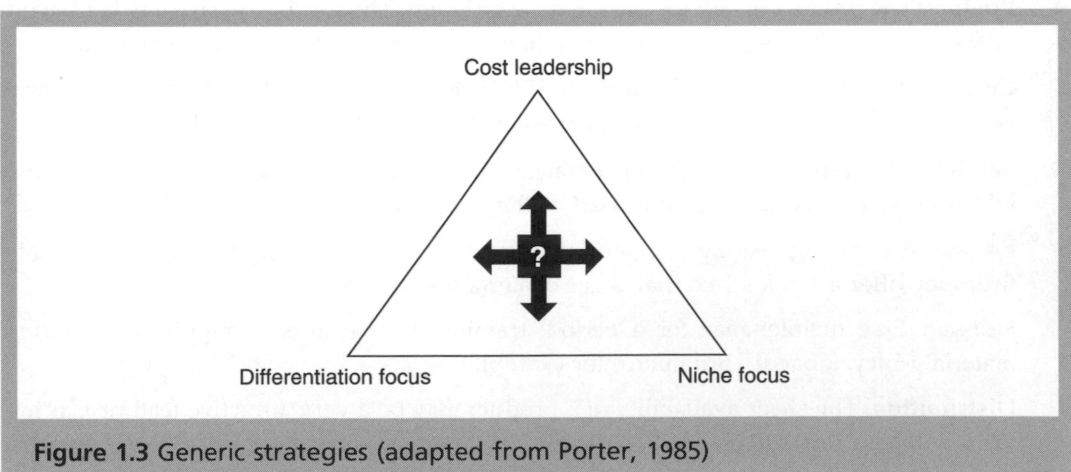

Figure 1.3 Generic strategies (adapted from Porter, 1985)

and extend it to 'leisure in the home', the TV, video player and home computer all compete for the attention of the customer.

Often the most important question is – who are our potential customers most likely to spend their money with if not with us?

1.6.1 Porter's Five Forces of Competition

Another valuable way of looking at the market is to evaluate the profitability of the industry or sector. This will depend on where the competition is coming from. The best-known model is that of Michael E. Porter that shows that the profitability of the average firm in an industry depends on five factors – the forces of competition. While this model may have been developed as far back as 1980, it is a valuable analytical tool as, although the forces may differ over time, the model remains sound. According to the model, the state of competition in an industry depends on five basic forces (see Figure 1.4):

1. **Competition between existing firms** – intense competition reduces profitability. Competitive intensity tends to be high if there are a large number of competitors, if the market is stable or declining, if the fixed costs are high, and where competitive products are perceived as very similar.
2. **Threat of new entrants** – if it is easy for a new competitor to enter the industry, profits will be depressed. Barriers to entry that keep profits high include high capital investment, patents, economies of scale, restricted distribution channels or brand loyalty.
3. **Threat of substitute products** – an industry's effectiveness is less if the product is easily substituted by alternative technology or the technology of other industries.

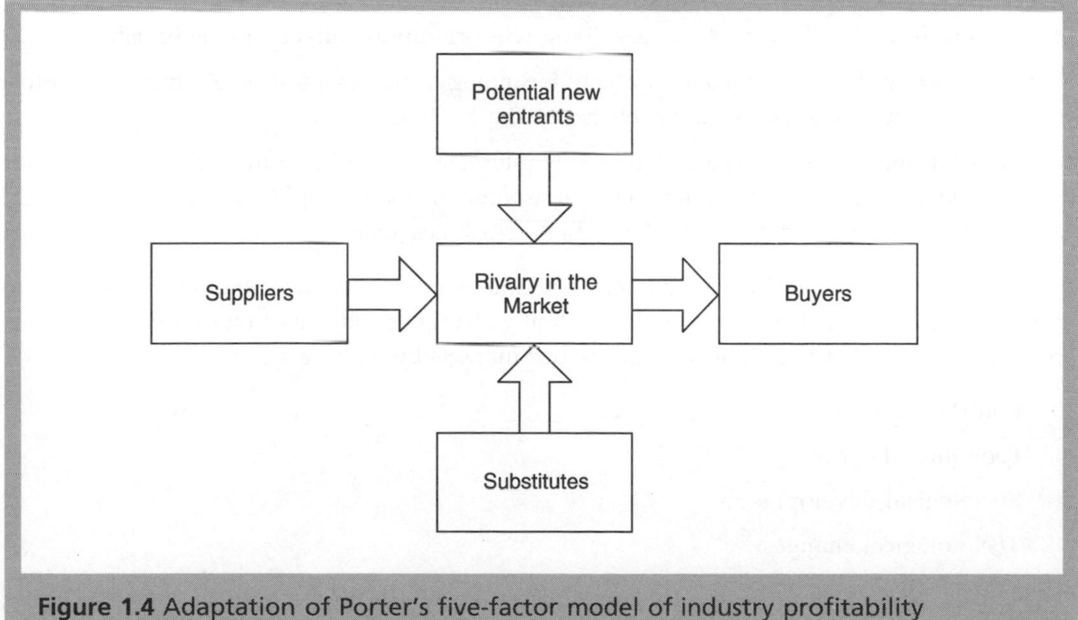

Figure 1.4 Adaptation of Porter's five-factor model of industry profitability

4. **Strength of buyers** – if buyers are strong, they will have bargaining power to squeeze the profits of producers.
5. **Strength of suppliers** – if raw material suppliers, utilities or trade unions are strong, they can depress the profits to be earned in the industry.

The Porter model shows what determines the average profits in an industry. The company's ability to obtain profits above this level depends on it building a sustainable competitive advantage.

Whatever its collective strength, the goal of an organization is to find a position in the market where it can defend itself from the forces that influence it. Knowledge of the underlying forces of competition provides the groundwork for strategic action.

1.7 A Dynamic Activity

A firm with a marketing policy (and all firms have one, whether they recognize it or not) is dealing all the time with a whole series of variables. Among them are the following:

- **The general economic situation**. Boom or recession, growth or stagnation, a developed or an underdeveloped economy – all will have a profound effect on what is possible and on how marketing can operate. For example, the UK foot-and-mouth outbreak in 2001 followed by the atrocities in New York on 11th September the same year had a severe adverse effect on the British hotel industry. The number of UK holidaymakers and American visitors dropped and businesses cut back on travel costs.
- **Customer needs**. The social climate will affect the needs customers feel to be important, as will the level of development of a society.
- **Competition**. What competitors are doing will profoundly affect what is possible.
- **Technology**. The introduction of a new technology, such as plastics, electronics or information technology, will completely change the existing situation.
- **Legislation**. Governments are increasingly intervening in the operation of the marketplace and hence changing the commercial environment. For example, changes to Legal Aid practices in 2001 had a profound effect on British law firms.

These and other factors change all the time, both independently of each other and in reaction to each other. The external environment is constantly changing and the acronym PEST is used as an analytical tool that highlights changes in our markets by looking at:

- Political decisions
- Economic changes
- Sociological developments
- Technological changes.

Collectively, these factors have a kaleidoscopic effect, which means that the total marketing environment is constantly changing. Companies must be aware of these changes and react to them. Going on doing as we have always done must lead sooner or later to a situation where we apply yesterday's answers to today's problems, and disaster must follow. This will be explored further in Chapter 2.

Because marketing is concerned with what people will do tomorrow, it is always subject to risk and uncertainty. (Risk means that we know that certain actions may have a number of different outcomes, and we have to calculate the odds in favour of the outcome we desire; there are other areas where we just do not know – that is uncertainty.) There can never be total knowledge about the future; we can, however, make sure that we do know what the present situation is and where events appear to be leading. Information is a precious commodity in all business activity, and nowhere more so than in marketing.

The factors listed above are often referred to as the non-controllable variables – those that companies and individuals cannot control but have to build into their marketing planning. The marketing mix (see Section 5.3) contains the controllable variables that can be changed to provide us with the appropriate response.

1.8 The Marketing Process

We can view marketing as a constant series of actions and reactions between the customers and the marketing organizations trying to satisfy their needs. The customers make their needs and/or problems known and the firms make it their business to receive the information. The firms use their resources (money, materials, skills and ingenuity) to develop ways of satisfying the needs. Firms must then communicate the existence of the 'solutions' back to the customers whose needs created the 'problems' (see Figure 1.5). Customers will gladly pay for solutions to their problems or satisfaction of their needs.

The remainder of the first section of this book is devoted to examining this fundamental process in more detail. Chapter 2 takes a more complete look at the changing external climate of marketing, while the third chapter looks at internal drivers of marketing change – technological

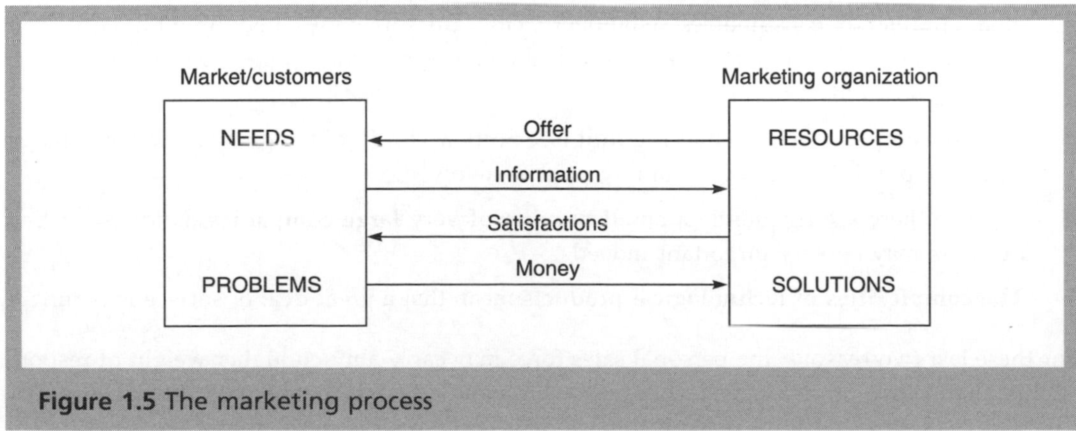

Figure 1.5 The marketing process

innovations. These two forces come together in Chapter 4 as we review the fundamentals of market research – the process that tracks the customers' or stakeholders' needs. We bring these pieces together to form a product and service 'mix' in Chapter 5 and make the case for a strategic operational plan before moving on to the second section of the book.

1.9 Special Marketing Situations

There is a natural tendency for people to see their own particular industry, market or type of operation as being quite different from every other. Thus seminars are held and books written on, for example, the marketing of financial services (banking, insurance etc.), on knowledge businesses like accounting or law, or on industrial marketing. Clearly the type of customers one is dealing with and the nature of the needs they are trying to satisfy or the problems to which they seek solutions have a strong influence on the way organizations respond. This book, however, supports the approach of most serious marketing thinkers – there is no fundamental difference in the marketing process. The same analysis has to be done, the same questions asked. The marketing answer will be different, but there are few if any clear lines along which these differences split. Marketing pop records to teenagers is different from marketing pharmaceuticals to doctors. Banks, however, may find themselves offering their services to students using techniques very similar to those used to promote clothes or electronic equipment to the same market.

If there is a clear distinction it is probably between purchases made for personal satisfaction (which we may refer to as consumer purchases) and purchases made on behalf of an organization (loosely called industrial or business-to-business marketing) (see the following section).

1.9.1 Industrial Marketing (Business-to-Business Marketing)

There are some differences here, which are mainly concerned with:

- A rather **more rational, deliberative and scientific approach**. This should not be exaggerated. 'Industrial consumables' (stationery etc.) are sometimes bought with very little thought; expensive consumer purchases (cars, houses etc.) may sometimes be approached very scientifically.
- **A more complex decision-making unit** (see Section 11.5.1), although again in some major domestic purchases the whole family may be involved.
- Because there are frequently **a small number of very large companies**, holding existing business may be very important indeed.
- **The complexities of technological products** mean that a great deal of service is required.

For these last two reasons, the personal sales force may carry a much higher weight of responsibility than other promotional techniques such as advertising in the promotional mix (see Chapter 9). Figure 1.6 shows the key characteristics of industrial marketing.

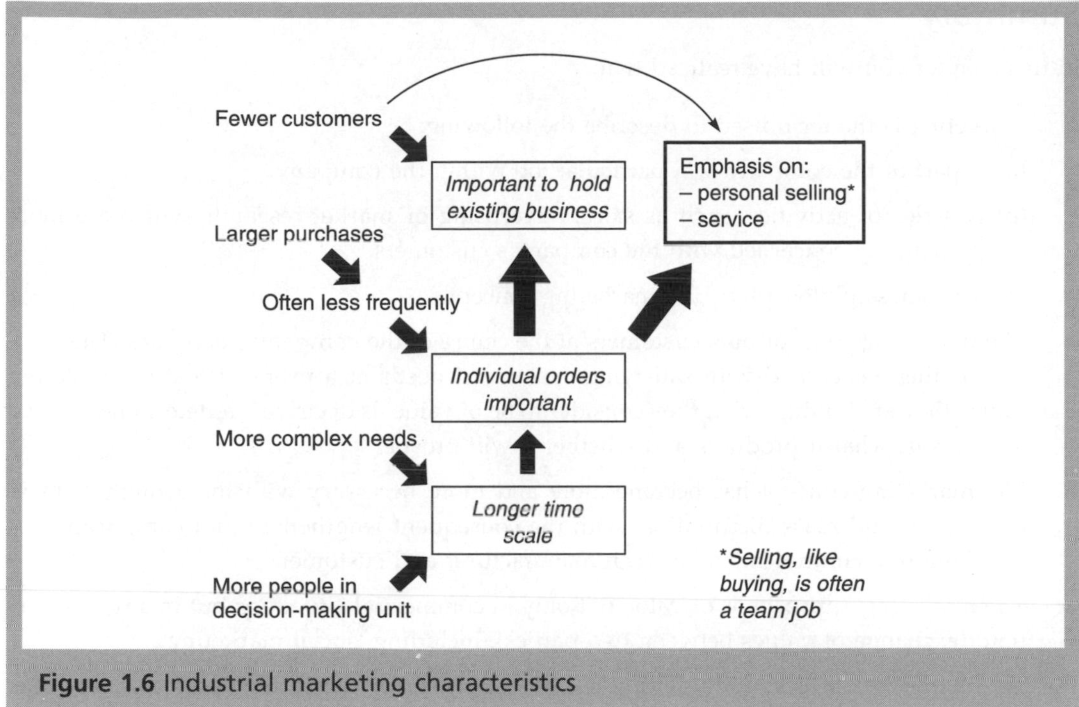

Figure 1.6 Industrial marketing characteristics

1.9.2 Marketing Services

Great play is often made of the difference between goods (tangible products) and services (intangible products). This distinction has limited value when it comes to marketing considerations, since what customers buy in any case is the 'satisfactions' delivered by either a tangible or an intangible product (see Section 3.2).

There are, however, particular pressures associated with the marketing of particular kinds of intangibles. Some of these are as follows:

- **Perishability.** Electric generating capacity not used today cannot be sold tomorrow, for example, and an empty airline seat or hotel room represents revenue and profit lost forever. A common response to this problem is differential pricing, such as off-peak fares or 'bargain breaks' in hotels (see Section 13.7).
- **Heterogeneity.** It can be difficult to ensure a standard product of uniform quality when it depends on the skill and consistency of individuals, e.g. hairdressers, waiters and football teams. What customers get for their money may depend on how a particular individual performs on a particular occasion. Training and performance monitoring by management have important roles to play.
- **Intangibility** itself makes it difficult in some instances (e.g. insurance, medical care) for would-be customers to test the quality of the product in advance, so techniques such as free trial and testimonials from satisfied users may assume great importance. It is also more than usually important to communicate benefits strongly.

Summary

In this chapter you will have realized that:

- Marketing is the term used to describe the following:
  (a) A part of the company or a particular job within the company.
  (b) A series of activities, such as sales, advertising or market research, which are more particularly concerned with the company's customers.
  (c) A business philosophy – the marketing concept.
- The marketing concept puts customers at the centre of the company's activities. The business is then concerned with satisfying customers' needs at a profit. 'What the customer thinks they are buying, what they consider to be of value, is decisive – it determines what a business is, what it produces and whether it will prosper.'
- The marketing concept has become more and more necessary with the growth of mass production and mass distribution, with the consequent lengthening and complication of the chain of communication between manufacturer and customer.
- The marketing approach is of value not only in commercial situations but in any 'transaction' (exchange of values between two parties), including 'social marketing'.
- The marketing process starts with a customer's need, for which they seek a satisfaction. The search leads ultimately to a decision – but the marketer is also concerned with the customer's post-purchase feelings as to whether their need has been adequately met.
- The marketing process operates in conditions of imperfect competition, and a key aspect of it is the identification of the competitive differential advantage.
- Marketing is a dynamic activity, which must constantly respond to changes in a whole series of variables, including legislative changes, the economic situation, customers' needs, competition and the development of technology.
- Marketing is best viewed as a process in which companies deliver solutions to customers' problems (hence satisfaction of customers' needs) in return for payment.

References

i In *The Orientation Triangle* by Byron Osing and Stanley J. Paliwoda. *Marketing Business,* April 2001.
ii In *Management: Tasks, Responsibilities, Practices* (Peter Drucker).
iii In *Marketing Management and Strategy* (Prentice-Hall, 1994).
iv *Wealth of Nations* (1776).
v Godin, Seth. *Permission Marketing* (Simon & Schuster, 1999).
vi After Brown, S. *et al. Operations Management* (Butterworth-Heinemann, 2001).
vii From Stanton, M. *Fundamentals of Marketing* (McGraw-Hill, 3rd Edition, 1971).
viii Porter, M. *Competitive Strategy* (New York: Free Press, 1985).
ix In *Marketing Business,* March 2001, p. 50.

x ibid.
xi Maslow, A. *Motivation and Personality* (Harper & Row, 1954).
xii Porter, M. *Competitive Advantage* (Macmillan, 1985).

Further Reading

Baker, Michael, J. *The Marketing Book* (Butterworth-Heinemann, 5th Edition, 2002). The many contributors set the scope and nature of the marketing function.

Donaldson, Peter. *Economics of the Real World* (Pelican, 1973). This originally accompanied a series of programmes on BBC TV. Without jargon, it is a good layman's introduction to economics.

Drucker, Peter. *Managing for Results* (Butterworth-Heinemann, 1994). Marketing in relation to business management is dealt with superbly in Chapter 6: 'The Customer is the Business'.

McDonald, Malcolm and Wilson, Hugh. *The New Marketing* (Butterworth-Heinemann, 2002). Built around the concept of value exchange with customers.

Doyle, Peter. *Value-based Marketing* (2000). Covers the principles of value creation and developing, implementing and organizing value management.

Questions

1. Charles Revson is quoted as saying 'In the factory we make cosmetics. In the drug store we sell hope'. Explain what this statement means.
2. How is the marketing concept relevant in the following situations? In each case discuss what would be the 'product', who the 'customer' is, what form distribution would take and how 'promotion' would be carried out.
   (a) An 'AIDS awareness' programme by the government of an underdeveloped country.
   (b) The Blood Transfusion Service.
   (c) A new inexpensive method of developing renewable energy for the home.
3. How would you define the 'value added' by the following?
   (a) The London Underground.
   (b) Your local college of further education.
   (c) A shopping precinct or covered shopping centre.
   (d) An online music store.
4. What customer needs are satisfied by the following?
   (a) The Royal Opera House, Covent Garden.
   (b) Chinese takeaway restaurants.
   (c) Marketing textbooks.
   (d) The BBC WebPages.
   (e) Laptop computers.

Chapter 2

The changing climate of marketing

Introduction

By the end of this chapter you will:

- Appreciate the rapidly changing nature of the marketplace.
- Have gained a perspective on the influences on consumers that affect their buying patterns.
- Have a grasp of the many and complex issues that impact any marketing situation.
- Be aware of the growing importance of 'consumer issues' such as health, environmental and 'Green' concerns, as well as increasing insistence on value for money.

'Indeed, the tendency to drift into set patterns or formulas, avoiding the painful necessity for original thought, has betrayed what should be a fundamental element in the marketing attitude – the flexibility to adjust rapidly to changes in a constantly monitored environment.'

Colin McIver. *Back to Marketing*

2.1 The Complex Life of the Consumer

In Chapter 1 we saw how the object of marketing is to satisfy consumer needs, and that those needs consist not merely of purely physiological urges (to eat, sleep and be warm), but include other needs such as to be loved and respected, to feel secure and not threatened, and to develop one's personality to the fullest extent possible. We took the existence of these needs for granted and went on to discuss the means by which they are satisfied.

We shall now examine briefly some of the factors that shape these needs and give emphasis to one desire or another. Only by understanding these mechanisms can marketing ultimately be more than a mixture of carefully measured trial and error ('if we sold the goods they must have been what the customers wanted').

At present the mechanisms are not wholly understood. The science of social studies (also called behavioural studies) carries out many research programmes, and the results of these investigations are gradually becoming available. They are still fragmentary, not always easy to relate to the marketing situation and too complex to do more than touch on here. But students of marketing should be aware of a pattern of knowledge that is beginning to take shape.

Figure 2.1 shows some of the many influences that go to shape a person's needs and responses. The material in Section 1.5 is part of this picture.

There are a number of 'models' of the way buyer behaviour operates. The simplest is the 'economic model', related to the perfect competition theory outlined in Chapter 1. It takes the view that people act in a purely rational way to optimize the satisfactions gained from their expenditure, bearing in mind cost on the one hand and value on the other. This is probably true

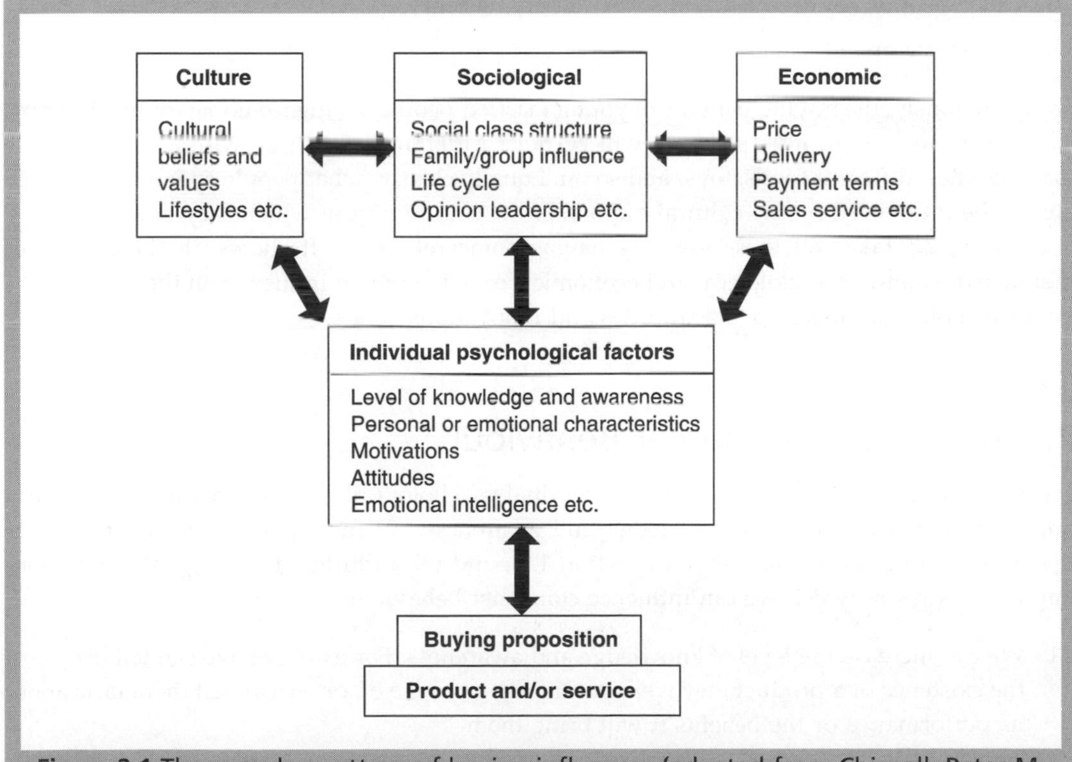

Figure 2.1 The complex pattern of buying influences (adapted from Chisnall, Peter M. *Marketing – A Behavioural Analysis*, McGraw-Hill, 1975)

to some extent of industrial purchases (although how far it is true even there is disputed). But it is largely discounted by most marketing experts in the consumer field, especially for low-cost everyday purchases.

Much more favoured is the 'social-psychological model', which takes the view that human beings are social animals much influenced by the groups to which they belong – their family, workmates, social class etc. Friends, neighbours and other acquaintances, particularly those we would like to emulate and to whose lifestyle we aspire, are our 'reference groups' and have considerable influence on our behaviour. ('Keeping up with the Joneses' is one everyday expression of this approach, 'peer group pressure' another.)

It is known that some individuals set the pattern within their own circle of acquaintances. They are the 'opinion leaders', the trend-setters – the first to have a home sauna, a video camera or a mobile telephone (see Innovations in Chapter 3).

Several researchers have drawn attention to a difference in purchasing behaviour as people move through their life cycle. This is defined variously, but often by the following stages:

1. Single.
2. Young married or cohabiting couples with no children.
3. People with young children.
4. Couples or single parents with older children.
5. Older people, children left home (the 'empty nesters').
6. Sole survivors.

Fairly obviously, the buying patterns of young married people setting up home for the first time (carpets, furniture, records, pictures) will be quite different from those with a young family (baby clothes, different foods, toys) and so on. Equally clearly, what people spend their money on will be influenced by the cultural outlook of the community in which they live.

Figure 2.1 takes all these ideas as having some relevance. It shows all the influences mentioned – cultural, sociological and economic – each having an influence on the individual's own psychological make-up, his attitudes and motivations.

2.2 Influencing Consumer Behaviour

Listed in Figure 2.1, under the heading 'Individual psychological factors', are three particularly important items: (1) level of knowledge and awareness; (2) motivations (which are closely related to the needs we discussed in Section 1.5); and (3) attitudes. This suggests three very important ways in which we can influence consumer behaviour:

1. We can increase the level of knowledge and awareness. For example, we can tell people of the existence of a product they were previously unaware of, or we can tell them facts about its performance or the benefits it will bring them.
2. We can show people how our product will help to satisfy their needs. This is the basis of the 'emotional appeals' used in advertising.

3. We can change their attitudes. The view taken of mobile phones in the early 1980s was that most people saw them as unnecessary or even a rather expensive extravagance or gimmick. By 2001, they were largely taken for granted with an average of 60% penetration in Europe.[i]

To **change attitudes** can be a very desirable objective, sometimes in a positive, sometimes in a negative, way. Examples of changing attitudes in a negative way are the government campaigns against smoking, drug taking and 'drinking and driving'. Marketing will more often be concerned with positive change in order to win acceptance of a new idea or a new way of doing things.

Attitudes can be changed by the following means:

- Reasoned argument leading the audience to judge the suggested conclusion as 'true' or 'false' (a recent example is the use of accident statistics to attempt to change people's attitude to Gatso speed camera placement to control traffic speeds).
- Positive emotional appeals (e.g. 'Stop smoking and you will feel fitter and food will taste better').
- Negative emotional appeals (e.g. 'Don't stop smoking and your lungs may end up looking like this').

It is important to make it easy for people to **identify with products and services**. This means that brands must have a clear identity (or 'personality') that is a function of all forms of promotion as well as of the product itself (its name, packaging etc.) or, if it were a community service, all forms of promotion and livery etc. The identity of the product or service can be considered to have three parts:

- The presence of the brand (the extent to which it can be easily remembered).
- The individuality of the brand (the extent to which it is seen to have different or unique characteristics and properties).
- The nature of its identity (the kinds of values that people have about it).

All this means that what matters is not merely what people know about a product or service but how they feel about it and how they are able to relate it to their own personalities and lifestyles. This is likely to be just as much a function of the right side of the brain (creative/intuitive) as the left (rational/logical) and often more so. This will be explored more in Chapter 9.

2.3 The Changing Social and Economic Climate

A failing of many marketing textbooks and a weakness in the make-up of many marketing practitioners is that they assume that things will go on in the same way. That is because society as a whole tends to take that view. But in recent years there has been a spate of books and articles talking about the rate of change and pointing out that marketing is dealing with a dynamic, not a static, situation.

Randall Tobias, former Vice Chairman of AT&T, offers this comparison to explain the astounding rate of advancement of technological change: 'Computer power is now 8000 times less expensive than it was 30 years ago.'[ii] And likewise, John Naisbitt, CEO of Global Paradox, makes this comparison: 'If we had similar progress in automotive technology, today you could buy a Lexus for about $2. It would travel at the speed of sound and go about 600 miles on a thimble of gas.'[iii]

Many marketing people have drawn attention to 'the increasing tempo of business' and 'the speed of technological change'. They often rightly point out the increasing speed of change. But the assumption usually is that the 'direction' of change will be broadly the same. As long ago as the late 1960s, authors like Alvin Toffler[iv] and Herman Kahn[v] highlighted the problems of moving ever more rapidly in the same direction. In fact, the very warnings they were uttering suggest the strong possibility of a change of direction. Indeed, 'The Limits to Growth', a summary of the famous Club of Rome study of the earth's resources, pointed out the absolute necessity of a change of direction, or at any rate a reduction in speed of change if we are to continue in the same direction. Growing populations and diminishing resources make continuing at the same speed on the present course impossible to sustain, in their judgement. Since publication of the Club of Rome report, its warnings have been at least partially averted by the reactions it provoked. There has been increasing pressure to control use of the 'finite resources of the globe'. The increasing cost of some of these resources, owing to rising demand, has of course also contributed.

As recently as November 2001, the latest round of World Trade Organization (WTO) talks in Qatar's capital, Doha, ended with little commitment to environmental concerns, bar an agreement to phase out agriculture export subsidies and plans for further discussions.

The 142 members of the WTO ended almost six days of talks in Doha with little visible success on furthering an environmentally friendly trade agenda. The European Union and United Nations had been driving for such an agreement, and they only achieved a commitment to 'reductions of, with a view to phasing out, all forms of export subsidies and substantial reductions in trade-distorting domestic support'. They also had an agreement to a mini-trade round in 2003 to include new negotiations on industrial tariffs and the environment. The failure to integrate sustainable development into all WTO agreements frustrated the European Commission and environmental groups.[vi]

Earlier prophecies drew attention to the widening gap between the wealthy industrialized countries and the underdeveloped 'Third World'. OPEC (the oil-producing countries' cartel) showed that the balance can be quickly changed. Two of the fastest-growing countries in the world in recent times, each with considerable natural resources, have been Iran and Brazil – both classified as Third World (underdeveloped) countries, at least until recently. Yet as long ago as 1975, Brazil was Volkswagen's largest market outside Germany and then said to be the only profitable one.

More recently, many of these Third World countries (the term is becoming less popular and an alternative 'The South' – as opposed to the rich countries of 'The North' – is in wide use) have run into severe financial difficulties because of their huge foreign debts. Throughout 1983 crisis threatened the international banking systems that had provided the money and could no longer expect the anticipated rate of repayment. Over the next decade there were huge write-offs of these 'bad debts' by the leading banks and the threatened crisis was, though painfully, averted.

A small group of senior central bankers from the emerging markets met at the BIS (Bank for International Settlements) in December 1999 to discuss the management of foreign debt and liquidity. Recent crises have revealed major shortcomings in these policies and the dangers of excessive foreign debt, particularly short-term debt. Two days of discussion highlighted the various issues confronting policy makers.

The issues discussed included the idea of 'national liquidity', the question of how much government debt should be issued domestically and how much externally, the development of domestic bond markets and the relationship between government debt management and reserve management. They also examined possible policies towards the management of the private sector's external debt. Such policies include prudential rules for banks, capital controls, disclosure requirements and regulations on corporate borrowing.

At the same time 'The North' is experiencing huge unemployment due to economic cut-backs and structural change as industry and commerce uses more microcomputers and robots. Moreover, high employment industries such as shipbuilding are moving to countries like South Korea that not so long ago might have been regarded as part of the Third World.

The 'island economies' of Hong Kong and Singapore were other examples of economic success among countries of the Third World or 'The South'. However, in these early days of the new millennium they face an uncertain future. (The future of Hong Kong still remains uncertain while the hand-over of control from the UK to the Chinese People's Republic settles down.)

Certainly, marketing is all about change. But change does not just mean more or less of the same, or even stops and starts heading in the same general direction. Some of the changes can be very surprising. For example, who can be sure what will be the main form of short-distance transportation twenty years from now? The events of 11th September 2001 in New York have changed forever our futures but no one quite knows how.

We saw in the previous section that the prevailing culture and social climate have a big influence on people's needs and on their purchasing decisions. So does the economic situation. If there is social change, we must watch out for totally different marketing opportunities.

VIGNETTE

Electronic Relationship Management (e-CRM)

The exponential expansion of the Web has led to more and more homes coming online (over 8 million by the end of 2001) and an ever-growing proportion of business-to-business operations and customers emerging. The sheer noise of developments is drowning out the reality of less-than-ideal performance and rising customer dissatisfaction with a number of companies' e-commerce operations.

Technology has been and is driving the development of e-commerce, making online purchasing and communications available to more of us and in more everyday, everywhere situations. Digital TV, for example, will introduce online shopping to millions more people (especially housewives/husbands) as a result of being accessible via familiar technology (such as remote controls) and in familiar and friendly surroundings (the TV in the living room). Equally, the m-commerce market (purchases via the mobile phone) is set to be worth US$200 million by 2004, according to a study by Strategy Analytics. Exponential growth indeed.

In the rush of digital dementia, the business of getting online and building traffic flows is subsuming a basic fact: that e-business, more than any other business method, lives and breathes because customers prefer to use it and are satisfied by the performance of companies using it. Make no mistake, in e-business the customer is king, and poor online service and bad experience will be met by a simple click of farewell. The competition is but a click away. In no other business channel is the customer more central to a company's success or failure than in e-business. As Kevin Marshall, MD of BMW (GB) said in a recent issue of *Management Today*, 'Any business that does not recognise that it is owned by its customers will simply disappear . . .', while Jeff Bezos, founder of Amazon.com comments, 'it is our customers who tell us what we want to do next' (he had 13 million of them at the last count).

Companies who decide to adopt e-commerce should take careful note of these views, or face the inevitable consequence of customer dissatisfaction and alienation. The travel industry is an example of a category for which e-commerce is perfect, with 45 per cent of Internet homes surfing for travel research. But, if the visitor gets a 'sorry, that one's gone now' message, which may appear quite reasonable for the occasional retail travel agent shopper, it may totally destroy the trust of the daily Web visitor. Online share dealing has become very popular, as e-commerce suits the customer well. However, the eTrade UK Internet share-dealing service discovered this to its cost when the surge in private investor dealing overpowered its ability to cope.

However, every player needs to have a fallback system to capture interested customers and prospects, and retrieve the situation.

It is important to remember that for businesses, the real value of going online is the creation of more revenues, the reduction of costs, and the development of greater profitability. In classic direct marketing terms, it is about increasing customer lifetime values (the value to the business over the time that a customer stays with the business) from a given number of key customers. Hence, the successful customer-centric e-business will, as with its traditional *alter ego*, be dependent on the relevance of the position (unique differential), process (protocol and systems) and people (know-how, enthusiasm, energy), coupled with customer value management and process quality management. Collectively, this is electronic relationship management (e-CRM).[vii]

Questions

1. It has been said that mobile phone users spend more time looking at their phone rather than listening or speaking to it. What implications will this have for both the mobile phone manufacturers and for the networks?
2. With the development of more and more one-to-one interactive media, what might be the effect on the socialising skills of the next generation?

2.4 The Changing Attitude of Consumers

Another kind of change marketing has had to contend with is the growing awareness of consumers' rights and increasing unwillingness by consumers to accept what they regard as a poor deal. The title of Robin Wight's book, *The Day the Pigs Refused To Be Driven To Market*, aptly expressed the situation. In the press, and on radio and TV, many articles and programmes give space and time to consumers' complaints and to attacks on poor goods and unsatisfactory marketing practices.

This seems strange when, for many years, the marketing concept has been accepted as an important principle by a large number of manufacturers and retailers in this country. Changing organization structures, in-company training and management education programmes witness a serious intent to carry this concept through into practice. Yet, more than ever before, there is this vociferous and growing consumer protest movement, usually referred to as consumerism.

If marketing was all that it claimed to be, why do we need consumerism now?

There is, of course, nothing new about movements and legislation to protect the interests of consumers. The first Weights and Measures Act in the UK dates from 1878 and the Sales of Goods Act from 1893. Philip Kotler[viii] recognizes in the USA three distinct consumer movements over the last hundred years or so – the early 1900s, the mid-1930s and the mid-1960s – each leading to the strengthening of government controls over the buyer/seller relation.

As early as 1962, President John F. Kennedy identified the four 'rights of the consumer':

1. The right to safety.
2. The right to be informed.
3. The right to choose.
4. The right to be heard.

The current wave of consumerism has thus been rising up for many years now. Earlier waves tended to be responses to particular, limited situations and subsided when these were dealt with. The present one is much more widely based, shows no sign of abating and has largely triumphed with a whole flood of government legislation to its credit.

In all the EU countries, in Scandinavia, Australia and many other nations, there are strong consumer movements and legislation to protect the consumer. In Japan, women's organizations with memberships totalling several millions have produced price-shattering boycotts of colour TV sets and cosmetics. In many countries all round the world the consumer movement and the legislative reaction to it is well established. Even in the Soviet Union there are consumer clubs that try to improve the quality of production.

In Great Britain there is the Government-sponsored Office of Fair Trading as well as many privately based groups that speak for the consumer. Each of the main local government areas offers consumer advice to its public free of charge.

The present consumer movement is thus stronger, more widespread and longer-lasting than similar previous manifestations. The reasons for this are many and include the following:

- Rising incomes, standards of living and education, with a consequent greater concern for quality of life.
- The increasing complexity of technology and marketing, putting the buyer more and more at a disadvantage in relation to the seller.
- The stresses and strains developing in the economic/political system – the population explosion, inflation, pollution and loss of faith in political institutions.

- The 'impersonality' arising from the increasing size of companies and institutions, coupled with automation and computerization.
- The influence of writers such as Galbraith, Packard and Rachel Carson, with political leaders ready to seize upon the points raised.

2.5 Consumerism and the Marketing Response

For whatever reason, consumerism seems here to stay, and is a force that marketing people must reckon with. How does marketing respond to consumerist attitudes?

On the face of it, it should reinforce consumerism rather than conflict with it since the essence of the marketing concept is to generate customer satisfaction. However, the term 'customer satisfaction' is ambiguous. It has been suggested that most businessmen take it to mean that consumer desires should be the orienting focus of product and market planning. However, in efficiently serving customers' desires, it is possible to hurt their interests in the long run. Here are four examples of this situation, all of relevance today:

1. Large expensive cars satisfy their owners' immediate desires, but pollution, congestion and parking problems reduce their long-term satisfaction.
2. The US food industry produces new products with high taste appeal but low nutritional value.
3. Packaging provides short-term convenience but causes its users long-term problems of pollution and wasteful use of resources.
4. Cigarettes and alcohol are classic products which obviously satisfy consumers but which ultimately hurt them if consumed in excessive amounts.

So, while consumers buy as consumers they increasingly express their discontent as voters. The public use the political system to correct the abuses that they cannot resist through the economic system. The problem is to somehow reconcile company profit, consumer desires and consumer long-term interests.

The understandable automatic reaction of businessmen to the consumer movement is to condemn it – many businessmen feel that they have been serving the consumer extraordinarily well. To many in the US, consumerism looked like a threat to their businesses. Many consumer demands create additional costs, impinge upon the freedom of business operations and push business in the direction of uniform standards and sameness.

If this was the typical American reaction, British businessmen felt much the same. The average business sees itself as satisfying its customers' needs in the best way it can at reasonable cost. The criticism by Which? and the Automobile Association of car-servicing standards is a case in point. The reaction of many members of the trade was that they were being subjected to a quite unfair attack.

Now that consumerism has largely made its point, industry finds itself under attack from many other 'lobbies' (Greenpeace, Third World protagonists and conservationists, to name but three). There is still the danger that industry's response will be entirely negative. Yet all of the new threats also present new opportunities (just as the resistance to 'unhealthy' processed foods has given rise to a whole series of new markets for high fibre and low fat dietary foods). Any signals from customers as to what they do and do not want must be eagerly listened to by marketing people.

In the UK, Lever Brothers provide an example of a manufacturer taking considerable pains to maintain continuing dialogue with representative consumer organizations and political spokesmen on sensitive issues such as unit pricing. Any communications from individual customers or from consumer organizations gain immediate attention, and are systematically analysed to determine what response is necessary – not merely as a defence mechanism but as a means of anticipating and reacting to changing attitudes in the marketplace.

One could take a dim view of consumerism. At first a growing number of pleasant conveniences for housewives in the 1950s, then a car for everyone with the gradual erosion of public transport. Then the ubiquitousness of 'things' and chemical products technologically unimaginable a few decades earlier. Then the growing availability of consumer credit and debt, the over-dependence on labour-saving devices, total dependence on the car and absolute necessity of full-time work. This leads to the two-income household to pay for more and more, then the importation of cheaper and cheaper goods and the disappearance of manufacturing jobs, and now the decline of service work with professionals next to be downsized ... where will it end? When America looks like some faded Third World fragment of the old British Empire, an overpopulated wasteland of pollution, eroded landscapes and hungry people digging into landfills for salvageables?

We shouldn't let this or anything like this happen. Things may be starting to turn around in our favour. But it takes work and time and attention to detail and a willingness to try new things for our own and our children's benefit. There are serious changes ahead. We can control some of these for our benefit or we can just react to them after they have happened.

Simply stated, there's a lot of money being made and a lot of power being gathered by the people that promote consumerism. You pay for it in gradually limited economic mobility, pollution, threats to your health and a declining standard of living, as measured by the things that really matter.

VIGNETTE

Consumerism

The dominant message found in all the corporate ads is BUY, BUY and BUY. The collective impact of this message has had its effects over the past fifty years of intimately linking our most basic needs to consumer items and channelling all our energies into the marketplace.

Henry Ford, who introduced the Model T in 1909, probably would have died of a stroke if he had looked into a crystal ball and seen the May 1973 issue of Playboy, which featured a pictorial on sex and the automobile. In the photospread we see a woman, apparently in ecstasy, stroking a steering wheel. Even if the first car on the road did more than just revolutionize transportation, Playboy shows us that in our modern world people driving their 'babies' don't always need human beings to love.

The aphorisms, verses, lecture and fables of the great apostles of individualism continuously blasted the early American. Benjamin Franklin, for example, spent much of his life talking about his rise from obscurity to affluence.

Perhaps more than anyone else, Horatio Alger is responsible for the American rags to riches saga. In his 135 books, he always portrayed his hero as someone who achieved success through his diligence, honesty, perseverance and thrift. If you worked hard and saved your money, you succeeded.

Despite the ideology of the self-made man, the end of the nineteenth century and the early years of the twentieth were increasingly difficult times for American culture. The growing American corporations appeared to be slowly changing the criteria for personal success. Henry Ford was able to maintain a commanding lead over his competitors by simply offering his customers the assurance that his cars would get them to their destination and back. After the basic mechanical features of the automobile became more reliable and production problems were overcome, the consumer needed an innovative jab. In 1927, when General Motors introduced the LaSalle, the first 'styled' car, Ford lost his number one position. Henry wanted back in and came out with his restyled Model A. We all know what has happened since.

Vance Packard was not the first to attack the Great Success Story. When *The Hidden Persuaders* was published in 1957, however, public attention was more aroused than ever. Packard heavily documented his argument that two-thirds of America's largest advertisers had geared their campaigns to a depth approach, using strategies inspired by what was called motivation analysis. Consumers were seen as bundles of daydreams with hidden yearnings, guilt complexes and irrational emotional blockages. Using research techniques that were designed to reach the subconscious mind, it was hoped that advertising would mass-produce customers for the corporations just as the corporations mass-produced products.

According to sociologist C. Wright Mills, people in the 1950s were increasingly told by carefully designed mass media formulas who they were, what they should be and how they could succeed. People were becoming increasingly lonely and simultaneously mimicking media happiness.

There is hardly a family that is not under the constant, everyday pressure of 'what the house needs next'. If it is not a new TV it is a new dishwasher; if not this, then new rugs or curtains. For many couples who are estranged but will not face up to it, all of this consumerism and household planning often serves the function that a child does – it keeps the couple 'together'. That is, it fosters the illusion that they are on an adventure together, pooling their wits and energies to reach a common goal. Many couples feel compelled to show they have made it together by what they have accumulated. When the debts begin piling up, and economic strain becomes a constant feature of the relationship, rather than cut back on the good life, the husband, as mentioned before, begins to work more or, as is a growing necessity these days, the wife begins to work. The cycle is apt to grow more vicious if, rather than admit that their way of life is the source of the problem, the wife – who is forced to work to help pay the bills – identifies with ideologies to justify her activity, and adds to the problem by getting farther and farther away from its root.

The Western World, as we have heavily illustrated throughout this book, has almost wholly accepted the illusion of material progress as a guarantor of happiness. The common denominator of materialism is an uncritical acceptance of the glittering competitive and success-oriented consumer life as the only reality. The corporations, their advertising, and the mass media have skilfully created consumer illusions, as our everyday cultural world has built a screen in the human mind, shielding us from our possibilities as a species. Our well-conditioned interests in and overwhelming concern with the world of material objects and gadgetry leads us to depend on technical solutions to all our problems ... [ix]

Questions

1. Justify whether you agree or disagree with the opinions drawn from this adapted article.
2. The consumption of certain products (for example alcohol and nicotine) is known to carry some health risks. Discuss whether or not a government's advertising campaigns against misuse of such products is justifiable in a free society.

2.6 The Green Issue

Throughout the 1980s and beyond (with its origins much earlier) there has been increasing public concern for the long-term viability of our planet. These concerns were focused through political parties, especially in Germany, where the Green Party had considerable political success for a short time. (Unfortunately, in Germany and elsewhere, the parties were supported by people of widely ranging views and attitudes and found it difficult in the long run to focus their ideas into a sustainable programme that would command continuing support. In the meantime, the established parties had 'climbed on the bandwagon' by incorporating many of the 'Green' ideas into their own programmes.)

Some of the issues involved were the decimating of several animal species (especially whales) to provide food and the rapid reduction of the earth's forests (especially in Amazonia).

Some marketing organizations also saw opportunities linked to the Green issue. Products such as tissues were offered as made from recycled paper. Some cars now feature the fact that an increasing proportion of their components can be recycled for further use.

At one stage the glass industry in the UK was under severe attack for curtailing the established practice of buying back 'empties' for re-use. One response to the criticism was the introduction of 'bottle banks' where users could take their bottles to be recycled.

Some of these commercial responses are perhaps largely cosmetic, e.g. 'recycled' paper ignores the fact that the trees used for paper manufacture are harvested and replanted anyway, while the re-use of newsprint calls for toxic bleaches to remove the ink.

For further information visit the Green Party Statement of Core Principles on the Internet at: http://www.greenparty.org.uk.

2.7 Social Responsibility and Business Ethics

For many centuries legal judgements between buyer and seller were largely made on the basis of the dictum *caveat emptor* – 'let the buyer beware'. The consumerist movement and the resulting legislation have changed this to the point where many businessmen ruefully feel it is now a question of 'let the seller beware'. However, the matter goes much further than the question of buying and selling.

Businesses are now increasingly expected to exercise 'social responsibility' in all their actions. For example, some of the sports shoe manufacturers came under fierce criticism for employing cheap labour from Asia. Quite apart from any legal requirements, it is no longer acceptable for a business to be carried on in a way that pollutes the environment or causes excessive noise – things that a few years ago would have been regarded as 'necessary evils'.

This all means that far-sighted companies are themselves attempting to assess the social implications of any contemplated action well in advance of decisions being taken. Since marketing people are likely to be involved in such decisions, they too are bound to be drawn into social responsibility discussions.

Along with the growing consumerism pressures and the blossoming of social responsibility, there is also an increasing interest in codes of practice and ethics. It is more and more realized that to be recognized as responsible professionals, managers must subscribe to and adhere to clear-cut standards.

Our Commitment

London Underground aims to deliver the best possible service for all its customers. You want a quick, frequent and reliable train service, a safe, clean and welcoming station environment with up-to-date information and helpful, courteous staff. This means a continuous, demanding programme of improvements to meet rising expectations.

Our Targets

To drive and measure these improvements, performance targets covering many aspects of our service have been agreed with Government as part of the Citizen's Charter programme. If you would like to know more, please contact our Customer Service Centre, which is open between 0830 and 1730 Mondays to Fridays, on 020-7918 4040. We regularly publish our performance against targets. Train service performance information is posted at every station and details of other targets are available from the ticket office.

Our Refund Pledge

If you are delayed more than 15 minutes because of our failure, we will give you a refund voucher to the value of the delayed journey. Please claim by filling in this form. We cannot give refunds in circumstances that prevent us from safely running trains such as a security alert, freak weather or because of action by a third party; nor when we have publicised in advance an alternative route, for example because of planned engineering works. Special conditions apply if we have an industrial dispute. Extra claim forms are available from any station or the Customer Service Centre.

Your Feedback

If you have any complaints or suggestions on how we can improve our service, please contact your local manager. The address and telephone number are displayed in the ticket hall.

Figure 2.2 London Underground Charter – taken from their passenger leaflet

Thus the Chartered Institute of Marketing has prepared a code of practice for managers, as have the Institute of Management, the Market Research Society and the Institute of Public Relations. While the majority of people accept that most of these codes are at present too broad and unspecific in terms to be wholly satisfactory, they are a beginning and a public statement that the principle is accepted.

The Chartered Institute of Marketing Code of Professional Standards can be found at: http://www.cim.co.uk/cim/index.cfm.

2.8 The Charter Initiative

John Major, at the head of a newly elected Conservative Government in the UK in 1992 announced his intention of providing 'Citizen's Charters'. All Government-funded providers of services were required to fall in line. Figure 2.2 is an example of such a charter from London Underground and published in 2001.

Summary

- Buying behaviour is the outcome of a number of complex factors – economic, cultural, sociological and psychological.
- The most valuable study from a marketing point of view is that of the social-psychological area.
- To influence consumer behaviour, one may have to: (a) increase customers' knowledge, (b) show how needs can be met and (c) change customers' attitudes.
- Attitudes can be changed by (a) reasoned argument and (b) positive or negative emotional appeals.
- The social and economic climate is liable to change, not merely in speed but in a discontinuous way, and marketing people must be alive to the opportunities this presents.
- A particular kind of change is represented by the following:
  (a) The growing strength of consumerism.
  (b) Insistence on the need for social responsibility in business.
  (c) The establishment by professions and quasi-professions of their own ethical standards and codes of practice.
- The pressures of consumerism are giving rise to codes of practice.

References

i AdStats, from World Advertising Research Centre, *AdMap*, Issue 418, June 2001.
ii From *New Work Habits for a Radically Changing World* (Price Pritchett, 1994).
iii Also from *New Work Habits for a Radically Changing World* (Price Pritchett, 1994).
iv Toffler, A. *Future Shock* (Bodley Head, 1970).

v Kahn, H. *The Year 2000* (Macmillan, 1967).
vi See http://edie.net November 2001 – the site of the Environmental Data Interactive Exchange.
vii Based on an article in the journal *Admap*, Issue 405, April 2000, p. 46.
viii In a paper in the Harvard Business Review (May/June 1972).
ix Adapted from Altchuler, R. and Regush, N. *Open Reality: The Way Out Of Mimicking Happiness* (Pitman Publishing Group 2001).

Further Reading

No one book covers the subject matter of this chapter adequately, but any of those mentioned in the References is good on particular aspects.

The Limits to Growth (Pan, 1974). The one all students should have some familiarity with, in view of its challenge to the belief that things must necessarily go on the way they are.

Atkins, S. *Cause Related Marketing* (Butterworth-Heinemann, 1999). Making the case for cause-related marketing, it's an essential read for people involved in fund-raising and charities and looks at the mutual benefits for business and society.

Questions

1. Identify two current advertisements that seem to you to contain inadequate or misleading information. Say why you think this and what changes you would want to see made.
2. To what extent does the marketing concept take into account the potential conflict between consumer wants, consumer interests and long-term societal welfare?
3. During the past decade there has been a number of changes in the pattern of distribution of goods and services to the consumer. Identify two major changes that have taken place and state what you consider to have been the causes.
4. Discuss some of the main factors that give rise to changes in consumer needs.

Chapter 3

Making changes and innovations

Introduction

By the end of this chapter you will:

- Understand the need for the continuous management of a company's product range.
- Appreciate what it is that constitutes a product and why new products often fail.
- Be aware of the factors that cause markets to change and so demand a response from marketing managers.
- Understand the concept and importance of 'the product life cycle'.
- Appreciate the increasing importance of market segmentation, niche marketing and focused marketing.
- Realize why there is a need for new products in almost all circumstances and appreciate the criteria that new products must meet.
- Understand that products can be innovative, adaptive or imitative.
- Be aware of the crucial stages in the successful introduction of new products.

'If you try to manage change the same way you've managed a stable, routine situation, you're going to have real problems. It is time to switch gears.'

Price Pritchett and Ron Pound. *The Handbook for Supervising Organisational Change*

3.1 The Management of Products and Services

Every company has to make decisions about the products it sells – how many products, of what kind, at what price levels, suitable for which markets – and also what type of service will be provided. These decisions will have a profound influence on the company's long-term success or failure. They have to be taken in relation to the best use of the company's financial and manpower resources, the kind of market opportunities that exist, the economic climate, the changing technological situation and the activities of competitors.

H. I. Ansoff[1] has defined four main product-market strategies for a company seeking increased business, as follows:

1. **Market penetration.** The company seeks increased sales for its present products in its present markets through more aggressive promotion and distribution.
2. **Market development.** The company seeks increased sales by taking its present products into new markets.
3. **Product development.** The company seeks increased sales by developing improved products for its present markets.
4. **Diversification.** The company seeks increased sales by developing new products for new markets.

This is a useful model (see Figure 3.1) as it can be used to evaluate the level of risk of a company in its approach to its markets. Clearly market penetration is the least risky, as 'doing more of the same' keeps to the same knowledge base of the business. However, markets move forward and, as we shall see, the product may become obsolete or the service offered 'just like everyone else' and become no longer required. So, the alternatives are two-fold. This situation requires that the company either develops new products or services (or 'enhancements'), or it must take its

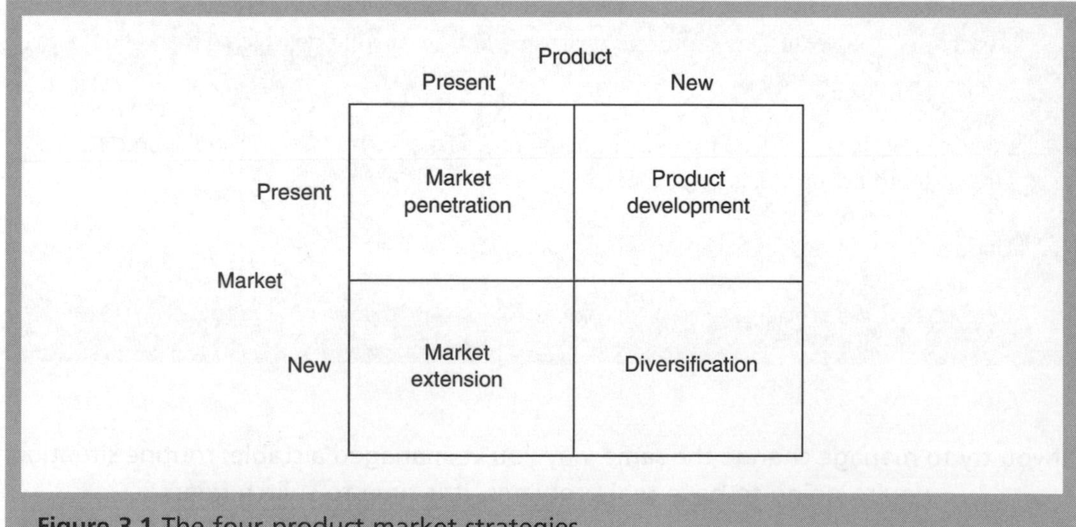

Figure 3.1 The four product-market strategies

existing products to serve new markets. There is a risk with either strategy – new products require investment and learning new markets, and finding new distribution channels also requires investment. The level of risk, i.e. the money involved, will differ from one company to the next. A software company manufacturing accounting software for business users may consider offering their accounting software for the home user. This would be market penetration and the task of entering a new market may be more difficult than developing new business software for, say, human resources or operational management.

Clearly, the most risky strategy would be diversification. Taking our software company that moved, say, into consumer markets with their software, then thought it might get into the manufacture and supply of home computers to run their software. This would be diversifying away from its core business.

So, the controlled management of products over time becomes crucial to minimize the risks when making changes to the business base.

3.2 What is a Product?

It is not the product as such that customers are interested in, but what it will do for them. What the customer buys is a set of satisfactions, and those satisfactions are the product. Products must be evolved not purely in terms of engineering or techniques, but in terms of design, presentation, packaging, brand-image and all the attributes which, together, give the customer the satisfactions being paid for. A box of high-quality chocolates, an expensive perfume or a fashion shirt cannot be divorced from the packaging, presentation and atmosphere created around it by advertising and other forms of display. All these things together make up the product. It is in relation to 'products' in this sense that we consider in this chapter the background against which policy questions concerning products have to be decided.

The word 'product' is used here as a piece of convenient shorthand. It is not used to mean only tangible 'things', but includes services (the intangibles) as well as things that can be touched and seen and tasted. Thus, a hairdressing, car hire or business consultancy service is just as much a product as a washing machine or fish fingers. Banks and insurance companies, for example, offer a range of products, such as specifically tailored pension schemes or student bank accounts, designed to meet the needs of specific groups of customers. A product has been defined as 'A bundle of physical, service and symbolic particulars expected to yield satisfactions or benefits to the buyer'.

Products are often referred to under the three main categories of durables, consumables and services.

- **Durables** – Tangible goods that are used many times over a long period are durables. Cars, domestic appliances, hi-fi equipment and mobile phones would all fall into this category.
- **Consumables (or non-durables)** – These are goods normally consumed over a short period. Foodstuffs are typical examples, as are drinks, tobacco and confectionery; but stationery items, heating oil, sewing cotton and many other goods are also consumables.
- **Services (intangible products)** – Services are made up of intangible 'activities', benefits or satisfactions that one party can offer to another and does not result in the ownership of

anything. Its production may or may not be tied to a physical product. Insurance, travel and entertainment are typical examples.

- **Further classifications (industrial purchases)** – We also distinguish between consumer products bought for the use of the purchaser and the family, and industrial products bought for use by an organization. Sometimes, the goods can be the same ones used in a different situation (ballpoint pens, chairs and light bulbs are random examples of goods with consumer and industrial uses). We can go on further to distinguish between industrial durables (machinery and equipment) and industrial consumables (such as raw materials, stationery and fuel).

3.3 Reasons for Changes in Customers' Needs

Since the sole purpose of a product is to provide satisfactions for customers, every marketing organization is in a highly dynamic situation. This is because customers' needs are constantly changing. Their incomes, their lifestyles, their customs, their fashion sense and so on are dynamic and not static. Therefore, our marketing policies must be dynamic not static, and the products we offer must come constantly under review and must frequently change.

Here are some of the reasons why customers demand new satisfactions.

- **Rising incomes and expectations** – In the developing industrialized western world in particular we have been living in a phase of increasing affluence, which in turn has led to an atmosphere in which expectations constantly change. Post-war, the British were renowned for their cold houses; now even people with relatively modest incomes would expect to live in centrally heated homes. Not so long ago things like television sets, tape-recorders and hi-fi equipment were very unusual pieces of equipment to find in a home; now they are almost universal and other items such as video games, DVDs (digital versatile discs) and mobile telephones are spreading rapidly. Changes like this are made possible by technology but are stimulated by the fact that, once the basic necessities of life are satisfied, rising incomes make a whole range of other satisfactions possible.

VIGNETTE

The Rise of DVDs

By the end of 2001, the DVD player had become the fastest-growing consumer entertainment product ever. The devices, which are compatible with televisions and home computers, offer sharper pictures and sound than VHS videotapes. The DVD has sold over 3 million units in its first three years since launch in Britain – it took the compact disc player and video recorder some seven years to achieve the same sales. In the UK, around 2 million machines were bought in 2001 alone. In the US, sales of DVD players outstripped video players for the first time in November 2001.When first launched, DVD machines were around £1000 each but with advancing technology, a basic model will now cost a little under £100.

- **Increasing education and sophistication** – Universal education to an increasingly high level, social trends like the widespread custom of holidaying abroad, and the fact that virtually everybody sees a wide range of different lifestyles and activities on television, all lead to a much greater readiness to accept and demand new things. Coupled with this demand for new things is a rising expectation in the standard of performance of existing things. Cars are not new, but cars with navigation devices, electronic sensors and many other comforts and safety devices are still relatively new. Universal viewing of television has developed an appetite for knowledge, which is being met by providing new distribution methods for information through the Internet and mobile phones.
- **Changes in social habits and customs** – Rising incomes, more education and foreign travel have all led to a much more fluid social situation, where habits and customs change rapidly. This leads to a ready acceptance of new forms of entertainment, new styles of dress, new eating habits etc. Instead of formal dinners or 'high teas', family television has led to informal easy-to-prepare meals. At the same time, a much wider range of tastes and eating experiences has evolved. For example, baked beans and sardines on toast have been joined by pizza, paella and many other dishes that would have been unknown to most British television viewers only a short time ago. There has been a phenomenal growth of 'fast foods' and 'takeaway meals'. Small towns and even villages have a Chinese and/or Indian restaurant. Mexican food is becoming increasingly available and Cajun and Balti dishes appear on many menus.
- **Fashion** – Traditionally, fashion changes started at the top end of a fairly well-defined social scale and gradually worked their way down. Nowadays the social pattern is much more difficult to define, and fashion changes take place much more rapidly. This is partly due to the fluid social situation, but even more to the much greater range of communication systems now available. Television and radio stations, together with an ever-increasing variety of specialist magazines and books, feed avid social appetites.

All these influences lead to the demand for constantly changing products to meet the developing needs of consumers. Other factors at the same time make these changes possible and also reinforce the rate of change.

- **Technological change** – It is a well-documented fact that the pace of technological change is increasing very rapidly. New materials and processes make the satisfaction of old needs possible in new and cheaper ways. As more and more simple tasks can be carried out more efficiently by computer-controlled equipment, robots etc. the whole pattern of employment is changing – often referred to as de-industrialization as many of the older industries decline or even disappear. At the same time, many new jobs appear in fields such as leisure facilities, information technology and financial services.
- **Worldwide change** – Events of 11th September 2001 in New York have signalled changes on a global basis. Where one might look to one's own country or community as a local market, we cannot escape the fact that we are now in a 'global village' where our neighbours might not be quite what we thought they were.

- **Business factors** – Because customers are becoming increasingly receptive to changes, so industry and commerce are responding to these changes. This is especially true in retailing. Thus, the commercial situation itself is becoming increasingly dynamic as companies vie with each other in being the first to offer a new or revised product for which a demand is anticipated. This leads to marketing management tasks, since many of the new products meet a rapid death. The latter part of this chapter deals with the management of new product development.

Unfortunately, many people prefer to think and behave as though we were in a static environment whereas a highly dynamic one is the reality. Equally, one often hears people romanticizing about the past or harking after a period of stability. None of the above factors seems to offer stability. At this point, it is also worth referring back to the PEST analysis in Chapter 1.

3.4 The Product Life Cycle Concept

Because we live and work in this dynamic situation, managers must accept as the normal state of affairs that all products have a limited life. This fact is commonly expressed in the form of the product life cycle curve shown in Figure 3.2. Products during their existence go through the phases indicated on the curve, as follows:

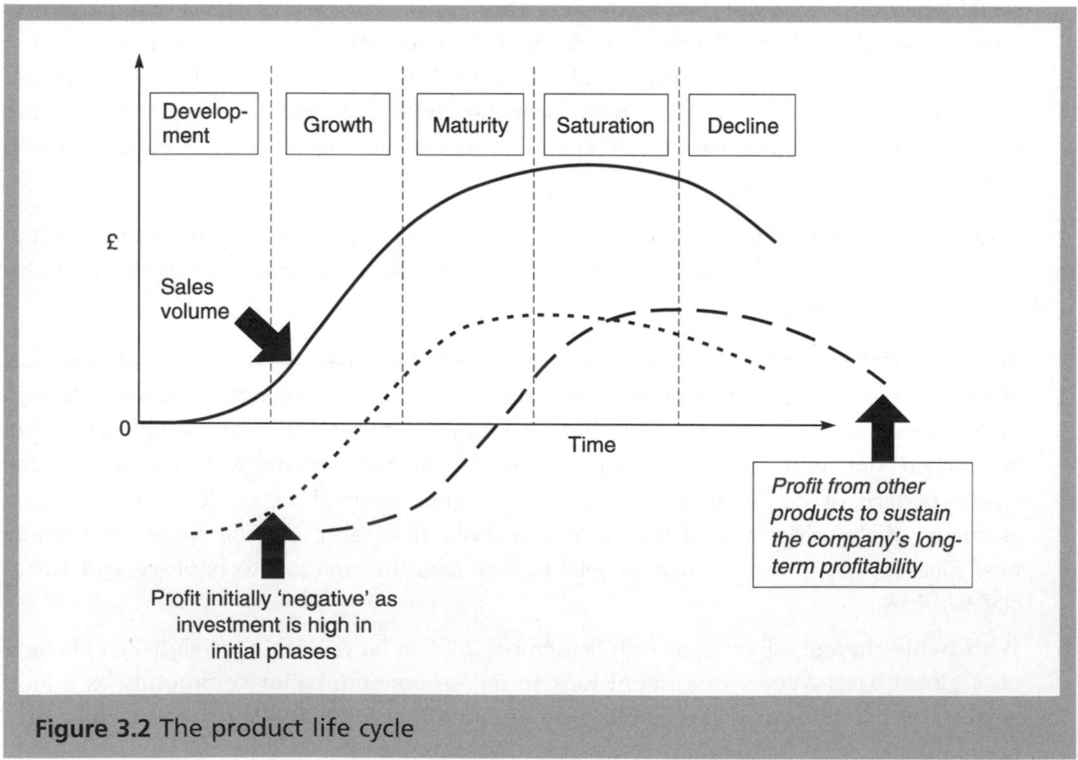

Figure 3.2 The product life cycle

1. Starting before, sometimes long before, a product reaches the marketplace, there is a **development phase**. Market research must be undertaken, the product designed, prototypes built, plant laid down. While costs can be very high, income will initially be nil and will probably grow only slowly. Profits are a long way off yet. Many products are slow to 'catch on' and this part of the curve typically does not rise steeply. For example, a new pharmaceutical product will spend about twelve years of its twenty-five year patent period in development before launch.
2. During the **growth phase** the product reaches general acceptance, and sales increase steeply. Profits mount as development costs are recovered and unit costs decrease with greater volume of production. Many pieces of home entertainment and information technology hardware form ready examples of products with high prices at launch which then drop a year or so later.
3. As the **product reaches maturity**, initial demand is beginning to be satisfied, competitors may have arrived on the scene, and there will be greater reliance on replacement sales. Sales increase more slowly, and profits come under pressure and may start to decline. By the latter part of 2001, mobile phone sales started to plateau in the UK.
4. When the **market is fully saturated**, sales will 'peak off' and profits decline still further. DVD players are now replacing VHS video recorders, and CDs are replacing the audio cassette.
5. Finally, **sales** will go into definite **decline** as the product is superseded by a new item or 'thing' and margins come under very severe pressure as it becomes increasingly costly to maintain sales at a reasonable level. Again the technology market is strewn with obsolete products from Betamax video recorders and 8 mm film cameras, to vinyl records. In fact, sometimes the old technology forms a collectors' niche.

The curve as illustrated is, of course, a generalization. The curve for any particular product may be steeper or flatter, and the time-scale may be longer or shorter. Some products seem to go on for a very long time indeed (Guinness and Coca-Cola, to name but two). For this reason the pattern must be applied with care. In addition, we must be careful what we mean by a product in this context.

For example, the market for glass has risen steadily over the past 50 years, but within this period the sale of lamp glasses has declined and that of milk bottles has risen steeply (to decline again in some countries in the face of competition from waxed cartons or plastic, and the change from doorstep delivery of milk to bulk purchase from the supermarket).

In the UK total consumption of bread has declined steadily since World War II. During this period, sliced wrapped bread was introduced, became very popular and is now in decline. Many different types of bread are being eaten in its place (e.g. croissants and pitta bread).

Nonetheless, the typical pattern stands as a warning that it is dangerous to rely too heavily for too long on one product. Instead, as profit from one product declines, profit from its successor needs to rise to fill the gap. Ideally, this will give a steadily rising profit for the company as a whole, even though some products have entered the 'decline' phase of the product life cycle.

It must be emphasized that the product life cycle diagram is not a rigid description of exactly how all products always behave. Rather it is an idealized indication of the pattern most products can be expected to follow.

There is nothing fixed about the length of the cycle or the lengths of its various stages. It has been suggested that the length of the cycle is governed by the rate of technical change, the rate of market acceptance and the ease of competitive entry. Thus, each year numerous new fashion styles are introduced, many of them to last only a few months. At the other extreme, a new aircraft must have many years of life if it is to be commercially worthwhile.

The main importance of the life cycle concept is to remind us constantly of the three following facts:

1. Products have a limited life.
2. Profit levels are not constant but change throughout a product's life in a way that is to some extent predictable.
3. Products require a different marketing programme at each stage of their life cycle.

3.5 Service Life Cycle

The usual industry or product life cycle can also be used to give some idea of a service life cycle. Maister's 3Es model[ii] is an illustration of this for the professional service firm in areas such as law or accountancy, for example.

This model can be applied to the firm, to different practice areas, and to an individual's know-how. It relates to the services provided by professionals, and is based on the three key benefits that clients want from professional services: **expertise**, **experience** and **efficiency** (see Figure 3.3).

This is useful in the analysis of professional services as it looks at the services *from the client's perspective*. Maister emphasizes that the three categories are not discrete but represent the opposite ends and midpoint of a spectrum. He suggests that each category requires a different approach to marketing, recruitment, structure and economics.

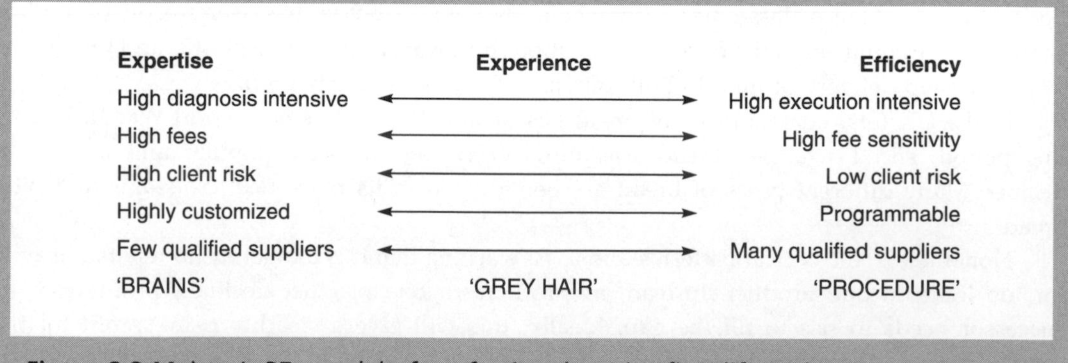

Figure 3.3 Maister's 3Es model of professional service firm life cycle

Too many professional service providers, he argues, consider that their services fall into the expertise category, whereas their clients' assessment differs. If a client considers the service to be largely procedural, like house conveyancing (or vaccinating a dog), and capable of being performed by any number of suitably qualified lawyers (or vets), then it will be an efficiency service. Competing for that client's work will mean being geared up as an efficiency practice and being subject to price competition. On the face of it, it would be irrational to insist that the service requires a high degree of diagnosis and tailoring, for which an expensive professional should be retained, if the client essentially wants a commodity service provided at a lower appropriate level of seniority. The only other alternative would be to try to add value to the procedure in some way by moving towards the left and demonstrating the value of experience – for example, to deal with unusual planning matters or to provide a comprehensive health check in the cases of businesses mentioned above.

The model represents a life cycle because of the tendency for any expertise to become diffused and performed by more people who are developed by the original innovators to handle that sort of work: it becomes experience. And as experience becomes standardized and proceduralized (and possibly even computerized), it evolves into providing efficiency. Over time, therefore, expertise and experience are rationalized and become routine; there is a shift from the left to the right. Indeed, it is possible that the service moves off the model to the right as clients become self-sufficient or find alternative suppliers. In this case, the fourth 'E' would be the extinction of that type of work. For lawyers, licensed conveyancers are taking over their work and we shall expect to see the introduction of private property 'sellers' packs in early 2002. In veterinary practices, we are beginning to see the vaccine-only clinics develop around pet superstores.

The strategic dilemma for professional service providers is whether they adapt the structure, marketing and organization of their practices to reflect the evolution of the services they provide, or whether they try to retain the structural components in place and seek new services that are suited to that structure. This would require frequent innovations in services.

3.6 Implications of the Product Life Cycle

If we have to accept that no product will go on earning profits indefinitely, then we must plan so as to have a whole succession of new products coming 'through the pipeline'. Figure 3.4 shows the profit implications of the product life cycle.

The existence of the product life cycle leads to other concepts that can help counterbalance its negative effects, or at least be aware of them. Three such concepts are described below.

- **Product elimination** – From the product life cycle concept, it follows that all products must be kept under review to assess their present and likely future contribution to profits. A common mistake of marketing management is to keep in the range products that have little or no prospect of contributing to profits. Products are kept in the range until they fade away, meanwhile consuming valuable resources, which could be more profitably employed elsewhere. These marginal products lower the company's profitability and it is essential to control them.

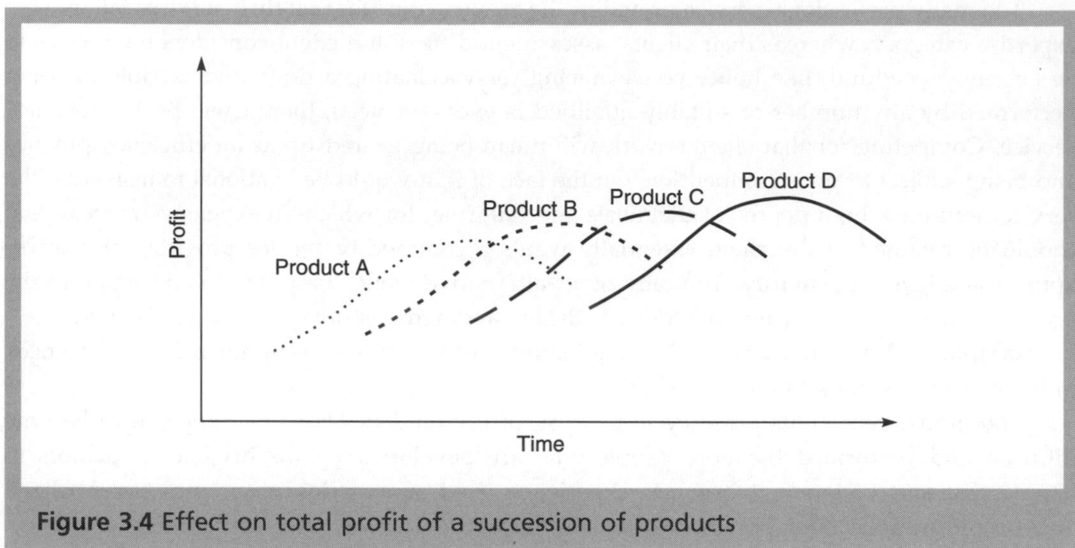

Figure 3.4 Effect on total profit of a succession of products

- **The product portfolio matrix** – Figure 3.5 illustrates a useful device for considering the implications of the various products within the portfolio – the matrix developed by the Boston Consulting Group.[iii] Note that the matrix is based on relative market share, that is the sales of a product *relative* to the market leader. The other axis is market growth. This positions products into four categories, with 'star' products being those with a big relative share of a high-growth market. 'Problem children' are those new launches that are in growing markets yet have a low relative market share – and what does one do with

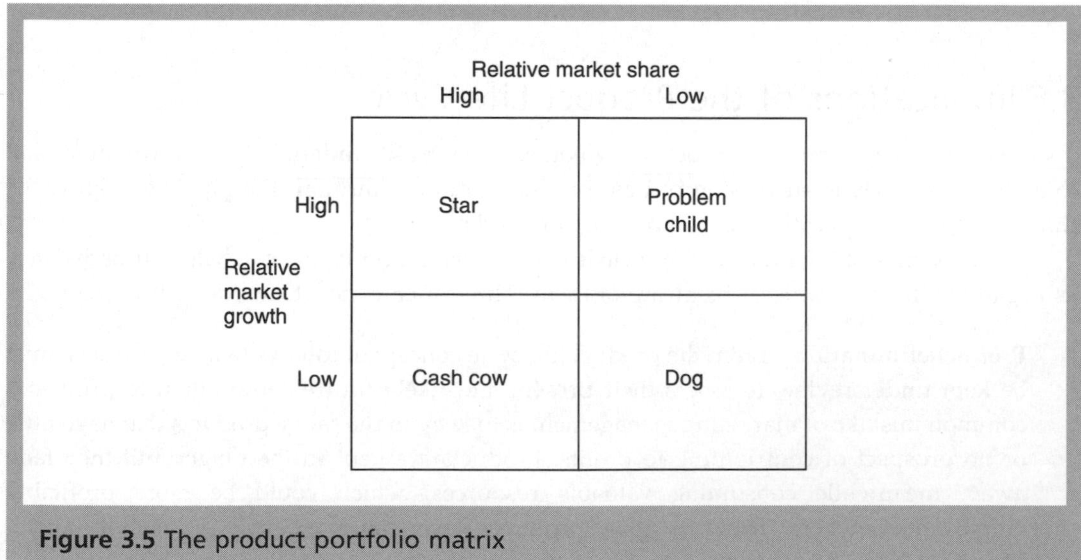

Figure 3.5 The product portfolio matrix

them? Are they going to turn out all right? Clearly, they will draw time and effort from the organization. 'Cash cows' have a high relative market share yet are in low-growth markets. While they still need some food (cash and resources) they generate funds which can be used to support the stars or, possibly, turn problem children into stars if the circumstances allow. 'Dogs' are clear candidates for product elimination but a number of them collectively may still provide useful profits, provided that investment is kept to a minimum. The sequence from problem child through star to cash cow and finally dog mirrors the product life cycle described earlier.

- **Product modification** – The basic product life cycle concept supposes a need for a planned succession of products. Often, however, a better alternative is to modify the product in such a way as to extend its profitable life. Technology-based products such as computers can achieve this by new microchips to deliver additional functions or 'add-ons' such as extra memory capacity.

VIGNETTE

Persil Evolution

Persil washing powder is an example of a product that has been around for many years (in this case about ninety) but has had its profitable life extended by many, often small, changes at frequent intervals to the product itself (occasional changes in the basic formulation as well as additives to build in extra desirable properties). Over a long period of time the product has become totally different from how it was originally. A new product has been achieved by evolution rather than revolution.

3.7 The Product Mix

A further outcome of the product life cycle is that few companies can rely on only one product. Most need to offer a series of products forming a product range. (American textbooks and some British ones that follow American terminology use the term 'product line', but 'range' is still the more common term in most British organizations.) In some situations, in any case, a marketing organization will be forced to have a range of products rather than just a single one.

VIGNETTE

Product Range

It is almost inconceivable that a shirt manufacturer would offer only one type of shirt. They are almost bound, by the nature of things, to offer various collar sizes and a selection of different patterns and colours. If we carry this process too far, we shall have an almost impossible and highly uneconomic task. Financing and controlling stock is just one of the problems that follows from a very wide product range, so decisions have to be made as to where to draw the line.

Continuing the shirt example, we have to decide how many different patterns of cloth to use and, for each pattern, how many different colour-ways. Are we going to offer collar sizes in centimetre steps or two-centimetre steps? Are we to offer slimline styles as well as the full-cut style? Are we to offer different collar styles as well as different patterns? Each time we add one element of difference, we may add twenty or thirty additional products to our range.

On the other hand, a manufacturer who decides to economize on research and development, on manufacturing costs, storage and distribution costs, may find himself in trouble for other reasons. For example, electrical appliance dealers often prefer to buy a range of different products from one supplier rather than having to deal with many. One advantage is that they can gain better quantity discounts. The supplier with a narrow range of products is then at a disadvantage.

VIGNETTE

Product Range in Depth

An example of a product range in depth would be a car manufacturer offering one model of car using the same body shape and basic engineering, but offering a wide range of engine sizes, colours and finishes, and optional extras. A car manufacturer with a wide range would offer a larger number of models, but each would have a much more limited choice of colours and options. There is no fundamental reason why a product mix should not have both breadth and depth, except of course that we then become enmeshed in the rather alarming complexities referred to above. Generally, compromises have to be made.

There are, of course, a number of product attributes that have to be decided upon as part of the product mix decision. Some of these are described below.

- **Product size** – In the case of a household detergent, for example, or a packaged food or a garden fertilizer, how many sizes will be available and what choice of sizes should be made? In some continental countries people buy many of their household goods in 1 kg or 2 kg packs, whereas in the UK much smaller packs are standard although we are moving towards the larger pack sizes. Should a manufacturer offer these larger family packs in addition to those already carried?
- **Packaging** – The style of pack has to be decided upon. Are we to have cardboard cartons, plastic drums, glass jars or a choice of two or more? A package may have a number of quite different functions to perform, including:

(1) *Protection*. Fragile products (glassware, delicate equipment and many foodstuffs) need packaging that will resist crushing during transit or withstand shocks during handling. Other products need protection against contamination, dust, light, heat and many other conditions.

(2) *Identification*. Distributors and retail customers need to be able to identify the product readily, especially if there are many competitors (e.g. cigarettes) or many varieties (e.g. car accessories). (While working with Durox Building Products, we discovered that it was the clarity of packaging colours on the pallet loads, which made it so much easier for builders to recognize the different building block sizes, that stole a march on the competition.)

(3) *Display*. Both individual packs and 'outers' may have to contribute to distinctive displays in shops or in cash and carry warehouses. Increasingly, there is little room available for display items as such, and packs often have to do the job. At the same time, the pack can carry through the brand image in a compelling way.

These requirements may carry different emphases in different parts of the country, or in different types of outlet. Which factors then are to have top priority and how many different packs will be necessary to meet the minimum requirement?

- **Presentation** – Is the product to be packed and presented in stark simplicity or with frills and elaboration? What will this do to the price and are we to choose one of the options available or offer customers a choice? In some fields manufacturers offer a wide range of brands presenting slight variations on the same basic product (see Sections 3.8 and 3.9).

VIGNETTE

Cigarette Product Ranges

Cigarettes are a case in point. Each manufacturer has a wide variety of brands, which will vary in flavour, size, tipped or untipped, coupons or no coupons, style of packaging and other ways. Each one of these changes represents an additional item in the product range, and the product mix has to be carefully worked out to appeal to the maximum number of customers with the minimum of manufacturing, marketing and distribution complications.

3.8 Product Differentiation

One of the problems confronting marketing organizations is that very rarely do they have sole rights to a particular product. For example, they may just be involved with brand marketing and distribution (as with many soft drinks), or hold a brand franchise (as with many fast-food restaurants). On the other hand, it is obviously desirable to be able to offer customers something that is unique and clearly different from anything else on the market. How does one do this with a product that is essentially exactly the same as everybody else's?

The answers are many, but brand image, packaging and all the variables listed above represent ways in which this differentiation of product can be achieved. It is important to note that these are often key elements in the competitive fight. We may expect competition to take place mainly through price, but there are two strong reasons why this is not the case.

First, to compete mainly through price could lead either to all competitors in a particular market eventually arriving once more at the same price (i.e. once again with no choice offered to customers), or to price competition, leading to damaging results for some, or perhaps all, of the competing companies. Second, price is only one of the factors influencing customer choice. It is not always the case by any means that customers will look for the cheapest article that will meet their needs. They may be perfectly happy to pay a little more, even sometimes a lot more, for the product so packaged and presented that it appeals to their sense of visual appeal or just sense of fun.

The 1960s British housewives who preferred a plastic daffodil to 3p off a packet of detergent have gone into the history books. In the late 1990s ESSO petrol dropped the famous tiger tokens in favour of a 'price watch' to regain market share. But in 2002 BP fuel continues to match them on price but have continued to offer premier points redeemable in Argos stores and catalogues and have maintained loyalty.

Thus, research and development goes into finding slight product differences that may give one product an 'edge' over the others. Ultra-low sulphur fuel, Shell's Optimax, or engine protection; seeds in 'harvest fresh' packaging or made into pellets for easier sowing; chocolates ready-packed with gift wrapping – all these are examples of product differentiation.

At the same time, advertising and presentation can achieve similar results by creating a different brand image, one that has greater appeal for more people (see Psychographic segmentation in Section 3.9 below).

3.9 Market Segmentation

A further choice to be made by companies deciding on their product mix is whether to attempt to provide a product or range of products that appeals to the maximum number of people. Alternatively, a company may decide to select a small group or groups of people in the marketplace and concentrate on pleasing them. The process of selecting carefully analysed 'segments' of the market and designing products to meet the requirements of that particular group of people is known as market segmentation.

In the new millennium, there are moves towards managing the relationship with customers individually over time – the ultimate segmentation.

Nonetheless, a large organization aiming at a major market share will try to satisfy many different segments. There are various ways in which markets can be segmented, some of which are given below.

- **Demographic segmentation** – This means by age or sex. For example, a shoe manufacturer might concentrate (as some have) on children's shoes, on high-fashion shoes for women or on men's safety shoes for industrial use, rather than attempt to provide shoes that will be reasonably satisfactory for everybody in all situations.
- **Segmentation by personal taste** – With products such as food, not everybody's tastes are the same, and a product that satisfies most people will leave others not completely satisfied. People less than completely satisfied by the 'standard' product form a ready market for a product formulated rather differently to meet their particular requirement. The attempt to meet these differing tastes is seen, for example, in the instant coffee market, which offers a range of special blends in addition to the 'standard brew'. Taste may also be a factor, of course, in terms of design, styling, colour etc.

  'Segmentation by benefits' emphasizes the different attributes of a product that appeal to different segments. For example, the same car may appeal to some people because of its economy and to others because of its safety features.
- **Geographical segmentation** – Concentration of effort can be achieved by aiming products only at those regions or countries containing a high proportion of customers for a particular product.
- **Segmentation by ethnic groups** – In societies where there are different ethnic groups, it will often be necessary and profitable to produce distinct product ranges to suit their different tastes and requirements. Obvious examples are ranges of food products and cosmetics.
- **Psychographic segmentation** – With many simple consumer products, such as cigarettes, drinks and toiletries, people may have strong brand preferences, even though the measurable physical performance of the various brands may be virtually indistinguishable. Brand name, packaging, promotion etc. are used to give the brand an 'image' that enables individual psychological and emotional preferences to be expressed (see Section 2.2). A related approach is segmentation by lifestyles.

  Focused marketing is the term often applied to the whole process (of which segmentation is part) of developing specific marketing mixes for selected groups of people, rather than trying to be 'all things to all people'.
- **Niche marketing** – It sometimes pays for a company to focus its efforts on a very small, carefully chosen segment or 'niche'. In that way it can satisfy the needs of one particular group of people extremely well and extremely profitably. Humbrol Paints, for example, supply through model shops small pots of paint in the appropriate colours for the use of hobbyists who make small-scale models of ships, aeroplanes etc. Similarly, W. Jordan (Cereals) Ltd, although it is to some extent in competition with Kelloggs etc., with whole-food products it holds its own through concentration on distribution to health stores. While one might consider niche markets as being like little harbours where the supertankers cannot reach, the question to ask is not 'is there a niche in the market?' but 'is there a market in the niche?'.

3.10 The Need for Innovation

Developing new products and launching them in the marketplace can be a difficult, costly and even dangerous business, as we see later in this chapter. So why do it? Why not leave well alone and be content with profit from existing products, concentrating effort on expanding sales of these products and finding new markets for them?

One reason is that seizing new opportunities as they emerge is a way to increase profits. (To be first in the field with a successful new product gives one the chance of creaming off large profits before effective competition develops.) But the main reason, as we saw earlier, is that it is dangerous to assume that profits from existing products will continue at present levels forever. The product life cycle concept tells us that they will certainly not continue forever. At different rates, over varying time-scales, all products eventually achieve market saturation and then start to decline. Even while sales volume holds up, profits may well not; and retaining sales volume and profits may call for regular updating of existing products.

For most companies, therefore, a programme of product review and development is essential; and, for all companies, to ignore this area of activity is highly dangerous. In consumer durables we have seen the successful introduction of digital video cameras, with DVDs not far behind. Innovative services (intangible products) include direct purchase of insurance by telephone and 'Internet banking'.

3.10.1 Driving Innovation

Based on extensive research with innovators in a variety of industries, we have concluded that innovation is a *better thing to do* or *a better way to do it* that contributes to the organization's capacity to achieve its goals. Innovation generally involves the deliberate introduction of new methods, structures, processes or products to an organization to enrich its ability to conduct its business. This means consciously framing improvements and driving them through the organization to ensure their implementation. To be considered an innovation, a development or idea must meet four criteria:

1. **It must represent a unique response or practice.** In other words, it hasn't been done before in that organization.
2. **It must represent a break from past practice and a new approach for the organization.** This means a deliberate break with the status quo – not always easy to do, especially for those people who created the status quo.
3. **It must be visible to others within the organization and on the outside.** If it is not visible, it may be too private to make a difference to the entire organization.
4. **It must offer the potential for a lasting presence and make an impact.** If the impact does not last, the idea was more a flash in the pan than a real innovation.

Successful innovation requires the ability to define where to go and the ability to help others to get there; it requires both inventing new responses to a problem or opportunity and leading others through the implementation process in a way that maximizes the odds of success. In other words, research with successful innovators shows that there are two phases of innovation:

invention and implementation. Each of these represents a cluster of management practices or activities that contributes to success.

There are a number of ways that we can drive innovation in the organization. Creativity is the fuel, vision the direction, commitment the engine and management the road map for the innovation process. Most innovators represent a mixture of these four functions. Creativity alone – that is, invention without implementation – may be a waste of resources; implementation (vision, commitment and management) without creativity may lead to stagnation. The most effective and innovative leaders have relatively equal shares of the four components. These are the people who are always looking for ways to improve upon past successes – who are anticipating the need to change before they are forced to change. Any profile that is dominated by only one element of the model is likely to stifle innovation.

Leading a successful innovation – taking an idea and making it a reality – does not require a mystical capability available only to a few inspired and gifted people. However, innovation does require *access to* a minimum level of capability in each of the components. Each component can be translated into specific behaviours that will help managers at all levels and in all types of organizations to improve their effectiveness in a changing world.

We often think of innovation as a dramatic breakthrough or a departure into unknown territory that miraculously proves to be highly profitable. It's true that innovation represents a 'better' thing to do or a 'better' way to do it, but achieving these things doesn't necessarily mean that an organization must move away from its basic strengths and resources. In fact, a closer look at successful innovations in large companies shows that most build on certain core resources the organization already possesses, such as:

- The organization's customer relationships.
- Its existing products or services.
- The ways in which customers use its products and services.
- Its processes for making, marketing and delivering its products and services to the customer.

So, in order to identify opportunities for growth, expansion, cost reduction, or other new directions, managers must think carefully about these core resources and strengths – about *what* they are doing now, *for whom* they are doing it and *how* they are doing it.

VIGNETTE

Arm & Hammer Baking Soda

Church & Dwight's innovation with its Arm & Hammer baking soda involved thinking about properties of an existing product – what the product actually did for the customer and how he or she used it. This kind of thinking led Church & Dwight to seek many new applications for its existing product and these applications – meant to appeal to their traditional customers – dramatically increased Arm & Hammer's sales and expanded the company's overall business and its profits. One such innovation was Arm & Hammer toothpaste.

This approach, obvious as it may seem at first glance, requires a lot more than unstructured brainstorming. It requires managers to examine in a disciplined fashion the relationships among their products and services and their customers, and how customers use the products and services. At the same time, it requires managers to go beyond the 'givens' (the constraints) inherent in those existing relationships. In other words, Church & Dwight had to go beyond the fact that baking soda was traditionally useful for only one application – baking.

The invention cube shown in Figure 3.6 is a tool that will enable you, when examining your own business or business unit, to identify innovative ways of expanding constructively on the foundation of existing capabilities. Just as length, width and depth measure the volume of a cube, the potential to increase the capacity of your business is measured on three dimensions: customer groups, products/services and applications. Looking at all three dimensions of your 'business cube' at once will enable you to examine the strengths and weaknesses in each area and to explore various ways of enlarging the capacity of what you do.

The cube is a visual device to help you begin thinking in three-dimensional terms. To the degree that you can expand what you do in any one dimension, you increase the potential capacity of your business. For example if you are able to identify more customer groups for your existing products/services or applications the shape of your cube will change because you have enlarged its volume. It is possible to expand in more than one dimension simultaneously

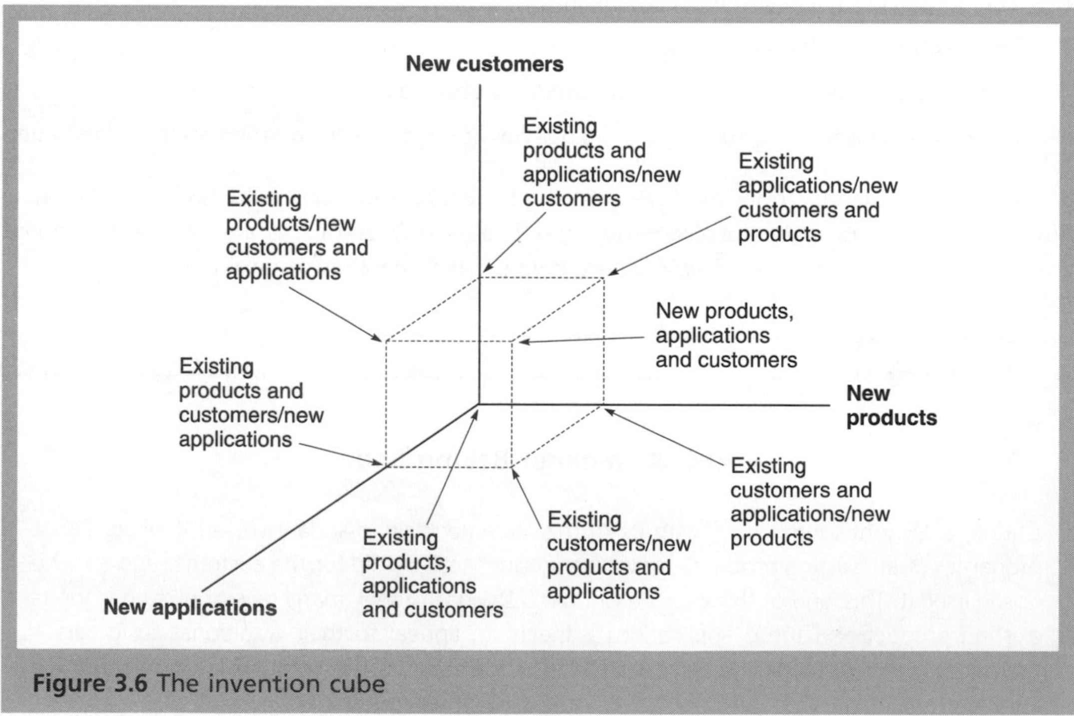

Figure 3.6 The invention cube

in that some ideas pose new customers, new products/services and new applications. This allows you to enlarge the volume of your cube in all three respects.

The invention cube allows you to free yourself from the constraints inherent in existing relationships among your current product, customers and applications, while building on the strengths you now have in each of these areas.

3.10.2 Innovation and the 'Hows' of Your Business

We have said that innovation is a 'better' thing to do (product to make, service to provide) or a 'better' way to do it. So far, we've been focusing on the things your business does – that is what products or services it provides to given customers for given applications.

There are other kinds of innovations to consider as well and these involve the way your business operates – how you produce your products or services, how you sell and distribute them to your customers, and how you help your customers use your products or services in ways that meet their needs. You'll find that the invention cube (in addition to helping you answer the questions about products, customers and applications) can help you identify innovation opportunities in the 'hows' of your business. For example: how you make the product (production processes), how you get the products to the customer (sales and distribution), and how you help the customer use or apply the products (services).

VIGNETTE

Innovations in Banking

Let's look at a simple example of the kinds of innovations that can occur in the 'hows' of a business. Most of us deal with banks; and banks and other financial institutions are currently seeking innovative ways of meeting their customers' needs. The questions about what products, what customers and what applications are less relevant in banking, since products, customer groups and applications don't vary widely from bank to bank. Therefore, many banks are now paying particular attention to differentiating themselves through the 'hows'. For example:

- In their *internal production process,* many financial institutions are cutting costs and speeding service through increased computerization and the use of electronic funds transfer systems among banks. In addition, many larger banks are centralizing operations and moving labour-intensive functions to areas where labour costs are low.
- In *sales and distribution,* banks are expanding the hours and their ability to reach customers through automated teller machines in the bank and in high-traffic areas like supermarkets and airports. In addition many banks are revamping their sales organizations to target sales efforts on particular customer segments – small business owners, for example.
- In their *customer service* activities, banks are providing expanded and more flexible services through automated teller machines, the use of touch-tone phones, lines of credit

for overdraft protection, Internet access and so on. Often the tools that banks provide for customer service (like the ATM and Internet) also enable them to increase the number of services they sell to a given customer. In other words, 'service' means ways to help customers use your products or services.

Questions

1. How should a bank provide a better personal service while driving for efficiencies through the use of information technology?
2. In the case, it was stated that 'Service means ways to help customers use your products or services'. Discuss this statement in the context of an on-line bookstore like Amazon.

Figure 3.7 shows the invention cube, labelled this time to reflect the three 'how' dimensions of innovation. Again, expanding along any one dimension (or along all three dimensions at once) will increase the potential capacity of your business.

In summary, we've looked at ways to be innovative in the things a business does (what products it provides for given customers and given applications) and in how the business operates (its production processes, sales/distribution systems and service activities).

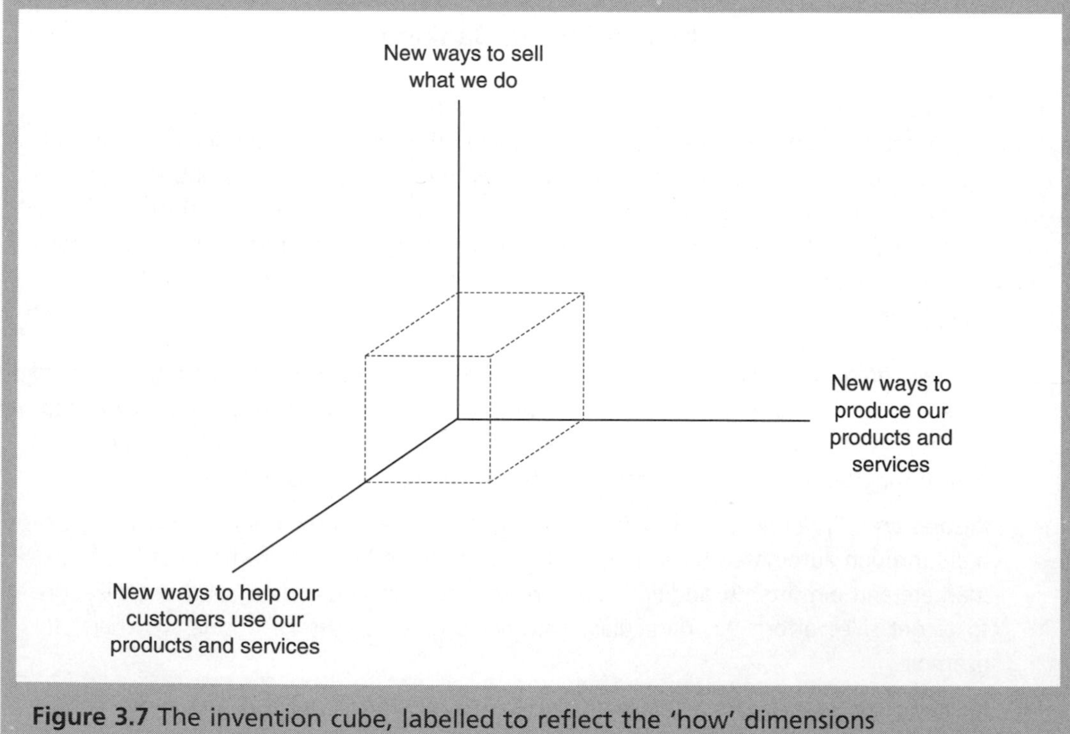

Figure 3.7 The invention cube, labelled to reflect the 'how' dimensions

There are three methods of obtaining new products: (a) modifying an existing product; (b) acquiring a new product; and (c) developing a new product. We now briefly examine the first two of these before looking in more detail at the business of product development.

3.10.3 New Products From Old

We first need to be clear what a new product is. We can consider three clear kinds of new product, as follows:

- **Innovative** – These are unique products for which there is a real need, not being met satisfactorily by an existing product. Penicillin, when first introduced, fell into this category, as did the telephone, the internal combustion engine and chloroform. We can also describe as innovative those products that, while replacing existing goods that have been satisfying existing markets quite well, offer totally different solutions. Examples would be television partially replacing the cinema and the radio, the zip fastener and later Velcro instead of strings or buttons, and solar power for other energy sources.
- **Adaptive** – These offer significantly different variations on existing products. They include such items as instant coffee, freeze-dried foods, self-adhesive wallpaper and typewriters with a memory. Another kind of variation is represented by package changes, styling modifications, and new designs and colours.
- **Imitative** ('me too') – These products are already being sold by someone else but further sales opportunities exist for an additional brand, with or without minor modifications.

The divisions between these categories are obviously very fuzzy. Indeed, some authors have distinguished as many as a dozen different ways in which a product can be 'new'.

The truly innovative product is rare. Adaptive new products can sometimes necessitate a great deal of new technology and extensive research and development, though a 'new' product can often be produced by changes to an existing one. These may range from relatively minor changes, which effectively extend the life cycle of a product, to much more extensive improvements.

3.10.4 Acquiring New Products

There are various ways in which new products can be 'bought'. A company needs to decide whether it will make or buy, i.e. whether it will itself manufacture the products it markets or whether it will simply be a marketing organization, leaving the manufacturing to specialists in that part of the operation. A company must similarly decide whether it is better to do its own product development or to 'buy in' this particular expertise. Thus new products can be acquired in the following ways:

- Buying patent rights.
- Acquiring manufacturing rights.
- Arranging to act as a marketing organization for a company wishing to concentrate on manufacturing.

- Acting as marketing agent in one country for a company manufacturing and marketing in another.

3.11 The Criteria New Products Must Meet

What we have said so far should not be taken as an indication that all new products are worthwhile, and that they all make a contribution to company profit. The majority do not (see Section 3.15), so that great caution must be exercised in devoting time and money to their development and launching.

Fortunately, some clear-cut criteria can be applied and, if they are observed, the chances of success are likely to be greatly increased. (It should be noted, however, that there is no way of totally avoiding the risk inherent in launching a product of which consumers have no previous experience.) These are the criteria:

1. **There must be an adequate demand**. It is quite pointless to produce a product that is unlikely to be bought in sufficient quantity for the revenue to cover development, production, marketing and distribution costs, and also make a contribution to profit.
2. **The product should be compatible with the company's marketing experience and resources**. A washing machine manufacturer could add a dishwasher to the range and market it successfully with their existing organization and through the same distribution channels. Customers' motivations and purchasing habits could be expected to be familiar. But a similar manufacturer deciding to sell paint or biscuits would be entering a totally new marketing area and would somehow have to acquire a completely new body of expertise. They would need different retailers and an appropriate pricing structure, quite new physical distribution problems would have to be faced, and the advertising approach and way of thinking would have to change (see the Ansoff matrix in Section 3.1).
3. **The product should fit fairly easily into the company's present production pattern**. The plant and machinery, technical expertise and servicing facilities may all be quite different for a new product field.
4. **The financial implications of launching the new product must be carefully thought through and appropriate arrangements made**. For example, if the new product needs high stock levels, the extra finance must be available; and if its sales are seasonal, the cash-flow fluctuations must be provided for. Developing and launching a new product generally means very heavy costs, so that a long time may elapse before it reaches break-even point. The cash to sustain this period of heavy 'losses' must be available.
5. **Adequate management time must be devoted to a new product**. Without such attention it will wilt and die.
6. **Any necessary legal and other procedural clearances must be obtained well in advance.**

Finally, there is no point in trying to launch a new product unless it has some clear marketing advantage that can form the basis of a unique selling proposition to be featured in promotion, and it can reasonably be expected to make a profit contribution in line with the management time and other resources it will absorb.

3.12 Why New Products Fail

Having established in the previous section what criteria new products should meet, we can see that any not meeting these criteria are likely to fail. Many new products do fail. It is impossible to reach an agreed figure, however, because definitions of what constitutes success or failure will vary. So, too, will the definition of a new product. Does a new surface design for the pack and a change in price and advertising image give us a new product or just a revamp of an existing one? Where to draw the line between revision and new product is impossible to say. However, no one disputes that the failure rate of new products is extremely high.

A favourite occupation of researchers and authors is listing the reasons why new products fail. Many products will, of course, fail because they do not meet the criteria for success listed in Section 3.11. These can be briefly summarized as follows:

1 Ensuring an adequate demand exists.
2 Ensuring the product 'fits' the company's marketing capability.
3 Ensuring it fits the existing production capability.
4 Ensuring suitable finance is available.
5 Allocating adequate management time.

Most authorities would add two further points when considering why new products fail: 6, lack of a coherent policy for new product development; and 7, lack of a suitable organization for developing the new products. The most important reason for failure by far is probably that there is a natural enthusiasm in all concerned to take a product forward even on the slimmest possibility of ultimate profit.

The answer to this is a rigorous procedure for 'screening' new products so as to counteract as far as possible any natural tendency for over-enthusiasm. This we consider shortly. If we do take steps to screen products in order to ensure that only the likely ones reach the marketplace, then something like the pattern in Figure 3.8 will emerge.

As we go from generation of ideas towards commercial development, the cost generally rises sharply. Thus it is important to have well-defined procedures to ensure rigorous control over how far along the sequence any given product is allowed to proceed. This is in order to counteract the tendency to have 'natural enthusiasm' for products with little chance of ultimate commercial success.

As Figure 3.8 indicates, many bright ideas for new products are available or can be stimulated, but very few are ever going to produce the 'crock of gold' at the end of the rainbow in the marketplace. The road thither is long, hard, dusty and very costly.

In the following sections we look at each of the stages indicated in Figure 3.8 in turn.

3.12.1 The Generation and Screening of New Product Ideas

New products can come from many sources and through many kinds of individuals with widely differing backgrounds. We can, however, think in terms of three main categories of 'new' products, as follows:

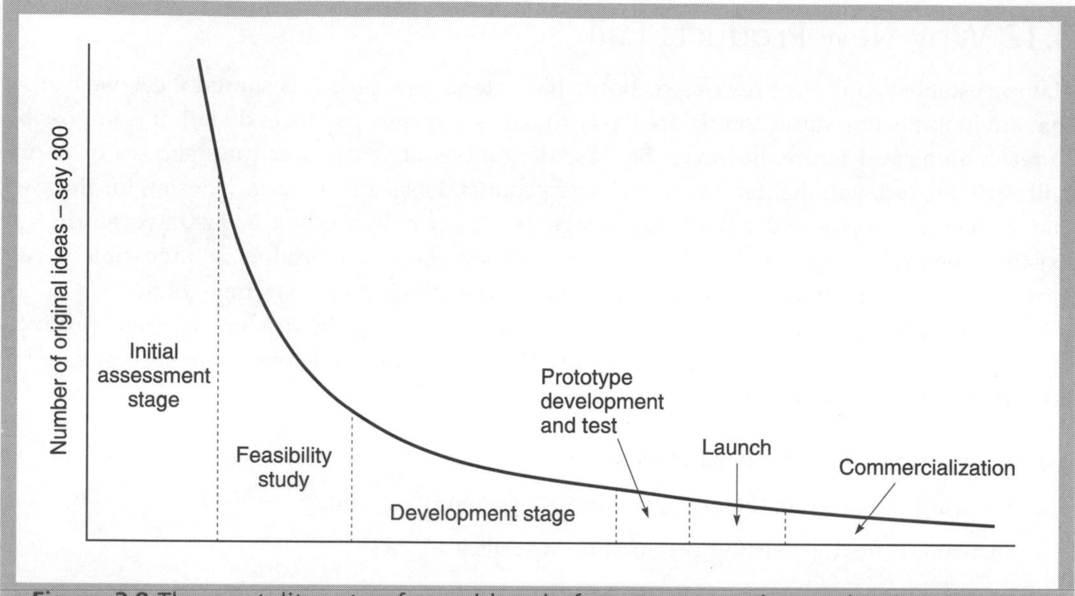

Figure 3.8 The mortality rate of new ideas before a new product makes it onto the market

1. **Products developed to fill a known 'gap'** in the range of existing products available to meet a known need. An example would be the considerable development currently going on to fight degenerative disease with stem cells rather than current pharmaceuticals.
2. **Products arising out of scientific research** probably devoted originally to quite different ends, or from 'pure' research in pursuit of knowledge with no commercial end at all in view. One famous example is penicillin, whose effect was first noticed by accident during a study of many different moulds. Another example is 'Post-it' notes from 3M where the search for a new industrial adhesive found one that didn't stick particularly well – except to itself!
3. **Creative ideas with no very logical origin**. These range from a technical breakthrough departing from the orthodox approach (e.g. the jet engine and hovercraft) to more trivial and less technical but nonetheless useful ideas, such as oven-ready french fries, ready-planted flowering shrubs for 'instant gardening', and self-assembly 'knock down' furniture. Generally speaking, of course, it is products that are developments of existing ones that arise from a study of the marketplace and new technology that gives rise to products with high novelty. Thirty years on, Viewdata ('Teletext') information displayed on home TV screens is still to some degree a 'product in search of a need' and there are many 'high-tech' products in a similar situation.

Each of the above ways of originating new products has its own method of approach, which we will now take a look at.

When it comes to **finding gaps in the market**, the aim is to identify a need in the market and then find the product to fill it. There are three main approaches, as follows:

1. **Examine other markets**. For many years it has been commonplace for British companies to keep a close eye on international markets, the United States in particular. If a product is selling well there, it has a fair chance of also succeeding in Great Britain. Indeed, many of the products now established in the market here were first developed in the United States, including ballpoint pens, aerosol sprays, credit cards and 'finger-lickin' good' Kentucky Fried Chicken. The USA is, of course, not the only source, nor is there just one-way traffic (as Schweppes, Jaguar cars and others have demonstrated by taking established British products to the USA and elsewhere).
2. **Segment the market**. Since people do not have identical preferences, it is unlikely that one product will completely satisfy everyone. A new product that gains a large market share may, therefore, suggest the possibility of a number of market segments. Thus, instant coffee was originally marketed with a single flavour. This was reasonably acceptable to most people. Now we see the development of special blends – mild, roast and so on – to suit smaller groups of people prepared to pay a premium price to obtain something that suits their personal taste more closely than the 'standard' flavour. Jamaica 'Blue Mountain' is an example of one of the premium instant coffees.
3. **Gap analysis**. This is a rather complex technique of examining products on the basis of how people view them – what people 'think' they are. For example, if people viewed all existing chocolate bars as crunchy, but said they preferred a soft bar, then a gap might exist for a new chocolate bar brand promoted as 'the soft one'.

VIGNETTE

Chocolate with 'Bite'

The 'fictional' example concerning chocolate bar texture became almost totally real a year or two after the first edition of this book was published when research showed that customers were less than totally satisfied with existing chocolate bars. Cadbury Schweppes and Mars (with their Galaxy brand) had responded to rapidly increasing raw materials' costs partly by increasing prices and partly by reducing the thickness of the bars whilst keeping the other dimensions the same. Thin chocolate tastes different from thick and has a different 'bite'. Responding to research indications, Rowntree-Mackintosh (now part of the Nestlé group) developed, tested and launched 'Yorkie' – a premium-priced chocolate with a narrowed but thicker shape, which made a chunky chocolate bar with 'bite'. It won them a very large share of a market in which they were previously barely represented.

Achieving new products through **scientific development** was the second of the three categories listed above. This is a question either of a company maintaining its own research and development team or of it keeping closely in touch with development teams in universities, research establishments and worldwide publications carrying reports of technological development. The former method is much more expensive, but can be more directly applied to the areas in which the company is interested.

The previous two categories of new product generation both rely on some kind of systematic search. But the **creative ideas approach** is almost by definition not systematic. Here we are looking for a new departure rather than a logical development from what already exists.

Many people think there is a mystical secret to creative thinking. Nothing could be further from the truth: creative thinking is simply the process of allowing your own brain to work for itself without the restrictions of procedures, traditions or the opinions and tastes of others.

3.12.2 The Business Analysis of New Product Ideas

Far too many ideas have money spent on their development simply because they seem good ideas, that is to say they appeal to someone, who then becomes committed to them. The best way to avoid this temptation is to ask at a very early stage what is the likelihood of adequate profits accruing if the product is successfully developed and launched? Crucial questions will include the following:

- What is the likely demand and at what price?
- Can the product be manufactured and distributed at a cost that will fit the price/demand situation and also yield a suitable profit?
- What will be the yield of capital and manpower invested in this way as against the comparable return from alternative ways of employing the resources? (In economic language, what is the opportunity cost?)

3.12.3 Product Development

This is the process of technical development in the laboratory, on test-rigs, in a pilot plant, or whatever is necessary in the particular circumstances. Depending on the product, safety tests, quality tests, servicing and maintenance routines may need to be worked out alongside many other factors. It is most important to keep clearly in the mind of everyone concerned the needs of the ultimate users. This will avoid developing a product which either does not meet the requirements of the marketplace in one respect or another, or which does so superbly but at so high a cost that competition cannot be met or that profits cannot be made.

3.12.4 Test Marketing

This is dealt with at greater length in Section 4.17. Here it is enough to recognize that a full launch on the national scale of a new product is (a) very costly and (b) potentially dangerous.

As an interim stage, it is often sensible to launch the product initially in one carefully selected part of the country only. It is then often possible to check whether all aspects of the marketing mix are fully effective. If the optimum has not been struck, changes can be made in the national launch. In particular, if further product improvements need to be made in response to customer reactions, this can be done without too much damage to the company's reputation or too great a loss of future sales. A national launch of what turns out to be an imperfect product (or a wrongly priced or promoted one) can be an irrevocable and disastrously costly affair.

In 2000, when dot-com businesses were the new Holy Grail, advice to test (by direct marketing) a new pet superstore website on a small clearly defined sector – those people known to have Internet access and who had already bought from pet catalogues – was not taken, in favour of the full-scale national launch. Unfortunately, the finance for full development ran out and the business went to the dot-com graveyard with many a finger burned.

3.12.5 Launch and Commercialization

Only when all signals are green so far does it normally make sense to launch the product fully, although there may well be situations where it is wise to skip the test-market stage. A reference back to the product life cycle (Figure 3.1) will quickly show that up to now each stage has produced a larger and larger loss. Only at some time – possibly a very long time – after the launch does revenue, and eventually profit (if all goes well), begin to be generated.

A further significant point, is that even after the launch, we may well still need to think in terms of a series of stages. The life cycle concept suggests this, and a further useful concept is that of 'adopter categories'. Especially with innovative products, some people will adopt the new ideas quickly and eagerly, whereas others will be slower to take to them. Five distinct groups have been suggested,[iv] as follows (see Figure 3.9):

1. *Innovators* – The venturesome 2½ per cent who are willing to take the risk of trying something out first. They tend to be younger, of higher social status and more affluent than the other categories.
2. *Early adopters* – About 13½ per cent of the market, including more opinion leaders than the other groups. They tend to be younger, more creative and more mobile than the groups below.

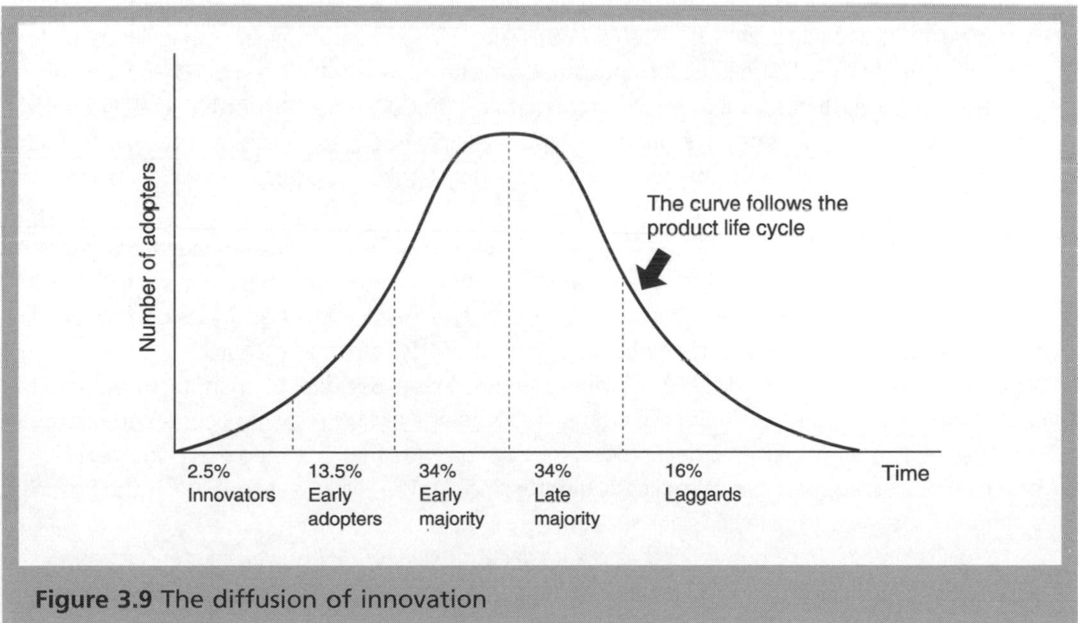

Figure 3.9 The diffusion of innovation

3. *Early majority* – About 34 per cent of the total market. A bit above average in social and economic standing.
4. *Late majority* – Another 34 per cent, more sceptical than the previous group. Adopt only under economic necessity or pressure from their peers. Older, worse educated and below average in social and economic status.
5. *Laggards* – The tradition-bound 16 per cent. Suspicious of innovation. They tend to be older than the rest and at the lower end of the social and economic scales.

While the innovators and early adopters are considerably influenced by promotion and by the apparent advantages of a new product, the later groups will tend to wait for the situation to develop until they feel virtually forced to follow suit. This is one reason for the slow and gradual development of the product life cycle, and why a long-term, carefully monitored development plan with financial targets is essential.

CASE STUDY

The following case history is one outlined by Mr James Dyson of Dyson Ltd.[v]

James Dyson's first product, the Sea Truck, was launched in 1970 while he was studying at the Royal College of Art (by 2001 sales to date had exceeded $500 million). A few years later came the award-winning Ballbarrow that can go where no wheelbarrow has ever been before. It became market leader in three years. Then there was the Wheelboat – that travels at 64 km/h on land and water – and the Trollyball – the most practical boat launcher. Even the integral hose, seen on most upright vacuum cleaners, is a Dyson invention.

In 1978, James Dyson noticed how the air filter in the Ballbarrow spray-finishing room was constantly clogging with powder particles (just like a vacuum cleaner bag clogs with dust). So he designed and built an industrial cyclone tower, which removed the powder particles by exerting centrifugal forces greater than 100,000 times those that gravity could exert. Could the same principal work in a vacuum cleaner? So, James Dyson set to work and 5 years later (after 5127 prototypes) the world's first bagless vacuum cleaner from Dyson arrived.

It may sound like 'taking coals to Newcastle', but James Dyson's vacuum cleaner was first sold in Japan, the home of high-tech products. Known as the 'G Force', it won the 1991 International Design Fair prize in Japan. The Japanese were so impressed by its performance that the G Force became a status symbol, selling for $2000 a piece!

Using income from the Japanese licence, James Dyson decided to manufacture a new model under his own name in Britain. In June 1993 he opened his research centre and factory in Wiltshire, not far from his home, and developed a machine that collected even finer particles of dust (microscopic particles as small as cigarette smoke). The result was the DC01, the first in a range of cleaners to give constant suction.

Dyson scientists were determined to create vacuum cleaners with even higher suction. So they set to work developing an entirely new type of cyclone system. They discovered that a smaller diameter cyclone gives a greater centrifugal force. So they developed a way of getting 45% more suction than a Dual Cyclone® and removing more dust, by dividing the air into eight smaller cyclones, hence the name Root^{8}cyclone®.

'I like your vacuum cleaners but when will you make one that you don't have to push around?' This casual remark set James Dyson's mind working. Producing something that bounced aimlessly off the furniture and picked up very little dust would have been easy, but James Dyson insisted that the Dyson DC06 robot should not only clean properly but should also guide itself more logically than a human would. It took three on-board computers, fifty sensory devices and 60,000 hours of research to create efficient, methodical robot cleaning.

To Dyson, 'design' means how something works, not how it looks – the design should evolve from the function. That is why the people at Dyson who design products are called 'engineers'. Sadly, most education systems (according to Dyson) still encourage children towards academic subjects and away from 'getting their hands dirty making things' (strange from a country that started the industrial revolution). It may take time, but Dyson hopes to change that.

The Dyson Washing Machine

Dyson engineers constantly re-examine products of all types. One of the things they looked at was the washing machine. They found that its wash action does not flex the fabric very much. That is why it takes a long time to release dirt. In fact, washing by hand gave better results than a single drum machine. So, Dyson set about replicating a hand wash action to manipulate and flex the fabric to release dirt more quickly. In 2000, the Contrarotator® was created – the world's first washing machine with two drums. Suddenly you could wash faster, with better wash results and bigger loads.

The Patent Nightmare

The Dual Cyclone® was nearly never made due to patent and legal costs. Unlike a songwriter who owns a song he or she writes, inventors have to pay substantial fees to renew their patents each year. During the development years when James Dyson had no income, this nearly bankrupted him. He risked everything, and fortunately the risk paid off. Then in 1999, Hoover tried to imitate a Dyson and James Dyson was forced back to court to protect his invention. After 18 months Dyson finally won a victory against Hoover for patent infringement.

Questions

1. If you build a better mousetrap, the world will beat a path to your door. Discuss.
2. Consider technical innovations, particularly in home entertainment, and discuss whether or not innovations 'fulfil a need' or whether they 'create the market'. Use the XBOX from Microsoft as a recent example.

Summary

- A product is a whole collection of physical and other attributes offered to customers to satisfy a need.
- The product life cycle concept expresses the fact that products exist in a constantly changing situation. Product management is a dynamic, not static, process.
- A company's product range and product mix must be kept constantly under review. New products must be developed and old ones eliminated on a regular basis to ensure that the company can satisfy current customer needs.
- It will rarely be possible to please all the people all of the time. The techniques of product differentiation and market segmentation can help to ensure that a company's products have a specific appeal to selected groups of people.
- New products can be obtained by modifying existing products, by acquiring new products or by developing new products.
- A new product development plan must ensure that products are only taken to an advanced stage if they fit the criteria of: (a) an adequate demand, (b) compatibility with existing marketing capability, (c) compatibility with existing production capability, (d) adequate financial resources and (e) adequate manpower resources.
- New products fail for a variety of reasons, but notably through over-enthusiasm.
- New product ideas can come from: (a) analysing market gaps, (b) new technology, and/or (c) creative thinking.
- New products take time to find their way right through to the marketplace because buyers vary from innovators and early adopters to late adopters and laggards.

References

i Ansoff, H. I. *Corporate Strategy* (Pelican, 1975).
ii Maister, D. H. *Managing the Professional Services Firm* (Free Press, 1997).
iii In *The Management of New Products* (Booz, Allen and Hamilton, 1968).
iv In *The Fundamentals of Marketing* (McGraw-Hill, 35th Edition, 1971).
v Adapted from 'The Story of Dyson', Dyson sales literature, 2001.

Further Reading

Doyle, P. and Bridgewater, Susan. *Innovation in Marketing* (Butterworth-Heinemann, 1998). Describes both systems innovation and the launch of new products.

The Advertising Works series, published annually from 1980 in connection with the advertising awards scheme. Contains many examples of new product launches.

Mercer, David. *Marketing* (Blackwell, 1992). Has a very good new products chapter highlighting the strategic aspects.

Piercy, Nigel. *Market-Led Strategic Change* (Butterworth-Heinemann, 3rd Edition, 2001). Written in a witty and direct style, it is a seminal text on the subject.

Questions

1. How would you describe the 'product' as perceived by the customers for the following?

   (a) Easter eggs.

   (b) Expensive lingerie.

   (c) Trailer caravans.

   (d) EuroTunnel.

2. What changes in customer needs do you anticipate might arise from changes to the taxation of company cars on the basis of exhaust emissions coupled with a period of economic stringency?

3. Suggest ways of differentiating products in the following fields:

   (a) Web-based entertainment.

   (b) Shoes.

   (c) Motorcycles.

   (d) Airlines.

4. Suggest examples of products that have recently been improved in terms of: (a) quality, (b) features and (c) style. Qualify your reasons for the examples you suggested.

Chapter 4

Market and marketing research

Introduction

By the end of this chapter you will:

- Understand the importance of marketing research.
- Appreciate that marketing research forms part of a wider marketing information system.
- Appreciate how marketing research is organized.
- Know what are the main research methods and their limitations.
- Understand the differing types and sources of marketing research.
- Realize the key part that marketing research can play in test marketing.
- Appreciate the need for marketing research to be cost-effective.
- Understand the basis of sampling and know the main methods of sampling.
- Be aware of the basic principles of questionnaire design.

'Market research is the systematic collection from external sources of any information about markets, and the analysis of this information for market planning and business decisions generally.'

Dictionary of Market Research, ISBA/MRS

4.1 Why Marketing Research is Necessary

All business is conducted under conditions of risk and uncertainty – particularly about the future. Obviously, the future cannot be totally known, the uncertainty cannot be completely removed, or the risks precisely calculated. However, it is asking for trouble not to use whatever information is available. Many facts can be known and unnecessary risk can thus be avoided.

For example, while a firm can very easily know how its own sales are progressing, this information is relatively meaningless without knowledge of the total size of the market and whether that is increasing or decreasing. Often information on the total market is freely available – from government statistics, trade associations or similar sources. If it is not freely available in this way, market research techniques can be used to get it. But, as we shall see later, this is just one example of the vital necessity for information about the market situation.

The overwhelming reason for carrying out market research, however, is to keep open the channels of communication between customers and ourselves so that we can more effectively understand and then satisfy their needs.

4.2 Marketing Information Systems

In a well-ordered and sophisticated marketing-oriented organization, marketing research will be part of a totally integrated marketing information system encompassing information derived from:

- The internal accounting system, especially sales analysis.
- Market intelligence, i.e. the capturing of information from many sources, including the media, industry reports etc., regarding matters such as the economic situation and competitor activity.
- Market research of all kinds (see below and Section 4.8).

(For further information on marketing information systems in support of marketing decision making, see Section 4.4.)

Key questions need to be asked for several areas of research, as follows.

Market research:

- What is the size of the market (in terms of volume and/or value) and is it decreasing or increasing?
- What are the market shares of ourselves and our competitors and are these changing?
- How is the size and trend of the market influenced by various factors (economic, social and seasonal)?
- What is the composition of the market in terms of age groups, income groups, size of company or geographical area? (For market segmentation, see Section 4.24.)
- What are the main distribution channels and how do they function?

Competitor research:

- What competitors are there and how do their product ranges, prices etc. compare?

- What are their marketing strategies?
- How are their products distributed, advertised, packaged etc.?
- How does their sales force operate?
- Are any new competitors likely to enter the market?

Product research:

- Who are our customers and what are their needs?
- Which products do consumers prefer and why?
- Are proposed new products acceptable?
- Do consumers have complaints about products presently on the market that could indicate a possible new product opportunity?
- What is the customer reaction to new product concepts?

Advertising/marketing communications research:

- Who reads which publications; who watches/listens to which TV/radio channels?
- Are existing or proposed advertising campaigns communicating effectively?
- What are the motivations that activate consumers and is our advertising correctly interpreting them?
- How do customers react to proposed advertising themes (copy testing)?

4.3 How Marketing Research is Organized

Marketing research is a specialized job. While in principle it can be carried out by anyone, there are serious potential pitfalls:

- The necessary objective, unbiased approach needs to be acquired or 'trained into' people. Salespeople, for example, are usually not suitable for obtaining research information, because their training and instincts are such that they are enthusiasts for a particular point of view – partisan for their own product. If not, they might well be less effective as salespeople.
- Some of the techniques employed demand skills and disciplines that have to be learned.

Usually therefore, marketing research is a task for specialists. These specialists are found in three main groups.

1. **'In-company' departments.** Many companies have their own marketing research departments. This has the advantage that the people concerned can specialize and over the years acquire great knowledge of the fields in which they operate and the best techniques for gathering information for their particular purposes. It can thus be a very economic way of providing the necessary information. The disadvantages are a possible tendency to bias, which can, of course, be guarded against and resisted; and the fact that it may be difficult to

give them a full workload at all times, so that the operation may become uneconomic. But they do provide additional security of information.

2. **Advertising agencies.** Advertising agencies need to prepare advertising campaigns within a total marketing plan and in the light of the fullest possible knowledge about markets. They also need much detailed information on readership and audiences, on motivation and on reactions to advertising themes. For these reasons many agencies employ their own marketing research specialists, who work for the agency and its clients. Indeed, the agencies had much to do with the whole development of market research in this country. The trend over many years now has been for these market research units to be operated as quite distinct departments or completely separate companies. They work for a whole range of clients, in addition to those of the advertising agency, and normally charge for their services in the same way as would a market research agency (which is what they have in practice become).
3. **Market research agencies.** There are many individuals and companies offering their services as market research agencies. Some offer a very wide range of services, whereas others are highly specialized. The Market Research Society publishes a list of these with an indication of their capability in its annual Yearbook. Among the specialist services available are: (a) retail audits and panels, (b) motivation research and (c) audience measurement. Some organizations specialize in one stage of the research process, such as interviewing or the processing and analysis of data.

4.4 Sources of Marketing Research Data

The items of information gathered as the basis of marketing research are usually referred to as data and we speak of primary data and secondary data. The former is information collected by means of a research programme carried out for a specific purpose. The latter is information that already exists, because it was collected as part of a previous research operation or for some different purpose.

Secondary data can be found inside a company, in sales records in particular. When used for marketing research, such data probably need reorganizing. For example, sales of a particular product will often be listed customer by customer, whereas the research might call for a geographical breakdown. Alternatively, many external sources of secondary data are available, in government departments, trade associations, professional bodies, the press, specialist research agencies and so on. The increasing availability, power and flexibility of computers makes it increasingly easy for this information to be made immediately available to decision makers. An increasing range of databases can now be accessed online.

Some research agencies operate syndicated research programmes in special fields. These are research programmes set up on a co-operative basis and paid for by contributions from each of the companies taking part. Usually it is possible to 'buy into' such a programme and thus gain access to data already collected. Alternatively, agencies sometimes themselves mount a programme of research and offer the results for sale to anyone interested. Trade associations often make certain information freely available to their members but sell it to 'outsiders'.

Increasingly all this kind of information is built into a total 'marketing information system' which is constantly updated.

Identifying relevant sources of secondary information, extracting the relevant data and analysing it is usually referred to as desk research.

4.5 How Marketing Research is Conducted

A great deal of time and money can be wasted unless marketing research is conducted in a carefully planned manner. Some kind of logical sequence, such as that outlined below, should always be observed.

1. **Identify the problem.** It is vital at the outset to be quite clear what information is needed and for what purpose. Usually it will be required to provide the basis for a management decision. The nature of that decision and the precise way that the additional information will help in taking it will dictate the kind of information required. Without such definition marketing research is liable to be used to gather a vast quantity of information at great cost but with low utility.
2. **Agree terms of reference.** At what time is the information needed, how much is it worth spending to obtain it, precisely what areas are to be studied and what is their relative importance?
3. **Plan the survey.** Factors to be decided upon at this stage include the following:
   (a) *Define the market* in which you are interested; this is the 'universe', the total number of people from which the sample will be selected.
   (b) *Decide on the sampling technique.* More will be said about sampling later in the chapter – sufficient here to say that marketing research uses extensively the technique of assessing the response of the many by studying that of a carefully selected few, just as a farmer judges the ripeness and quality of a wheat crop by examining a few grains from different parts of the field.
   (c) *Decide on the survey methods* to be used.
   (d) *Draft the questionnaire.* Most surveys use a series of questions (the questionnaire), which must be constructed with great care to elicit suitable responses from those being interviewed. The principles are discussed in later in this chapter.

Planning the survey will also include working out a detailed timetable and allocating manpower and such other resources as computer time. It will also have to be decided whether a single- or multi-stage survey is necessary, and whether there is need for a 'pilot' survey in advance of the survey proper.

4. **Execute the survey**. The survey has now to be carried out.
5. **Analyse the results**. Information is normally gathered in a way that means it can be directly entered in electronic form or can easily be translated into it. Thus the results of telephone research will normally be keyed directly into a computer. Manually completed questionnaires can be completed and scanned so that the precoded results can be automatically fed into a computer for analysis.

6. **Report to management**. Market researchers differ as to whether they merely report results, go further and interpret them, or go further still and offer recommendations. While one can disagree about whose job it is, ultimately the results of marketing research must be translated into management decisions. There is thus an intermediate and vital stage between delivery of the 'raw' facts and management coming to a decision, which means interpreting the facts and assessing their importance.

4.6 The Limitations of Marketing Research

It is tempting to think that all management decisions would be easier if only there were more information, and that marketing research is the key to better marketing management. There is some truth in this but marketing research does have severe limitations. First, it can be very costly. This can mean that obtaining the information on which to base a 'better' decision would absorb any profit the decision might produce. Second, it can be time-consuming. Time is often all important in marketing decisions. A good guess at the right time may be better than precise knowledge two months too late. Third, it solves nothing by itself. All over the world there are shelves full of market research reports that have not been acted upon. Marketing research is only valuable if it helps in making effective decisions. This takes us right back to the beginning and the vital importance of being quite clear at the outset why we need further information.

4.7 The Purposes of Marketing Research

4.7.1 The Value of Market Research[i]

Market research is a cost-effective way of finding out what people think, want, need or do. Normally, it is information unavailable elsewhere. Businesses use market research to help them produce goods and services in line with their customers' needs, and to evaluate the success of marketing strategies. Most successful organizations recognize that inadequate research significantly increases the risk of failure in the marketplace.

Social and government bodies also use market research to gauge public opinion, as an input to policy generation or to measure the success of government communication campaigns.

Market research is effective because, by talking to or measuring a relatively small number of people, you can find out about a much larger group. However, it only works if the people are representative of the total group of interest, if the right questions are asked, and if the answers are interpreted correctly. For this reason, research needs to be conducted by skilled and experienced practitioners who can design, conduct and deliver information and insight to their customers.

4.7.2 The Continuing Need for Facts

There are two important truths about market research:

1. Facts alone achieve nothing; they have to be processed. They need to be used imaginatively and creatively to produce good management decisions, which must then be well implemented.

2. But it is also true that decisions based purely on ideas (or hunch or flair), without the support of facts, can go sadly astray.

Managers need facts on which to base their decisions and their judgements – just as a judge in court would do, just as a scientist would do in testing a hypothesis, just as a general needs intelligence about the enemy's strength, position and movements before planning his own campaign. But there is a dimension in which business decisions differ from those of the judge or the scientist, although not from those of the general. Generally judges and scientists make a once and for all judgement. But, as we saw in Chapter 2, business managers are dealing with a continuing situation. They cannot stop events at a particular point while they consider all the relevant facts and then make a decision. Even while the decision-making process is going on, the facts will be changing – a new competitor enters the market, an existing one changes their prices or introduces a new product, the pattern of distribution alters, or a new advertising medium becomes available. In one part of the company's global market the economic situation may change, for the better or for the worse; even the manager's own decisions change the situations in which they are operating.

So, market research ideally needs to be built into the total activity of the business as a continuing operation, providing a steady flow of facts. There are, of course, many different kinds of fact. There are 'objective' and 'subjective' facts, as illustrated below.

- **Objective facts** – Examples include actions (buying habits) and demographic facts (age, sex, marital status).
- **Subjective facts** – Examples include knowledge (of a certain brand), perception (of an advertising message), notions (image of a brand or company), opinions (views, fashions, anticipations), intentions (to buy certain types of goods, say), wishes (to possess) and motives (mainly subconscious).

In varying degrees, and depending very much on the particular situation, all firms need facts of all these kinds to assist in making sound decisions. Gathering such facts in order to improve decisions is what marketing research is all about.

Clearly, the ease of gathering facts and their reliability when gathered varies considerably. Facts about the numbers and ages of the population are readily available and highly reliable. Those concerning what people intend to do or why they behave as they do (motives) will almost certainly have to be specially collected; the cost may be high, the reliability low and the difficulty of correct interpretation very considerable.

4.7.3 Marketing Research for Predicting the Future

It must be stressed that marketing research can never be an infallible crystal ball. Facts about what is happening are relatively easy to obtain, but facts about what has happened are more difficult to come by (people find it difficult to remember and what they do remember may become confused). Facts about what will happen are even more of a problem, for people often have not thought about the situation in question and may well find it difficult to project themselves mentally into it. They may have intentions which, when the time comes, are not carried out (because other influences come to bear, because the situation changes or simply because, like the ordinary human beings they are, they change their minds). This is probably one reason why political opinion polls sometimes give a totally misleading prediction of 'voting intentions'. The intentions may not be the same as the behaviour a few days or even hours later.

What will happen in given circumstances is, of course, what managers most wish to know. All that marketing research can offer (a not inconsiderable offering) is a firm basis for a clear appreciation of the present situation and perhaps a clearly delineated trend over time supported by some indication of what might happen in the future – a far better basis for a decision than no real knowledge at all.

4.8 Types of Market Research

If it is necessary to obtain primary data by survey, three methods are available. They are: (a) personal interviews, (b) telephone interviews and (c) postal questionnaires. In general, the cost decreases as we go down this list, but so do the reliability and extent of the information that can be obtained.

- **Personal interviewing** is the most versatile and can fairly readily be carried out on the basis of a properly selected sample (see later in the chapter). A large number of detailed questions can be asked, and the answers can be supplemented by the interviewer's personal observations if required. But the cost per interviewer is high, and the degree of planning and supervision required adds further to such costs.
- **Telephone interviewing** enables many people to be reached quickly over a wide geographical area. For this reason it is widely used in industrial marketing research. Its drawbacks are that, generally speaking, only short interviews of an impersonal nature can be carried out. Since, in the UK at any rate, telephones in the home are virtually universal, this method is increasingly widely used. Answers can be keyed straight in for computer analysis, giving further cost reductions.
- **Postal questionnaires** are relatively very cheap. However, the response rate (number of people who return properly completed questionnaires) is usually very low, which introduces its own form of bias.

For particular purposes, various forms of the following surveying techniques have proved valuable.

- **Panels** – When continuing research is required, the panel method is often used. This differs from the *ad hoc* enquiry (see Section 4.8.2) in that the same group (or panel) of informants is used to provide a series of answers over a period of time. This arrangement is particularly valuable when the need is to establish trends. Disadvantages are that it is difficult to maintain a panel that is truly representative over a long period; panel members may gradually become self-conscious and the information they provide no longer a spontaneous expression of their personal views. Panels are used extensively in listener/viewer research and the retail shop audit panel is a well-established source of information.
- **Discussion groups** – A small (typically around eight) and carefully selected group of people are brought together to discuss a particular topic. The interviewer does not normally pose specific questions but intervenes only to ensure that the discussion stays on

subject and that all-important aspects are discussed. Because interpretation of results can be difficult, interviewers (or more correctly discussion leaders) are frequently qualified psychologists.

Discussion groups cannot be regarded as properly representative and statistical analysis is normally impossible. However, they have the advantages that: (a) they are relatively inexpensive and (b) the dynamic group situation may bring out information that would not have been foreseen by someone constructing a questionnaire. The technique is particularly valuable for obtaining information rapidly and inexpensively, for example, as a guide to copywriters and product development groups and as an aid in constructing questionnaires for pilot surveys.

- **Motivational research** – This had a strong vogue some years ago but is now much less popular. It uses methods adapted from clinical psychology in an attempt to establish motives for behaviour and opinions. The methods used include word association, ink-blot tests and sentence completion tests. While in theory such methods can give deep insight into human attitudes, in practice much doubt has been cast on the validity of the results. Certainly, to carry out such tests thoroughly is very expensive of highly trained manpower, since interviews must be individually conducted and each can last several hours.

4.8.1 Primary Data

If the information required for a particular marketing research project does not already exist as secondary data, we have to determine the best way of collecting it. There are three fundamental approaches to the collection of primary data – observation, experiment and survey. It is the third approach that most people normally associate with market research, and later sections deal with it at length. However, the first two approaches also have an important role to play in certain circumstances.

Observation is based on the idea that it is sometimes better to watch what people do rather than to ask them what they do. This has the advantage that it eliminates any problem of interviewer bias and avoids the difficulty that people do not always remember their actions (especially trivial ones) very clearly. For example, a hidden camera may be the best way of establishing how customers move through a shop, and a tape recorder the best method of establishing the sales approach used by salesmen. Similarly, a physical count is normally used to establish the volume of traffic on key roads and the volume of different brands sold by important retail outlets (increasingly via electronic point of sale, or 'EPOS' installations).

Simulation of a real situation in an **experiment** may often be a better way of assessing likely future behaviour than asking people hypothetical questions. It is notoriously difficult to get reliable answers about possible future behaviour. But, if for example, we want to know which of two possible packages housewives would prefer, we can put them side by side in a real or dummy shop, give a group of housewives a shopping list and money to spend and see which pack they choose. Similarly, a way of assessing children's preference for one toy as against another is to give a group of children a selection of toys to play with and see what happens (the way in which they play can also yield valuable insights). Test marketing is of course an example of using experiment as a means of obtaining marketing research data.

4.8.2 *Ad Hoc* and Continuous Research

A great deal of marketing research is carried out on a continuous basis. Many government statistics are gathered quarterly, annually or at some other regular interval. Many commercial studies are carried out on a 'panel' or 'audit' basis. The great value of this is that we can plot trends and see whether a particular factor is increasing or decreasing, whether any of the elements being plotted are departing from what the trends were indicating, and so on. Any departures from the 'expected' trends may point to new factors of importance in the marketplace.

On the other hand, this is costly, and not every aspect of every market justifies the expense. Many marketing investigations are thus carried out on an irregular, infrequent or even a once-and-for-all basis. The term usually applied to such cases is *ad hoc* research.

4.8.3 Panels and Audits

Panels consist of permanent samples of the universe concerned (see later in the chapter for a full discussion of sampling). Members of these panels agree to give regular interviews and/or regularly record information in special 'diaries'. They are usually paid a small fee. This has obvious advantages in that sampling is itself costly, and using the same sample over and over represents a saving. But the main reasons for the use of panels are as follows:

1. Comparison is easier and more reliable, since we are comparing over time the behaviour and/or attitudes not just of similar people but of the same people. It is even possible, if desired, to study individual behaviour over a period of time.
2. Because they are specially recruited and instructed, panel members are usually more 'forthcoming' than people interviewed 'out of the blue', and can be asked to carry out more complicated and extensive procedures.

Disadvantages of panels are that members may become self-conscious and no longer truly representative. Indeed, it may be that willingness to participate is in itself a non-characteristic response. Another problem is matching the succession when, for one reason or another, people leave the panel.

However, panels are used to gain regular information on such matters as household purchasing patterns, TV viewing and radio listening habits and current stock patterns. An example of the last item is the 'pantry check', where interviewers make regular calls to a panel of households to check what products they are using (providing valuable information on such matters as changing preferences for pack size, quantities bought at a time etc.).

Panels are not confined to individual members of the public or to households. The **retail audit** technique uses panels of shops to establish brand shares and volume of sales from retail outlets to customers (which, because of changing stock levels, may be quite different from the volume of deliveries from factory to retailers).

A. C. Nielsen, owned by Dun and Bradstreet, and operating in thirty-four countries, are leaders in this kind of research. Starting with their Food Index, then moving on to a Drug Index (based on audits of grocery and chemist shops), they now regularly publish indexes for confectionery, home appliances, DIY, liquor stores and cash-and-carry wholesalers. Visit the A. C. Nielsen web pages for a description of how their Lifestyle Track system operates (http://acnielsen.com).

A wide variety of consumer and retail panels is available and the companies offering them (along with other kinds of marketing research facilities) are listed in the Market Research Society Year Book. The Retail Audits Ltd entry, for example, includes: 'RAL operates 10 national audit panels and has national distribution checking services, covering such outlet types as chemists, grocers, garages, hardware, fertilizers, CTNs, licensed premises, electrical, toys and stationery.'

The results of retail audits, consumer panels and many other types of research are available to anyone who wishes to buy them. This cost-sharing approach, known as **syndicated research**, enables very extensive research to be carried out in a way that would be uneconomic if each client had to commission it separately.

Some research companies operate a regular survey (often using a panel of interviewers), where a small number of questions can be bought by a series of different subscribers. Thus, the same survey might cover car servicing, shaving habits and a variety of other topics. These are often referred to as 'omnibus' surveys and they provide cost-effective access to a large representative sample. Those making up the sample are often consumers, but some companies run specific omnibus surveys in selected industries or sectors.

The results are confidential to individual clients; the only shared data are demographics such as age, sex, class/income and region, which are used to cross-analyse your selected information. Taylor Nelson Sofres is one of the world's leading market information groups providing continuous and custom research and market analysis in over eighty countries. The surveys they offer are among consumers. To find out more about the variety of their survey initiatives, try their web pages (http://www.tnsofres.com/uk).

Omnibus surveys will collect interviews to match the profile of the population, in terms of such variables as sex, age, class/income and region. Furthermore, in countries where there is a high unlisted telephone number element of the population (in Great Britain, for example, where many urban telephone numbers can be ex-directory), randomly computer-generated telephone numbers will be used to ensure comprehensive coverage. Most face-to-face research uses a random location sampling method. At the data analysis stage, fine-tuning of profile by weighting is the norm.

Some of the notable omnibus services in existence are:

- Omnimas®,[ii] which has been around for three decades and is the largest weekly consumer omnibus survey in Great Britain. The survey interviews 2100 different adults aged 16+ per week, which can be increased to 4000 in the same week, depending on the organization's needs.
- Ncompass™, the international omnibus from Taylor Nelson Sofres. This gives access to cost-effective worldwide consumer behaviour and opinions – fast.
- PhoneBus®, one of the UK's speediest and smartest consumer omnibuses, which runs twice-weekly providing data from 1000 or 2000 adults in Great Britain aged 16+. It provides a four-day turnaround.

4.9 Qualitative Research

Marketing research is not only based on statistical analysis of the responses of large numbers of people (quantitative research) – sometimes disparagingly referred to as 'head counting'. Often it is valuable (and frequently more cost-effective) to have information which, although having little or no statistical validity, does give important insights.

We referred in Chapter 2 to motivational research and to group discussions – these are two of the techniques used in qualitative research. Here the aim is to explore in some depth the reactions, opinions or behaviour of a few people. While these people are chosen so as to be reflective of the universe, they are not numerous enough for the information obtained to be totally acceptable as being representative of the universe. However, information and insights obtained in this way are often used as a starting point for drafting questionnaires. The latter are used in surveys that do give a statistically accurate view of the whole. Even where this is not the case, however, qualitative research can often have great value in helping us to understand why people behave as they do, instead of merely telling us what they do – which is largely what is obtained from such research as retail audits.

4.10 Advertising Research

Marketing research carried out as an aid to advertising decisions has become so extensive as to be a subject, and an industry, in its own right. Two main areas of this research are important:

1. **Advertisement research.** This includes testing proposed advertisements to determine whether they are likely to have the desired effect (advertisement pre-testing), and also research to assess what the effect actually was (advertisement post-testing).
2. **Media research.** This consists primarily of identifying the size and nature of the audiences for the various media, but also tries to determine such matters as the effect of varying the size and position of advertisements.

4.10.1 Advertisement Research

Many of the standard techniques of marketing research – questionnaires and group discussions, for example – can be used to yield information about the ways in which people have reacted to advertising or how they will be likely to react. Interviewees can, for example, be shown a publication and then asked questions about which advertisements they can recall. This, of course, is a 'post-testing' technique, but a similar 'pre-test' can be obtained by making up a folder or dummy magazine containing one or more projected advertisements (perhaps along-side existing ones) to obtain reactions to them before incurring the cost of placing them in publications.

Television commercials can be tested in a similar way before or after showing over the air. In one method members of the public are invited to a private film show. Following a brief feature or cartoon film, a number of commercials are screened, including the one being tested. There are then a number of techniques enabling the audience to record their reactions, one of the simplest being the questionnaire, perhaps supplemented by group discussion. Sometimes a 'brand-awareness' questionnaire is completed before and after the showing, giving a measurement of change in awareness brought about by seeing the commercial or commercials under test.

At the more complicated extreme, a whole battery of physiological tests have been used, measuring such things as sweat response (with a 'psychogalvanometer') or pupil dilation (by means of a special camera). Such techniques were much in vogue among some researchers at one time but are very seldom used nowadays. Many of these 'ironmongery' techniques are far too expensive for other than experimental use and, in any case, few of them are universally regarded as totally reliable. Increasingly, group discussions are used whenever possible as they provide a great deal of information at low cost.

For more information on advertising research refer to *The Fundamentals of Advertising* (2nd Edition).[iii]

4.10.2 Media Research

In the UK, a number of joint bodies supported by the advertising industry are responsible for basic readership/audience research concerning the main media:

- **National Readership Surveys Ltd** – For newspapers and magazines, NRS Ltd commissions readership research. The NRS is a non-profit-making but commercial organization, which sets out to provide estimates of the number and nature of the people who read UK newspapers and consumer magazines.
- **Broadcasters' Audience Research Board (BARB)** – This is the primary source of television audience data in the UK. The shareholding of the company is made up of the BBC, ITVA, Channel 4, Channel 5, BSkyB and the IPA (Institute of Practitioners in Advertising). BARB is currently responsible for two research services:
  (a) *Audience measurement*. This service provides quantitative data on a continuous basis giving television-viewing estimates within all UK domestic households. Both broadcasting organizations and the advertising industry use these data.
  (b) *Audience reaction*. The reaction service provides qualitative data on appreciation of television programmes. The service is confidential to subscribing broadcasters (BBC and ITV).
- **Radio Joint Audience Research Ltd (RAJAR)** –This is a company specifically established to manage the UK's agreed system of radio audience measurement. It is jointly owned by the CRCA (Commercial Radio Companies Association) on behalf of commercial radio companies and by the BBC. RAJAR commissions regular research based on weekly diaries kept by all members of selected households. This information forms the basis of quarterly reports on radio listening. The Quarterly Summary of Radio Listening contains detailed breakdowns of the areas served by individual BBC stations and each of the commercial stations. Internet access is via http://www.rajar.co.uk.
- **Commercial Radio Companies Association (CRCA)** – This is the trade body for commercial radio companies in the UK. It is a voluntary, non-profit-making body, incorporated as a company limited by guarantee, and was formed by the first radio companies when independent radio began in 1973.

- **Association for Survey Computing (ASC)** – Originally known as the Study Group on Computers in Survey Analysis (SGCSA), the ASC was formed in 1971 in order to improve knowledge of good practice in survey computing and to disseminate information on techniques and survey software. It is a non-profit organization, affiliated to the British Computer Society and the International Association for Statistical Computing. It has a wide-ranging membership at both individual and corporate levels, and has close working links with the Royal Statistical Society, the Social Research Association and the Market Research Society. Although based in the UK, it has a growing international membership.

4.11 Product and Package Testing

So far we have considered marketing research in connection with products already 'in the marketplace', but an important use of research is in screening products so that only those likely to be acceptable to customers reach the market. Not only the product as such but its packaging and everything about it can be subjected to testing before the product launch.

Some of this is by completely straightforward questioning of carefully selected samples of people. Often, however, subjective reactions are provoked, and rather more subtle techniques need to be used. For example, groups of people can be asked to choose between a number of alternative products with (unbeknown to the group) only minor differences, such as colour or design of pack. This 'blind' approach can give more reliable results than open questions such as 'Which of these three packs do you prefer?'.

Getting a suitable sample to taste a product or various products and give their views can be a valid test. Two commonly used ways of doing this are:

1. Invite people in from a busy shopping street to a rented room (e.g. in a church hall), give them a cup of tea and a snack, and then ask their reactions to the taste of the snack. This approach is known as a **'hall test'**.
2. Give people a sample to try in their homes and call them back a few days later to collect their views (**'placement test'**). This is a more expensive method but has the advantages that the whole family's reactions can be gathered, and that it is carried out under more natural conditions than the 'hall test'.

4.12 Test Marketing

In a sense, the reason for all marketing research is to reduce the level of costly failures. The best possible way to know whether your marketing mix is correct is to try it on the customers and see whether they buy (and go on buying) it in sufficient numbers. But a failure at this stage can be very costly indeed. Yet research can only attempt to measure whether some of the ingredients in the marketing mix are likely to be successful; as we said earlier, no research can predict what will actually happen.

The compromise between a full-scale, potentially very risky, national launch of the product, and research that at best can only give useful pointers is a test marketing operation. That is to say, one part of the total market is chosen for a launching of the new product. If this is successful, we can then go on to the complete national launch or a step by step, area by area build-up to the national marketing stage (a 'rolling launch'). If the test is unsuccessful, then less money and effort have been wasted than would have been the case with an immediate national launch (see Section 3.12.4).

Test marketing is of value not only with new product launches. Successful marketing necessitates correctly adjusting a large number of variables – weight and kind of advertising, price levels, distribution patterns and so on. Changes in any one of these may improve or worsen the competitive position. Thus, before making changes of this kind throughout a market, it may be valuable to first test the proposed changes in one section of the market.

There are some key points to consider when selecting a test market area:

- It must be as representative as possible of the market as a whole, in terms of age, class, sex, size of households; in terms of proportion of large and small shops, independents and multiples; in terms of relative weight of one's own sales organization; and in terms of behaviour patterns. For example, are people in the area typical of the whole in their purchases and usage of the type of product concerned? One area may have higher car ownership or keep fewer pets than another.
- As far as possible, it should be self-contained. A town with a big shopping centre, serving a wide 'hinterland' area, for example, presents problems when it comes to analysing the significance of sales patterns generated during a test.
- The area should offer advertising media that can be duplicated when sales become national. For this reason (and for reasons connected with the previous point) a television coverage area is often chosen. Even so, there are problems of overlap (people in some areas have the choice of two or three TV transmitters). Other problems are that the local press does not have exactly the same characteristics as the national newspapers, but the latter offer few regional test facilities (although a number of colour magazines do now offer, at a price, the facility of including an advertisement only in those copies delivered in a particular area).
- Size – the larger the area, the better (but more expensive) the test. Small areas are not only more likely to be atypical but also tend to present greater problems of overlap and non-availability (without colossal wastage) of national media.

It should be noted that test marketing is not a precise instrument. The conditions listed above are difficult to achieve in any completeness; there are usually many variables, and attributing success or failure to particular variables is almost impossible. There are also other problems. For example, an extensive test gives competitors an opportunity to beat you by launching their products virtually before your tests are completed. It is not even unknown for competitors to devise ways of 'spoiling' a test.

For all these reasons, test marketing is no longer thought to be the panacea and the near-necessity it was once considered. In many situations (especially where the price of failure is not very high) it may be more cost-effective to go straight into a national launch, particularly with products (e.g. in the fashion world) which have a short life cycle.

A well-considered and probably substantial programme of research must accompany test marketing if it is to be of great value. Thus, it is of little use to find that sales of a new snack food are too low to be profitable if we do not know why. Research may tell us that customers do not like the taste sufficiently, that they regard the price as too high, that too few retailers are prepared to stock or display it, or that the advertising was noticed by too few people. With an array of facts such as these we are in a much better position to make further changes or to develop the next new product more successfully.

4.13 The Full Scope of Marketing Research

The above are some of the more important types of marketing research, but there are many others. The full scope of marketing research is summarized in Figure 4.1.

4.14 The Positive Use of Marketing Research

There is a tendency to view the use of marketing research in a negative or a passive way. Thus, it is used to help solve problems, such as why our brand share is falling or why customers prefer an alternative product. It could also be used to tell us what the best advertising medium for the desired audience is or to monitor progress – what our brand share is now, or what the overall market trend is.

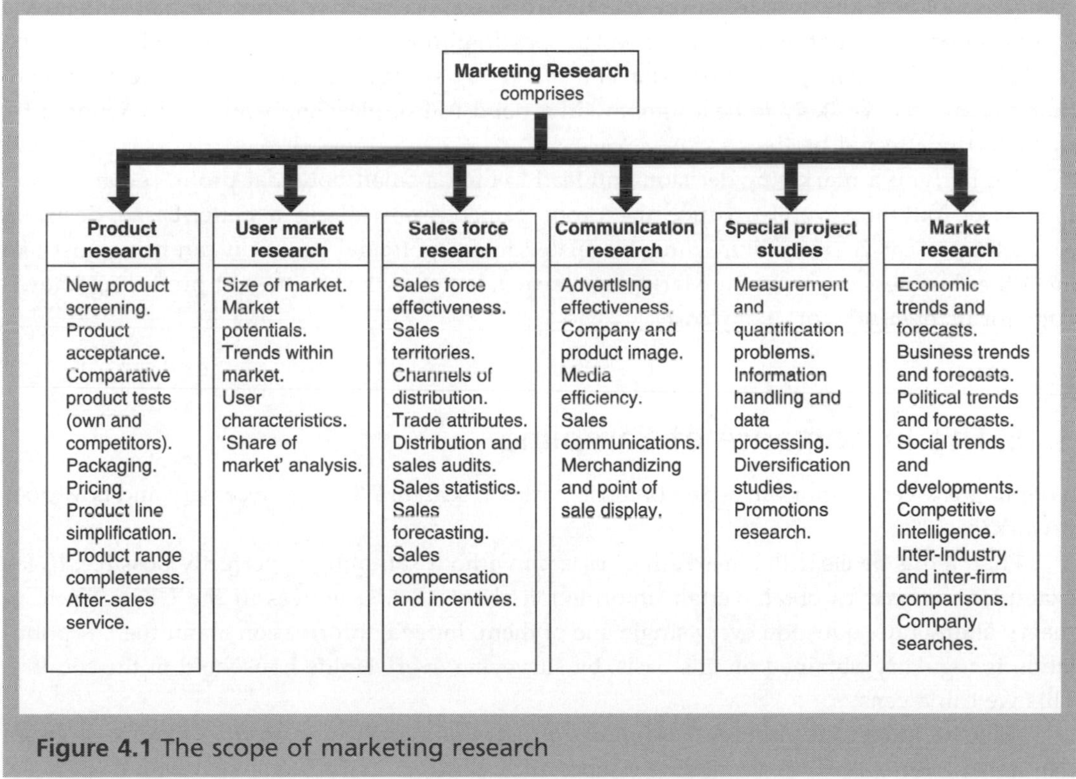

Figure 4.1 The scope of marketing research

But research can also be used positively in order to expose marketing opportunities, which can then be exploited. Here are some examples of possible questions to ask.

- What are the ways in which our product is used? (Johnson's were able to open up a whole new market when they discovered that adults were using their baby talcum powder.)
- What customer needs are not at present well met by our products or our competitors'? (See gap analysis in Section 3.12.1).
- What might be the customer reaction to an advertising approach no one is currently using?

Using research to expose gaps in the marketplace can reveal opportunities potentially far more profitable than simply plugging away with existing products to known customers in the traditional way.

4.15 Cost-effective Marketing Research Decisions

In Section 4.6 it was pointed out that the two main limitations of marketing research are time and cost. It is particularly important not to become over-enthused by the undoubted value of research to the point of ignoring its cost implications. For example, we have said several times that knowledge of brand shares is an important use of marketing research, and to know one's own and one's competitors' brand shares is an important matter. But it is not important for a company holding a tiny share of the market. To know precisely whether the market share is 2 per cent or 3 per cent will hardly be worth spending money on, since the knowledge will be unlikely to affect management decisions on marketing strategy. At anything up to 5 per cent brand share, one is likely to be a minnow in a pond full of big fish, being totally ignored by them and unaffected by their actions.

Similarly, if a marketing decision will lead to only a small potential profit, research costs may wipe out or severely reduce the profit gained from taking a better-based decision. Marketing research expenditure must be related to the potential benefit it can bring, just like any other business expenditure. Marketing research is not in the business of producing knowledge for its own sake or at any cost.

4.16 The Importance of Sampling

Sampling is a very important aspect of most market research. Why is it necessary and how does it work?

First, let us be clear that marketing research without sampling is perfectly possible. If, for example, we need to obtain certain information about all housewives in the UK, we can, in theory at any rate, question every single one of them. Indeed, information about the UK population is regularly obtained on this basis, by surveying every single household in the country. This we call a census.

In some industrial markets the number of users of a particular product may be so small that it is perfectly feasible to interview them all. Indeed, it could be dangerous not to do so, since any one of them may be a sufficiently large user to have a significant effect on the total picture (computer manufacturers, for example).

However, normally a census is not the preferred method of obtaining information (a) because of the cost and (b) because of the time it would take. For most products, to interview all households would cost far more than the potential profit over many years. Because of the time it takes to carry out a full census, even government population statistics are now regularly gathered in the UK on a sampling basis – with a full census only occasionally. Using the figures from a full census means inevitably working with out of date information, and it will often be preferable to have up to date information, even if it is slightly less accurate.

4.17 The Basis of Sampling

The use of sampling is based on the concept that, if a small number of items or parts (the sample) are selected at random from a larger number of parts of a whole (the universe), then the sample will tend to have the same characteristics in approximately the same proportion as the universe. The 'universe' is sometimes called the 'population'.

'Random' has a special meaning in this context. It does not mean, as in everyday usage, aimless or haphazard. A random sample is one selected in such a way that every single individual unit in the universe from which it was chosen had a full and equal chance of being included in the sample. Its implications are perhaps best understood by looking at examples of sample selection that are *not random*:

- A sample of householders obtained by selecting numbers from the telephone directory cannot be random, since people not on the telephone, or who are ex-directory, have no chance of being selected and so are not representative of the universe.
- A sample of marketing people selected from the membership list of the Institute of Marketing cannot be random, since it excludes those who are not members.
- Questionnaires inserted in a motoring magazine for completion and return by readers cannot provide a random sample of all car owners because: (a) it excludes non-readers; (b) it excludes readers who did not see that particular issue; and (c) it excludes those who are too busy or disinclined to fill in the questionnaire and return it.

We said in the definition at the beginning of this section that the sample tends to have the same characteristics as the universe. However, it may well not precisely match the characteristics of the universe – how closely it matches will depend largely on the size of the sample.

We can see in principle why this will be so by considering the simple case of tossing a coin. The proportion of 'heads' to 'tails' must be 50:50 if we toss the coin enough times. But we know from experience that, purely due to chance, there are 'runs', so that, in a small number of tosses, we may get a higher number of heads than tails or vice versa. The more times we toss, the more likely we are to reach the 50:50 balance. Similarly, with a sample, the nearer it approximates in size to the total universe, the less likely we are to get chance deviations from the total pattern.

Fortunately, as the sample size increases, we fairly rapidly reach the point when there is a high degree of 'match' with the total universe, and further increases in sample size give only relatively small increases in accuracy. Provided we have a good idea of the total size of the universe, we can, using statistical formulae, calculate the size of sample needed to give the desired degree of accuracy. Since specialists within the marketing research team would normally carry out these calculations, we do not need to concern ourselves with precisely how they operate.

The main point to grasp here is that the use of sampling techniques enables us to trade off an acceptable loss in accuracy for a substantial reduction in cost and in time taken to provide the information. Since it is rare that 100 per cent accuracy is necessary in any case, and since percentages in the 90s are fairly readily obtainable with relatively small samples, this is a good bargain.

4.17.1 Size of Sample

The following examples give a good general idea of what all the above actually leads to in terms of sample size. Surveys with more than 15,000 (0.025 per cent of the adult population of the UK) are very exceptional. A nationwide sample often contains no more than 2000 cases and is rarely greater than 5000 cases. Samples of only a few hundred cases are often regarded as sufficient for the purposes of a particular survey.

The aim is to include the optimum, not the maximum, number of cases. The choice of optimum size may be decided according to various criteria:

- **The budget available**. After deducting other project costs such as research design, questionnaire development, data processing, analysis etc. the remainder determines the size of the sample that can be surveyed. There are limits, of course. If the money available is enough for only a clearly inadequate sample, a decision must be made. Either more funds must be found or the project cancelled. While this may seem a highly unscientific approach, commercial realism dictates that plans are based on financial resources. The 'budget available' approach forces the researcher to carefully consider the value of information in relation to cost.
- **Rules of thumb**. Some individuals specify they want a sample of a given number of respondents. While the choice may be based on some consideration of sampling error, in other cases it is based on nothing more than 'gut feel'.
- **Number of subgroups to be analysed**. The total sample size may be viewed as acceptable until the various subgroups to be analysed are considered. For example, if a sample of 400 was chosen as acceptable on an overall basis, once one analyses the data by sex and age, the subgroups may become too small to be of value. Thus, the larger the number of subgroups that need to be analysed, the larger the required total sample size. It has been suggested that the sample should be large enough so that there will be 100 or more respondents in each major subgroup and a minimum of 20 to 50 respondents in each of the less important subgroups.
- **Traditional statistical methods**. These are the more traditional approaches for determining the size of simple random samples, and are based on an estimate of:

  (a) How widely the characteristics of a population vary (the population variance).

(b) The amount of sample mistakes or bias that the researcher is willing to accept from the sampling process (sampling error).

(c) The desired level of confidence that the sampling error will fall within acceptable limits (confidence limits).

In practice this means that consumer research surveys use several hundred respondents, and for large surveys several thousand. Industrial and other specialized surveys are often smaller, but still require adequate samples.

We have been talking in terms of sampling individuals. Samples are, of course, drawn not only from groups of people but from other 'populations' or 'universes', such as shops, farms, posters, sites etc. People can be sampled in such groups as customers, readers of publications, shoppers etc.

4.18 Types of Sample

So far we have been talking of sampling in terms of random sampling of the entire universe. But we have also referred to the need for marketing research to operate within cost limitations. This latter point means that, in practice, other approaches to sampling are frequently used. The main division is between the following:

1. **Random sampling**, where each unit in the universe has the same chance of being included in the sample. Units are selected by precise means and the interviewer is given detailed instructions on who or what to include.
2. **Quota sampling**, where the interviewer selects the individuals to be interviewed, but is given detailed instructions concerning their characteristics (age, sex, class, occupation etc.), the number of each category to be interviewed and the conditions of interview (at home, at work etc.)

Random sampling needs a 'sampling frame', i.e. a complete and up to date list of all members of the universe, such as that provided by the electoral roll (although it, like any sampling frame, is never totally accurate). The units to be included in the sample are then selected along the lines of the following example.

On any given section of the electoral roll, randomly select (by means of a more sophisticated version of the 'drawing lots' principle) a starting point, such as the 10th household. The interviewer is instructed to interview the head of that 10th household, then the 25th, 40th, 55th and so on, or the 30th, 50th, 70th and so on – the interval depending on the total sample size required. The interviewer must interview the person specified and must, if necessary, call back repeatedly until he or she finds the interviewee at home. Strict rules are laid down to cover such contingencies as death or permanent absence, and the interviewer can only include someone else in the sample instead if so instructed.

In the case of a quota sample, the interviewer selects the people to be interviewed, although strict criteria are laid down to ensure as far as possible that the final sample, when all the individuals interviewed by the different interviewers are put together, does represent the universe.

The main advantage of a quota sample is that the cost per interview is much lower than with a random sample, as particular individuals do not have to be found and interviewers can conduct more interviews in a day. The disadvantage is that, unless very well trained and reliable interviewers are used, personal bias in selecting people for an interview may affect the sample adversely. For example, there is a natural tendency for interviewers to select people they know or suspect will readily respond, and to choose locations near their home or that are easy to travel to.

4.18.1 Stratified Sampling

Sometimes it is specified that there are to be proportionately more sampling units from some levels or strata of the universe than from others. Thus, in order to be able to make the necessary subdivisions, it might be necessary to sample a higher proportion of rural households than urban ones (which are a much bigger stratum).

In industrial market research it is often possible to stratify companies according to number of employees or turnover. A number of different strata can be fixed – for example up to 500 employees, 500–2000, 2001–5000 and over 5000 – and a different percentage taken from each category according to its size and importance.

One important factor that may lead to the use of stratified sampling arises when one or more strata are so small a proportion of the universe that they would yield only a very low number of interviews. Suppose that, in a total sample of 1000, one stratum is expected to yield only fifty interviews, when the subdivision required in the analysis of results may call for at least 200 in the smallest group. It is then necessary either to increase the total sample to 4000, and thus considerably increase the cost, or to add 150 interviews within the particular stratum, at much lower cost. In tabulations of results proportionality can be restored by 'weighting' the various strata according to the size of sample taken from each.

4.18.2 Multi-stage Sampling

If the universe is a big one, such as a whole country, selecting a relatively small number of units over the whole universe will mean that widely scattered (and therefore costly) interviews have to be carried out. A way of reducing this problem is to divide the universe into sections (such as administrative areas), sample the sections on a random selection basis, and then take a random sample within each section. Clearly, there can be a number of stages – for example, counties, and then towns within selected counties, electoral areas within towns and, finally, individuals within selected areas – the selection of each stage being established on a random basis.

Cluster sampling is a form of multi-stage sampling in which sales areas, residential blocks or similar groupings are chosen randomly and then either all units within the 'cluster' interviewed or else a further random selection made within each cluster. Area sampling is a similar process, in which a geographical area of some kind is selected randomly.

CASE STUDY[iv]

In December 2001, a number of UK newspapers were taken in by a survey of the social behaviour of young adults. This survey was collecting information on the attitudes and behaviour of today's youngsters towards promiscuity and sex before marriage. *The Sun*, *The Mirror*, *The Express*, and *The Times* reported on the 'Brook Survey'; the last of these newspapers used a headline that stated 'Young think ten lovers is normal'. The findings were reported faithfully by the main national news agency, the Press Association, and a string of newspapers; they were said to reveal a 'culture change'. The Brook Group itself used the results as a platform for a national campaign to expose 'society's double standards and hypocrisy' about young people and sex. They showed a desperate need for more sex education and contraception, it said.

The verdict of independent analysts after seeing the research was very scathing. It was discovered that the survey involved just 99 women and 40 men at Southampton University, where all but 24 were students and many were thought to have links with the university's Centre for Sexual Health Research. One commentator said that the research '... was not capable of any interpretation beyond its own boundaries. To be presenting percentages on the basis of the views of 40 men is ridiculous'.

A partner in the MORI polling group said: 'A total of 139 people is too small a sample on which to base conclusions.'

While the Brook research claimed that 64 per cent of men and 54 per cent of women thought it 'OK for a person to sleep with more than ten partners' before marriage, the National Survey of Sexual Attitudes and Lifestyles, published the month before, found that just 20 per cent of men and less than 15 per cent of women had more than ten partners. This survey was based on 11,000 interviews with young people.

Question

1. Discuss why you feel that the 'opinion polls' prior to an election so often do not give an accurate prediction of the outcome.

4.19 Questionnaires and the Problem of Bias

Although sampling can be a complex process, it is in some ways easy to handle (by experts, that is) because it is susceptible to precise statistical analysis. The limitations arise not so much from inadequate techniques as from the difficulty of obtaining suitable sampling frames.

Some other aspects of marketing research are much more a matter of judgement, and questionnaire design is one of them. There are some simple rules, which are briefly listed below, but experience, care, good judgement and careful cross-checking are necessary if bias is to be avoided.

4.19.1 The Problem of Bias

In all marketing research there must be a constant fight to prevent bias creeping into the results, i.e. to avoid the situation where the results are not in fact representative of the universe. Bias is any force, tendency or procedural error in the collection, analysis or interpretation of data that produces distortion.

Among the sources of bias are:

- **Faulty sample selection**. The various sections of a universe may not be represented in the sample in the correct proportions. An extreme case might be using the telephone directory to select a sample that should include the same proportion of poor people as in the population as a whole, when the poor have fewer telephones than the rest.
- **Prejudiced interviewing**. There was a 'classic case' of an ardent prohibitionist who interviewed down-and-outers. They blamed liquor for their situation to a much greater extent than did similar people questioned by less prejudiced interviewers. Generally speaking, it is desirable for interviewers not to be too different from respondents in age, education and socio-economic status.
- **Leading questions**. Bias here springs from questions that suggest the answer required. There is a strong tendency for people to give the 'accommodating answer' – the one they believe the interviewer wants. If the sponsor of the research is known, the respondent's attitude to the organization may well affect the answers given. Questions that have strong connotations of social acceptability (such as 'How frequently do you bath?') are likely to lead to respondents giving the answer they believe they ought to give. Other sources of bias are questions that are ambiguous or not clearly understood.

It is partly because of these problems that it is customary to include a pilot survey as part of most market research projects. This enables questionnaires to be tested and many potential difficulties overcome.

4.19.2 The Content of Questionnaires

In most surveys the interviewer is provided with a questionnaire (but see Section 4.20). The purposes this fulfils are:

1. To list the questions the interviewer is to ask, in the precise words to be used and in the right sequence.
2. To provide space for recording the answers, usually in such a way that they can be readily analysed. Frequently a scanner will be used, so that it can read off the marks and transfer them directly for computer analysis.
3. To record details of the respondent – age, sex, occupation etc. – and sometimes such other factors as whether he or she is a car owner or not, or a householder or not, depending on the needs of the particular survey.

4.19.3 Types of Question

Questions asked in interviewing are of four main types:

1. **Dichotomous**, i.e. answered by a simple yes or no (usually with a 'don't know' column as well).
2. **Multiple-choice**, where a number of possible answers are listed and the interviewer indicates which are selected (sometimes more than one).
3. **Scaled-response** – a type of multiple-choice that is designed to capture intensity. So, the respondent is given a range of possible answers from across a scale of four or five points. For example, in response to a statement the respondent is asked to indicate whether they 'strongly agree', 'agree', 'disagree' or 'strongly disagree'. A fifth point would be 'neither agree nor disagree' in the middle of the range, but some researchers might not favour a neutral reaction.
4. **Open-ended**, where no particular kind of answer is presupposed and the interviewer has to write in the respondent's answer.

Open-ended questions have the disadvantage of being slow, difficult to analyse, and yielding answers that are perhaps irrelevant or incoherent. On the other hand, they allow the possibility of much fuller answers, with shades of meaning, they reduce the possibility of bias from answers suggested by the researchers, and they may overcome the reluctance of some respondents to answer direct questions. The selection of types of question will depend on the kind of information being sought and the depth required, the type of respondent, and the cost limitations imposed on the research.

4.19.4 Some Rules for Framing Questions

In order to reduce bias, care has to be taken in working out the sequence and wording of questions. Some of the 'rules' are as follows (but judgement and experience play a large part):

- Questions on matters of a private or emotional nature should come at the end of an interview, as should complicated questions and those requiring thought, so that these are not asked until the respondent's interest is engaged.
- Conversely, easy questions and those most likely to capture a respondent's interest are placed at the beginning.
- Questions should be short, easy to understand, and phrased in appropriate colloquial language, albeit chosen not to confuse possible respondents.
- There should be no ambiguity and 'double-barrelled' questions should be avoided ('Did you drink coffee with lunch and dinner yesterday?' holds two questions).
- Leading questions (i.e. where it appears obvious what answer is expected) must be avoided.
- Questions that rely heavily on the respondent's memory (e.g. 'Which magazines have you read during the past six months?') must be avoided.
- Questions must be as precise as possible. For example, in the previous point what do we mean by 'reading' a magazine? From cover to cover? A quick glance? Editorial or advertisements, or both?

- There are severe limits to the length of questionnaire that will hold a respondent's interest. To go beyond these limits increases the risk of ill-considered or flippant answers.

4.20 Structured and Unstructured Interviews

So far we have considered interviews in which the interviewer asks specific questions listed on a questionnaire (or, for example, in postal surveys, in which the respondent is asked to read and answer the questions). These are known as 'structured interviews'. Often, especially in industrial marketing research, it is not possible, or not the best technique, to do this and an 'unstructured interview' is used. In these the interviewer has a general idea of the ground to be covered (and may be given a list of questions for his/her guidance), but extracts the information through a guided conversation with the respondent instead of through specific questions. The respondent is encouraged to talk about the area of interest in his own way. The interviewer makes notes or (with the respondent's permission) uses a tape recorder.

4.21 The Socio-economic Classification

Although the idea of 'class' is becoming increasingly suspect, at any rate in this context, it is often convenient to be able to break down the population into groups. Since there is often a degree of correlation between occupation and lifestyle (the latter in turn having some influence on buying habits etc.), the classification now commonly used is based on the occupation of 'chief income earner', which has replaced the earlier 'head of household'. This is described in great detail in a document published by the National Readership Survey, for which it was originally developed. In outline the classification runs as shown in Figure 4.2.

By using this classification (usually simplified into A, B, C1, C2, D, E), data produced in different surveys can achieve a higher degree of comparability than would be the case if a

Classification (using chief income earner)	% of UK population
A (Higher managerial administrative or professional)	3.1
B (Intermediate managerial administrative or professional)	18.1
C1 (Supervisory, clerical, junior administrative or professional)	27.8
C2 (Skilled manual workers)	22.4
D (Semi-skilled and unskilled manual workers)	17.0
E (State pensioners, widows, casual and lowest grade earners)	11.6

Figure 4.2 Classification of the UK population based on occupation of the chief income earner (National Readership Survey (NRS Ltd) July 1996–June 1997)

different classification were used. It is for this reason that the system continues in use, although many people have reservations about it.

A number of new methods of classification are now available, including Media Graphics, which classifies people according to the types of newspapers and magazines they read and the TV programmes they watch. Another system, Sagacity, is based on life cycles. People are grouped into dependants (still living with their parents), independents (supporting themselves), family stagers, empty nesters and the retired. This is crossed-linked to broad social gradings. However, no other system has yet achieved the universal acceptance needed for it to replace the established one.

4.22 Using Secondary Data

Because it avoids the cost of sampling and interviewing, the use of secondary data (see Section 4.4) has obvious advantages. Naturally there are snags, too, for the sources are not always obvious or easy to locate, and the information is not always available in a form that makes it easy to use for the purpose in hand. There is also the question of whether the cost of re-analysing data will be so high that gathering fresh primary data will, in the long run, be cheaper.

Sources are an easier matter to deal with. There are a number of 'sources of sources', i.e. books of reference that indicate where various kinds of information may be found. Most government statistical offices issue a guide to what is available in their own files, as do organizations such as OECD, UNO, GATT and the European Commission.

The Internet has opened up the field of information and a number of sources are listed at the end of the chapter. Always remember that, while the information is available, its reliability must always be confirmed.

4.23 Analysis and Interpretation

The results of the fact-gathering part of a marketing research operation will be a large pile of completed questionnaires in the case of a survey, or masses of figures gathered as secondary data from various sources. The way this material is analysed and presented is a crucial factor in how valuable the research will be.

Questionnaires must frequently be edited as a first stage in processing: that is, they must be carefully scrutinized by an experienced person who will reject obviously unreliable questionnaires, and correct or complete any answers not clearly written in by the interviewer (but where it is obvious what is meant). In appropriate cases the editor will check that the various answers in the questionnaire are consistent with each other, that the answers are not merely frivolous and so on.

The questionnaires screened in this way will then be processed to extract the data in tabular form. This is almost invariably carried out by computer as even small surveys can be processed using standard software.

Once the information is available in the form of tables of figures, their significance must be examined and interpreted. This interpretation will emerge finally as a report, which will draw attention to the similarities, discrepancies, changes and other important features the analysis has uncovered. This stage must also be carried out when secondary data are being used, although most of the actual processing of figures may already have been done.

Opinions vary on how far marketing researchers should go in pointing out what can be inferred or deduced from the figures they present. Normally, people unfamiliar with figures of this kind will read the report, so they will need some guidance as to what the figures mean. How much 'help' is required depends on the individual situation. However, the key point is one made at the beginning of the chapter. Marketing research is only of value when it enables better decisions to be made. So taking a management decision will normally be the final stage in the process.

4.24 Market Segmentation

The proper analysis of market characteristics and segmentation is of prime importance in any industry. In the fast-paced fields of telecommunications and technology, understanding who and where your target market is and how this market views your company can be a powerful asset in staying at least one step ahead of the competition. Common objectives (and the underlying questions that go with them) involved in such an analysis include:

- To identify distinct target segments on which to focus marketing efforts.
- To profile your company's image *vis-à-vis* the competition.
- To determine which product/service attributes have the greatest influence on your company's reputation and market presence.
- To profile those individuals not attracted to your company's products and services in order to guide future product/service development efforts.
- To customize promotional and advertising strategies to specific segment requirements.
- To develop effective point of sale materials that match distribution channels with appropriate segment targets.

Three statistical techniques that are commonly employed to answer the types of questions related to the above points are cluster analysis, correspondence analysis and CHAID. These procedures are often used in preliminary data analysis and exploration, but by themselves each offers an appealing graphical representation of the data that is often straightforward and easy to understand.

4.24.1 Cluster Analysis

Cluster analysis is a simple yet insightful analytical technique used to find natural clusters or groupings of objects. As a market research tool, cluster analysis is often employed in preliminary analysis to find natural, homogeneous market segments that can be identified and analysed further with more advanced statistical techniques. In cluster analysis, objects are grouped on the basis of the similarities (associations) and distances (dissimilarities) of their observed variables. Cluster analysis does not require a specific size or number of groupings to be found. That is, no knowledge of group membership or possible number of natural clusters need be predetermined. Cluster analysis can be used to cluster either individuals or variables into natural groupings.

Cluster analysis techniques can be applied to a wide variety of marketing questions. Any question that seeks to define or associate individuals or variables into similar groups is appropriate fodder for cluster analysis. Some common applications include perceived benefits analysis, product positioning, and usage information.

All of the traditional survey techniques have been employed to gather data to be used in cluster analysis. The advantages of 'cyber survey instruments' (i.e. using the Internet) – speed, high response rate, low cost etc. – can be incorporated with this analytical method without a loss of statistical validity.

4.24.2 CHAID Analysis

CHAID (chi squared automated interaction detector) is a market segmentation technique. It was designed for use with variables that can be split into definite groups called **categorical variables** (e.g. gender, employment status, race etc.) and those ranges or **continuous variables** which have been divided into categories (e.g. income, education, age etc.). CHAID divides a population into two or more segments that differ with respect to some designated criteria.

Although it is not a sophisticated procedure, CHAID is an extremely versatile tool that can be used with nearly any market segmentation query. Uses could include finding a selected portion of a target market that would be most receptive to a new marketing campaign or new product based on previous spending habits. Another use might be to reduce marketing costs by combining market segments that have different demographic characteristics but where the differences are not statistically significant.

As with most other basic statistical procedures, CHAID analysis has been applied to data that have been gathered in many different fashions. However, for CHAID analysis to be fully utilized, relatively large sample sizes must be used. This requires a cost-effective way to gather the data and often a phone or mail survey approach is used for this purpose. When applicable, an online or cyber survey (using the Internet) would be a viable option due to the large reach and relatively low cost.

4.24.3 Correspondence Analysis

Like CHAID, correspondence analysis is a technique that can be used with both categorical data (e.g. gender, brand name, marital status etc.) and continuous data such as rating information. Correspondence is a powerful tool for developing a graphic overview of how product and company characteristics tend to define the relative image of competitors in the market. What are the main factors that distinguish company A from company B? Correspondence analysis generates an excellent visual overview of the answer to this question that can prove to be an invaluable tool in crafting market strategies.

Correspondence analysis is an exploratory technique used to analyse tabulated data presented in columns and rows – such 'rectangular' arrays of data are called 'correspondence tables'. These correspondence tables may represent any indication of similarity, affinity, confusion or interaction between row and column variables. The simple cross-tabulation table of frequency counts is the most common form of correspondence table. As the number of categories increases for each variable it becomes increasingly difficult for the mind to process the variable relationships presented in tabular form.

Correspondence analysis can be applied to almost any situation where interpretation of variable relationships is needed. Virtually all data collection methods can be used with this procedure and, where applicable, online or cyber survey methods.

4.25 Market Penetration/Customer Satisfaction

The need to understand what drives a consumer to buy or not buy a particular product is a major concern in any industry. The ability to accurately measure the consumer's feelings toward a particular brand or product is tremendously important in marketing. If a company can accurately gauge how their product, service or brand is perceived in the areas of customer satisfaction, reliability, trust, loyalty, or some other measure of gratification, they can change or implement marketing strategies accordingly.

Although these are not tangible concepts, certain statistical techniques can be used to quantify them for use in answering the following types of questions:

- What are the criteria that influence customer decision-making?
- Is there an optimal allocation of resources that will enhance customer satisfaction?
- What is our standing in relation to our competitors in the areas of customer loyalty, satisfaction and trust?
- Do our customers see us as an industry leader or laggard?

When concerns in these areas need to be addressed, researchers can incorporate statistical techniques that include **strategic planning model**s and **factor analysis**. These advanced procedures can generate accurate, quantifiable and predictive relationships concerning intangible factors using measured variable information.

4.25.1 Strategic Planning Model

Strategic planning model (SPM) analysis is a statistical regression technique that defines new variables, often called factors, or latent variables, that are combinations of the observed or measured variables. These 'new' variables are then used in a regression equation to predict the way that a group of people might behave. The technique is similar to factor analysis, but a major difference is that with SPMs both dependent and independent variable data values are used to work out the factors and their coefficients, not just the independent variable values. This technique is best used to predict what a group of people might do when the sample does not follow usual assumptions about the population.

Regarding survey methods, SPM analysis can be used on data gathered with any of the traditional methods. A special benefit of SPM analysis is that it requires relatively small sample sizes to achieve viability. Thus, focus groups, one-on-one personal interviews, and executive interviewing with a comparatively small number of participants can be used. This feature also lends itself to the use of cyber or online survey methods where a small sample size representing distinct but abbreviated populations could be obtained at little or no extra cost.

4.25.2 Factor Analysis

Factor analysis is a statistical method used to find correlations (similarities) between measurable variables. These variables with a high degree of similarity, that are presumed to be measuring the same concept and/or idea, are then combined to form new composite variables. Customer loyalty, customer satisfaction, perceived brand reliability and brand value are difficult to measure directly in a survey, but using factor analysis several survey questions that all deal with different aspects of these issues can be united to obtain an overall impression of each of these intangible, but genuine, concepts. These new factors, or composite variables, can then be analysed with other statistical procedures as if they were directly observed.

As stated above, factor analysis is often used to quantify intangible traits and/or show the relationships between these traits. Marketing questions such as: 'How is a new product perceived with regard to value?' 'What is the public perception of our business practices?' 'Is our company respected compared to our competitors?' can be best answered using factor analysis techniques.

In the past, traditional market research survey techniques have been used to gather information needed to answer these types of questions. However, the benefits of an online or cyber survey may be well-suited to provide the data at lower costs and in a more timely manner.

4.26 Neural Networks: A Preliminary Definition

A neural network is an interconnected assembly of simple processing elements, called units or nodes, whose functionality is loosely based on the animal neuron. The processing ability of the network is stored in the inter-unit connection strengths, or weights, obtained by a process of adaptation to, or learning from, a set of training patterns.

Artificial neural networks are computer programs that simulate biological neural networks. In order to process vague, noisy or incomplete information, researchers are turning to biological neural systems as a model for a new computing paradigm. Biological neural systems process this type of information seemingly effortlessly.

Artificial neural systems are unlike artificial intelligence programs. Artificial intelligence programs use deductive reasoning to apply known rules to situations to produce outputs. Each new situation may require that another rule be implemented. The programs can become quite large and complicated in an attempt to address all possible situations. Artificial neural systems, however, automatically construct associations based upon the results of known situations. For each new situation, the neural system automatically adjusts itself and eventually generalizes it.

Artificial neural systems are trained from experience. An artificial neural system is constructed and then simply presented with historical cause and effect situations. The artificial neural system then shapes itself to build an internal representation of the governing rules. Later, after the artificial neural system is trained, it can be presented with a hypothetical situation to produce a prediction of real event results.

4.26.1 Applications of Neural Networks

Amongst many other applications, 'neural nets' have been used to:

- Predict staffing requirements at different times of year and in different conditions. (Brooklyn Union Gas Corp. predicts in advance the number of crew members who will be needed for service calls based on the time of year, predicted temperature and day of the week.)
- Predict which customers will pay their bills. (Again Brooklyn Union Gas Corp. uses this facility.)
- Spot odd trading patterns. (This is how Ivan Boesky, the rogue trader, was caught.)
- Predict sales.
- Predict costs.
- Predict a company's corporate bond rating.
- Test beer. (Anheuser-Busch identifies the organic contents of its competitors' beer vapours with 96 per cent accuracy.)

In general, a neural net can capture the hidden relationships in historical data, which allows you then to predict future trends in that data.

4.26.2 What Does a Neural Net Do?

A neural net simulates some of the learning functions of the human brain. It can recognize patterns and 'learn'. It can be used to forecast and make better business decisions. It can also serve as an 'expert system' that simulates the thinking of an expert and can offer advice. Unlike conventional rule-based artificial intelligence software, a neural net extracts expertise from data automatically – no rules are required.

Braincel, developed and published by Promised Land Technologies, Inc. of New Haven, Connecticut, is a PC software tool that generates neural nets. Braincel, combined with Microsoft Excel or Lotus 1-2-3, creates the first 'intelligent spreadsheet'. It makes possible a sophisticated new level of problem solving and analysis that can give planners, business executives, engineers, scientists and others a major competitive advantage.

It can solve problems that were previously considered impossible to solve, offering an easy to use and more powerful alternative to statistics, expert systems and programming languages. One can use Braincel for problems where the data are too complex, fuzzy or fast-changing for rules or statistics.

For example, Braincel can create forecasts of stock market prices and sales, and carry out failure diagnoses, forecasting of inventory levels, demand forecasting of equipment or personnel, selection of effective direct-mail strategies, financial portfolio analysis, auditing analysis,

analysis of scientific data, and many other pattern-recognition tasks – it can even generate tips for horse racing!

Summary

- Marketing research must be conducted according to a carefully conceived plan and in the light of a clear understanding of how the information to be obtained will contribute to improved management decision-making.
- Information consists of secondary data from existing sources and of primary data, which are obtained by: (a) observation, (b) experiment or (c) survey. Secondary data can often provide the necessary information at lower cost.
- The three types of survey are: (a) personal interview, (b) telephone interview and (c) postal questionnaire; they are listed in order of decreasing cost but also of decreasing yield and reliability.
- Continuous research (such as consumer panels, retail audits and TV audience research) is based on a panel of respondents, selected on sampling principles.
- Much research is syndicated, i.e. the cost is borne by a number of subscribers rather than by one company.
- Test marketing is done to simulate, on a large or a smaller scale, what is likely to happen in the marketplace as a whole. It can be used as an insurance against expensive mistakes but is often in itself very costly.
- Marketing research can be used not only to monitor a position or explore problems, but also, more creatively, to identify profitable opportunities
- Most market research uses statistical sampling methods to obtain a close approximation of the views or behaviour of an entire universe by interviewing a relatively small representative selection from it.
- Sample size is determined by: (a) the degree of accuracy required, (b) the cost that is acceptable and (c) the size of the smallest sub-unit of those interviewed that has to be analysed. In practice (c) is most often the decisive factor.
- The two main sampling methods are random and quota sampling. With random sampling, each unit in the universe has an equal opportunity of being included and interviewers are instructed who to interview. With quota sampling, the interviewer selects people to be interviewed, but does so according to instructions designed to ensure that each group within the universe is proportionately represented.
- Stratified sampling and multi-stage sampling are ways of arriving at a representative sample without incurring the cost of a widely scattered sample of the entire universe.
- Bias – the tendency for distortion to creep in for various reasons – must be guarded against in all marketing research. Common sources of bias are: (a) sampling errors, (b) prejudiced interviewing and (c) faulty questionnaire design.

- Interviews may be structured (based on specific questions the interviewer must ask) or unstructured (consisting of 'guided conversation').
- The socio-economic classification (A, B, C1, C2, D, E) is commonly used in order to stratify members of the public in terms of occupation and income.

References

i Adapted from the web pages of A. C. Neilsen at http://www.acnielsen.com.
ii Adapted from the web pages of Taylor Nelson Sofres at http://www.tnsofres.com/uk.
iii Wilmshurst, John and Mackay, Adrian. *The Fundamentals of Advertising* (Butterworth-Heinemann, 2nd Edition, 1999).
iv Reported in the *Daily Mail*, 11th December 2001.

Further Reading

Baker, Michael, J. *The Marketing Book* (Butterworth-Heinemann, 4th Edition, 1999). Updated text with contributions from top UK marketing educators and writers – has a good chapter on 'Developing marketing information systems'.

Crouch, Sunny and Housden, Matthew. *Marketing Research for Managers.* (Butterworth-Heinemann, 3rd Edition, 2002).

Dictionary of Market Research (Incorporated Society of British Advertisers and the Market Research Society, 1987).

Smith, David and Fletcher, Jonathan. *Inside Information* (John Wiley and Sons, 2001). This text seeks to allow marketers to draw on market research theory to create practical information for making informed market decisions.

Questions

1. What sources of secondary data would you consider if you were seeking information on the following markets?

   (a) Snack foods (peanuts, crisps etc.).
   (b) Combine harvesters.
   (c) Dishwashers.
   (d) DVD players.

2. 'Although an up to date knowledge of the market is essential for successful marketing, research seldom provides all the answers and is never a substitute for executive decision-making.' Comment on this statement, indicating the scope, value and limitations of marketing research.

3. Which of the three main survey methods (personal interview, telephone and postal) might be most appropriate to each of the following situations?

(a) An electronics journal aimed at technical people in industry and with a worldwide, controlled circulation wishes to gain knowledge of the job function and seniority pattern of its readers.

(b) A manufacturer of highly specialized machine tools wishes to know how they are rated by customers and non-customers in comparison with competitors' products.

(c) A company preparing aseptic manufacture of cancer treatment for hospital pharmacies wants to know how to improve its services.

(d) A brewery wishes to know whether a proposed new beer will be preferred to existing beers.

(e) A food company wishes to gain some insight into the probable acceptance and likely market segments for a meat-flavoured man-made protein.

4. There will always be more marketing information that could be useful than funds available to collect it. How would you go about ranking possible marketing research projects in order of priority?

Chapter 5

The right mixture and the vital spark

Introduction

By the end of this chapter you will:

- Appreciate the need to achieve the appropriate interaction of a whole series of factors in order to satisfy customers' needs.
- Understand how this is expressed in terms of the marketing mix – the 'four Ps and S'.
- Realize how the mix has to change to meet the requirements of different customer groups and types of product or service.
- Understand why alternative versions of the marketing mix may be appropriate in changing circumstances.

'Marketing mixes have to be changed from time to time in response to new factors in the marketing picture. The firm can react to environmental changes in an expedient or a systematic fashion.'

Philip Kotler. *Marketing Management*

5.1 Satisfying Customers' Needs

In Chapter 3 we saw what characteristics products have to have in order to meet customers' needs, and then saw how best to develop suitable products. But now, we must put products into perspective and recognize that, in order to satisfy customers' needs, we have to consider not merely the product as such but other things as well.

We saw in Section 1.6 that the competitive climate within which marketing operates gives rise to the need to seek a competitive differential advantage. It is naive to assume that competition can be met only by producing a 'better' product. (In any case, what is 'better' for some customers may be 'less good' for others – the person whose pocket will only support a Mini may recognize that a Rolls is 'better' in some respects, but the Mini is 'better' for them.) We have to take into account the whole range of customer requirements. These will include not merely product performance, but also price, convenience of purchase and the way the product or service is presented. Figure 5.1 describes the marketing process very simply.

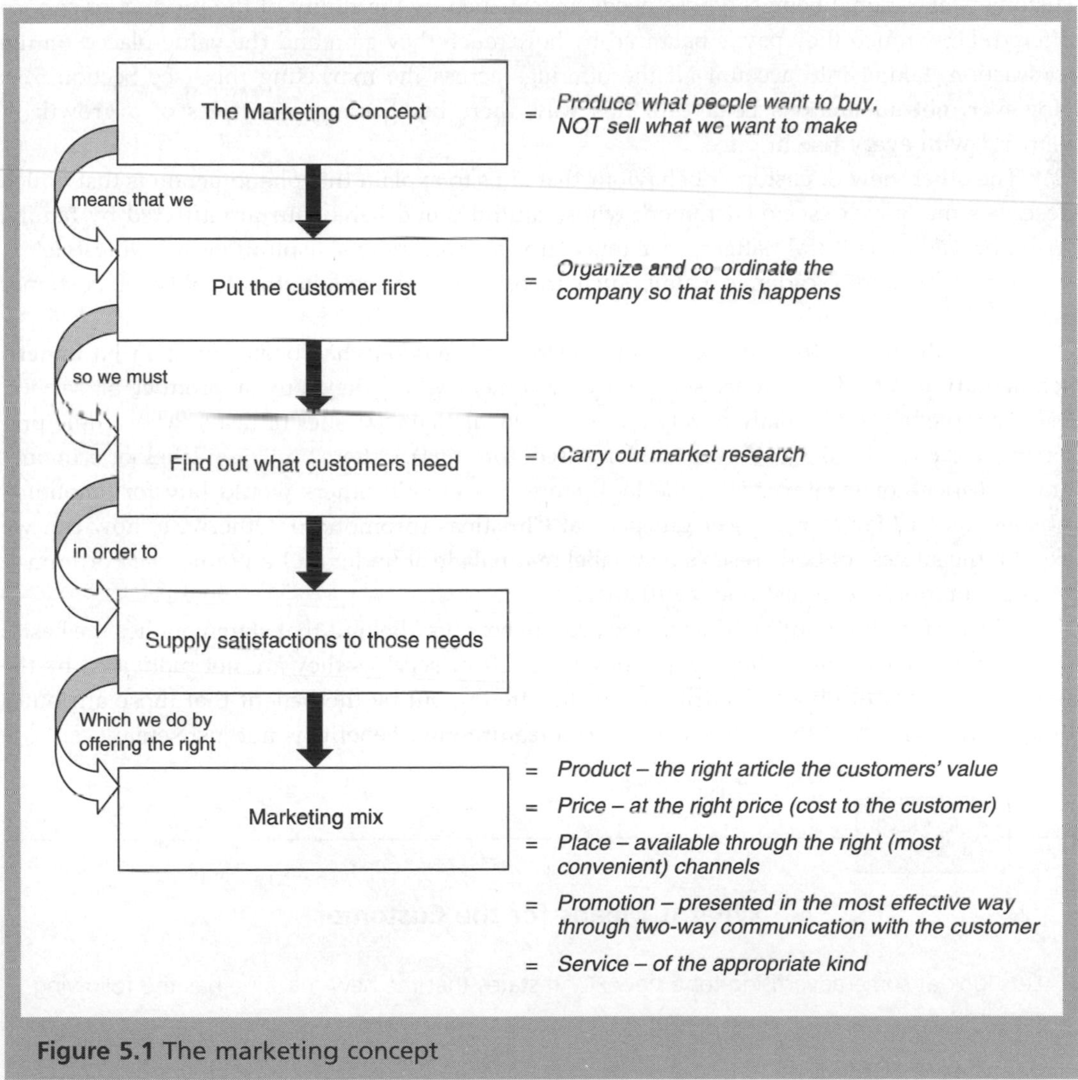

Figure 5.1 The marketing concept

5.2 Analysing Customer Behaviour

One can look at the market in two ways: *what* is bought and *why* it is bought.

'What' comes down not only to products but also considerations of the structure of markets in the form of volume, value, the physical character of the product purchased, frequency, price paid and so on. From this will come information on segmentation, distribution, and outlets that are turning over product quickly. With services, we have such things as who takes what service, what else they do at the same time, their characteristics and circumstances, and so on.

The second part of analysing customer behaviour is trying to understand 'why' customers behave the way they do, because if we are able to explain the behaviour of our customers, we are in a better position to satisfy their needs.

There are two principal theories to explain customer behaviour. One theory refers to customers as rational beings, whose needs are satisfied by the utility of the product or service offered. How much they pay is balanced by how much they gain and the value placed on the transaction, taking into account all the offerings across the marketing mix (see Section 5.3). However, not all markets behave in this way, there being many examples of a growth in demand with every rise in price.

The other view of customer behaviour that aims to explain this phenomenon is that which describes the 'psycho-socio customer', whose attitudes and behaviour are affected by family, work, prevailing cultural patterns, reference groups, perceptions, aspirations and 'lifestyle'.

While of some academic value, such theories rarely explain the totality of customer behaviour.

One valuable method of explaining customer behaviour has been found to be **benefit segmentation**, i.e. the benefits sought by customers when they buy a product or service. Some people buy marmalade purely on its functional characteristics of taste, for example preferring 'old english thick cut' over 'golden shred' (product). Others buy 'own label' or economy brands (price), or whatever is at the local store (place). Still others would buy for emotional reasons, like a Marks & Spencer gift pack at Christmas (promotion). Otherwise, how can we explain the success of both Tesco's own-label marmalade at under a £1 a pound *and* Fortnum & Masons' marmalade at just under £10 a jar?

'Customers don't buy products; they acquire benefits.' Behind that statement lies the basics of successful marketing. When people buy products or services they are not motivated by the physical features or objective attributes of the offering but by the benefit that those attributes bring with them. And the difference between features and benefits is not just semantics.

VIGNETTE

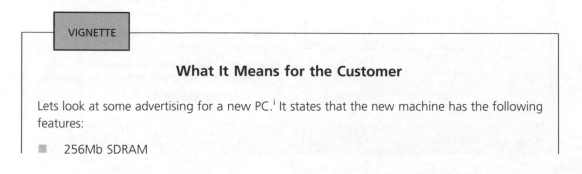

What It Means for the Customer

Lets look at some advertising for a new PC.[i] It states that the new machine has the following features:

- 256Mb SDRAM

- DVD-ROM (16x)
- High Resolution 15" Digital Colour Monitor
- New 64Mb nVidia GeForce 2MX-400 Graphics Card
- 56k Modem V90
- CD Re-Writer (12x 8x 32x)

All this listed under the banner headline '1.5GHz', representing best value at £799.99 including VAT, it appears. Given that it is loaded with WindowsXP Home Edition, one assumes that it is targeted at the domestic rather than industrial or business user.

However, many companies fall into the trap of talking to customers about the features of their product or service rather than what those features mean to the customer. The advertisement example above assumes that the reader – a potential buyer – has a clear idea what a '64Mb nVidia GeForce 2MX-400 Graphics Card' is and what it does, and possibly why it is better than the 1MX card.

So, being expert in the technical products is not enough and makes a great assumption that the potential buyer is as knowledgeable as the supplier is. The customer may not be able to work out the benefits that a particular feature brings and it is, therefore, up to the supplier to explain the benefits that accrue from each of the features mentioned. A simple formula to ensure that this customer-oriented approach is adopted is always to use the phrase 'which means that' to link a feature to the benefit that it brings:

'This computer has a new 64Mb nVidia GeForce 2MX-400 Graphics Card which means that you can play the latest computer games or . . . with the DVD-ROM (16x) which means that you can watch the latest films with the sharpest pictures'.

By applying the formula 'which means that' you should aim to turn **features** (of the product or service) into **advantages** (for the customer) and **benefits** in terms of what the product or service does for the customer.

From this customer-orientation comes the definition of markets in terms of the benefits sought. So, from the earlier example, Fortnum & Masons' marmalade is not a food product but a luxury gift item and is packaged in that way. Similarly, a premium fountain pen is often a gift item in the mind of the customer, and so they are distributed in that way and are found in good jewellers rather than in stationers next to Biros and similar writing implements. Knowing how customers define the market can significantly alter your marketing strategy.

See Section 14.3.1 for a more detailed look at internal influences on buyer behaviour.

5.3 The Marketing Mix

The 'marketing mix' is a term developed originally by Neil H. Borden to describe the appropriate combination, in a particular set of circumstances, of the four key elements that are at the heart of a company's marketing programme. They are commonly referred to as the 'four Ps': product, price, place and promotion. It is easy to see why, if any one of these elements is wrong, the marketing programme will fail and the company will not profit from the operation as it should. Later, in Section 5.7, we explore a possible enhancement of this description. But for now, lets us consider each component of the four Ps' marketing mix.

If the **product** or service (see Section 3.2) offered does not perform in the required way, customers will not buy a second time, and the word will get round to prospective customers so that they will not buy even once. A car with poor performance or excessive breakdowns, a 'tasty snack' that does not seem very tasty to its consumers, a magazine that does not interest its readers, or a video rental shop that is never open when customers want to use it, are all examples of faulty products. (Clearly, to some extent, other items in the marketing mix can act to compensate for shortcomings in this area. I may decide to accept more breakdowns in a car if it is cheap enough, or buy the snack I do not like too well if the shop I am in does not stock the one I prefer.)

No matter how good the product, some people will be unable to pay more than a certain **price**. Others may be able to afford it but believe that another way of spending that sum of money would give them greater satisfaction. Conversely, as we have just seen, simply being cheap is not enough – the product must come up to some level of expected performance. In some situations (luxury goods, for example) a high price may even make the product more desirable than a lower one. The likely response of demand to a change in price ('elasticity' in economic terms) will affect our decisions on pricing policy (see Chapter 13).

We must not expect customers to shop around too much in order to find our particular product. It should be available at the **place** convenient to them. In some cases their attachment (brand loyalty) to a particular manufacturer's product may be so strong that they will go miles to find it and refuse to accept alternatives; but this is unusual. If one type of beer is not available, many people will take another, or if one newspaper is sold out, will buy its rival. The biggest single factor in deciding which brand of petrol people buy is which garage is most convenient for them to stop at. Coca-Cola is the world's best-selling soft drink largely because it is readily available virtually everywhere. Sometimes the best way of making the product easily available is to give people easy access direct to the product (mail order, freephone ordering using credit cards, TV and Internet shopping etc.).

The potentially negative factors must be avoided. For instance, not many people will 'shop around' to find a product that few stores have in stock. They will be reluctant to do business with a company whose telephones are not answered promptly, efficiently and courteously. Someone once defined marketing as 'making it easy for people to buy'. There is some truth in this observation, yet many organizations seem to go out of their way to make life difficult for their customers – complicated forms or administration, inadequate telecommunications systems, and unhelpful staff are just some examples.

The term **promotion** is used here to include personal selling as well as all forms of advertising and sales promotion, packaging and display.

A well-presented product will score over one that is badly presented. Men would be unlikely to buy as a present for their partners a perfume, however good, which was offered in a cheap plastic bottle inside a grubby brown box. In the case of gifts, presentation can be all-important. Easter egg packaging may well cost more than the chocolate it contains. The way some kinds of consumer products are spoken of by salesmen or in advertising may give them the aura customers seek, whereas an oil rig or a machine tool must above all else carry out its function, and its presentation is relatively unimportant. Note 'relatively' unimportant, because even in the extreme case it is likely that promotion will have some part to play.

So far we have established the point that a failure in any one of these four factors (product, price, place and promotion) may damage the chances of success in the marketplace no matter how good the others are. The opposite point also needs to be made. Getting any one of them right adds to the total chances of success. Getting them all right will have a synergistic effect. In other words, the total combined effect will be greater than we might expect by adding up the individual effects – the whole is greater than the sum of the parts.

There is, however, a complication: what we do to one element in the marketing mix can have an effect on one or more of the others, especially the price. Thus, if we want to improve the product's performance, we may have to build in features that will add to its price. On the other hand, the fact that the product performs better may make it more acceptable to more people; this in turn will lead to higher sales, bigger production runs and lower unit costs and prices.

Price and promotion are linked in this way also. Promotion can cost a great deal of money and, for example, heavy advertising expenditure can be justified only if either the advertising convinces customers that the higher price (necessary to cover advertising costs) is justified by the benefits the product offers them, or if the advertising leads to higher sales and therefore lower unit costs (with the savings thus achieved paying for the advertising without an increase in price). Both these situations can apply at the same time, of course, so we may have an and/or rather than an either/or alternative here.

There are some instances when **service** is such an important factor in delivering customer satisfaction that it will be seen as an important part of the marketing mix. The mix then becomes the 'four Ps and S'. Service can be provided at any stage – before, during or after the sale. Thus the provision of a free design service, the ability to try on clothing in comfort while children are happy at the play table provided, or a speedy emergency repair service can all offer a reason for customers to prefer one company to another. As competing products become increasingly similar in many markets, it becomes more likely that service levels will determine the final choice.

5.4 Marketing Mix Decisions

We have seen that being able to satisfy customers' needs profitably depends on making right decisions in the four main areas of product, price, place and promotion. In practice, this will mean answering a whole series of key questions. Again, we have to bear in mind that the questions cannot be answered in isolation, but that each may have a bearing on the others. The questions to be answered will vary from situation to situation, but will commonly include the following:

- **What should the product range be?** Should we standardize on a few items, offer a wide selection or make to customers' requirements? How much stock should we carry? How many variations should we make available? Even, what *service* products should we be offering?

- **What is our pricing policy?** Shall we offer products that are 'expensive' or those that are 'economical'? Shall prices be standard or subject to negotiation in view of customers' special requirements? What about wholesaler/retailer margins, and quantity discounts?
- **How shall we sell?** Shall we sell direct to customers or through wholesalers/agents/ retailers? Which retailers? What kind of salesmen, and how many? What after-sales service shall we offer?
- **How shall we distribute the product?** Shall we use our own transport? Or send by road/ rail/air/sea? Shall we despatch direct from the factory or do we need regional depots (build our own or rent)? How important is speedy delivery and how shall we achieve it?

An example of how these questions interact with each other is the physical distribution decision. There is a complex array of interlinking factors. If customers do not expect quick delivery, the problems may be relatively small. Deliveries can be made from a stock held at the factory or even delayed until a new batch of the product is made. Already, though, we are having to balance the cost of holding stock so as to meet orders fairly quickly against possible problems arising from cutting costs by not holding stock. Thus, if we hold no stock, either customers must wait (and perhaps choose to buy elsewhere), or production schedules must be disrupted (adding to costs) in order to meet an acceptable delivery date.

If delivery time is really important, we shall certainly have to carry stocks and they may have to be held near our customers. Supermarkets have a high turnover and carry small stocks which need replenishing regularly and at short intervals. This leads many major food packagers to establish regional warehouses from which the appropriate mixed loads can be taken for delivery to supermarkets and other customers over a relatively small radius. The decision must be taken on whether this system (where goods must be handled twice) is cheaper than direct deliveries from the factory or perhaps several different factories. Clearly, there is no standard answer, and the 'right' answer may well change with circumstances (see Section 15.6).

The kind of product will have a great bearing on the kind of selling and the distribution channels used. Some standard household goods – bed sheets, for example – can be sold direct to customers through the post. The purchasing decision is an uncomplicated one – cost is low, quality is not difficult to establish, styles are standard and the colour range limited.

Cars, on the other hand, represent a very difficult and complicated purchasing decision on the part of the customer, for a great deal of money changes hands (after their house, it is the biggest single outlay most people make). There is a wide choice of prices, styles and performance, and generally a used car is being sold as well as a new one bought. After the purchase is made, it will need servicing. All this usually points to the need for personal selling as a key element in the marketing mix; and clearly it is logical to link after-sales servicing with this part of the process. So we have a need for each main centre of population to have a sales/servicing point. The decision still has to be made whether the company marketing the cars sets up units of its own to do this or whether it employs independent distributors to do so. This is partly a matter of cost – either the manufacturer must find the capital to operate these distribution points or, through substantial discounts on the retail price, make it attractive for others to do so. In most cases, in Great Britain anyway, the latter system is used.

However, with the Internet providing a massive resource of information, and with the prices of cars in the UK being too high compared with many other European markets (exacerbated by the strength of sterling and individual country tax regimes), there has been widespread buying of new cars through other channels in the early years of this century. It has been suggested that, with the demise of dealerships as the sole route to market, manufacturers may soon be using supermarket channels to sell cars.

5.5 Examples of Mixes

Four examples may help to illustrate the different marketing mixes that emerge from differing situations. They are 'typical' cases, but it must be remembered that, within the categories referred to, there will still be considerable individual differences. One company may spend less on its sales force and more on advertising than another one will.

Example 1: Fast-moving consumer packaged goods – Typical food and confectionery products fall into this category. There is a mass market that can be economically reached through advertising, which therefore plays a big part in the marketing mix. Pricing may be very critical, since many retail outlets are used. The sales force may be very large (although, in some cases, the fact that a very high proportion of customers can be served through a few large supermarket chains may change this picture). The product is likely to have a low unit price and 'impulse' buying may play an important part, so that packaging and point-of-sale activities are important. Advertising budgets are commonly about 10 per cent of retail turnover and sales force costs about 5 per cent, but both may be even higher.

Example 2: Consumer durables – Cars, washing machines, freezers and similar goods present a different picture. Impulse buying is unlikely, and frequency of purchase is much less. Price, while still important, may not be so critical, although 'discounting' is common as a means of competition between retailers. The ability to inspect the product may be important, and the availability of after-sales service certainly is. A smaller number of distributors than with fast-moving consumer goods is therefore common, but these outlets are much more than the simple purchasing points they are with the fast-moving goods. Advertising and sales force costs may represent 5 per cent and 2 per cent of sales respectively, but retailers' margins will be higher. Retailers themselves employ large numbers of sales staff and spend their own advertising money.

Example 3: Industrial capital goods – Heavy capital equipment for industry is likely to be supplied to order rather than from stock. Technical performance of the product is all-important and price may well be a secondary consideration. There are probably a small number of customers and therefore a small (though highly trained and specialized) sales force. Because of the specialist role and the lengthy selling process, sales costs can be high. Advertising is likely to play a very minor role (advertising costs may be 0.5 per cent or less, but sales costs may vary from 2 per cent to 10 per cent, although there is really no norm). Distribution is almost certain to be direct to the customer, while installation and after-sales services may call for a large engineering division quite apart from manufacturing. Similarly, research and development (R&D), design and other such costs will be high.

Example 4: Financial services – Until fairly recently financial organizations such as banks and building societies relied heavily on people seeking them out and then being sufficiently satisfied with their services not to move their business elsewhere. During the 1960s and 1970s the market developed rapidly and competition was on the basis of a wider and wider network of branches supported by increasing promotional expenditures. In the 1980s and 1990s more attention was paid to developing different products (offering savers higher interest rates, 24-hour cashpoints and, more recently, computerized instant access banking through the Internet). This prompted many banks to close their no longer used branch networks, until such time as it was recognized that customers still wanted to talk to people for many financial matters – and famously Barclays set up a campaign to announce that they had stalled their branch closure programme.

5.6 Alternative Mix for Service Industries

It is sometimes not entirely easy to express all the important aspects of a successful offering to the customers within the framework of the 'four Ps and S' formula, and alternative versions have been proposed. Booms and Bitner, for example, add three extra 'Ps': people (on the basis that, in the hotel and catering business, for example, the quality of staff is an important ingredient in customer satisfaction), process (the way the service is administered) and physical evidence (where ambience, decor etc. have important roles). Today, the division between products and services is less defined and the 'other Ps' become more important to the marketing organization.

5.7 The Marketing Mix in the New Millennium

Philip Kotler has suggested that satisfying customer needs through the four Ps does not go far enough (in an interview for *Marketing Business*, Dec./Jan. 1991/1992). We should, he says, be 'delighting customers' by using the 'four Cs':

- **The first C** – In Kotler's view, the product, viewed from the customer's point of view, becomes **customer value**. In her book, *Successful Marketing Communications*,[ii] Kathy Ace suggests that the first C should be 'choice', since customers do not see products, portfolio management techniques, matrices and product life cycles – they see that they have to make a choice. Whatever choice they make, customers go after what they value. So, identifying what customers value will be paramount.
- **The second C** – Both Kotler and Ace concur that price is the **cost to the customer**, which may include time, effort, inconvenience etc. as well as money.
- **The third C** – Place, from the customer viewpoint, is **convenience**. Customers do not see channel management decisions, outlet selection or distribution strategy.
- **The fourth C** – Promotion is all about **communication** with the customers in that it should be viewed as a two-way mechanism rather than a one-way 'promotion'. Customers like to be heard and really listened to, rather than promoted to.

In the early part of this new century and beyond success will be determined by the ability to go beyond the bare satisfaction of needs and on to the creation of 'delighted customers'. This approach ties in with the concept of total quality management (TQM), which requires the commitment by everyone in the organization to constant improvement in quality. (One major Japanese company includes in its quality precepts the statement 'perfection is not enough'.) Since quality is determined by customers' perceptions and preferences, it is only by working closely with customers that we can deliver the customer value that will make them 'delighted customers', to use Kotler's phrase.

- **The fifth C** – We suggest that, from the customer's viewpoint, when he or she interacts with a person delivering a service, it is the **competency** of that person that is crucial. The customer experiences how capable the people are – whether they are competent not only in caring for the customer, but also capable of making decisions that solve the customer's problems, and able to find the product and deliver a personal, often individual, service. So, from an organization management approach, we see that a competency framework to personnel recruitment, job descriptions, performance appraisal, and training and development will be better able to deliver exceptional service to customers, or 'best value' as defined for public service organizations. Cathy Ace makes the case for 'care' as the fifth C.
- **The sixth C** – It is not the process that is so important to the customer. Having purchased a product, the customer does not want to be told that there is a system – even if based on the quality standard ISO 2001 – that they must follow if they wish to complain. The concern with many of these processes is that they do not track customers' interactions with the organization until they have the problem. That is not what the customer wants. More important, we suggest, is the way that the organization manages *all* the customers' interactions, thus building a relationship over time. Rather than process, we suggest the focus should be on **customer relationship management**. See Chapter 18 for a further treatment of this subject.

  Cathy Ace makes the case for 'corporate competence' being sought by the customer – many customers' view of an organization is that it is corporately incompetent and regularly unable to deliver its promises. However, as a buyer, one does not worry if an organization is 'corporately incompetent' as that probably means that they are not making much of a profit. From their point of view, the customer requires that the people they deal with are competent and that the 'relationship' is managed for the 'lifetime' of that customer dealing with the organization.
- **The seventh C** – Finally, physical evidence of the service delivery is today becoming less important. You may never see the Virgin One office in Norwich, nor be particularly bothered by their bright yellow and red stationery when you open a flexible mortgage with them. However, the way that they do business and how their interactions with you fit with your way of doing things is paramount. Therefore, we suggest the **context** of business activities is highly significant. What are the values, meanings, associated surroundings or setting for the interactions? In what context are you considering your new financial arrangements? How does the account fit in with your lifestyle, job and recreational activities, your savings and plans for the future? In this situation, context is all-important.

Moreover, by considering the context of the customers' needs, the total picture involving all seven Cs is brought into play. It is this co-ordinated and holistic approach that delivers exceptional customer value, rather than a piecemeal approach.

For a further thought on the subject, see Cathy Ace's text where she suggests that the final C should be consistency. She makes a good case for the fact that, when customers deal with organizations, they want to reduce the risk of that association and expect consistency of service. They expect the brand values to be maintained and be consistent. However, while consistency is important, customers still like to be treated as individuals and want the context of their experience with the service provider to match the context in which they are consuming the service.

It has been suggested that, for some companies, optimal quality means that the product provides the consumer with an experience that meets, but does not exceed, expectations. According to this viewpoint, there is no sense in incurring added costs in providing what amounts to excessive quality. However, other firms strive to exceed consumers' expectations in order to produce high levels of customer satisfaction and, in turn, brand loyalty.

5.8 The Importance of Timing

Another important factor, which runs through all marketing decisions, is timing. The best product in the world will fail if it is launched before there is a ready market for it (e.g. the WAP mobile phone market has been very slow to 'take off', and many efforts have been unsuccessful). To be too late may give competitors a chance to establish themselves in the market.

The launch of an expensive new product that coincides with a recession, and hence low consumer expenditure, will encounter far more difficulty than if it is timed to meet an upswing in the economy. To get into the shops by Christmas, a new toy must be 'sold in' to retailers by August, and probably needs to be shown at the Toy Fair in the previous January.

5.9 What is in a Name?

Company names are far more complex than they seem to be to outsiders and probably far more important to the health of the brand than even the experts recognize. So why do financial institutions decide to change their names? It may be that name changes can be used to refresh the brand or, as in the case of the emergence of the Midland Bank as HSBC, to signal that there has been a change in ownership. But renaming can be extremely costly and can risk alienating customers.

Barclays spent a lot of money on consultancy fees before deciding to stick with its name. The equity that a good solid bank or insurance company has in its name is unquantifiable and, unless firms want to cast off unwanted baggage in a name, experts argue that it is often best to stick with what you have got. This is not, however, always the case. The development of 'Egg' by Prudential as a stand-alone new brand has been successful in attracting a younger target market, and has added value to its parent.

5.10 The Vital Spark

There is grave danger inherent in the writing of books about marketing, and indeed in the whole idea of marketing as a course of study, that by analysing each aspect of it and trying to understand the mechanics and thought processes behind it, we begin to believe that marketing is the fact finding, the analysis, the careful weighing of one alternative against another. It is not. To study all these processes may be an aid to successful marketing, just as the study of strategy may help a successful general. But marketing, like war, is about activity. It is doing, not merely thinking. To be successful at it, one must be creative as well as analytical; aggressive as well as meticulous.

As J. H. Davidson[iii] puts it:

> "Many companies mistakenly regard marketing as an amalgam of specialist activities rather than as a total approach to business which should permeate the whole organization. The pressure of detailed routine has turned most marketing people today into maintenance men. All this is the very opposite of offensive marketing, which is a set of attitudes and techniques designed to exploit the marketing situation fully. It requires a company to innovate every major new development in its markets and to respond to competitive moves by counter-attack, not by imitation."

Davidson also speaks of the need for developing marketing 'from a limp theory into a dynamic practice'. Students should grasp this necessity from the outset. Marketing is about winning votes from customers in the marketplace, it is about beating competitors to the punch, it is about making optimum profits.

Above all marketing is about spotting customers' needs faster than anyone else, satisfying them better than anyone else and, in the process, making better profits than anyone else. It is about exploiting opportunities more than about avoiding problems.

The study, the analysis, and the weighing of facts and alternatives are all important, but the creative, aggressive, competitive spirit is equally necessary. The right marketing mix is the fuel, but it needs igniting by this vital spark.

CASE STUDY[iv]

The advent of airline global deregulation allowed for the entry of new airlines into the European market. One of the growth sectors has been in budget airlines; among the most successful has been easyJet.

In 1995, business entrepreneur Stelios Haji-Ioannou launched easyJet, positioning the new company as a low-cost, no-frills airline, operating a high frequency, point to-point, short haul scheduled service around Europe.

The UK-grown brand has been built on a staple diet of press, outdoor, radio and online advertising. The campaign objective of much of the 'off-line' advertising has been to drive the customer online and this strategy has proved very effective. Around 90 per cent of bookings are now made through the airline's website.

The airline has created a role for itself as the consumers' champion, engaging in many outspoken, high profile battles with large corporations, such as British Airways, SwissAir and

Barclays Bank, to protect passengers' rights to uninhibited low-cost air travel. The airline recently agreed to another series of LWT's observational documentary, Airline. The programme aired showed the problem some passengers had dealing with a company representative over a cancelled flight. The company's feeling is that, although there are risks associated with appearing on TV in this kind of programme, there are long-term brand benefits as the show attracts 10 million viewers every episode.

An omnibus survey commissioned by the airline in January 2000 indicated that overall awareness of the brand stood at 80 per cent in the UK, up from the August 1999 figure of 71 per cent. It is difficult to pinpoint an overall market share figure as competitors vary by route, making meaningful comparisons difficult. However, in December 1999, easyJet had nine aircraft operating fourteen routes, but by the end of 2000 these figures had increased to eighteen and twenty-eight respectively. The airline currently has twenty-one aircraft flying thirty routes, with another five routes and three aircraft due to be added this year. By 2004, the airline aims to be flying fifty to sixty routes.

In 1998, easyJet passenger figures totalled 1.7 million, rising to 3.5 million in 1999 and continuing the climb to today's figure of 7 million – level with British Midland's. In November 2000, easyJet floated on the London Stock Exchange. It is now among the FTSE top 200 companies and has a value over £1 billion.

The huge success of easyJet led founder Haji-loannou to look at the opportunities for using the brand to enter new market sectors. In 1999, he established easyEverything.com, a network of cyber cafes, of which there are currently 20 throughout western Europe and one in New York, receiving almost 2 million visitors a month. In Spring 2000, easyRentacar.com, the car rental business, was created, and easyValue, an Internet site that offers impartial comparisons for online shopping, is the latest venture in the virtual world. Haji-loannou is also launching easyMoney, a financial services business.

easyJet plans to keep its business model simple and concentrate on offering an attractive product that offers real benefits to consumers, and on stimulating demand for it. (Expect more to come under the easy.com banner!)

Question

1. Discuss whether you feel that the development of many 'no frills' services will have a damaging effect on service standards across the travel and tourism industries.

Summary

- The success of a product is dependent on a whole number of factors: the product itself, the price structure, the method of distribution and the promotional policy. In the second section of the book, dealing with the practice of marketing, we examine each of these areas in more depth. It is important to recognize from the start, however, that we need to consider them all at one time and in relation to each other.

- It is not sound to deal in isolation with such questions as: What should our prices be? How much should we spend on advertising? What kind of sales force should we have? A co-ordinated approach is required.
- The answer to each of these questions is related to all the others and must be considered in the light of the total market situation, taking into account such things as:

  (a) The type of product and how it is bought (impulse or considered, consumer or industrial, frequently or infrequently).

  (b) Size of market and complexity of distribution and service required.

  (c) Competitive activity, and whether the market is relatively static or fast-changing.

  (d) Capital/cost flow implications and sales/production required to produce acceptable break-even points.
- The marketing mix represents only those factors over which management has control. Decisions must be taken in the light of all the many other factors that are not controllable, such as the social, political and economic climate, which influence available spending power and consumer choices, as well as the level and type of industrial investment. (See PEST analysis, Section 1.7.)
- Getting the marketing mix right is not merely a question of passively evaluating all the factors and 'getting the sums right', important though that is. Elements of creativity, aggression and competitiveness provide the vital spark that leads to higher profits through satisfying customers' needs better and faster than anyone else.

References

i Fijitsu Computers' Advertisement, *Daily Mail*, 4th December 2001.
ii Ace, Cathy. *Successful Marketing Communications* (Butterworth-Heinemann, 2001).
iii In *Offensive Marketing* (Penguin Business Library, 2nd Edition, 1987). Conveys the nature of successful marketing excellently. The book contains numerous practical examples, now with the benefit of hindsight, many of which illuminate the way the elements of the marketing mix can be used in varying patterns to achieve successful results in different situations.
iv Adapted from *Marketing Business*, September 2001, p. 14.

Further Reading

Ace, Cathy. *Successful Marketing Communications* (Butterworth-Heinemann, 2001).
Christopher, Martin. *The Customer Service Planner* (Butterworth-Heinemann, 1992).
Mudie, Peter and Cottam, Angela. *The Management and Marketing of Services* (Butterworth-Heinemann, 1999).
Kotler, P. *Principles of Marketing* (Prentice Hall, 1994).
Stanton, W. J. *Fundamentals of Marketing* (McGraw-Hill, 3rd Edition, 1994).

Questions

1. What kind of emphasis would you expect in the marketing mix for the following?

   (a) Water skis.

   (b) Motor oil.

   (c) Yoghurt.

   (d) Management textbooks.

2. On what basis would you decide whether to spend more money on promotion when this would mean increasing the price of the product?

3. Compare and contrast the 'seven Cs' approach of this text (customer value, cost to the customer, convenience, communication, competency, customer relationship management and context) with that of Cathy Ace (choice, cost to the customer, convenience, communication, care, corporate competency and consistency). What would be your approach to defining the marketing mix? Support your answer with examples from your experience as a customer.

4. Choose a manufacturing or service company and say what factors determine the product or service it offers.

Part 2 – Section A

The Practice of Marketing – *Communications*

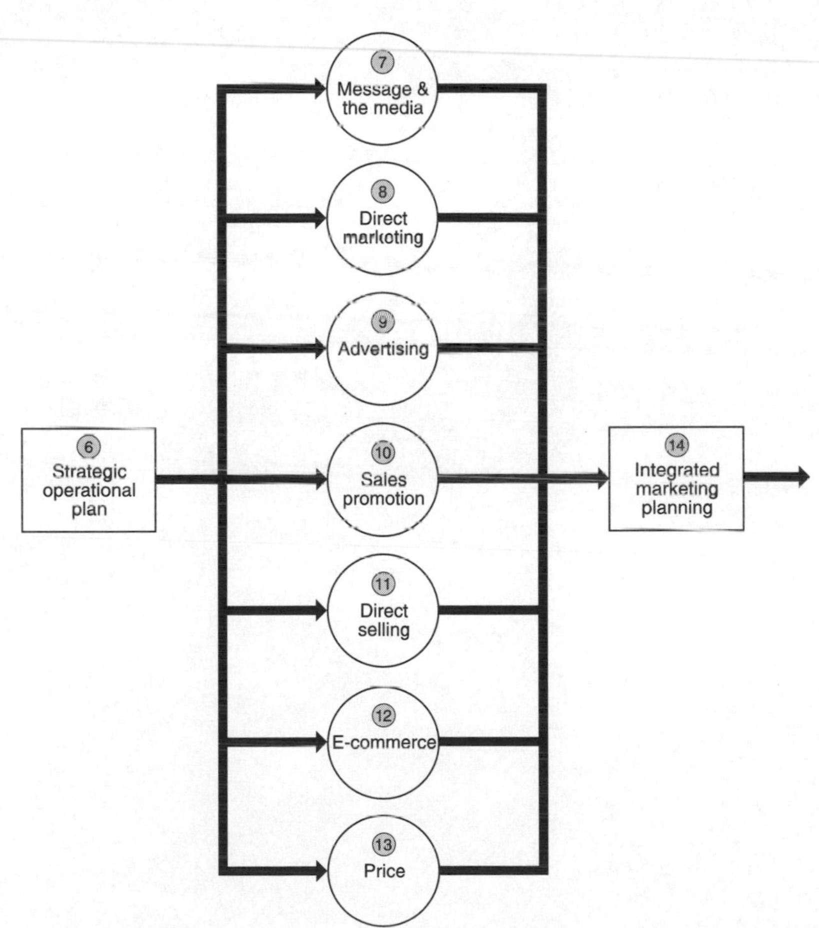

Chapter 6

The strategic operational plan

Introduction

By the end of this chapter you will:

- Appreciate where 'the marketing department' fits into an organization.
- Understand the limitations of what the marketing department can achieve unless the whole organization subscribes to the philosophy of the marketing concept.
- Be aware of the key roles a marketing department may have in co-ordinating and planning, and in the application of specific techniques.
- Realize that there are many different ways in which the marketing department can figure in the organizational structure.
- Realize the central and crucial importance of properly conducted marketing planning.
- Understand how marketing planning can best be dealt with.
- Be aware of the key stages in the marketing planning process.
- Appreciate the importance of getting the most effective balance in the marketing mix, adopting the appropriate position in the marketplace and communicating a very strong competitive advantage.
- Have an insight into some of the main sales forecasting methods.

'Transition and change will confront you with many new pressure points. Some of the company's priorities will change, and you will have to integrate those shifting priorities into your own work. There will be many people and problems vying for your time.

Those who make the most noise should not necessarily get the most attention. It is easy for a manager to end up in a fire fighting mode, getting sidetracked by low priority issues that chew up a lot of time and energy yet have little pay-off . . . Careful planning and organizing is essential during times like these.'

Price Pritchet and Ron Pound. *Managing and Supervising Organisational Change*[i]

Robert Townsend in *Up the Organisation* wrote:

"Marketing departments, like planning departments, personnel departments, management development departments, are usually camouflages designed to cover up for lazy or worn-out chief executives. Marketing, in the fullest sense of the word, is the name of the game. So it had better be handled by the boss and his line, not by staff hecklers."

With that in mind, we can move on to open the chapter with a fundamental question.

6.1 Why Have a Marketing Department?

The point was made in Chapter 1 that if marketing means anything, it is an attitude of mind that must permeate the company from top to bottom; and Chapter 5 spoke of the 'total approach to business' and the need for a 'vital spark'. Yet many companies have a marketing department, probably headed by a marketing director, which seems to indicate that they see marketing as just one of the functions that a business has to carry out. Which of these apparent contradictions is the right approach? The answer is that both are right. It is perfectly true that a company cannot 'do' marketing by having a few people labelled 'The Marketing Department'. On the other hand, such a department can make sense, for three main reasons.

First, unless the chief executive does it personally, someone else has to be responsible for ensuring that the whole company does work to pursue its marketing aims – that everyone does understand what they are doing and why. In particular, there is a built-in tendency for each main specialist department to go its own way and pursue its own aims. It is not at all uncommon for the sales department and production department, for example, to be at loggerheads over quality standards, over delivery times, over stock control policies etc. Since all these should be features of a detailed marketing policy, it can make sense for a marketing director to exercise a co-ordinating role – to ensure that everyone understands the company's marketing policy, subscribes to it and faithfully carries out their part of it.

Second, if everyone is to work to a detailed plan, someone must produce that plan. Again, if the chief executive is not to produce it personally, someone must do it for him. It is sensible to give that person the title of Marketing Manager or Marketing Director. Since it can be a big task – collecting marketing research information, preparing and assessing promotional plans, working out sales and profit forecasts and possibly specifying new product needs – we may have the beginning of a sizeable marketing department rather than an individual. This is the 'planning role' of the marketing department.

Third, while it is true that everyone in the company should be marketing-oriented, striving to provide customer satisfactions at a good profit, it is also true that some are more directly concerned with customers than others. The purchasing manager's main focus of attention will be on suppliers and their delivery dates, quality standards and negotiating the best price for the company. Production managers will have their eyes particularly on equipment and raw materials, on production schedules and machine allocation, on the recruitment, training and motivation of skilled work-people. In many parts of the company, in fact, the customer is the distant horizon. On the other hand, there are other groups of people in the company who are mainly dealing with customers, and who are much more immediately concerned with their needs. For sales, advertising, market research and product development people, customers are the main concern. Consequently, it often makes sense to group all these people and departments together, thus making it easier for them to work closely with each other, and easier to direct and co-ordinate their activities as a group of specialists. This is marketing in its 'functional role'.

So, if we find a marketing department within a company, we should expect to find it carrying out one or more of these three roles:

1. Co-ordinating.
2. Planning.
3. Specific functions or techniques.

We go on to examine each of these roles. But first a word of warning. The 'Marketing' title does not necessarily indicate that the company has embraced and understood the marketing concept. Marketing has been through a fashionable phase, and has become one of the 'in words' of management (and the media). It is tempting for an ambitious sales manager or a would-be 'with it' chief executive to change the name on the organization chart and the office door so that the 'Sales Department' becomes the 'Marketing Department' overnight. Nothing has really changed. There was an estate agent that considered printing the brochure as 'doing the marketing' for a house sale, while his staff remained blissfully unaware of the property's details. When potential buyers visited the agent's office they didn't even know they had the house to sell, let alone anything about the property.

Conversely, there are many companies that, consciously or not, have adopted the marketing concept but do not use the word 'marketing' at all. The chief executive or the sales director may be acting as a marketing director without calling it that or even recognizing that that is what it is. Eddie Stobart, CEO of the haulage firm of the same name, does not have a marketing department and yet is one of the most successful haulage businesses in the UK that, by the end of 2001, ran over 1000 vehicles. In a service business like a law firm, there may be no marketing department as such, yet every person is responsible for delivering what the firm offers to meet clients' needs. And that includes the senior partners, all fee-earners and legal executives, as well as the secretarial and support staff.

6.2 The Marketing Department in Its Co-ordinating Role

It is an interesting exercise to draw up company organization charts showing the role of the marketing department in varying types and stages of organization. Predictably, the ultimate in organization charts usually winds up as showing the marketing department in charge of virtually everything, except perhaps preparing company accounts and arranging overdrafts (finance), finding staff – mainly for the marketing department – (personnel), and operating the factory (production). This is unfortunate for the two following reasons:

1. It underrates the importance and relative weight of the other parts of the organization.
2. The use of organization charts, while having a value, is increasingly seen in management theory as a stultifying concept. Informal communications in a company are often more important than the 'chains of command' ones. A person's authority and influence can be much wider (or may be narrower) than is easily expressed in a set of boxes and lines on a chart.

In so far as the organization chart concept is of value in assessing the role of the marketing department, much of its responsibility would normally need to be expressed in 'dotted line' terms. That is to say, its direct authority may well be very limited but its responsibility for consulting, guiding and co-ordinating other departments is very much wider. Compare this to Porter's value chain in Chapter 1, page 13.

Thus, the simplest form of company structure looks something like Figure 6.1 (to play the organization chart game for a minute), especially if the company is production-oriented.

As mentioned above, the chances of conflict between the various sections of the business, perhaps especially between sales and production, are infinite. They will only be resolved if: (a) there is a clear company plan which all are aware of, and (b) the chief executive or someone on their behalf, but with authority over all departments, ensures that proper co-ordination is maintained.

There is a further problem with this type of organization as soon as moves are made towards a customer-oriented approach to business. The sales manager is probably a specialist, since his or her task will have been to sell what the factory is producing. What is to happen if, for example, market research or advertising are embarked upon? Either they will become the responsibility of the sales manager/director, who may have no knowledge of (and perhaps little sympathy with) them, or they will have to come under the chief executive or another board member, or be put into one of the other departments – an anomalous situation.

The tendency is, of course, for one of three things to happen:

1. A separate department is created operating alongside sales – often named the marketing services department.

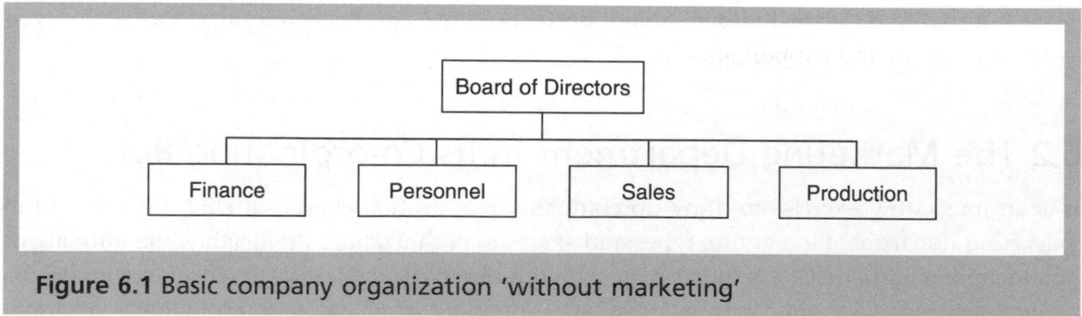

Figure 6.1 Basic company organization 'without marketing'

2. The sales manager/director takes on wider responsibilities and becomes the marketing director.

3. A new senior person is brought in to head both sales and marketing services, probably with the marketing director title.

If option 1 is the choice, either both departments must be headed by a board member (in which case, she is in effect the marketing director) or the situation quickly turns to option 3. Either way, we then have a situation where the company structure has become something like Figure 6.2.

This partly resolves the problem, but does not get over the need to ensure that all departments work together to a common plan. Assuming that there is a marketing plan (see Section 6.9), the 'dotted line' responsibility of the marketing department now comes into play (Figure 6.3).

The dotted lines indicate the relations with other departments and the marketing department's responsibility for ensuring that they contribute to the development and the execution of the company marketing plan. For example, it is no good preparing a marketing plan for a product that cannot be economically produced on the existing equipment, unless finance can be made available for new equipment, and unless the necessary new staff can be recruited and trained at the appropriate time. Once the plan is agreed, then continuing co-ordination is necessary to ensure that agreed production schedules can be met (or the plan modified accordingly), that the turnover and profit targets agreed with the finance department still look reasonable in the light of experience, and so on.

There are a number of situations where a different structure for the organization will be more effective. Among them include:

- The customer demands are sophisticated and require a team response.
- There are many and complex variables in the business environment.
- There are complex internal resources that must be co-ordinated to meet customer requirements.
- The technology is complex and undergoing change.

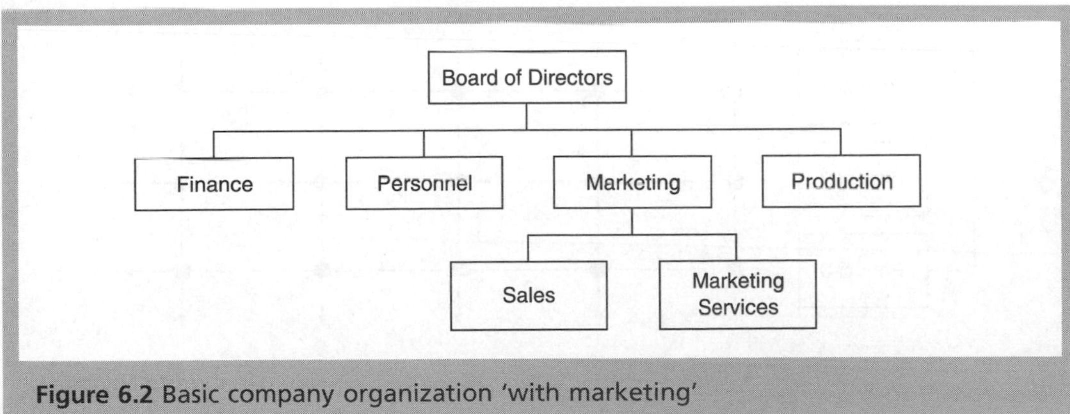

Figure 6.2 Basic company organization 'with marketing'

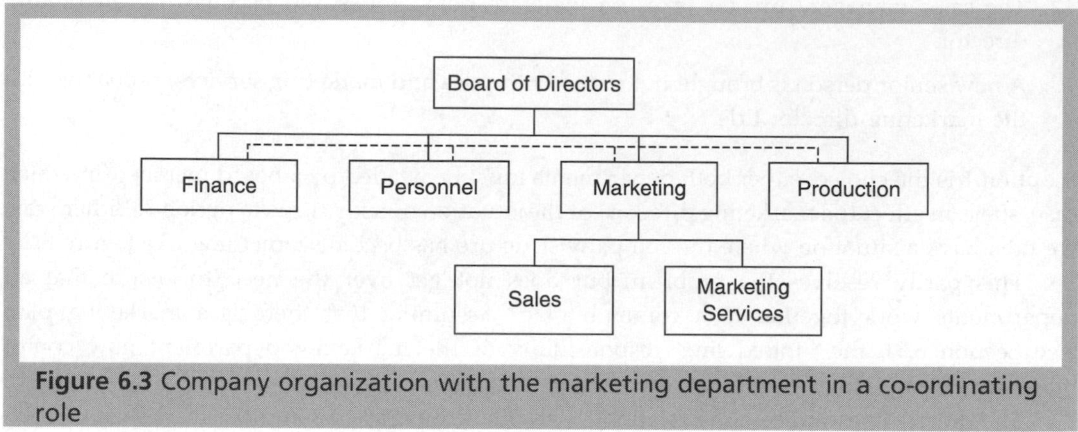

Figure 6.3 Company organization with the marketing department in a co-ordinating role

When these conditions occur, then a matrix structure (Figure 6.4) provides a solution to the demands placed on the organization. A growing number of organizations have experimented with a horizontal chain of people working in a multidisciplinary or cross-functional team setting. Where there are one or two such teams operating at the same time, things can be relatively manageable. It's when several of these cross-functional teams are put together into a matrix that requires people to relate to one another vertically, horizontally and diagonally – all

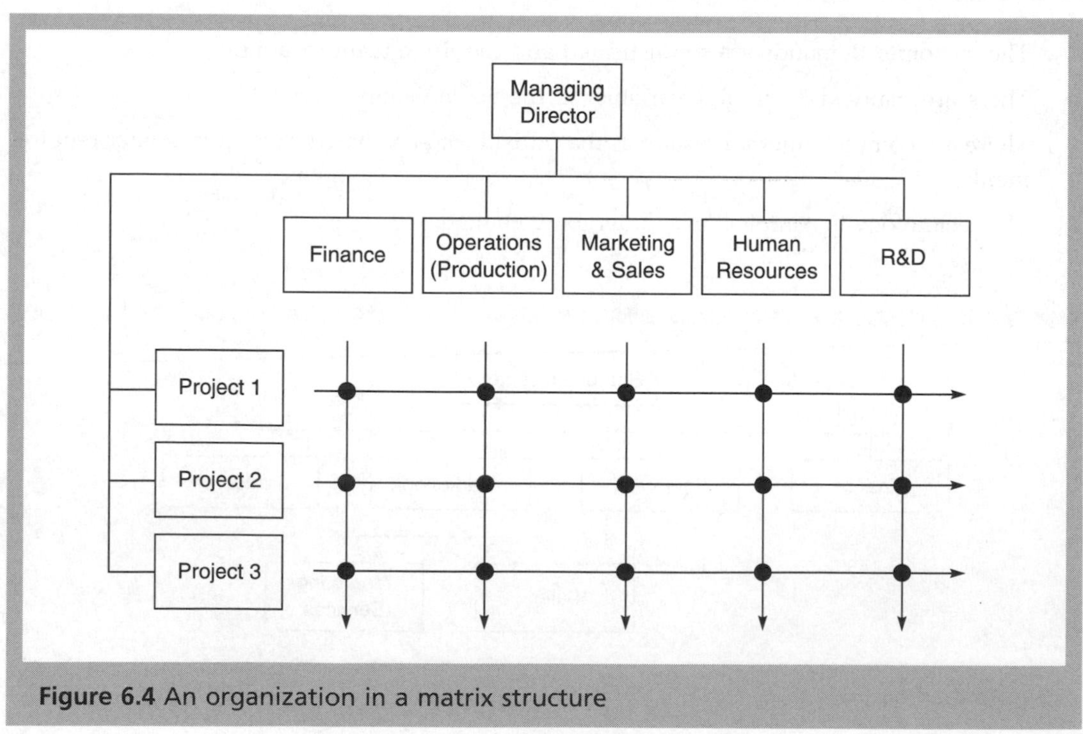

Figure 6.4 An organization in a matrix structure

at the same time! – that the terrain becomes unfamiliar and complex. The Financial Service Authority (FSA) in the UK adopted the matrix structure approach early in 2001 to be better prepared to deliver its services in the changing financial markets.

6.3 The Marketing Department in Its Planning Role

The whole idea of marketing planning is dealt with later in the chapter, so little will be said here about the details of the planning process. But it is important to be clear about the role of the marketing department in planning. Planning means deciding what to do now in order to bring about a desirable situation in the future. It calls for the following steps:

1. Assessing what the true present position is.
2. Deciding what the most desirable future situation is.
3. Assessing alternative ways of getting there.
4. Selecting the most attractive of these alternatives.
5. Making detailed arrangements for pursuing the chosen course.

In terms of marketing plans, items 2 and 4 are clearly matters for top management decisions. Management will also want to be deeply involved in 3. The remaining items may well be the direct responsibility of the marketing department (consulting as necessary with other specialists inside and outside the company).

Thus, an important part of the task of most marketing departments is the detailed continuous monitoring of the present situation and the preparation, from time to time, of detailed plans showing how top management's objectives (expressed in terms of profit levels, sales targets or market shares) can be achieved. On the basis of these proposals, top management will make its decisions about future action.

6.4 The Marketing Department in Its Functional Role

As well as co-ordinating the work of its own and other specialists, and preparing plans for top management, the marketing department will normally have its own specialized functions to carry out. Some of these, such as market research, will be necessary in order for it to perform its planning, monitoring and co-ordinating functions. Others, such as sales and advertising, will play their part in implementing the plans when the top management decision has been taken. Those specialist functions that are grouped under the marketing department heading will vary from company to company, depending on the individuals employed, the kind of business the company is in, and the extent to which it has embraced the marketing concept.

6.4.1 Core and Peripheral Functions

Broadly speaking, there are two groups of functions that can be part of the marketing department: the core functions, at the centre of the marketing activity, and peripheral ones, which can often be performed quite adequately in some other part of the company, even though they have a close connection with the 'customer end' of the business.

The core functions are the following:

- **Marketing research**. Seeking, recording and processing all necessary data about the economy, the market, competitors, and the effectiveness of sales and advertising programmes.
- **Product planning**. Determining the product mix and ensuring that the company's products are in line with customers' requirements, including packaging and pricing.
- **Sales**. Field selling; selection of distribution channels; forecasting, budgeting and analysis of sales; sales office administration.
- **Advertising and promotion**. Advertising, trade and consumer promotions, point of sale and merchandising material, editorial publicity and sales literature.

The peripheral functions might extend to the following:

- Product development.
- Physical distribution.
- Credit control.
- Stock control.
- Recruiting and training sales and other marketing staff.

Clearly, of these, product development, physical distribution and stock control could be controlled by production; credit control by finance; and recruiting and training by personnel. In many companies they are. There is no 'right' organization – it depends on the company, the people and the circumstances, and it will constantly be changing as these change. This is why the organization chart approach has its critics – they see an organization as a fluid and constantly changing pattern, not as a fixed base structure that can be pinned up on a board for all time.

6.5 Organizing the Marketing Department

As well as being part of the total organization of the company, the marketing department must within itself be organized so as to operate as efficiently as possible. Organization of the field sales force is a subject in its own right, and is dealt with in Chapter 16. Here we look mainly at the remainder of the marketing department functions, although of course they cannot be divorced from each other in this way in reality.

The need for a clear-cut organization emerges as the size of the marketing department increases and the number of people and specialist functions proliferate. The number of people and tasks that can be effectively supervised (the 'span of control') is limited, although there are different views on whether a wide or narrow span of control (one person supervising a larger or smaller number of other people) is better.

The wide span of control eases the co-ordination problem (since one manager is in charge of a wide variety of specialist functions), and the danger of dilution of objective is less. The manager, however, may be forced to control more than he can effectively have personal knowledge of.

A narrow span of control makes it possible to have a manager with intimate knowledge of the work of his section. On the other hand, the proliferation of control centres adds to the co-ordination task, introducing the risk of each section developing its own goals and objectives and to some extent losing sight of (or being in conflict with) the general objectives.

There are four basic ways in which the work of the department can be subdivided: (a) by function, (b) by region, (c) by market and (d) by product.

6.5.1 Organization by Function

Here the marketing director will have a series of managers for each main function, as shown in Figure 6.5. As the number of functions increases and the span of control becomes too wide for comfort, a further subdivision might be introduced (Figure 6.6). This type of organization tends to be found where the product range is fairly narrow and where the markets are concentrated and clear-cut – especially in industrial or business-to-business markets.

6.5.2 Organization by Region

Here the breakdown would be by geographical region, with countries, continents, counties or arbitrary areas being the units. The marketing director has a territorial manager for each region. Each manager might have his own functional organization as above, or have responsibility within his area only for some functions, the rest remaining centralized and responsible to the marketing director. This is clearly the likely organizational approach for multinational companies or those with a very large field sales force backed by many supporting functions over a very large area – especially where local variations are an important feature.

6.5.3 Organization by Product

A proliferation of products, perhaps all selling to the same or similar markets, introduces a different situation. Here the need is not so much for specialists in regions as for specialists in products.

Each major product or group of products has its own marketing organization. This can be set up in one of two main ways, as follows:

1. **Product divisions**. Each main group of products has a separate marketing division, each with its own sales force and marketing specialists. Thus a large electronics company might

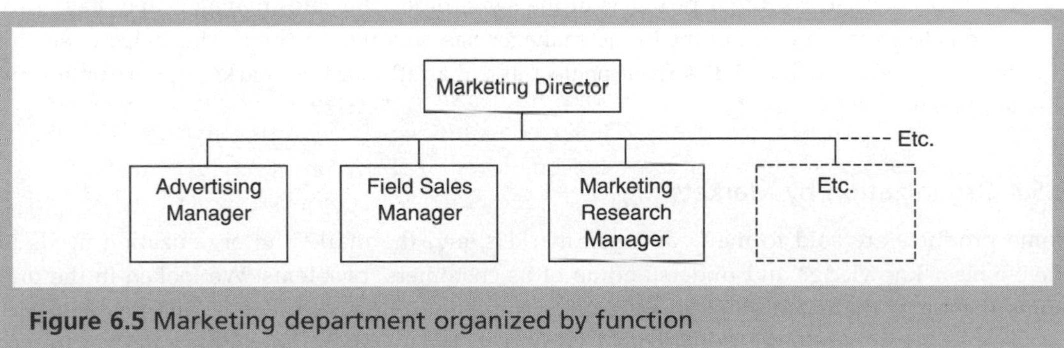

Figure 6.5 Marketing department organized by function

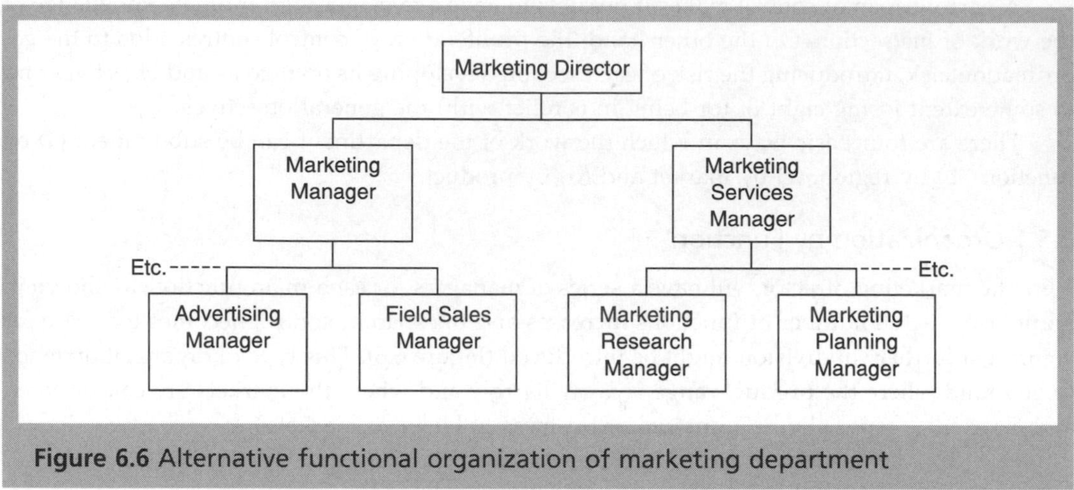

Figure 6.6 Alternative functional organization of marketing department

have divisions handling: (a) telecommunications products, (b) radio and TV products, (c) aircraft control systems and (d) radar systems. Meanwhile the other functions within the company are split differently so that one factory, for example, might be manufacturing items to be marketed by all four of the marketing divisions, another making items for (a) and (c) only, and a third producing for (b) and (c). The position of the marketing division is then somewhat analogous to that of an independent marketing organization 'buying in' products from the various factories.

2. **Product managers** (also called **brand managers**). Alternatively, there can be a single sales force, with a product manager for each product or group of products. The product managers' tasks vary somewhat from company to company but normally include the co-ordination of all advertising, promotion, packaging and product improvements for their personal products or brands. To a greater or lesser extent they will help in preparing the marketing plans and setting sales and profit targets for their brands. This pattern is very common in companies in fields such as confectionery, cigarettes and detergents, where there is a proliferation of brands. The main purpose is to ensure that each product or group of products is the responsibility of a person whose attention and enthusiasm is not diluted by their concerns for other products at the same time. The sales manager may have fifty brands to worry about, but the brand manager has only two or three. This helps to ensure that no product wilts or dies from neglect and that all possible market opportunities are exploited.

6.5.4 Organization by Markets

Some products are sold to many different markets, and the marketing organization needs to have a clear knowledge and understanding of its customers' problems. We looked in the previous section at the example of an electronics company selling products in the fields of telecommunications, radio and TV, aircraft control, and radar. Let us now look at an electronics component manufacturer selling to many different companies making some or all of these four kinds of product, and add computers to the list. To design and market such components successfully, the sales force must be able to talk technicalities with the designers and production engineers of their customers. But it is virtually impossible for one person to be thoroughly conversant with all five of these areas – each a technology in its own right – so that the marketing organization may be subdivided by markets, as shown in Figure 6.7.

6.5.5 Organization by Customer

In many areas of business the increasingly typical situation is of very large companies dealing with other large ones, e.g. British Aerospace dealing with Defence departments and airlines, food companies and others dealing with supermarket chains. In these circumstances the organization may be on a customer by customer basis, often using project teams including a mix of, say, sales, production, technical, marketing and finance – whatever is most appropriate at a particular time for dealing effectively with that customer. The group dealing with another customer might have a totally different composition. Thus, as early as 1994, in an article in *Marketing Business*, Malcolm McDonald said: 'Moving away from the transactional, where customers are to be scrutinized, predicted and controlled, the concept of relationship marketing aims to foster a genuine partnership with customers, and even further down the buying chain.' See also 'Customer relationship marketing', Chapter 18.

6.6 Buying in Specialized Services

It must not be assumed that all the functions referred to in this chapter are necessarily staffed wholly by people on the company's payroll. Advertising, as an example, can be carried out wholly within the company or wholly outside. Typically it is a mixture of the two. Similarly, market research, public relations or new product development may be wholly or partly bought

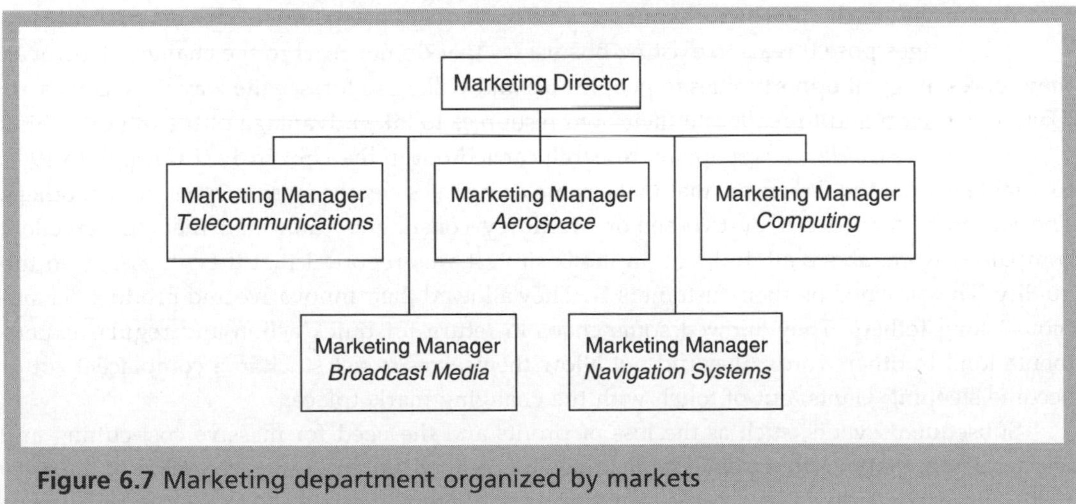

Figure 6.7 Marketing department organized by markets

in from specialist organizations. It is not even essential for a company to employ its own sales force. In some cases suitable intermediaries can take care of all necessary personal contact with customers; or the in-company sales force can be supplemented as necessary, for example by hiring a 'commando sales force' to help with the launch of a new product or to 'sell in' a special promotion to retailers.

6.7 Making the Future Happen Through Sound Marketing Plans

Marketing, indeed business as a whole, is all about making the future happen. Unfortunately, far too much of the average executive's time is spent reviewing the past or dealing with today's problems. Yet only action that affects tomorrow's situations can secure tomorrow's vital profits. As Chapter 2 stressed, marketing deals with a dynamic situation.

While trying to make the future happen is risky, it is a rational activity. And it is less risky than coasting along on the comfortable assumption that nothing is going to change, or following a prediction as to what 'must' happen or what is 'most probable'.

We have touched on two very important points:

1. We cannot safely assume that things will continue exactly as they are, nor that present trends will continue.
2. Taking steps to control the future can be a rational activity.

The word normally used in management terms to describe this rational approach to controlling future events is 'planning' (the dictionary definition of 'plan' is 'arrange beforehand'). Planning is an essential aspect of marketing and a prime function of marketing management.

A wise sage once said: 'You need to manage change, rather than to let change manage you!' However, if one tries to manage change in the same way that one managed a stable, routine situation, then a crisis will ensue. As Albert Einstein is reputed to have quoted: 'You cannot solve problems with the same thinking that caused them in the first place.'

As we saw in the first two chapters of this book, there are plenty of drivers of change.

All changes pose threats to existing businesses that do not react to the changes. However, they represent great opportunities to people able and willing to foresee the way the changes are likely to develop and to reallocate their own resources to take advantage of the opportunities.

In Search of Excellence[ii] reports on research carried out in the USA in 1977 through to 1980, to establish what the factors are that make some companies clearly more successful than others. The research, carried out by two senior McKinsey consultants, indicated that 'the excellent companies were, above all, brilliant on the basics'. It was reported that they: 'insisted on top quality. They fawned on their customers ... They allowed their innovative and product "champions" long tethers. They allowed some chaos in return for quick action and regular experimentation.' In other words, they did not allow themselves to get stuck in a complacent rut or become sleeping giants, out of touch with the changing marketplace.

Subsequent events, such as the loss of profits and the need for massive cost-cutting and restructuring, that overtook some of the 'excellent companies' during the recession of the early 1990s, threw some doubt on whether any company has totally established a successful formula for all time. Indeed, in a later book[iii] Tom Peters, one of the authors of *In Search of Excellence*, acknowledged: 'There are no excellent companies . . . No company is safe. IBM is declared dead in 1979, the best of the best in 1982 and dead again in 1986. People Express is the model 'new look' firm, then flops twenty-four months later.' Peters then goes on to emphasize, and demonstrate throughout the book, that these 'excellent' firms don't believe in being excellent. He makes the point that they only believe in constant improvement and constant change – they 'thrive on chaos'.

So, obviously, if we always do what we always did, then we'll always get what we always got. Unfortunately, if what we got was good, then someone else is sure to notice and take some of it away! In order to stay ahead of the competition, we need to develop a sustainable competitive advantage. And at a seminar run by Tom Peters recently, he stated that *'the only sustainable competitive advantage is the ability to learn faster'*.

6.8 Corporate Planning

It has become fashionable for the term 'corporate plan' or 'corporate strategy' to be used to describe a plan for the whole future activity of a business. Generally the plan is for five years (although it depends on the industry and the particular needs of the company concerned). More detailed one- and two-year plans are then developed.

The planning process comprises a sequence of steps along such lines as the following:

1. Assessing political, economic, social and technological trends on a national and international basis (PEST analysis – see Chapter 2), and then identifying corresponding opportunities in the marketplace and threats from market forces and the competition.
2. Evaluating the company's own particular strengths and weaknesses.
3. Relating these to the likely situation developing from point 1. In particular, trying to pinpoint opportunities that the company's strengths are well suited to exploit.
4. Setting quantified objectives.
5. Working out strategies to achieve these objectives.
6. Preparing detailed plans and assigning tasks in order to carry out the strategies.
7. Identifying the measures needed to evaluate the success of the various initiatives.

Note that the last step is perhaps the most crucial. In a study reported in *Marketing Business*,[iv] it was stated that 75 per cent of marketing executives in the US and the UK say that their company is unable to measure a marketing campaign's return on capital employed (ROI).

Clearly, as time goes on, the assessments of likely trends will need to be modified. The company's relative position – its strengths and weaknesses in relation to competition and the developing situation – will change. So the corporate plan must be regularly updated.

Only the most sophisticated companies use this approach in its most developed form, although more and more are moving towards it. If, however, we are to control the development of the company to any extent at all and not simply be carried along by events, then some degree of planning is surely essential. Quite apart from anything else, we must assume that, if we do not plan for change, we shall eventually run out of business. The life cycle of our existing products (see Chapter 3) will have run its full course.

6.9 The Marketing Planning Process

The planning process outlined above can be usefully explored in more detail with the help of Figure 6.8.

6.9.1 Corporate Planning

Marketing plans are a detailed expression of 'how to get there' (i.e. how to make the future happen). But first there has to be a corporate vision of where 'there' is. Thus, top management must take a clear view of where the company as a whole is heading.

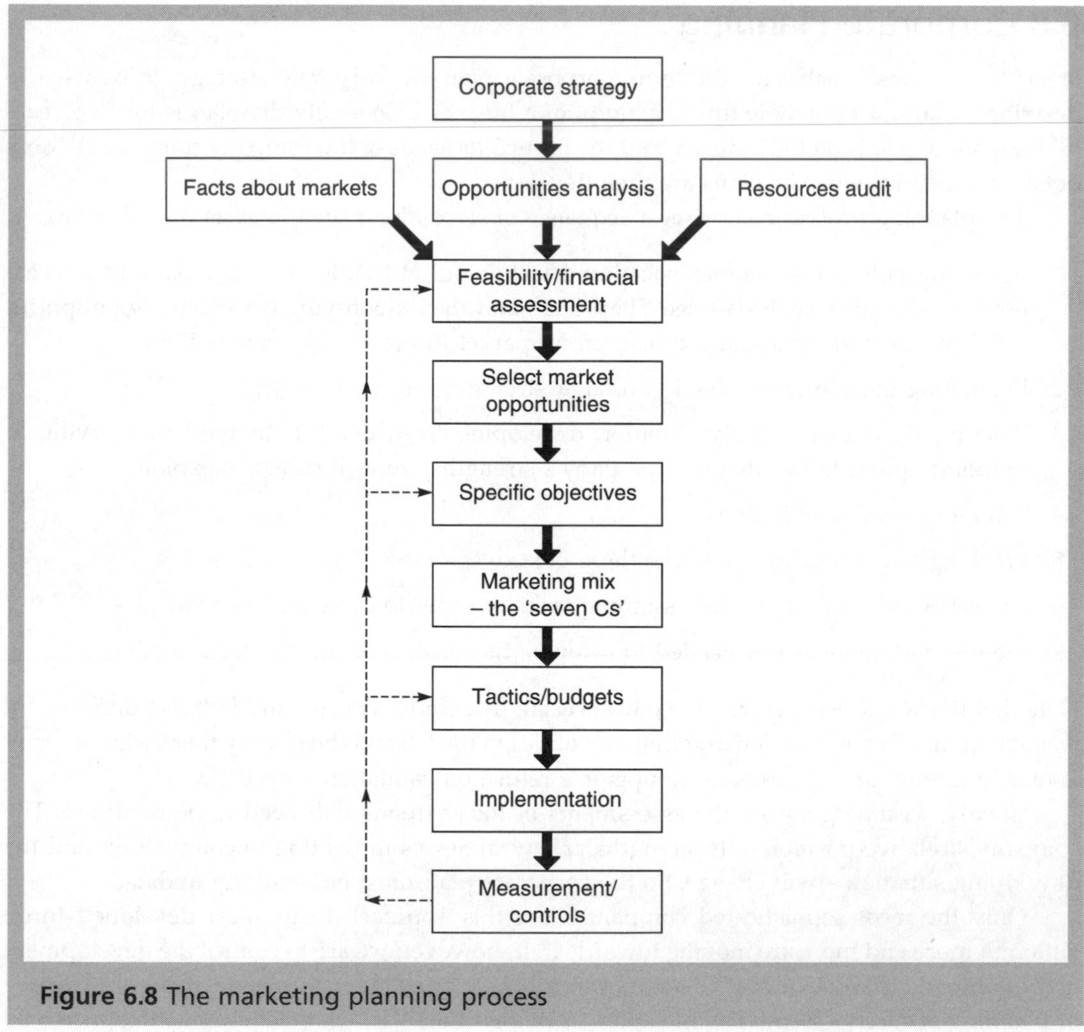

Figure 6.8 The marketing planning process

It is usual that the successful management of a business will depend on successful decisions at three levels: strategic, administrative and operational. Moreover, strategic decisions are primarily concerned with external, rather than internal, problems of the firm and specifically with selection of the product mix of the firm and the markets into which it will sell. Or, in other words 'what business the firm is in and what kinds of business it will seek to enter'.

In the rapidly changing environment that the world now represents, decisions do have to be made. No company can simply drift along doing whatever comes next. There needs to be a clear idea of the answer to the question 'What business are we in?' (see Section 1.2). Otherwise the necessarily limited resources any company has to operate with will be dissipated rather than concentrated and hence not totally effective. This need to be clear where the company is heading and what business it is in (sometimes referred to as a 'mission statement') is at the heart of the corporate planning aspect of top management's long-range decisions.

Once this general direction has been clarified (our business is in entertainment, or food and drink, or business systems), then specific product/market decisions can be taken. This involves balancing market opportunities on the one hand against the company's resources on the other (see the TOWS matrix, Section 6.10.2).

6.9.2 Resources Audit

A key aspect of successful management is to ensure that a company's resources are fully employed in profitable ventures. On the other hand, disaster can come if a company takes on ventures that over-stretch its resources.

A careful review or audit of resources needs, therefore, to be carried out on a regular basis so that management is very clear what resources it does and does not have to operate with. It is convenient to carry out this audit under a number of headings:

1. **Production capability**. What experience/equipment/know-how do we have in providing particular products or services, and in what other areas could these be relevant?
2. **Marketing capability**. Similarly, what is our experience in distributing and promoting to particular markets, and what distribution channels and systems do we have available?
3. **Human resources**. What kind of people do we have – with what skills, experience and abilities?
4. **Financial resources**. Any new project is almost certain to need both capital investment to launch it and continuing finance to see it through the early stages of the life cycle and into a profitable state. 'Over-trading' – taking on more trade than a company can finance – is still one of the commonest causes of bankruptcy. Stock manufactured but not sold, and goods delivered but not yet paid for, can be voracious eaters of capital.
5. **Image**. Most companies have an 'image' of some sort – that is their market sees them in a particular light and this can be a valuable asset. Therefore, new ventures should, where possible, reinforce this clear and favourable image, not conflict with it and thus confuse customers (see Section 6.11).

The above concentrates on knowing positively which resources we have, but it is of course also important to be clear what resources we do not have. A common experience of the authors and other consultants is to be asked to advise on marketing a new product only to find that the company can easily manufacture it but is in no way geared to market it (and is usually also short of finance for the long haul required to establish itself in a market which is totally new to it).

From this analysis companies often develop a list of their strengths and weaknesses – the first half of the 'SWOT' analysis. However, there is a need to evaluate the usefulness of the strengths in terms of what the market demands and also to evaluate the weaknesses in terms of whether or not they will significantly compromise the business. (A classic mistake of many firms is to include a loyal customer base as a strength of the business – it is not. The business *reputation* or *brand name* may be a strength, and the *database* would be a legitimate strength, but the customers themselves are external to a business and therefore represent an 'opportunity'; see Section 6.9.3 below.) From this position, priorities of activity can be developed.

6.9.3 Selecting Marketing Opportunities

Alongside the resources audit an analysis of market opportunities will be taking place. Similarly, there are likely to be identified a series of threats that come from other companies or changes in the marketplace. This is based on a constant review of 'facts about markets' provided by the company's marketing information system and review of the PEST analysis (see Chapter 4). These findings are summarized under 'opportunities' and 'threats' – the second part of the 'SWOT' analysis.

Out of these many opportunities a selection has to be made of those which are:

1. **Feasible**, given the company's resources (see Section 6.9.2). (For example, the fast-food boom provides many market opportunities, but they may not be feasible for a company whose experience is in some totally different direction such as heavy engineering.)
2. **Potentially profitable**.

The latter needs to be established as early as possible. Often no one does any real figure work until enthusiasm for the project has caused many hours of precious manpower to be spent and much expenditure to be committed. If the project is then aborted because it is not financially attractive all of this time, effort and money has been wasted. It should therefore be established at the outset whether the venture looks likely to be profitable (the calculations will need refining at least once as the project goes along).

One common failing in this area is that many people only look at those opportunities that are obvious extensions of what they are already doing. There are often other, more profitable opportunities, that would be preferable if only someone had established that they existed. This is why 'facts about the market' must be gathered on a continuing basis and market opportunities compared against one another.

6.9.4 Where the Marketing Department Comes In

In the sequence shown in Figure 6.8, the first steps are mainly the responsibility of top management (often assisted in large organizations by a 'corporate planning team'). They will call on the marketing department for facts, figures and forecasts and will draw on past marketing experience. But the direct responsibility is theirs. When we get into deciding which marketing opportunities to go for, the marketing department becomes more deeply involved, although top management would normally take the main decisions. Once, as a result of the feasibility and financial studies, specific opportunities are selected, then it becomes primarily a marketing task to elaborate those decisions into specific objectives and to work out and implement the details of how they are to be achieved.

6.10 A Strategic Planning Process

All too often, the 'SWOT' analysis is undertaken as part of a strategic planning review but there are insufficient links made between the analysis and the plans developed. There is no value in reviewing the business, defining the strengths and weaknesses, and reviewing the market to uncover the opportunities and threats, only to put that analysis in the drawer and then go off and write a business strategy in isolation.

The following is a strategic planning process usually conducted in a series of facilitated workshops with the senior people in an organization.

6.10.1 'SWOT' Analysis: Overview and Theory

The 'SWOT' analysis is a simple and well-established analytical tool for teams of top managers. It involves considerations of internal and external aspects of the business, the market, the competition and the overall environment. The output should be a series of prioritized strategies that lead to action plans.

SWOT is an acronym for strengths, weaknesses, opportunities and threats:

- **Strengths.** These are INTERNAL properties of the business. They are what it does best, especially where it has competitive advantage over the competition. The syntax of a strength is 'Strong professional image' or, say, 'High quality client service'. Each should be evaluated into high, medium and low. See the accompanying web page for more detail.
- **Weaknesses.** These are INTERNAL features of the business. They are aspects that detract from performance and are in the control of the business. The syntax is the same as for strengths.
- **Opportunities.** These are EXTERNAL to the business entirely. They are NOT in the organization's control, but are observed. If exploited, they greatly increase business performance and success. The syntax is 'Expanding market in Pacific Rim' or 'Government changes environmental laws'. Again, these need evaluating in some form of grading. See the accompanying web page for more detail.
- **Threats.** These exist OUTSIDE the business and are outside its control. They are situations that do exist or could credibly exist. They are wide and deep in their extent. They are embedded in the landscape in which the business operates.

  (A special note about Combinations. A single issue can be both a 'strength' and a 'weakness'. For example, a successful and profitable product line is clearly a strength. It is a weakness if the business focused on it to the exclusion of all else and the market changed. So, too, can an issue be an opportunity and a threat. For example, a nice little local war can do wonders for the sale of light arms – an opportunity clearly. However, if the 'wrong side' won, the market has vanished! The top managers must agree on the position and be aware of the implications of the combination.)

The SWOT analysis continues with the following stages:

- **Reaching consensus.** This will require negotiating forms of words to meet the views of all members. Often weaknesses turn out to be threats and strengths become opportunities because the team members have different perspectives on the issues. Scoring (see below) is done *after* four agreed lists have been posted.
- **Scoring.** Each point on each list is taken and consensus is reached.
- **Brutality.** When the scoring has been completed, record but delete all the lower categories. They are day to day managerial issues; they have no long-term significance and are just corporate noise. Indeed, they may need to be addressed in the immediate term but they get in the way of strategic planning. They are for progress meetings not 'top team' meetings.
- **Strategy development.** The goal is to produce a set of strategy statements that score as follows. Strategy must be based on a number of internal strengths that grow, and it must exploit a number of appropriate opportunities. It removes at a stroke any weaknesses or shrinks them, and steers round threats. In the individual work phase, each team member should try and produce about five to ten strategic statements each. They score each one with the agreed ratings. When considering the number of strategies, three is ideal, five is the maximum. If the team wants ten, these are not strategies but short-term plans. Back to the drawing board at five and re-strategize. Often several team members' strategies can be consolidated into a much more powerful general case. This is a very effective consensus device.

In terms of frequency of undertaking the strategy review, it is usual to review annually with the whole process repeated afresh, but to monitor activity at least quarterly.

6.10.2 TOWS Matrix and Strategy Development

As a further enhancement, in this part of the process we look again at some traditional techniques to reflect current thinking. We review the classic SWOT analysis and extend its use to draw out the best strategic alternatives. This technique ensures that the work that goes into the auditing process is not just put 'on file' or in the desk drawer when the SWOT is complete. We turn the SWOT on its head and make the analysis work for us so we can use it as a tool to assist in the strategy development process.

The important point to remember is that, no matter how thoroughly these subsequent activities are carried out, unless the objectives of product development or market extension are based firmly on an analysis of the company's capabilities, they are unlikely to be successful in the long term.

The TOWS matrix is a useful extension to the basic format. It facilitates the development of the most appropriate strategies to make the most of as many of the company's resources and opportunities as possible, limiting the disadvantages of its weaknesses and minimizing the effect of threats in the marketplace.

The basic process requires the company to review the marketing audit and to define the strengths of the business and its weaknesses, and to define the external opportunities and threats.

Having focused on the key issues, the information is recorded in a matrix as shown in Figure 6.9. The matrix then permits the development of **proactive** strategies that can be readily seen to accommodate, for example, as many strengths as matched opportunities (strategies 'a' and 'b' in Figure 6.9).

Similarly, **protective** strategies can be developed that take account of the strengths of the business that counter threats identified from the audit (strategies 'f' and 'g' in Figure 6.9). **Progressive** strategies indicate what can be achieved if the organization undertakes some key developments and improvements to overcome its weaknesses so that it can take advantage of the market opportunities identified. The **prohibitive** strategies are important as they indicate that the organization must stop threats from striking hard at its weakest point and damaging the business base.

In the example in Figure 6.9, nine possible strategies have been shown. The TOWS matrix allows visualization of the various options such that group discussion and appraisal of all strategic options can be undertaken.

It may be decided, for example, that while strategy 'a' or 'b' seems to offer the most advantages to the company, the less glamorous, defensive, strategy 'h' may be more economical or less risky than others. It may provide for a better future, as the damages are limited in the short term, allowing survival of the organization.

	Strengths S1 S2 S3 S4 S5...	**Weaknesses** W1 W2 W3 W4 W5...
Opportunities O1 O2 O3 O4 O5...	**PROACTIVE** STRATEGIES ST : a = S1 + S2 + O1 ST : b = S1 + S2 + S5 + O3 + O5 ST : c = S4 + O4 + O5	**PROGRESSIVE** STRATEGIES ST : d = W1 + W2 + W3 + O2 + O4 ST : e = W4 + W5 + O3
Threats T1 T2 T3 T4 T5...	**PROTECTIVE** STRATEGIES ST : f = T1 + T3 + T5 + S1 + S4 ST : g = T1 + T2 + T3 + S2 + S5	**PROHIBITIVE** STRATEGIES ST : h = T1 + T2 + T3 + W4 + W5 ST : i = T4 + T5 + W1 + W3

Figure 6.9 The TOWS matrix

6.11 The Central Importance of the Marketing Mix

Chapter 5 discussed the necessity of using the marketing mix – the 'four Cs and the S' – as a kind of checklist to ensure that we can deliver customer satisfaction in all the key aspects of the total marketing activity. Section 1.6 showed how a company's 'competitive differential advantage' could derive from any one of the key elements in the marketing mix. The time has come to examine another dimension of the marketing mix: that, in practice, it is not possible to examine one element such as cost to the customer without considering possible effects on other elements. For example, if we decide that the cost to the customer must be substantially reduced, we may have to reduce the quality of the customer value offering – perhaps the product or level of after-sales service – to help make the new situation feasible. If the item a customer values needs heavy marketing communications investment to help establish it in the marketplace with a strong image to which customers can relate, the cost to the customer may have to be increased to help finance this.

Figure 6.10 indicates the different approaches or strategies that can emerge from varying combinations of high, medium or low price with high, medium or low product quality. At one extreme, we can offer a low-priced, low-quality product. In some situations many people will happily opt for this combination. But others will prefer the opposite extreme of top quality at a premium price. 'Fly-by-night' street traders may operate with high prices and low quality but that will not be a suitable strategy for companies wanting repeat business from an established and loyal clientele.

		Customer value		
		High	*Medium*	*Low*
Cost to customer	*High*	Premium strategy	High-cost strategy	Hit-and-run strategy
	Medium	Penetration strategy	Average quality strategy	Shoddy goods strategy
	Low	Super-bargain strategy	Bargain strategy	Cheap goods strategy

Figure 6.10 Nine marketing mix strategies (adapted from Kotler, P. *Marketing Management*, Prentice Hall, 1976)

CASE STUDY

An interesting pattern has emerged with a wide range of marketing executives (male and female, old and young, from all sectors of British industry) attending the author's 'Introduction to Marketing' seminars over the period 1998–2001. They were asked to say how they, as customers, perceived the trading policies of three major UK retail chains.

Marks & Spencer were always placed towards the top left-hand corner but with much discussion over which part of which square. Many noted, that in recent years, they have struggled to respond to customers and were somewhat in the mid-top of the grid.

British Home Stores (BHS) were placed, virtually without exception, firmly in the middle of the middle square.

Woolworth's posed great problems and it was seldom possible for the groups (with numbers ranging from six to twenty in each group) to reach agreement. Some people still saw Woolworth as pursuing a 'cheap goods' strategy (firmly and clearly their policy at one stage but far from the recent facts at the turn of the century). Some still remembered and had been impressed by the 'Wonder of Woolies' advertising which showed a wide range of merchandise in an exciting 'show business' atmosphere – but had then been disappointed by the merchandise, store layout and staff behaviour when they had actually visited a store.

Further discussion elicited the feeling that both Marks & Spencer and British Home Stores had 'got it all together' in the mid-90s with merchandise, pricing, store layout, staff and promotion all a piece of the same picture and each presenting a coherent believable consistent story which appealed to many people. Woolworths, on the other hand, were still struggling (under a recently appointed new management) to 'get their act together' in a changing environment already very different from the one they had once dominated with their clear-cut '3d and 6d' (cheap goods strategy) approach of many years earlier. (Where '6d' refers to when there were 12 pennies to the pound, pre-decimalization; thus 6d is equivalent to 2½ pence today.) By 2001, groups had revised their perceptions of M & S and BHS but now increasingly put Woolworth in the 'Bargain strategy' square.

Question

1. From your own experiences of the three retailers (BHS, Marks & Spencer and Woolworths) what do you predict for their future?

For further discussion, see the accompanying web pages.

A very important aspect of the whole marketing planning process is thus arriving at that emphasis, right across the marketing mix, which enables customers to relate strongly and firmly to the company and its products and thus be happy to do business with them. Staying in tune with customers, both existing and future, is fundamental. A low price alone, a good product or a fantastic advertising campaign by itself will not do, unless all the elements of the marketing mix are individually correct, reinforce each other and are consistent with each other.

The tactics to be used and the budgets to be allocated (what needs to be done, when and by whom, using what resources) depend on this clear establishment of what is to be communicated (the 'competitive differential advantage' referred to in Section 1.6). Making these decisions and achieving this focus are an aspect of the positioning referred to in Chapter 9.

6.12 The Importance of Measurement and Control

In drawing up the marketing plan, it is vitally important to include at the outset ways of knowing how the implementation of it is proceeding against pre-set targets. For this reason the 'specific objectives' in Figure 6.8 need to be both quantified and measurable. Otherwise it will be impossible to tell whether the plan is working or not. The quantified objectives can be based on revenue and profit targets, market shares, return on investment or whatever combination is most relevant.

Measurement may involve rapid feedback of sales figures, retail audits (to give both turnover at point of sale and also market share information) and sometimes opinion survey type research – especially when the selling process is a lengthy one.

Figure 6.8 shows this information being 'fed back' up the line. Thus, in the light of actual achievement, tactics may have to be changed or objectives revised. It may even be necessary in the light of experience 'in the field' for the whole feasibility and financial viability of the project to be reviewed. It is better for this to be done early on and the project terminated so that losses can be cut rather than for the juggernaut to roll forward, consuming resources to no ultimate purpose.

When the Chartered Institute of Marketing launched its 'Better Marketing Measurement' campaign through *Marketing Business* (September 2000), it was in part in response to accusations that marketers were 'unaccountable, untouchable, slippery and expensive'. However, it was also in part to coincide with a growing interest, from within the industry, as to how marketing impacts company performance and shareholder value, and how its effectiveness can be measured.

A study into the link between corporate reputation and shareholder value, and how brand reputation can be measured, was launched by the Centre for Corporate Reputation and Relationships at Henley Management College (see *Marketing Business*, February 2001).

The growth of e-commerce is also furthering the measurement cause. If clear objectives are set and performance measures are in place, online marketing is one of the easiest disciplines to evaluate. (Measuring online marketing was explored in the e-commerce supplement in the December/January 2001/2002 issue of *Marketing Business*.)

6.13 Contingency Plans and Sub-plans

6.13.1 Contingency Plans

Sometimes, it can be foreseen that the original plan may have to be changed if certain situations are encountered in the market (e.g. a known possible competitor does in fact enter). In this case, contingency plans can be made in advance and swung in to replace the original plan when the situation changes. The availability of such contingency plans prepared in advance can avoid the necessity for hasty re-planning in a 'panic' situation.

6.13.2 Subdivisions of the Marketing Plan

The marketing plan, itself ideally developed within the total corporate plan, will contain a series of 'sub-plans'. Generally the corporate plan is designed for a lengthy term (say five years), and the marketing plan for a shorter term (say two years). The sub-plans will often be short term (one year or less). The following sub-plans are usual, with others perhaps being added in particular situations:

- The **sales plan** will detail how the selling effort is to be deployed – balancing the servicing of existing accounts against gaining new ones, and detailing the relative effort to be put into each part of the product range. It will indicate call rates, journey cycles etc. Items such as conversion rates of orders to calls and new accounts opened will be quantified.
- The **advertising plan** will indicate matters such as target audiences and the relative importance to be attached to them, expenditure in the various alternative media etc. Quantification will be in terms of number of new users of the product, increase in brand awareness, coupon response rate, or other criteria, depending on the situation.
- A **sales promotion plan** will cover all the other promotional activities where the message is not in a paid for medium. It will include the various mechanisms used and describe what activity will happen over what period, and will clearly make reference to the other communication plans.
- A **market research plan** will be necessary since, although one will undertake some form of research at the outset, it will be equally important to track the advertising and other communication techniques as part of the evaluation process.

6.14 The Importance of Budgets

We have referred to the importance of quantifying targets. Another aspect of this is that all phases of the marketing plan must be budgeted as accurately as possible, in terms of both costs and anticipated income. Since there eventually must be a profit (even though in the short or medium run a loss might be acceptable) it is essential at all stages to know what the expectations are in this respect. Incidentally, an important aspect of the 'controls' will be devoted to methods of monitoring income and expenditure against budgets. Break-even analysis (see Chapter 13) may play an important part in the development of plans and arriving at acceptable budgets.

Another aspect of budgeting, which has assumed greater importance in recent times, is 'cash flow'. Not only is it vital that an adequate profit should ensue from any marketing activity, but also the necessary funds to finance each stage of the operation must be available without undue cost and without crippling the firm in other directions.

With new ventures particularly, it is almost a certainty that in the early stages there will be a net outflow of funds (i.e. outgoings will exceed income). The timing and level of the flow of money in each direction – the cash flow – must therefore be carefully predicted and monitored if serious hold-ups and/or expensive borrowings are to be avoided. In all marketing planning, a key factor will almost certainly be the level of profit a project is likely to generate, either in the short or in the long term (see Section 3.5).

Reporting in the *Daily Mail* on 29th November 2001, Peter Markham wrote:

"The future of ITV's digital channel looked bleak as its owners admitted they could not cope with spiralling losses. ITV Digital ... plagued by low viewing figures since launch, has invested hundreds of millions of pounds in an attempt to rival BSkyB ... running costs were unacceptably high."

"Carlton and Granada have already spent £800 million on TV Digital. Another £350 million is needed before it can become profitable in 2004."

6.15 Marketing Forecasting

Forecasting demand is an important aspect both of arriving at a total long-range corporate plan and of preparing detailed shorter-term marketing plans. In the first case, management must have an idea of the size of any predicted market developments, in order to estimate the resources needed to seize the opportunity presented. In the second case, distribution, price and promotional resources (including size of sales force and level of advertising budget) all depend on an accurate assessment of the likely level of sales.

How then can accurate forecasts be made? There are basically two approaches: the 'top-down' and the 'bottom-up'.

The '**top-down**' approach works as follows:

1. Start from a forecast of general conditions (stage 1 of the corporate planning approach outlined in Section 6.8).
2. Use this to estimate the total market potential for the product in question.
3. Apply to this figure the proportion of market share the company can expect to achieve.

The '**bottom-up**' approach, instead of starting from broad economic estimates, begins with separate estimates for each of a number of market sectors or organizational units within the company. These are then added together to form the total market estimate. For example, a company might be selling electronic components to a number of different industries – home entertainment, telecommunications, aerospace etc. A projected new range of components could have a number of different applications within each industry. Estimating each and collating the estimates gives the total forecast.

It is of course likely that the 'bottom-up' approach will be more applicable where the new ventures are developments of existing business, and that the 'top-down' method may have to be used for a completely new departure. Note too that, inevitably, there is a fair amount of intuition and 'guesstimating' in these approaches. There is no way that we can achieve certainty about the future. All we can do is to be systematic instead of haphazard, and to subject all our guesses to careful scrutiny, to compare the unknown with the known to see if it appears reasonable. There are a number of well-established forecasting methods we can use.

6.15.1 Forecasting Methods

Survey of buyer intentions – Since forecasting is an attempt to gauge the quantities of future purchases, the most obvious method is to ask buyers what they intend to buy. In some cases this is a perfectly reasonable approach. For example, component and sub-assembly suppliers to major industries often work on a forward contract basis or at any rate work in close liaison with their major customers.

More often, however, buyers may be unwilling to disclose their intentions. In a volatile industry they themselves may not know what their future buying pattern is likely to be; even when they are clear on their future intentions, they may in the event not carry them out. In many cases, too, where there are several buyers with diverse interests, the cost of collecting the information may be too high relative to its value. It is thus likely to be of the greatest value in a fairly stable industry with few buyers.

Composite of sales force opinion – Since salespeople (or agents or distributors, for example) are closest to the market, they can be said to be in a good position to make reliable estimates. Clearly there are potential problems, in that salespeople are not generally trained to make unbiased estimates, and indeed may have (or believe they have) reason to introduce bias (e.g. they may want to minimize likely demand so that their performance will show up well against the targets set). But, especially where there is a high technical element, the salespeople, from their close personal knowledge of and relations with their customers, may well have a contribution to make, even if their views have to be weighed rather carefully for possible bias in one direction or another.

Expert opinion – Particularly where a new venture is concerned, or where long-range forecasting is employed, past and present experience may be largely irrelevant. How do you estimate what the use of embryonic stem cells will be in ten years' time for cancer or AIDS treatments when neither exists yet? How do you calculate the off-take of as yet undesigned components for engineering projects themselves still in the preliminary consideration stage?

One approach is to consult a number of experts in the field and ask them to guess what the future situation is likely to be. One refinement of this is the 'Delphi technique' (the name derives from the Delphic oracle of ancient Greece). A number of expert 'guesses' are built into a combined 'scenario', which is fed back to the individual experts for comment and revision. Stage by stage the scenario is modified until a 'consensus' is reached. Sometimes a number of alternative scenarios are developed, so that alternative plans can be built upon them.

Time series analysis – This method goes right to the other extreme and attempts to use past patterns to project future trends. The simplest example is the sales graph over a number of years, showing a consistent trend, which is then extrapolated to indicate the likely future development of the trend. This method has considerable attraction because, at least in its basic form, it is simple and also because it is based on facts. However, it has considerable inherent dangers, unless the underlying factors producing the trend are clearly understood. Otherwise an unanticipated change in one of the factors will completely wreck the forecast.

A series of sales figures plotted over time (time series analysis) contains the three following components:

1. **Trend**. The result of basic developments in population, capital formation, technology etc.
2. **Cycle**. House building, for example, shows swings (undulations in the curve) related to the general level of economic activity, which itself tends to have a cyclical pattern.
3. **Season**. Many products show distinct seasonal peaks and troughs – some, like toys, for obvious reasons, others less obvious.

Time series analysis uses mathematical techniques to separate out these components, and also to isolate any extraneous or 'random' factors (such as strikes, price wars, fads and abnormal weather conditions) that obscure the underlying patterns. Detailed analysis of this kind, which can be a formidable undertaking, is often only possible with the use of specially developed computer programs.

Market factor analysis – A market factor is an element in the market which can be quantitatively measured and which has a direct relation to the demand for a particular product. For example, the number of new houses being built (housing starts) is a market factor contributing to the demand for plumbing components, and the number of two-year-old cars is a market factor in the demand for replacement tyres. When the relation is as obvious as this, market factor analysis can be a very cheap and reliable method of forecasting.

Statistical demand analysis – Unfortunately, in many cases, the factors contributing to demand are not so obvious as those just cited. However, by means of statistical techniques, one can develop equations that may demonstrate a correlation between past sales figures and a single variable (simple regression analysis) or a number of variables (multiple regression). The variables may be population figures, income levels etc.

Depending on the precision of the 'fit' between sales and those predicted by the equation, the equation may then possibly be used to predict future sales on the basis of the variables in question. However, a high volume of computer analysis is needed for these calculations, and figures over many years are necessary before a 'fit' good enough to ensure accurate prediction can be obtained.

Executive judgement – Many would say that, despite the previous approaches, there is no substitute for all of them being tempered with sound executive judgement. Should forecasting be done solely by slide rule, computer or mathematical model? Equally, forecasting by executive opinion alone will not reduce the risk in decision-making. In some instances, it is simply intuition or guesswork.

Perhaps, in the end, the purpose of the more sophisticated techniques is to reduce the possibility of some of the wilder guesses being acted upon.

The role of marketing research – It will be realized that many of the above forecasting techniques depend on the availability of suitable information. Often marketing research techniques will have to be used to gather and analyse this data. In Section 6.12 we saw the importance of controls as part of the marketing plan. Here, too, marketing research normally plays a vital role in providing a flow of data, which will enable performance to be continuously monitored.

6.16 Conclusion

In this chapter and throughout this book we have seen that marketing is a vital aspect of the management of any business. Because it is concerned with the future and with the behaviour of many individual people, it can never be an exact science. However, that does not mean that it should ever be irrational. The use of careful study, logical thought patterns, detailed monitoring of results and quick reaction in the light of experience can avoid many costly mistakes and add greatly to profitability.

Summary

- The marketing department may have responsibilities for: (a) co-ordination, (b) planning and (c) specific functions.
- The main marketing functions are: (a) marketing research, (b) product planning, (c) sales and (d) advertising and promotion; but others may be added in particular circumstances.
- Organization within the marketing department may be by: (a) function, (b) region, (c) market or (d) product.
- A prime function of all management, and of marketing in particular, is to take rational steps – make plans – to 'make the future happen'.
- The ideal starting point is a corporate plan setting out quantitative objectives and strategies for achieving these objectives.
- From this a marketing plan can be developed, with sub-plans for sales, advertising, market research etc.
- Forecasting likely demand is a vital activity of marketing, both in providing a basis for the long-range corporate plan and in working out the shorter-term detailed marketing plan.
- There is a range of methods for forecasting demand, with varying degrees of accuracy and levels of cost.
- All plans must include budgets, and these form a vital element in the control procedures, without which no plan can function properly.
- We conclude with the thought that marketing can never be an exact science but nevertheless is a rational, as well as vital, activity.

References

i Pritchet, P. and Pound, R. *Managing and Supervising Organisational Change* (Pritchett, 2001).

ii Peters, T. J. and Waterman Jr, R. H. *In Search of Excellence* (Harper & Row, 1982).

iii Peters, T. J. *Thriving on Chaos* (Macmillan, 1988).

iv In *Marketing Business* (the magazine for the Chartered Institute of Marketing), January 2002.

Further Reading

McDonald, Malcolm. *Marketing Plans* (Butterworth-Heinemann, 5th Edition, 2002). The classic text on marketing planning.

McDonald, Malcolm and Morris, Peter. *The Marketing Plan in Colour* (Butterworth-Heinemann, 2nd Edition, 2000). Four-colour cartoon illustration throughout.

Wilson, R. M. S. *Strategic Marketing Controls* (Butterworth-Heinemann, 1996). Particularly useful on the financial control aspects of marketing planning.

Questions

1. Many 'professional people', including accountants, lawyers and architects, who until recently could only compete within very strict codes of conduct (amounting in some cases to a rigidly enforced cartel) are now able to compete more freely. What kind of marketing staff and organization do you believe would be most effective for them?
2. What would you suggest as the proper organizational relations between the research and development department of a company producing products for industrial use (e.g. machine tools) and its marketing department?
3. What do you see as the importance of executive judgement in the marketing planning process?
4. Consider the nine marketing mix strategies in Figure 6.10. Identify an example in each box, giving the reasons for your choices.

Chapter 7

The message and the medium

Introduction

By the end of this chapter you will:

- Understand what promotion means and its importance in the marketing mix.
- Appreciate the need to devise the appropriate promotional mix to suit each different marketing situation.
- Realize the necessity of setting clear promotional aims.
- Be aware of the crucial importance of positioning and branding.
- Understand the basis on which promotional mix decisions are made.

'Basically, promotion is an exercise in information, persuasion, and influence.'

William J. Stanton. *The Fundamentals of Marketing*

7.1 What Promotion Means

The word 'promotion' might have been used by Humpty-Dumpty, the character in Lewis Carroll's *Through the Looking Glass* who asserted that words meant what he wanted them to mean. 'Promotion' is such a word, used by different people, in different ways, to mean different things.

In this text it is used mainly as an all-embracing term to describe an important part of the marketing mix. When the right product, at the optimum price, is available in all the right places, through the most cost-effective distribution channels, we still have a problem. The people who might want to buy the product have to be told about it.

Just occasionally they simply have to be told of its existence – 'The new Ford Mondeo is now in stock at Bloggs' showroom'. More usually they need to be given information about the product. This may reinforce people's current attitudes or revise them in some way. They may need to be told what it will do for them (is it really the safest place to be, as advertising for the new 2001 model might suggest?); what shapes, sizes and colours it comes in; what its quality is and its price; and, perhaps, whether credit terms are available.

Very frequently there will have to be a considerable element of persuasion. People do not always readily grasp (or believe) the advantages of a new product, especially if its function is entirely novel and may mean a change in their habits. The acceptance of portable telephones was rapid but not immediate. In some other countries, with a less conservative outlook, however, the take-up rate was much faster (Hong Kong, for example).

The other reason why both information and persuasion are necessary is the existence of competition. No product can afford to be 'invisible' – the situation where people are aware of competitive products but not of this one. People must be aware of the product before they can buy it. Similarly, they must be persuaded that Product A is worth testing against Product B, which they may already use, and that Product A has some distinctive features.

The word promotion is used here firstly to describe the whole collection of methods by which the tasks of information giving and persuasion may be carried out. In the main, these consist of the following:

- Direct marketing (see Chapter 8)
- Advertising (see Chapter 9).
- Sales promotion (see Chapter 10).
- Personal selling (see Chapter 11).
- e-Commerce (see Chapter 12).
- Price as a promotional tool (see Chapter 13).
- Point of sale and merchandizing (see Chapter 17).
- Public relations (see Section 10.9, and the companion web pages for an international perspective).

Secondly, the word is used in a more abstract sense. The point was made in Section 5.2 that the way in which the customer perceives the product becomes a part of the product and is an important element in determining what that customer buys in order to satisfy their needs in the fullest possible way. The example was used of a perfume bought as a present. The chemical ingredients are an important but relatively small element in what is bought. Exactly the same ingredients could be used to provide a cheap 'popular' perfume and a moderately expensive 'exclusive' perfume. The difference between the 'popular' perfume and the 'exclusive' perfume lies not in the perfume itself but in how it is perceived. How it is perceived will be determined by such things as the following:

- The price.
- Packaging (materials used, the way they are constructed, the surface design and colour).
- The name.
- What is said about the perfume in sales literature and in advertising.
- The way it is displayed in shops and which shops stock it.

All these things we can describe collectively as 'the way the product is promoted'. Thus, the word promotion is used to describe both the methods used to communicate with customers and the total effect of the communication. One may talk of 'promotional methods' that go to make up the promotional mix – this is using the word in the first sense. One may also talk of the 'promotional aims' towards which the promotional mix is directed, which is using the word in the second sense.

7.2 The Promotional Mix

The word 'mix' is a particularly valuable and hard-worked one in marketing. We have already discussed the marketing mix (Chapter 5) and the product mix (Section 3.7). Now we must approach the concept of the promotional mix. The way in which the promotional methods listed above are used, and their weight and cost relative to each other and to the other ingredients of the marketing mix, will vary from one situation to another. The group of methods to be used in a given situation and the weighting attached to each method is referred to as the 'promotional mix'.

Arriving at the correct promotional mix is a very complex business, which we discuss in outline in this chapter and in more detail throughout this section. First we look at the kind of factors that influence the make-up of the promotional mix. We can see these clearly in relation to advertising and to personal selling, although similar considerations can be applied to other ingredients in the mix.

7.2.1 Personal Selling

This is an important element in the mix under the following circumstances:

- There are relatively few customers and they are easily identified and not too scattered.
- The product needs demonstrating or the benefits of its use need to be explained in relation to the customer's personal needs (e.g. life assurance and other types of investment).
- The product has to be specially made or developed to fit the customer's needs (life assurance again; also many technical products and products or services with a design element, such as office furnishing).
- There is a need to establish personal rapport (services such as business consultancy and advertising agencies).
- The product has high unit value, so that time spent with an individual customer can be easily paid for by the occasional sale.

- The salesperson buys as well as sells (cars, for example, are normally sold against trade-ins).

7.2.2 Advertising

This approach is favoured in such circumstances as the following:

- Product of low unit cost, selling to very many customers, widely scattered.
- The need to inform many people very quickly – such as a new product launch, a bargain sale or a special offer.
- Uncertainty as to who is likely to buy, or difficulty in locating potential customers.

Some products are easier to advertise than others are. Products that can be strongly differentiated lend themselves well to advertising, as do those with an emotional appeal and those that are strongly branded. Advertising works better when a product is on the 'upswing' part of its life cycle – it is more difficult to use advertising cost-effectively when the intention is to 'buck the trend'.

7.3 Deciding Promotional Aims

In theory it is possible to have a marketing mix that excludes promotion – where the right product at the right price, available through the right channels, will 'sell itself'. In practice it is hard to think of examples, although 'commodities', such as agricultural and mineral primary products, are often in that situation. Other products at first sight come near it – timber, plywood and hardboard, for example. These products are undifferentiated ('homogeneous' is the economics term). One piece of softwood timber, say, is likely to be indistinguishable from another. But this impression is only true at first sight, for two reasons.

First, it overlooks the fact that distribution is a multi-stage affair and so is promotion. So in the case of hardboard, for example, it is true that customers are influenced almost entirely by availability and are not very concerned which hardboard they buy. But the distributors have to be persuaded to stock one manufacturer's product rather than another's. The fact that this may be done through price/delivery negotiations does not alter the fact that a selling job has to be done. It simply means that, in this instance, personal selling at dealer level (perhaps supported by some modest point-of-sale material) is the main element in the promotional mix.

Secondly, however, it may mean that marketing of a particular type of product is still at a fairly undeveloped and unsophisticated stage. In the same field as hardboard, 'Contiboard' in the UK gained a large share of the market by taking an equally homogeneous product – chipboard – and giving it a high degree of differentiation by adding a plastic surface. The added value thus provided, and the additional benefits to the customer, were promoted in colourful leaflets, point-of-sale displays and advertising. This is an example of the point made above that differentiated products lend themselves to advertising.

Sometimes it is not the product that differentiates one supplier from another but service. It will then be the level of service that is featured in the advertising. Even the promotion itself and the brand image it creates may be the differentiating factor. This is often the case with professional services, for example. As far as the general public are concerned, one high street solicitor is often indistinguishable from another – a qualified solicitor who 'does conveyancing' or who can pursue a claim for compensation with respect to an injury (in this case 'the product') is no different to one from his or her neighbouring firm. However, the amount of contact and accessibility of the lawyer, the quality and quantity of information, and the proactive abilities of the support staff in dealing with enquiries, are some of the service differentials that clients can use to distinguish the 'product'. However, many firms are now developing a brand name – like 'Shoosmiths' in the Midlands or, nationally, Claims Direct – to promote their services, the brand image being a key differentiating factor.

It also illustrates the fact that a different promotional mix can be used with very similar products in the same field. Arriving at the most effective mix must start from a properly constructed marketing plan, going through a stage by stage analysis, along the lines set out in Chapter 6. Remember, one needs to be aware that we must be able to answer the following questions:

1. Who are our customers?
2. Which of their needs are we trying to satisfy?
3. How does our product or service provide satisfaction (what benefits does it deliver)?
4. In order to demonstrate this: (a) what facts do we have to supply (information) and (b) what emotional appeals do we need to express (persuasion)?
5. How can we best communicate these things to the ultimate customers?
6. What do we need to communicate to the various parts of the distribution chain and how best can we do it?

We should note that the distinction between 4(a) and (b) is more conceptual than practical, more apparent than real. The provision of the right facts is in itself a form of persuasion (we select the facts that will best make our case, just as a barrister, a lecturer or a journalist does). Also, for the customers, it is what they perceive and sense that is important. How they feel about, say, a car is to them a 'fact', and may be more important than some of the things an automobile engineer would regard as vital pieces of information.

In connection with point 6 above, we must note that what needs to be said to distributors will be different from what is said to customers. Customers will want to know 'How will this product meet my needs, what benefit will I gain from it?' (e.g. economy, convenience, enjoyment). Distributors will want to know 'How will this product increase my profits?' (e.g. faster turnover, bigger discount, more customers in the shop). Different levels of the chain of distribution may well need to be told different things. Thus, wholesalers will be concerned about warehouse space, ease of handling and transport, and minimal breakages; and retailers will want to know about advertising support, introductory discounts, estimated turnover, and profit margins.

Step by step analysis of this kind brings us to the point where we have established: (a) a number of audiences to whom we have to communicate (ultimate customers, the various levels in the distribution chain and others able to exert an influence); and (b) the kind of messages we wish them to receive (which will have been based on an analysis of their needs and matching them with a product, existing or specially developed, that we believe will meet those needs). The purpose of the promotional mix is, therefore, to ensure that the messages are conveyed in the most cost-effective manner.

7.3.1 Positioning and Branding

Quite apart from the communication of specific messages, there is often a more general job to be done, although it is all part of the task of being sensitive to how the customers are likely to perceive the product. Thus, we need to signal to customers whether the product is for the early adopters or for the majority (see Section 3.12.5), for old or young, male or female or both, for the 'big spenders' or for those on low incomes, for families with young children or for sophisticated couples on their own. An industrial product or service may be intended to satisfy the special needs of large corporations or small businesses.

Putting the product in its right 'slot' in this way is often referred to as 'positioning'. Thus we can position a product as 'upmarket' (for the more sophisticated and the bigger spenders) or 'downmarket' (for ordinary people with limited budgets). We can position it to appeal to older people rather than the young, or vice versa. The latter case can be an important one. All established products run the danger of finding themselves being bought entirely by older people. If nothing is done about it, all its regular customers will eventually die. Meanwhile younger people are reluctant to try a product that is thought of as what 'Mum and Dad' or even 'Grandma' buys. Some repositioning is necessary to ensure a continuing market for the product.

A recent example of repositioning a brand was Skoda cars. Along the way, Skoda won the Marketing Effectiveness Awards 2000. Often the hub of many jokes, Skoda was not considered a particularly good mark. However, after their advertising campaign that used the copy line 'It's a Skoda. Honest', their volume market share grew by 30%.[i] By January 2002, the copy line had moved on to 'It is a Skoda. Which for some is still a problem'.

VIGNETTE

Positioning a New Product

Mobile telephones, when they were first introduced and aimed at the 'early adopters', were presented as valuable tools for small businesses or sole proprietors such as builders or plumbers. With slogans such as Vodaphone's 'How to be in when you're out', they highlighted the potential benefits of extra business won through never having the telephone unanswered (or, alternatively, the savings of not needing to employ staff to answer the phone).

Later, 'mobiles' were offered far more widely (at significantly lower prices) to motorists, especially women, as an inexpensive way of always being able to summon help in an emergency.

By early 2002, over two-thirds of the UK population had a mobile phone. Some were positioned as a fashion accessory with exchangeable covers to match the clothes of the customer – way beyond the technical capabilities of the telephone! Moreover, with an average of 82 million messages sent per day in Europe, compared to 20 million per day just two years previously, the mobile phone has gone beyond a voice communications device.

Questions

1. How do you see mobile phones being positioned today?
2. What do you feel the position for third generation telephones will be over the next decade? (See Chapter 12 for more details of the development of mobile telephones)

In planning to market a new ballpoint pen we would need to consider whether to position it as an expensive/exclusive gift, as a reasonably priced working tool or as a cheap 'expendable'.

Branding can also be an important factor in communication. A brand in its simplest form is a name – 'Coca-Cola', 'HSBC', 'Black & Decker'. But other features, such as visual design, colour, typography and slogans, usually come into it. The use of a brand can bring a number of advantages, including the following:

- The product is **easily remembered** and **easily identified**, for example on the supermarket shelf.
- It becomes easier to provide **strong links between advertising** and other forms of **promotion**.
- **New products** can be more **easily introduced** under an existing, well-established and well-regarded brand name. Heinz do not have to start from scratch each time they add a new flavour of soup to their range or enter a new sector of the snack foods market.
- Alternatively, a producer with a **successful brand in one sector of the market can enter another sector with a different brand** (such as Cadbury's with their food products). Companies like IBM in computers or British Aerospace in aircraft or space satellite systems similarly have a head start with new products in the areas where they already have an established reputation.

These positioning and branding aspects will affect the messages we need to transmit to customers and potential customers. Perhaps even more important to realize is that they will affect the way in which the message is transmitted and will therefore have a strong influence on the promotional mix. If there is a need for branding, then there is a strong case for advertising. A manufacturer may of course supply more than one competitive brand (to gain maximum market share). A retail chain may supply lower-priced 'own label' brands, selling in competition with manufacturers' advertised brands, to divert customer loyalty to themselves rather than the manufacturer.

7.4 The Salesperson's Role

By far the most important means of communication between producers and consumers is personal selling. For every person employed in advertising there are at least 100 others taking part in the face to face communication that contributes to the selling process, whether 'on the road' as travelling salesmen or 'behind the counter' of a shop or office or (increasingly) over the telephone. The people that represent councils and local authorities are an important interface with the public – whether they are a part-time telephonist or a senior building inspector; both will represent the 'face' of the organization and will have a role in 'selling' best value.

Personal selling has the following two main advantages over the other forms of marketing communication (listed in Section 7.5):

1. It can carry out the **whole** of the **sales process**, which the others rarely if ever can (although note the exception of direct marketing, Chapter 8).
2. It is **flexible** and can be tailored to the requirements and attitudes of individual customers. Similarly, it can be receptive to the reactions a particular message is creating and can modify it accordingly. With advertising, by contrast, one message has to be transmitted to a wide audience, and there is no way of altering or modifying it in the light of individual reactions.

7.4.1 The Selling Process

The total selling process can be said to consist of a number of stages, although not all of them are present, in this order, in every selling situation:

1. Making the initial contact with a customer.
2. Arousing interest in the product.
3. Creating a preference for the product as against competitors or alternative uses of the customer's money.
4. Making a specific proposal.
5. Closing the sale.
6. Ensuring post-purchase satisfaction and generating future sales.

A good salesperson can do all these things, but only with a relatively small number of people, and therefore at high cost. Other forms of marketing communication can reach far more people, so that they deliver a much cheaper message, but usually they can only effectively carry out some parts of the total process.

Thus advertising can be very good at 1, 2 and 3 above, is not usually good at 4 and 5, and can sometimes be moderately good at 6. At first sight we might rule out 5 entirely (i.e. as an appropriate task for advertising), but advertisements for unit trusts, for example, do sometimes deal with the whole process right to the point of 'send cheque with order'. Many book clubs operate almost entirely by 'selling off the page', and music cassettes and discs are often sold in this way. This is called direct-response advertising or, for television, direct-response television (DRTV).

In general, though, we can contrast the good salesperson dealing at high cost with the whole process as against advertising dealing much more economically with some parts of it. Despite the contrast, however, each can be used to reinforce the other, and they will often be used together as important ingredients in the promotional mix.

7.4.2 The Different Selling Jobs

The term 'selling' embraces a wide range of different tasks in a variety of situations. Some salespeople, such as the following, are basically 'order takers':

- The salesperson who is really a **delivery person** (e.g. of milk or bread). He/she could in theory generate extra sales but in practice rarely does.
- **Retail counter** salespeople or **telephone call centre** staff, whose customers normally know what they want to buy in advance.
- **Travelling sales** staff calling regularly on established retailers or other customers who normally re-order to bring their stock back to its desired level. In some cases the retailer is virtually obliged to stock the product because of high customer demand generated by advertising.

At the other end of the scale, some salespeople have to do a very creative selling job, because the customer may not be aware of his/her need, or must have the fact that the particular product will satisfy his/her needs better than any alternative explained or demonstrated to him/her. Staff of a call centre that provides a contact point with customers may also sell other services. For example, telephone banking call centre staff deal with account queries and, at the end of the discussion, promote and try to sell their bank's financial services, such as insurance, mortgages, independent saving accounts (ISAs) etc. However, as the task may be complex, the call centre staff may redirect the caller to a specialist in a given department.

Some writers have distinguished between selling tangible and intangible products, but the principles are not substantially different. In some cases the salesperson will be primarily a technical expert, since he or she would not otherwise be able to show the customers how their needs can be met.

Not only does the selling situation differ, but also the salesperson's contribution to the total selling process outlined above will be different. Not every salesperson is expected to take orders, for example. Some have the task of preparing the ground by introducing customers to new products, while those who call regularly will take orders for both new and existing products. Many companies employ people called merchandizers, whose task is to ensure that products are properly displayed in the main retail outlets, that special promotions are prominently featured, and so on (although this is becoming less common as the more sophisticated retailers take on this responsibility themselves).

Thus, not only do we have to decide what emphasis should be given to personal selling in the marketing mix, but also what kind of salespeople need to be employed and in what role or roles. It should be clear from other sections that salespeople often work with other promotional methods. For example, advertising and direct mail can be used to produce 'leads' which the sales staff follow up.

7.5 Marketing Communications

This term is often used as convenient shorthand to embrace all the methods available for communicating with customers other than personal selling. Just to confuse the issue, it is occasionally (but not often) used to include that also, and it is useful to be able to make the distinction. We do make the distinction here mainly on the basis that personal selling is a highly individual ('one to one') affair, transmitting slightly different messages at each encounter, depending on the recipient. While it can be planned to some extent, how he or she conducts each interview must be left to the individual judgement of the salesperson.

Marketing communications, on the other hand, are normally 'across the board' communications to mass audiences, carried out on a planned basis with a common message throughout.

The purpose of communication is to help move a potential customer from a state of ignorance towards a position of decision and action. We use marketing communications methods to convey messages that will aid in this process, in the face of the forces operating in the opposite direction (Figure 7.1).

For each situation, we have to choose which selection of communications methods will help us. Some of them were listed in Section 7.4, and we deal with them in detail in later chapters.

A very important (perhaps the most important) means of communication, which is easy to overlook, is 'word of mouth'. People looking for ways of satisfying a need do not merely talk to salespeople and read advertisements and sales literature. They read relevant newspaper and magazine articles, listen to radio and watch TV, but, above all, they talk to each other. People contemplating buying a new car, or a new washing machine, talk to friends and relations and get their reactions. Neighbours compare notes on public services. People who buy a new product and like it recommend it to their friends. If they dislike it, they warn off their friends. There are problems about using this as a method of marketing communications, however, for it takes a long time, its workings are not clearly understood, and it is almost impossible to control. On the other hand, since messages received in this way are seen to be without vested interest, they are perceived as being trustworthy. It is, therefore, well worth seriously setting up special events, projects and new product trials that have, as their main

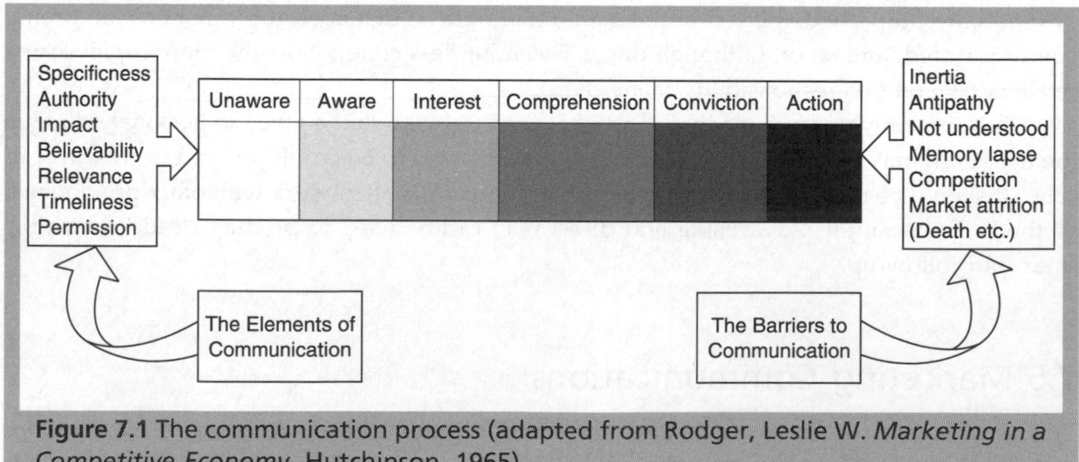

Figure 7.1 The communication process (adapted from Rodger, Leslie W. *Marketing in a Competitive Economy*, Hutchinson, 1965)

aim, simply getting people to talk. Conversely, every possible step should be taken to avoid adverse word-of-mouth criticism. The Tamagotchi cyber pet (an electronic 'pet' held as a liquid crystal image on a screen about the size of a key fob and controlled by a series of buttons to walk it, feed it, let it sleep etc.) was a runaway success. This product was introduced to children in the playground before a campaign was ever launched and the craze spread rapidly by word of mouth. On the Internet, this word-of-mouth technique is called *'viral marketing'*.

In essence, viral marketing creates an incentive for others to communicate your marketing message through the Internet or e-mail, via methods such as attachments or sign-up forms. Attachments allow one to add a degree of personality to a brand and encourage consumers to interact, as well as to find out more about you and your product or service. Just like their more dangerous cousins, viral marketing campaigns can spread across the entire Internet in a matter of days. No other method of marketing has been found that can generate such massive 'recommendation' marketing status with such a relatively small outlay. Viral marketing will be examined further in Chapter 12.

Very frequently, however, we shall find ourselves using more 'structured' methods of communication, because they are faster and their effects are more predictable and controllable.

7.6 Choosing Methods of Communication

There is no 'best' way of communicating with customers. To discuss whether advertising is 'better' than public relations or personal selling is meaningless. Each method has advantages and disadvantages, and, depending on the circumstances, one may be more cost-effective than another. Every marketing situation calls for its own special marketing mix and its own unique promotional mix. Valid generalizations are few, but Table 7.1 gives a rough guide to the way some of the main methods of communicating with customers rate according to a few key criteria.

7.7 Integrated Campaigns

It is important that the ingredients used in the marketing mix and the promotional mix, whatever they are, make a coherent whole. Each activity, each piece of promotional material (advertisement, leaflet, display stand or whatever) must be part of a well-conceived plan. Often the term 'integrated campaign' is used to describe this carefully worked out scheme, where all the individual pieces fit together and support each other. If this is not done, a conflicting effect can result, with a poor response from customers (who are confused rather than motivated by the varying messages they receive). An integrated campaign, on the other hand, can have a synergistic effect – that is, the total effect can be greater than the sum of the various individual activities. Outstanding examples, such as Esso's classic 'A tiger in your tank' (first used over thirty years ago, and with a tiger still 'watching prices' in 2002) and 'Intel Inside' benefit even further from the same message being stated in various languages – but in the same well recognized format – all over the world.

Table 7.1 Promotional methods compared

	Believable	Two-way	Fast	Cheap	Controllable	Action
Word of mouth	✓	×	×	✓	×	✓
Personal selling	×	✓	×	×	✓	✓
Seminars	✓	✓	×	×	✓	✓
Advertising	×	×	✓	✓	✓	×
Sales promotion	×	×	✓	✓	✓	✓
Public relations	✓	×	×	✓	×	×

Notes:

1. In the table, a cross means 'No, rather than yes', a tick 'Yes, rather than no'. The judgements are subjective and simply illustrate the kinds of assessments that have to be made – based on facts if known or judgements if not.
2. The criteria used are:
   - *Believable* – Do the receivers of the message tend to regard the source as believable?
   - *Two-way* – Is there good communication back to the company?
   - *Fast* – Does the message travel quickly from source to destination?
   - *Cheap* – Is the cost per message received relatively cheap?
   - *Controllable* – How much control does the company have over the message as received?
   - *Action* – Is the message very likely to produce immediate action?
3. Seminars, in this context, are meetings to which prospective customers are invited to hear a technical presentation of new products or techniques. 'Hard sell' is kept to a minimum.

7.8 Brands Under Threat?

There are a number of signs of dramatic changes in the economic situation that may affect the marketplace worldwide as well as in the UK:

- Protectionism is on the way out, with European airlines being one of the last major industries to operate under significant government protection; however, Swissair folded towards the end of 2001.
- Many of the traditional defences of manufacturers – such as control of distribution or the exploitation of technological superiority – are no longer effective. Vast increases in productivity and distribution have benefited not the manufacturers or the employees, as once they would have done, but the customer.
- A crisis has developed for the brand, the standard means of adding perceived value to a consumer product. Too many brands have allowed their pricing premiums to drift up in a period when the wider diffusion of skills in production technology has actually been

undermining the advantages of market leaders. This is particularly prevalent in computer manufacturing where there is less technological leadership from many of the well-known brands. In any case, some of today's big retailers have stronger brands than many of the big consumer goods manufacturers. Who has the more powerful brand, a retailer like Sainsbury or a food manufacturer such as Brooke Bond or Tate & Lyle?

- There is increasingly fearsome competition between efficient factories that is forcing down prices and reducing profits.

Readers might like to consider whether such considerations do or will affect their business. If so, how far can effective marketing (as described in detail in later chapters) go in keeping profits from falling too far and too fast?

Summary

- Promotion is the term used to describe all the methods available for communicating with customers and potential customers.
- This communication normally contains both information and persuasion.
- Promotion also means the way in which products are presented to customers so as to match their needs and their perceptions.
- The correct promotional mix is arrived at by considering what has to be communicated to which groups of people and then selecting the most cost-effective media to carry that particular message.
- As a generality, personal selling is favoured as an element in the marketing mix when dealing with a few people buying a product of high unit cost; advertising comes strongly into its own with low-cost items sold to a mass market.
- But there are many other factors and many other promotional methods, each with its own strengths and weaknesses.
- Normally a range of methods will be used, and it then becomes important that they are carefully planned to operate in support of each other in an integrated campaign.

Reference

i In *Marketing Business*, December/January 2001/2002, p. 22.

Further Reading

Further references on particular aspects of promotion are given at the end of Chapters 8–14.

Wilmshurst, J. and Mackay, A. *The Fundamentals of Advertising* (Butterworth-Heinemann, 2nd Edition, 1999). This provides an overview of all forms of promotion, along with the same John Wilmshurst's *Below the Line Promotion* (Butterworth-Heinemann, 1993).

Useful contacts also include:

- **BBC**, Television Centre, Wood Lane, London W12 7RJ. Tel: 020 8743 8000; www.bbc.co.uk
- **BSkyB**, Victoria House, 98 Victoria Street, London SW1E 5JL. Tel: 020 7705 5000; www.sky.co.uk
- **Channel 4**, 124/126 Horseferry Road, London SW1P 2TX. Tel: 020 7396 4444; www.channel4.com
- **Channel 5**, 22 Long Acre, London WC2E 9LY. Tel: 020 7550 5555; www.channel5.co.uk
- **IPA**, 44 Belgrave Square, London SW1 8QS. Tel: 020 7235 7020; www.ipa.co.uk
- **ITV Network Limited**, 200 Gray's Inn Road, London WC1X 8HF. Tel: 020 7843 8000; www.itv.co.uk

Questions

1. Suggest a suitable promotional mix for:
   (a) Wind-surfing equipment.
   (b) Pre-mixed cocktails sold in 'one glass' sized bottles.
   (c) Electric shavers.
   (d) A new range of expensive cosmetics.
   (e) Fire extinguishers for use in factories and offices.
2. Many salespeople argue that expenditure on advertising and sales promotion would be better spent on the sales force. Using examples, explain how advertising and sales promotion can help salespeople in their task of selling.
3. What is the function of a brand name in the marketing of a product or service? Is there any difference in its value in consumer as opposed to industrial markets?
4. How do you reconcile the idea that the marketing concept is concerned with satisfying customers' needs with the existence of persuasive advertising designed to convince people that they need something they have not previously thought of buying?

Chapter 8

The practice of direct marketing

Introduction

By the end of this chapter you will

- Appreciate the basics of the direct approach to individual customers.
- The theme will be picked up again throughout this section of the book – in Chapter 9 when direct response advertising is discussed, and in Chapter 11 dealing with direct sales. Chapter 12 will review current thinking on electronic commerce (e-commerce), an important vehicle for direct response communications. The final section of the book looks at delivering to the market where Chapter 18 will bring it all together in 'Customer relationship marketing'.
- Understand the difference between transaction and direct marketing, mail order, database marketing, one-to-one marketing, and customer relationship marketing.
- Recognize the place of a comprehensive information management system as the cornerstone of good direct marketing.
- Appreciate the scope of activities of the Direct Marketing Association and be aware of their Best Practice Guides.

'Direct marketing "happens" when a client company (the provider of a product or service) decides to set up a direct relationship with the purchaser of its product or service.'

Cathy Ace. *Successful Marketing Communications*

8.1 A Few Definitions

In Section 1.2.1 we looked at the history of marketing and saw that in the 1990s there was a shift towards treating customers as individuals. Over this time there was a move from the basic transactional basis of marketing, where customers simply exchanged money for goods or services. The recognition that it was possible to have a direct transaction between an individual and an organization enabled the development of a more quantifiable variety of techniques. Buying Christmas cards through the post from a catalogue received through the letterbox is a simple example. However, through the 90s the concept of customer relationship marketing developed. This required an understanding of the nature of customers and markets, the understanding of long-term customer satisfaction for competitive success, and the need for a long-term strategic orientation based upon a flow of information from customers and markets. In the new millennium, it was recognized that building that relationship meant that customers were now moving to granting 'permission' for an organization to market to them.

8.1.1 Transaction Marketing

As far back as 1972, Kotler[i] described marketing as '... the set of human activities directed at facilitating and consummating exchanges'. While the pressures on organizations in the new millennium have changed dramatically, marketing has changed in response. It has gone back to its roots to study the very nature of the exchange or transaction and has developed this into what today is called relationship marketing. While for some this is a new approach, it includes many ideas and techniques that have been practised for several years by many organizations. While marketing has constantly evolved since its inception and this evolution is likely to continue, the root of marketing – focusing on the exchange process – is unlikely to change.

The driving force for exchange is need satisfaction and therefore exchange has always been seen as a fundamental framework for studying marketing.

Exchange involves the transfer of something tangible or intangible, actual or symbolic, between two or more separate entities. At a very basic level we can say that people and organizations interact so as to maximize their rewards and minimize their costs in the transaction. Rewards can be tangible, such as products, or intangible, such as the pleasure derived from them. Costs can be actual monetary costs or negative socio-psychological consequences.

The assumption of exchange is that both sides are mutually satisfied by the transaction. However, it is possible that, after the event, the balance of exchange might not be felt to be fair. (Perhaps the product did not satisfy the need, or there was coercion or deception, or even the exchange is actively discouraged, as in the 'demarketing' of energy, smoking or alcohol.) If the exchange was not satisfactory, given an alternative, the dissatisfied partner will presumably not enter into another transaction with the original partner, but will look elsewhere.

It was recognized that, if the individual customer could be satisfied once, then knowing enough about the person, one might be able to exchange with them again, directly (and often through the mail). This required a database of customers and, as their needs changed and were tracked over time, the basis of relationship marketing was formed.

8.1.2 Direct Marketing

In its simplest form, direct marketing means that there is a direct two-way dialogue between individual customers and a company. Direct mail and mail order are the two most often used examples of direct marketing, yet they can sometimes be confused and the terms tend to be used indiscriminately in place of each other. Yet direct marketing is an all-embracing term that includes telephone marketing (telemarketing) and door to door distribution such as for cosmetics. It could also be used to describe such direct activities as 'party plan' where a salesperson invites a group of people to a social gathering to view the merchandise, often in their own homes (examples include Tupperware containers, Nutrimetics cosmetics, Ann Summers clothing etc.). Some would also include under direct marketing those organizations that have bought their own retail distribution outlet, such as Boots Chemists and Marks & Spencer.

More recently a variant has developed known as 'direct response marketing' or 'selling off the page'. Instead of ordering goods from a mailed-out catalogue, customers can order from an advertisement in a newspaper or magazine. The media has expanded to include independent radio, which is particularly useful for selling music; television, where the medium has coined the term direct response television or DRTV; and the newer electronic media like the Internet and mobile phones.

Whatever the system for viewing the products, the mechanism for ordering and delivery is essentially the same.

Direct mail, on the other hand, is simply using the postal service to deliver messages to a selected target audience. While the recipient may order directly, the original mailing shot – the letter and its enclosures – will be the first in a sequence of events. The recipient may be invited to send for further information, have a free trial period or viewing (perhaps of a book), invite a personal call (perhaps for a product demonstration), or visit a location (to test-drive a new car for example).

Direct mail, indeed, does not necessarily call for any immediate response from its recipient. Some organizations, like hotel chains and airlines, use it as a means of keeping in communication with regular customers – in which case it can be viewed as part of their public relations activity (see Chapter 10).

The two most crucial limitations of direct marketing are list building – as a direct marketing campaign is only as effective as the list of individuals targeted – and the content of the communications. Building a good list usually entails a great deal of research and keeping it up to date calls for more effort and dogged determination than most people are willing to give it. While information technology may speed the mechanics of keeping and updating a list, it does little to ease the management of the list. Moreover, while the essence of effective direct marketing is its personal touch, there is always a temptation to mass-produce stereotyped messages and material.

8.1.3 Mail Order

The National Mail Order Association in the USA has this to say about a definition of mail order:[ii]

"Volumes of words have been written defining mail order. Is it a business in itself, or is it a way of conducting business? They go into how to spell it; one word 'mailorder', two words 'mail order,' or spelled with a hyphen 'mail-order."

The NMOA doesn't care how you spell it, and they don't care to argue the point about whether it's a way to conduct business or if it's a business in itself. To the NMOA, mail order encompasses many different ideas, methods and opinions. In essence, they use the term 'mail order' loosely, as a way of describing any form of advertising or promotion that produces a measurable response and at the same time captures important customer or potential customer information that can be used to further expand sales opportunities. They see mail order as a marketing term that includes many other verbal descriptions and sales/marketing components such as: direct mail, catalogue marketing, data base marketing, direct response marketing, television marketing, infomercial marketing, niche marketing, and so forth. All these terms relate to one another and many times are used in conjunction with one another.

In mail order, there is usually no face to face contact and the whole transaction is carried out through the post. Although 'agents' sometimes hold a catalogue and earn commission, it tends to be passive rather than active selling.

8.1.4 Database Marketing

Database marketing (DBM) was a term developed in the late 1980s as the technology and the marketing techniques it employs developed. DBM is an interactive approach to marketing communication that uses individually addressable communications media (such as mail, telephone, the Internet and the sales force) to:

- Extend help to a company's target audience.
- Stimulate their demand.
- Stay close to them by recording and keeping an electronic database memory of customers, prospects and all communications and commercial contacts, to help improve future contacts.

DBM is a very customer-oriented approach to marketing. Its special power lies in the means it uses to harness the capabilities of computer and telecommunications technology. The key tool is the marketing database – an organized set of files providing a common store of historic customer data.

DBM can be differentiated from other forms of marketing in a number of ways.

- It communicates directly with customers through a variety of media, including direct mail, telemarketing and direct response advertising.
- It usually requires the customer to provide a response that will allow the organization to take some form of appropriate action such as described in Section 8.1.2 above. In all cases, however, it must be possible to trace the response back to the original communication. This is not always possible with other marketing approaches.

The concept of DBM is often confused with that of 'direct marketing'. Direct marketing has been defined as 'an interactive system of marketing that uses one or more advertising media to effect a measurable response and/or transaction at any location'.

DBM has increased the interest in 'direct marketing' although many still focus on the customer knowledge requirements rather than the management of the information. Some marketing people still believe that ' database marketing is just direct marketing done properly'.

8.1.5 One-to-one marketing

Focused on the individual customer, one-to-one marketing is based on the idea of an organization knowing its customer. Through interactions with that customer the organization can learn how he or she wants to be treated. The organization is then able to treat this customer differently than other customers. However, one-to-one marketing does not mean that every single customer needs to be treated uniquely; rather, it means that each customer has a direct input into the way the organization behaves with respect to him or her.

This could be summarized as:

- Know your customers by understanding how they interact with you.
- Allow each customer to let you know how he or she wants to be treated.
- Treat each customer in accordance with your understanding of how they interact with you and how they want to be treated.

Note what it doesn't mean (some explicitly stated, some implicit):

- It does not mean that every single customer needs to be treated uniquely (a marketing strategy per customer).
- It does not mean that companies should try and create the same one-to-one relationship with their customers that can exist between two human beings.
- It limits itself to marketing, though the scope of customer relationship management is usually considered to cover marketing, sales and customer service.

8.1.6 Customer Relationship Marketing

As business focus shifts away from product, towards understanding the customer and increasing their value, the commercial pressure to implement a customer relationship management (CRM) solution across all channels has become enormous. In this respect, CRM is a comprehensive set of activities that covers all functions of the organization interacting with and supporting a customer that ultimately build customer satisfaction by providing for those needs, wants and desires over the long term.

A CRM solution in an organization needs to:

- Efficiently manage 'sales', 'marketing', 'service' and 'support' operational processes.
- Produce customer intelligence and efficiently pass it on to all people and systems that need to improve customer-contact (so called 'front-office') effectiveness.

- Automate and increase marketing effectiveness, via personalised multi-channel campaign management.
- Automate and personalize service and support for each customer.
- Optimize the supply chain based on information on customer demand to reduce costs.

Clearly, such an approach needs to use the full gamut of information technology to track, store and predict individual customer behaviour (see Chapter 18 for a more full treatment of the subject). For the moment, let us turn to information management as it supports the fundamentals of direct marketing as, without it, direct marketing does not go beyond the simple transactional basis of marketing.

Over and above direct mail and conventional advertising routes, there is a plethora of tactics that can be deployed to catch the attention of your target market and/or persuade them to do business with you:

- PR – getting local, trade or national press write-ups about new products or other company news.
- Sponsorship – contributing towards the cost of an event or publication and getting your name and logo featured prominently in return.
- Corporate hospitality - treating existing customers or prime prospects to a 'jolly' in the hope they will think kindly of you in future.
- Conferences – speaking at conferences raises your profile considerably and attending them gives rise to the opportunity for some serious networking, plus a chance to get hold of a comprehensive delegates list. This can be worth its weight in gold in terms of identifying likely new customers and potential competitors.
- Exhibitions – be seen with the best of them at major trade fairs. You can stand to pick up quite a bit of new business and a considerable number of new leads as people wander up to your stand.

Any of the routes listed above – and many others besides – will work in conjunction with your direct marketing campaigns to enhance your efforts, reinforce your message and raise your profile in the eyes of your target customers.

8.2 Information Management

The type of information required for any form of database management to operate can easily be obtained from both internal and external sources, and will include customer, market and competitor information. While much of those data are already collected for invoicing or control purposes, they are often not in the appropriate format for use by the marketing department. Very often, their value is not recognized and such things as customer requirements, complaints and other communications are not held after the query has been dealt with.

Information about an organization's existing customers will form the core of the database, with sales invoices providing perhaps the most valuable input. While an invoice is created for financial purposes, it contains a considerable amount of information about customers that can be of immediate value to marketers. Table 8.1 shows what some of the data might be and the use to which they could be put.

The specific information held may vary by type of market. An industrial database might hold data on key purchasers and influencers, organization structure, industry classification and business size. A sophisticated database might hold postcodes to overlay specialist geo-demographic data and include lifestyle information.

The need for *ad hoc* external market research will decline as the sophistication of the information collection increases. The firm builds its own database of existing and potential customers on whom it can use carefully selected targeting and segmentation strategies, through its understanding of the market's purchasing behaviour.

Hence, the information that an organization holds in its database is potentially a valuable aid in decision-making. However, if it is to be used for decision-making, the database must be future oriented, like the marketing function itself. The marketing database for DBM must be the centre of an organization's MkIS (marketing information system) since it can provide for marketing decisions at all levels. Conceptually, DBM is a specialized form of marketing; at a physical level, it is a subset of the corporate information system.

See also 'Marketing Information Systems' in Section 4.2.

8.2.1 The Need for a System for Direct Marketing

It has been said that to manage a business well is to manage its future, and to manage the future is to manage information. It is not having information that matters; it is a question of how you

Table 8.1 Invoice information and possible marketing use

Information from invoice	Possible marketing use
Customer title	Gender
Job title	Job description identification
Customer first name	Sex coding, discriminates between members of the same household
Customer surname	Ethnic coding
Customer address	Geo-demographic profiling and census data
Date of sale	Tracking purchase rates, seasonality, repeat purchase identification
Items ordered	Benefit/need analysis, product clusters, dependencies
Quantities ordered	Heavy/light user, crude segmentation
Price	Lifetime value calculation of profitability
Discount (if any)	Price sensitivity
Terms and conditions	Special requirements, customer service needs

use it. Competitors can copy your technology, they can copy your information systems, they can collect the same information, but they cannot copy how you analyse it and how you use it to develop and drive your direct marketing strategy.

So, to turn data into strategically important information requires:

- First for you to identify what is strategically important to your business and filtering out what is not.
- Then you can identify those key sources of important information.
- Once you have done that, you can then ensure that the right people receive the right information.
- Finally, you need to safeguard strategic information.

While the above seems obvious, it is a sad fact that most organizations do not consider these fundamentals when designing their information systems. Therefore, many information systems never give the organization a strategic direct marketing advantage and do little to improve any of the other marketing decisions that the firm makes.

It is the authors' experience that much of the information gathered and communicated by both individuals and organizations has little relevance for strategic marketing decision-making. Much of the information that is used to justify a decision is collected and analysed *after* the decision has been made. Moreover, much of the information gathered in response to requests for information is not considered in the making of decisions for which it was first requested. We find that, regardless of the information that is available at the time a decision is first considered, more information is requested. On the other hand, complaints that an organization does not have enough information to make a decision usually occur while available information is being ignored. It seems that the relevance of the information provided in the decision-making process to the decision is less important than is the insistence on more information.

In summary, most organizations and individuals, it seems, often collect more information than they use or could reasonably expect to use in making decisions. At the same time, they appear to be constantly needing or requesting more information, or complaining about inadequacies in information. Such has been the case whether the information is stored in a cardboard box or in an integrated network of computers

So, an information system on its own will do little to overcome the problems mentioned above – indeed it may even contribute to them.

8.2.2 Problems of Marketing Information Systems

Advances in technology do not automatically lead to better quality information and improved decision-making. It has been variously quoted that the information supply available to us doubles every five years – since that was said in the mid-1990s,[iii] the information supply must now double every *three* years! Often one is faced with too much data and not enough information. Today, we find that:

- There is an excess of volume.
- Data are too detailed and irrelevant to needs.

- Data are in the wrong format for managers to use.
- The system demands expertise most executives do not have.

Almost every week there is a new website offering a collation of information for the business user, as any casual web-surfer will uncover. Unfortunately, with this bulging information resource, the quality of information – its fitness for the purpose intended – does not keep pace with the volume. However, for the business user, two helpful sites are www.business-intelligence.co.uk and www.enterprisenetwork.co.uk.

Recent research[iv] indicates a doubtful future for mobile business information. Based on a scale of 1 to 10, where 1 means of no importance and 10 means of highest importance, company surveys rated the importance of getting access to business information when on the move as just 4.9.

Turning to the causes of misinformation, we find that these fall into three distinct categories:

1. **The human dimension**. System designers often misunderstand what direct marketers – the end users of the information – actually want from the system. Technology often dominates the development and implementation of the system, often to the exclusion of crucial human aspects. These aspects relate to the nature of decision-making, concerns over loss of power or status, and fear of the technology.
2. **Organizational pressures**. Since marketing information systems must necessarily cross over organizational boundaries, there can be some resistance to this 'loss of power'. The specialization of roles in organizations can lead to a conflict of interest between individuals and departments, resulting in unnecessary or unsuitable investments.
3. **Technical issues**. These relate to such issues as software and hardware compatibility, types and capacity of processing and storage, decisions on networking, access, data security and integrity etc. Unfortunately, most users of information – the decision-makers – will steer well away from such questions and the IT departments will only raise them when they relate directly to users' applications. While in the past, technical issues led the use of IT in business, this is no longer necessary. Most good IT departments recognize that the technology should be made to fit the applications, rather than the other way round.

8.2.3 Information Systems and Decision-making

How sophisticated your information system needs to be will depend on the complexity of your requirements. It is also affected by the structure of your initial data, i.e. how much the information needs processing before it can be used within the system. The different data requirements for strategy, planning and control relate to the sophistication of the information system needed:

- At the fundamental level are simple **clerical tasks** that have been computerized to allow automatic processing. Such activities might include cheque processing from customers. They do not, on their own, need to form part of the marketing information system.
- The next level is **operational control** where information is required to ensure that specific tasks have been carried out. The information needs to be accurate, frequent and prompt,

but can usually be gathered from internal records and real-time monitoring. Such information might include sales in a defined period, customer contacts etc.

- At the next level of **managerial control**, which is the 'process by which managers ensure that resources are obtained and used effectively and efficiently in the accomplishment of the organization's objectives', information need not be so detailed or frequent. More qualitative impressions are allowed and information from external sources increases in importance; thus the information system increases in complexity and sophistication. At this level one might be looking at market penetration to various market sectors compared to the competition, the success of various direct marketing media, or the profitability of the various customer-facing parts of the organization.
- The top level is **strategic planning**, which is the 'process of deciding on the objectives of the organization, on changes to those objectives, on the resources to attain these objectives, and on the politics that are to govern the acquisition, use and disposition of resources'. At this level, marketers are making decisions about which markets to attack; on the strategy to be used for which segments; and on the relative investments in terms of time and money. The information to help them choose wisely is of a fundamentally different nature from that at the lower levels. It is likely to be much more qualitative, with assumptions about future growth and trends. It will be future-oriented and will extrapolate historical data; it will not require the same degree of detailed information as is used in managerial and operational control.

The development of marketing information systems has gone hand in hand with the development of customer relationship marketing, a theme that will be picked up again in Chapter 18.

8.3 The Direct Marketing Association

The Direct Marketing Association (UK) Ltd is Europe's largest trade association in the marketing and communications sector. They were established in 1992, following the merger of various similar trade bodies, to form a single voice to protect the UK direct marketing industry from legislative threats and to promote its ongoing development. This is reflected in their mission statement:

'To maximise value for our members, whilst maintaining and enhancing business and consumers' trust and confidence in the direct marketing industry.'

The Direct Marketing Association UK is the leading voice for the direct marketing industry (direct mail, telemarketing, e-commerce and more), championing best practice and self-regulation.

In a market where there is a need to protect consumers from inappropriate, unethical behaviour by unscrupulous or ignorant practitioners, the DMA is dedicated to the protection and development of the UK direct marketing industry. On behalf of their members, they lobby against adverse legislation from government and other regulatory bodies, and promote the expansion of national and international markets, working in partnership with government and other industry bodies.

They promote best practice through DMA codes of conduct and the DMA awards, and provide up-to-the-minute information, research and legal advice. They manage programmes that protect consumers against bad practice and increase consumer trust, including the DMA Preference Services schemes and Trust UK for e-commerce.

DMA campaigns promote the direct marketing industry in a positive light. They invite all DMA members to participate directly in shaping the future of direct marketing. Without the DMA, there is no one to defend direct marketing from unethical or unprofessional practitioners, who can bring direct marketing into ill repute, trigger restrictive legislation and create consumer mistrust.

The growth and complexity of their membership continues to reflect the evolution and diversity of the direct marketing industry. They now have more than 860 corporate members, and welcomed 116 new members in 2000 – a 13 per cent increase on 1999. Three-quarters of these are supplier members, including direct marketing agencies, list brokers and mailing houses. The other 25 per cent are client members, including household names such as BT, Marks & Spencer, Lloyds TSB and the Automobile Association.

All members operate under their Codes of Practice, which are in place to raise and maintain standards within the direct marketing industry. As part of the DMA's ongoing commitment to protecting its members and consumers alike, the DMA administers a group of Preference Services and has set up the DM Authority, which monitors the industry.

Today, they are the voice of the UK direct marketing industry and, as a member of the International Federation of Direct Marketing Associations (IFDMA) and the Federation of European Direct Marketing Associations (FEDMA), their reach is, on many levels, global.

CASE STUDY

To help fulfil its mission of developing consumer trust and confidence in direct marketing, the DMA works to maintain and promote a positive image of the direct marketing industry through trade, regional and national press, and radio and TV editorial and advertising coverage.

To support this effort, the DMA launched its 'Changing Opinions' campaign at the end of 1999 with the aim of:

- Promoting the real-life benefits of direct marketing.
- Informing consumers about the personal safeguards that exist, so they develop trust and confidence in direct marketing.
- Increasing consumer acceptance and use of direct marketing in their day to day lives.
- Building awareness and recognition of the DMA logo among consumers.
- Increasing the use of the DMA logo by DMA members, to help establish it as a quality kite-mark for adherence to the DMA's Codes of Practice.

By the end of 2001, this campaign had seen significant advertising coverage in national newspapers and magazines, through the placement of free 'filler' ads; extensive trade press coverage to encourage participation and support from the DM industry; a six-week period on the Charlotte Street.com website; over 10 million inserts distributed within IPC women's magazines in the lead-up to Christmas; and, consequently, over 3000 'Buying from Home' information booklets distributed to consumers requesting further information about direct marketing.

As the focus of the consumer campaign shifts to not only promoting the benefits of direct marketing, but also educating consumers about the rights and choices they have when buying direct, the campaign has been re-branded 'It's your choice'.

A national public awareness campaign is to be launched in early 2002, focusing on promoting the benefits of the new media such as mobile phones and email, alongside Internet safety issues.

A campaign-specific website has been developed as an information point for consumers to find out anything they need to know about direct marketing, data protection issues and their rights, at: www.its-your-choice.org.uk.

Questions

1. How do you feel the DMA might further improve the reputation of the direct mail industry?
2. What controls do you feel need to be in place to manage the increasing use of unsolicited e-mails or 'spam'?

8.3.1 DMA Codes of Practice

The Direct Marketing Association and its members operate within a range of Codes of Practice for the various sectors of the industry. These are comprehensive and detailed, providing an in-depth guide to practitioners. A copy of their Code of Practice for electronic commerce can be found at www.bh.com/companion/075065449X.

8.3.2 Best Practice Guides

As part of its ongoing commitment to raising industry standards and promoting consumer safeguards, the DMA issues Best Practice Guides, covering specific areas of direct marketing. DMA members are specifically asked to refer to these guidelines when planning their direct marketing campaigns. The guidelines should be read in conjunction with the DMA Codes of Practice which, alongside the Direct Marketing Authority, provide standards to which members should adhere. Most of the twelve Councils have published various Best Practice Guides that can be found on the DMA website.

8.4 Mail Order

Many people think about mail order as a business they want to be in; they hear of somebody that had a simple product and got rich working out of their home. Mail order marketing of products or services has all the ingredients of being the perfect way for the small entrepreneur to start or expand a business (e.g. being able to start at home no matter where you live, starting with limited capital, avoiding geographic selling boundaries etc.). However, it does have some pitfalls for the unwary. Before you start or invest money, there are a few things to bear in mind, derived from the National Mail Order Association six-point guide:

1. Keep in mind that mail order is **a way of advertising and selling** a product or service. In mail order, your catalogue or flyer is your shop, and the printed word is your salesman, and you go directly to the customer's home or business. This is in contrast to running a retail operation where you first try to get the customer to come to your store and then convince them to buy.
2. Specialize! If you look at a majority of companies that market via mail order, they **specialize in a specific product category** or group of products. This way they have a clear idea of who their potential customers are and how they can be reached. Products should be unique and not readily available at retail outlets. Make sure your potential customers are easy to identify and reach.
3. **Have follow-up products** that fit into the same category to sell to your customers. Very few people make a lot, or any, money on one product unless that product is one that is used up and people continue to reorder. Profits come from making a customer happy with their first purchase from you, so that they then buy a second time and so on. The second time they buy is most important. In essence they are saying, we approve of the way you do business, we are satisfied with your product or service, and we are ready to develop a purchasing relationship with your company.
4. **Persistence**. You must be in business for the long run. If you are starting from scratch with little capital, expect to build your business over a period of years. You must build up a base of satisfied customers who continue to purchase from you. As your customer base grows, so will your profits.
5. **Specialized knowledge**. Many people think mail order consists of putting an advertisement in a magazine or sending out thousands of letters and waiting for the cash to come rolling in. If it were that easy everyone would be in mail order. There are many tricks to marketing via mail order. You need to be familiar with many things so you can do them yourself or know how to hire someone who does. Every person considering the use of mail order to sell products or services should first invest in their personal education. A few hundred pounds spent on the right books and manuals can save a person from wasting thousands of pounds on things that never had a chance of working, or had major strategic flaws. Furthermore, you must associate with people who know the business well, and gain by their experience. And you must keep yourself up to date on the latest concerns to mail order marketers. These things include government regulations, postal rules and regulations, advertising secrets, promotional writing and graphics, cost-cutting tips, printing, availability of new products and lists, and much more.
6. **Know your product or service**. Many times the most successful mail order marketing companies start from a person's hobbies or interests. This way they know something about the products they are selling. For instance, if you want to market fishing-related items, but you yourself are not a fishing enthusiast, what will you base your buying decisions on? How will you know what a fishing person will be interested in?

8.5 Database Marketing Applications

We have looked at the development of database marketing and have reviewed the information requirements to make it work. We will now turn to the main applications of database marketing. They can be largely categorized into two sectors: tactical or short-term and strategic or long-term.

8.5.1 Tactical Applications

While an organization might use their databases for a variety of purposes, typical tactical applications might include customer loyalty and customer care programmes, generating and qualifying sales leads, cross-selling and price/promotion testing. The database should allow data capture of customer responses to a number of promotional activities on a selection of variables. This will then allow segmentation of customers to be drawn together by whatever variable is seen as having the most relevance for the next phase of a campaign. After analysing the most suitable (and potentially the most profitable) customer profile for a particular product, the marketer can then pull out of the database a list of likely prospects with the required characteristics. Promotional material can be targeted specifically to the needs of the identified group of customers, thus reducing marketing costs while improving response rates.

The database should also allow the marketer to test the effectiveness of different elements of the approach (such as product, medium, offer target market) to be carried out quickly so that, if necessary, prompt corrective action can be taken. The various direct marketing approaches such as that of a sales force, telemarketing, direct mail or e-mail can be co-ordinated by appropriate techniques, which then select the contact strategy most suitable for different groups of customers.

Finally, since all customer contacts are recorded on the database, opportunities for repeat sales and cross-selling of other company products are maximized. In this way, customer loyalty may be built up over time.

8.5.2 Strategic Applications

The strategic implications of database marketing have been undervalued. However, marketers have realized that building and maintaining relationships with customers has significant long-term implications and therefore affects the strategic and long-term planning of an organization's marketing. Since these relationships take a long time to evolve, they do become central to strategic planning.

Database marketing is itself a planning resource because:

- It generates a huge amount of market and customer data – reducing the need for market research.
- It allows direct marketing campaigns to be designed to obtain the required information.
- It can be of such sophistication that it will drive marketing policy.

Porter's five forces framework (See Section 1.6.1) provides a useful guide for identifying competitive opportunity areas, and a sound marketing database will operate strategically if the information it holds is used to:

1. **Change the basis of competition** – by collecting prospect or customer information, targeting direct marketing better, and by better control. In 2001, Laithwaite's Wine (formerly Bordeaux Direct) tracked customers' order volume, frequency and product type. So, knowing that a given customer usually purchased mainly red wines and knowing that they had an interest in good French wines but were not so keen on the 'new age reds', they were able to target, by e-mail, a pre-Christmas offer of a case of 'Andre Roux' Cotes-du-Rhone, 15% Special Reserve. (And very good it was, too!)

2. **Strengthen customer relationships** – by knowing each customer's needs more concisely, and handling their responses better. A detailed knowledge of customers' needs and past purchasing habits helps build a long-term customer relationship, ensures customer loyalty and increases the possibility of cross-selling – as any visitor to amazon.com will tell you!

3. **Strengthen supplier links** – by internal or external capture, optimize sales channels, measure supplier performance, and identify areas of inefficiency. A similar link-strengthening approach can be applied to suppliers. By building up relationships, typically by improving information flows on stock requirements, delivery needs etc., the quality of supply can be improved and the cost reduced. These benefits can be passed down the value chain in the form of improved value or benefits to the ultimate customers.
   Channels of supply to the market can also be changed by the use of telesales, mail order, the Internet etc. to reduce the costs associated with dealing with particular customer segments.
   Compac Computer Corporation launched a new programme in December 2001 called GP Online, which was based on Oracle e-Business Suite's Internet Procurement Software. It automates and streamlines spending while improving relationships with suppliers.

4. **Build barriers to market entry** – by improving the knowledge of the market, thereby allowing improvement in the service or value offered, by 'locking-in' customers, suppliers and intermediaries, and by being able to respond more rapidly to threats. A sound customer database can give a major competitive advantage over competitors who do not have such information. The ability to contact past, present and potential customers with personalized messages makes it simple to respond to a new competitor who is using traditional advertising techniques – the newcomer must use a mass market approach, based on common appeals, until knowledge of appropriate segmentation is obtained. Even then, the new entrant's costs per sale will be much higher than existing companies'. The higher costs for the attacking new entrant (it always costs more to attack than to defend a position) will, therefore, remain high, even before considering the investment required in building an equivalent customer database. This goes someway to explain why so many 'dot.com' businesses failed in the latter part of the last century.
   Note, conversely, that the knowledge held about a customer's lifestyle and needs may allow firms to jump industry barriers, as we have seen with complementary financial services such as banking, life and house insurance, mortgages, estate agent services etc.

5. **Generate new or substitute products** – by analysing any market gap, through dialogue with the customer, improving user innovation, or providing information as a product. Products and services are seen increasingly as being augmented products (a collection of

core as well as peripheral benefits of both a physical and psychological nature). For many products, such as cars, wine and perfume, the image is often more important than the reality. For others, the services associated with the basic offering are the main differentiating feature. Information can frequently be built into the product offering to enhance its appeal, as with automatic cash dispensers permitting customers access to information and services, or Internet banking and insurance services that offer immediate transactions. These services could not exist without database systems that are sophisticated in both technological and customer information terms.

8.6 Direct Marketing and the New Technologies

Many organizations often have to manage their customer relationships across international borders and on a remote basis. However, ensuring consistency of corporate and brand identities across the world has been a problem for decades. While the goal may be to communicate something specific about your product, it is evident that different countries have different national characteristics, languages and protocols. What works in one country will not work in another. So, while the use of e-mail, fax, the Internet and telephone technologies may be common throughout the western world, it does not mean that the way these technologies are used by marketing departments should be the same across national boundaries. Cold calling, for example, is acceptable in certain countries, frowned upon in some, and banned in others.

However, technology is making the world a smaller place and flexibility is opening up borders like never before. Armed with the services of an able translator and a database (perhaps an e-mail list) one is able to reach new prospects and keep existing customers up to date fairly easily. In specialist global industries, this ability to instantly reach people across the world is encouraging organizations to take up electronic marketing (see Chapter 12).

One recently reported case of successful use of new technologies described the operation of ICIS-LOR: 'ICIS-LOR is a leading global supplier of market information to the oil and chemical industries and uses a managed electronic broadcast service to deliver market information and reports to 3000 customers in ninety-four countries in exactly the form they want, when they want it. Each customer can choose to either receive reports by post (on CD or paper), e-mail or fax, or access reports themselves via bulletin boards, FTP sites, fax-on-demand or via the web.'[v]

The big advantage of many of the new technologies is that the communications systems can be totally automated. Automated e-mail and fax broadcasting techniques are useful in cases where customers are expecting information and need to be notified on time, every time. Where a more personal touch is required – like when a company is trying to qualify sales leads – the telephone is often the preferred option.

8.6.1 Telemarketing

This involves direct dialling to people with a given sales approach or using a team of people to answer enquiries from callers. Unfortunately, the technique has been overplayed – like so many others. Home-owners in the UK are particularly disenchanted by the early evening telephone call stating: 'your home is one especially selected that we feel would benefit from our double glazing ... ' Never mind the fact that you already have double glazing or that you live in a 300-year-old Cotswold cottage that is Grade II listed in a conservation area.

In the US, this so-called 'spam marketing' by the phone is used by stockbrokers working from a 'boiler room' who call 'carefully selected' individuals. The entire focus of this exercise is to trick the receptionist/secretary (or other gatekeeper) to get the target on the other end of the phone. 'Once there, the telemarketers lie to the prospect in the hope of getting a nibble (which is sort of an immoral spin on permission). Because the profit from these scams is so large, the perpetrators don't care that they are using an incredibly inefficient interruption technique to grab the attention of consumers.'[vi]

While the telephone is often the preferred option in qualifying sales leads, operating a cross-border telemarketing campaign is invariably more complex than cross-border electronic broadcast campaigns. Not only does one need people fluent in the language (which may require specialist staff); local laws may prohibit certain activity. Many organizations provide outsourced telemarketing and customer relationship management services. While they often centralize their resources for efficiencies of scale, many accept that local services would mean local telephone call rates. However, with offices connected to a VPN (virtual private network), the cost of making international calls can be relatively low. If one had, say, a dozen people undertaking a programme in France, the cost of a return flight from the UK and a single overnight hotel stay to oversee the campaign may exceed the advantage gained from lower call costs.

Establishing rules of engagement for an outbound calling campaign is crucial and the DMA has a Code of Practice but not everyone adheres to it and neither is it universally applicable. Not every country has a telephone preference service (TPS) or Fax Preference Service (FPS). This system allows an owner of any given telephone or fax line the ability to have their details removed from the databases. However, every country has its own regulations. Germany for example has very strict privacy laws. Companies must have an existing relationship and have the customer's permission to be able to make calls. This makes outbound cold calling difficult but not impossible. Therefore, one needs to be very aware of each country's requirements.

Recruiting the right people for telephone-based campaigns is crucial. Those skilled at customer care are not always the best for direct marketing campaigns since the skills are different. In a survey of 200 call centres,[vii] training, e-learning and personal development are the three main factors cited by call centre managers as key to improving call centre performance. Training was also identified as key to helping call centres improve staff retention.

Some companies use home-based telemarketing workers but it is difficult to maintain the quality and training levels without people in the same country, never mind the same office. Moreover, it may be difficult to provide technical service support to a network of home-workers' office machinery.

In order to provide information to customers when they want it and how they want it, many organizations are turning to a mixed media approach. Sometimes this may mean using traditional direct marketing techniques backed up by outbound or inbound telemarketing. On other occasions it may mean using automated e-mail or fax broadcast backed up by telemarketing, or a combination of all options. There are no hard and fast rules governing which media forms are most appropriate for which country. The Nordic countries and US favour e-mail, while Italy and Turkey favour voice communications. The UK is perhaps somewhere in the middle. It must be remembered that there are many differences in industry sectors (e.g. lawyers prefer to get it in writing, although the electronic media is becoming more acceptable), yet definitive conclusions are difficult to draw.

Automated e-mail and fax options are cost-effective for both inbound and outbound activities, but are not always appropriate. Being charged to 'fax back' an unsubscribe notice has made many business people very sceptical of faxed offers. For these reasons, the telemarketing industry continues to flourish.

So long as providers of e-mail, fax and telemarketing campaigns are honest about the merits of their respective trades, there is no reason for a conflict of interests. Providers need each other to give their customers a complete service.

8.6.2 Third Generation

The mobile communications industry has evolved in three stages:

[Analogue] ⟶ [Digital] ⟶ [Multimedia]

Three generations of mobile phones have emerged so far, each successive generation more reliable and flexible than the last:

- **Analogue**: You could only easily use analogue cellular phones to make voice calls, and typically only in any one country.
- **Digital** mobile phone systems added fax, data and messaging capabilities, as well as voice telephone services in many countries.
- **Multimedia** services add high-speed data transfer to mobile devices, allowing new video, audio and other applications through mobile phones – now music, television and the Internet can be accessed through a mobile terminal.

With each new generation of technology, the services that can be deployed on them become more and more wide ranging and truly limited only by imagination. We are reaching that stage with 3G. It has been suggested[viii] that '3G technology will drive all the players in the telecommunications, finance and retail industries to decide in what business they want to be. Long-term strategies are required to anticipate both the evolution of the telecom business and the development of new networks and infrastructures'.

While more will be said of the new technologies in Chapter 12, suffice to say here that there will be new ways of building an ongoing relationship with customers through direct means, which will need particular skills to ensure that a sustainable competitive advantage is achieved.

CASE STUDY

Telemarketing works but not always to good effect,[ix] as the following account illustrates.

It was discovered that charities using telemarketers to raise funds have exhibited 'glaring' problems in their business practices, according to a report by the New York Attorney General's office. The report, 'Pennies for Charity', found that of the $188 million raised in the state for charities by telemarketers in 2000, $129 million, or 68.5 per cent, went to the for-profit telemarketing firms.

Of 586 charitable telemarketing campaigns run in the state in 2000, only sixteen gave at least 75 per cent of the funds raised to the charities. The charities got less than half the funds in more than 80 per cent of cases.

So, while the technique worked to raise funds, significant profits were being creamed off it would appear. Some charities were using deceptive names, such as the New York Police Scholarship Foundation and the New York Firefighters Foundation, both of which are based in Florida and have no relation to New York agencies, according to an Attorney General spokesperson.

The report contains data only from 2000. While 2001 data won't be available until 2002, the spokesperson said it was encouraging that most of the money donated in response to the 11th September terrorist attacks appears to have been raised by the charities themselves rather than third parties.

However, what has been made clear during the past three months is that the American people demand that their contributions be used for the people served by the charities. The report shows that only 32 cents of every dollar raised in the average telemarketing campaign goes to the charity, and that was totally unacceptable.

Question

1. How do you feel the DMA might further improve the reputation of the telephone marketing industry?

Summary

- Direct marketing covers a variety of activities where there is a direct relationship – a two-way dialogue – between the provider and the purchaser.
- Transaction marketing looks at the basis of the interaction between supplier and purchaser.
- In mail order, as its name suggests, there is no face to face contact and the whole transaction occurs through the post.
- Database marketing needs a sound information system as its foundation and therefore has developed in line with information technology.
- Customer relationship marketing provides for customers' needs, wants and desires over the long term.
- Marketing information systems were discussed and the case put forward to question many organizations' practices.
- The Direct Marketing Association's activities representing the industry were outlined.
- The new technologies will change the way that organizations can have a direct relationship with the markets.

References

i Kotler, P. *Marketing Management: Analysis, Planning and Control* (Prentice Hall, 1972).
ii Adapted from Schulte, John D. From the NMOA website.
iii Pritchet, P. *New Work Habits for a Radically Changing World* (Pritchet, 1995).
iv See *Marketing Business*, March 2001, p. 5.
v In *Marketing Business*, an article entitled 'Breaking down the barriers' by Mickel Bak, December/January, 2001/2002, p. 38.
vi Godin, S. *Permission Marketing* (Simon & Schuster, 1999, p. 171).
vii Reported in *Marketing Business*, December/January 2001/2002, p. 7.
viii *Inform*, the news magazine of Compaq users and partners in Europe, the Middle East and Africa, published by Compaq Computer International, No. 3, 2001, p. 10.
ix Information was drawn from *Direct Marketing News*, 21st December 2001.

Further Reading

Bacon, Mark S. *Do-It-Yourself Direct Marketing: Secrets for Small Business* (John Wiley & Sons, 2nd Edition, 1997). This nuts and bolts resource helps small business owners develop marketing techniques tailored to their individual business and financial needs.

Thomas, Brian and Housden, Matthew. *Direct Marketing in Practice* (Butterworth-Heinemann, 2001). This is a practical manual for all senior managers and marketers getting to grips with the powerful techniques available to skilled direct marketers.

Questions

1. Much of the information gathered and communicated by both individuals and organizations has little relevance for strategic marketing decision-making. Critically evaluate your own organization on this basis.
2. Thinking of the new technologies, consider which products lend themselves to marketing through these channels.
3. What sort of information might be available from a checkout receipt from a superstore? Describe what use a marketer might put this to.
4. The Royal Mail (Consignia) is losing its monopoly on letter post. What effect is this likely to have on the direct mail industry?

Chapter 9

The practice of advertising

Introduction

By the end of this chapter you will:

- Appreciate when advertising particularly can have an important role in effective marketing.
- Understand what is encompassed by the term 'advertising' and how it differs from sales promotion.
- Be aware of the many different tasks that can be performed by sales promotion.
- Know some of the criticisms that are levelled at advertising and how they are countered by the industry.
- Know how advertising is planned.
- Be aware of the main methods for setting advertising budgets.
- Understand how advertising agencies operate.

'... it is no use advertising unless the advertiser has a good article. But the possession of the finest article in the world does not necessarily mean that success will be obtained unless advantage is taken of all the available facilities for making it known.'

Philip Smith. *Successful Advertising – Its Secrets Explained'* (1878)

9.1 What Advertising Is

It is important when discussing advertising to be fully aware of what it is we are talking about. Especially in critical comment, the view taken of advertising is often very narrow, whereas in fact advertising consists of a wide variety of types of message transmitted through many different media.

Generally, when people talk of advertising, they think mainly of advertising on television for household goods such as detergents, drinks and food, clothing and confectionery. However, if one looks at UK advertising the picture given in Table 9.1 emerges.

Some may find it a surprise that, of the £3571 million spent in the press, only £1510 million (14.3 per cent of total advertising expenditure) was spent in the national newspapers (*Daily Express, The Times, The Sun* etc.). A considerably larger amount (£2061 million; 19.5 per cent of total advertising expenditure) went into the regional newspapers (the local weekly, daily and evening papers).

So advertising is not just the beer, soap and car commercials on TV. It is also the shop in the high street advertising its sale in the 'local rag'; and the home-owner wanting to sell an old bedroom suite or a sailing dinghy through the 'small ads'. It is job announcements and company reports; the government urging us to stop smoking, wear our seatbelts and save fuel; the engineering company announcing a new machine; the mail order company offering its new catalogue; the poster telling us what is on at the local cinema or the Festival Hall; the card in the Underground offering to find us a job or clear our blocked drains; and the back of a bus telling us where we can buy our next car.

Table 9.1 Total advertising expenditure by medium and by type[i]

By medium	£ million	Percentage of total
National newspapers, including colour supplements	1510	14.3
Regional newspapers, including free sheets	2061	19.5
Consumer magazines	583	5.5
Business and professional magazines	1018	9.6
Directories	692	6.5
Press production costs	550	5.2
Total press	**6414**	**60.6**
Television, including production costs	3333	31.5
Outdoor and transport, including production costs	426	4.0
Cinema, including production costs	73	0.7
Radio, including production costs	344	3.2

Advertising is often the conspicuous part of marketing, the visible 'tip of the iceberg'. Most people know nothing of the complexities of the distribution process, of pricing policies or of product development. But they cannot help being aware of advertising, especially if they are television addicts (and the average person in the UK watches TV for some 3½ hours each day).

9.2 What Sales Promotion Is

This subject will be picked up again in Chapter 10 where we will find that this is another term used by different people to mean different things. The distinction made by a number of authors and one we shall follow here is that 'advertising' describes messages carried in media owned and controlled primarily by people other than the advertiser, and 'sales promotion' messages are carried by media controlled by the company itself.

Still left out on a limb by the above definition is **public relations**. This is not totally 'controlled' by the company itself but, although it includes messages carried in media owned and controlled primarily by people other than the advertiser, it differs sharply from advertising. In particular, the content of an advertisement is decided by the advertiser, although the law and the media owner may impose some limitations. With a public relations message, however, the company initiating it has no control at all over the way it finally appears in the medium. Advertising is clearly identified with the company sponsoring it; public relations frequently is not. In any case, messages in the media (press relations) form only one part of what public relations is concerned with. Public relations is a vast subject needing an entire book and is only partly directly concerned with marketing (see Section 10.9).

9.3 The Role of Advertising

The relative importance of advertising as part of the promotional mix is determined by the following.

- **The circumstances**. Advertising is more likely to be used in the following circumstances: (a) there are many customers, widely scattered, for a low-cost product (direct personal selling is then usually not economic and retailers do not really 'sell' the product); (b) many people need informing very quickly (e.g. about a new product, an improvement, a price change); (c) the distribution chain is long and complex (ultimate customers are remote from the manufacturer); (d) the opinions of many people are required in the buying decision (often the case with capital goods); and (e) the potential customers are not easy to identify and advertising can be used to 'flush them out'.
- **The task**. Advertising is particularly good at effecting some stages in the selling process (for example, arousing initial interest, creating brand awareness, giving post-purchase reassurance). It is less good at others (e.g. making a specific proposal, closing a sale). Whether advertising is the best means of communicating depends on what is being communicated and to whom.
- **The product**. Some products can be simply and easily explained in the short time available on radio or TV, or in the limited space of a press advertisement, or in the limited time that a

poster site next to the road is viewed. Others need discussion or specially designing to fit them to the customer's requirements.

- **Economics**. It is all a matter in the end of cost-effectiveness. Advertising should be used if it enables more people to be given the right message more effectively than in any other way.
- **Reach and richness.** Each form of communication has a combination of 'reach' (the number of people to whom the message is broadcast) and 'richness' (the power of the message to each individual that receives it). For example, TV advertising has great reach because it can carry sales messages into millions of living rooms in one fell swoop. However, it has limited richness, as the same message is delivered to whoever is sitting in front of the TV at the time.

9.3.1 Some Typical Advertising Tasks

Because of its strengths, advertising is commonly used to carry out certain marketing tasks. The following paragraphs describe and comment on these.

Announcing new products and product changes – A new product is introduced, an existing one changed, a new pack or a different price is brought in, the distribution is increased to include new retailers, a special offer is available for a short period. Customers and potential customers must be made aware of these changes, and quickly. Short of writing to or telephoning them all, advertising is the only way to do it, especially as in most cases customers cannot be listed by name and address. Even if they could, the cost would be astronomic, and it would still be difficult to achieve overnight. Some industrial markets, in which there are a very small number of well-known customers are, at first sight, different. In this case they can best be informed by the sales force or by direct mail. Even here, though, we often have the problem of the decision-making unit (see Section 11.5.1), not all of whose members will be easy to identify. Advertising may still have a job to do in such a case.

Aiding the salesperson – In industrial marketing, particularly, the reputation of suppliers is a very important factor in purchasing decisions. No one will be eager to buy an expensive and vital piece of equipment from a company they have never heard of. Buyers will be very reluctant to spend time with a salesperson from an unknown company. A similar situation applies in the consumer products field when salespeople call on retailers and other intermediaries. Selling will be easier if: (a) they know the company and (b) they have been informed in advance of the product it wants them to buy. Another factor in this field is that many retailers are reluctant to take in stocks of products unless they will be advertised to the ultimate consumers. Thus, one of the objectives of consumer advertising on TV or in the press may be to back up salespeople in their efforts to persuade dealers to stock the product during the crucial 'launch' or 'promotion' period. A subsidiary effect of advertising can often be that it boosts the morale of the sales force.

Entering new markets and expanding old ones – As we have already seen, customers have to be both informed and persuaded to try out new products. Except in markets where the cost per unit is high and the number of customers is low (typical of industrial products), advertising is again the only economical way of reaching them. Retailers are generally not good at selling products, especially new and untried ones. They normally act only as dealers, regarding it as the manufacturer's task to persuade customers to buy. Very rarely is it sufficient to put products on the shelves and wait for customers to come in. And, as we have already seen, retailers will be reluctant to do even this unless they can be sure of advertising support.

Advertising probably has a job to do when: (a) a product has been a success in one area and is now to be introduced to another and (b) many buyers already exist but more must be found in the same area(s) (e.g. by attracting customers from other socio-economic groups).

Keeping existing customers 'sold' – It is a mistake to think that, once a product is established in the market, it can simply be left to carry on. This is not so, for three reasons. First, customers who have bought a product need reassuring that it was a 'wise buy' in the light of all the alternative purchases they could have made. Section 1.5 spoke of 'post-purchase feelings' (see also Section 11.2.2 on Cognitive Dissonance). These are partly determined by the customer's actual experience of the product in use (does it do what he hoped it would do?), and are partly psychological. A well-known phenomenon is 'buyer remorse' – having made a purchase, it is quite common for people to be worried as to whether they have done 'the right thing'. Reading advertisements for the product they have just bought is one way they obtain the necessary reassurance (it has been established that a high proportion of the readers of car advertisements are people who have just bought the model being advertised).

Second, competitive or alternative products are constantly being offered; 'our' customers are constantly exposed to advertising, displays in shops and other invitations to buy. The advantages of 'our' product need constant reiteration. Third, established customers grow old and eventually die, and the new generation has to be told about the product afresh. Products such as Guinness, Bovril, and others, which have been flourishing for fifty years and more, owe their longevity largely to persistent advertising. Often, as in the Guinness 'Pure Genius' campaign, the opportunity will be taken to give the product an updated image to make it acceptable to the new generation.

Inviting enquiries – Many businesses depend very largely on inviting enquiries. Such companies are as diverse as hoteliers, mail order traders and seedsmen advertising their catalogues. They include insurance, unit trust and similar organizations offering details of their services; and manufacturers of industrial products offering to send a salesperson to discuss a would-be customer's requirements or provide a free quotation (e.g. for an office installation or car-leasing agreement). Generally advertisements of this type carry a coupon for the enquirer's name and address – it has been found that this considerably increases the enquiry rate and can also be used to add to the advertiser's list of addresses of potential customers. This technique is used when a constant stream of new customers has to be found, in contrast to the typical 'packaged household goods' product, where an objective of advertising will probably be to encourage repeat business – part of what Section 10.1.3 is all about. Most classified advertising falls into this category or the next (houses, used cars and other personal effects are advertised in the 'small ads' columns to attract enquiries from would-be buyers).

Selling direct – Some display advertising and much classified advertising aims to complete most of the selling process. Not only many unit trust advertisements but also many for household goods ask for the money and an order to be sent – often referred to as 'selling off the page' (see Section 8.1.2). Many classified advertisements expect to attract enquiries leading to sales that can be 'clinched' over the telephone (e.g. local advertisers of fencing, turf and other garden products). But this is the exception. Most advertising is expected to achieve only part of the total selling process.

Creating a brand or company 'image' – In Section 7.3.1, we spoke of the importance of 'branding' in some situations. The way a product is viewed by customers and those who might become customers can be a very important influence on the level of sales. People need to be able to 'relate' to a product, to be able to feel 'this one is for me'. So the way a product is presented, its personality, must all be expressed in its 'brand image'. Advertising lends itself well to this task, especially cinema and television advertising, where a wide range of aural and visual ('audio' and 'video' in the jargon of the trade) effects can be used to project the desired 'image'. The product can be made to look staid and reliable or young and 'cool', exciting and new or well tried and trusted, expensive and exclusive or economical for everyday use – just as the same actor can appear young or old, boring or dashing. Clearly the product when sampled must fit the image created, but this is rarely a problem. The same car, for example, may be fast and safe, economical on fuel and comfortable to sit in, dashing in appearance and also reliable. It may appear cheap to some and expensive to others. How we talk about it depends on who we believe to be our target market. If it consists of retired people, we may wish to stress the economy, comfort and reliability; if it is young business executives, we may emphasize the dashing appearance and performance. The car is the same, but with a choice of two quite different brand images.

Similarly, a company may need to present an 'image' of itself. Business buyers, in particular, have a liking to 'know with whom they are dealing'. Advertisements can present facts about the company – its resources, its financial status, its present customers, its product range and research facilities – which will create a picture or 'image' for its potential customers of what kind of company it is. Clearly, again, the desired image can, to some extent, be selected. The company can stress its financial standing and its long record in the business, its capacity for innovation and quick action, or its reputation for reliability and quality. Advertising can establish this image fast and with a wide audience – a task that might take years to achieve through salespeople or by customers talking to each other 'on the grapevine'.

9.4 The Social and Economic Justification of Advertising

Advertising (and sales promotion, since the two are not at all distinct in the mind of the general public) comes in for frequent criticism on grounds such as the following:

- It is a waste of money that would be better spent in price reductions or product improvements.
- It encourages people to spend money they can ill afford on things they would be better off without.
- It frequently appeals to the less attractive emotions, such as envy, snobbishness etc.
- The sheer weight of advertising 'forces' people to buy things they would not otherwise buy.
- It is an intrusion into our lives as we are usually busy doing something else, like watching television, reading a paper, listening to music or surfing the Internet, when we are interrupted by advertising.

Criticism along these lines has been made for many years and the history behind the situation is worthy of note. The criticisms led to the production of a British Labour Party Green Paper, which proposed in particular a tax on advertising and the setting up of a 'National Consumers'

Authority' financed from the proceeds of the tax. The advertising industry in the UK has, for a long time, believed in voluntary controls by the industry itself (see Section 9.6), and produced a spirited reply to the Green Paper.

This document, A Commentary on the Labour Party Green Paper on Advertising of March 1972, was published by the Advertising Association in October 1972, and contains the case in favour of advertising in reply to criticisms of the kind referred to above. Some of the points made are the following:

1. 'The consumer not only has the power to choose but exercises it ruthlessly.'
2. 'The consumer has spending power nowadays for many goods and services over and above the necessities of life. Industry responds by offering a wide variety of such products to suit as many tastes as possible. No one would want, or can afford, them all. People have to choose.'
3. 'The consumer can pick and choose what advertisement he wants to consider. It is well known that his mind and eye shrug off instantly those of no interest to him.'
4. 'The process of advertising . . . achieves no more than an interest to try the product and, if that product does not live up to expectations, it is not bought a second time.'
5. 'In general economics, the contribution of an efficient low-cost communication system lies in the fast pay-off of investment cost; the avoidance of wasteful production hanging about in the warehouses, the maintenance of steady production and therefore of employment.'
6. 'The special value of advertising is its cheapness and rapid spread of product information.'
7. 'Consumer attitudes may not be as the writers of the paper would like them to be. They are, however, the product of the material betterment of the mass of the population over the last century. They are the consumers' own choice, and industry and advertising have merely responded to their needs and wishes with products, services and communications. The communications have not created the attitudes; and to restrict the communications will not change the attitudes.'

This book is not the place to try to resolve the argument. However, most marketing people – at least in the UK – would take the view that our present economic system, in spite of difficulties and disruptions like the slow-down in economy as witnessed in the early part of the new millennium, is better than any other available to us. Certainly it is the one we have to work within at present. A key element in it is that consumers are offered a wide choice of products and services by competing organizations. Consumers' choices, in the end, contribute largely to the decisions as to which products and services will continue to be provided, since, without consumer support, companies cannot provide products and services at a profit. Most people are above the level of 'bare necessities', so that much of the purchases will be used to satisfy needs that are higher up the hierarchy of needs (see Section 1.5). There will be a wide discrepancy in what different groups of people believe they need. Advertising and sales promotion are among the ways in which competing companies signal to customers what is available to them. The customers then decide.

The debate continues.

9.5 The Ethics of Advertising and Sales Promotion

Even if the view is taken that advertising and sales promotion are in themselves a valuable part of the economic scene, it is still possible that individual advertisements or campaigns will use methods that are unethical. In the UK there is a unique system of voluntary controls, supported by all the major bodies concerned with advertising and representing advertisers, advertising agencies and media. In addition, radio and TV advertising must by law be vetted (the latter before transmission) by agencies of the Independent Broadcasting Authority.

The Advertising Standards Authority, financed by a levy on all advertising in the main media, will examine any advertisements or sales promotion activity complained of by a member of the public. The Authority has prepared a Code of Advertising Practice and a Code of Sales Promotion Practice, and ensures that activities offending against these Codes are amended or withdrawn.

In addition, there is much long-standing legislation, such as the Trade Descriptions Acts 1968 and 1972 and the Sale of Goods (Implied Terms) Act 1973, which limits what may be done or said in any selling situation. Other laws, such as the Hire Purchase Acts 1964 and 1965, lay down rules for advertising particular goods or services.

9.6 The Limitations of Advertising and Sales Promotion

It must not be thought that advertising and sales promotion are all-powerful activities. In spite of much loose talk, advertising is not 'brainwashing'; it cannot make people do what they firmly wish not to do. Its power of changing attitudes is real but certainly limited. Indeed, over-enthusiastic statements about a product will probably rebound, because those who try the product themselves will be disappointed with it.

A further limitation is cost. Advertising can be a very expensive activity. Only when it is accurately assessed and given its rightful place in the marketing mix, as part of a properly conceived plan, will it pay dividends. The 'accurate assessment' and 'properly conceived plan' will owe a great deal to sound knowledge of customers and their needs, and much hard work and good judgement in determining how best to meet those needs.

9.7 How the Advertising Business Works – The Story So Far

In Chapter 5 we saw that 'promotion' is an important element in the marketing mix – the combination of product, price, place and promotion that provides the satisfactions the customer is seeking. The way the product is promoted (e.g. as a 'fun thing', as an exclusive article, as a reliable mechanism) is inseparable, in the customer's mind, from the product viewed purely 'as it comes from the drawing board'.

In Section 7.5 we used the term 'marketing communications' as a convenient phrase to embrace the many methods by which companies may pass messages to their customers and prospective customers – messages that attempt to persuade as well as to inform (Section 7.3).

The precise way in which the various methods of communication (including personal selling) are blended together in the appropriate proportions to fit a given marketing situation is called the 'promotional mix' (Section 7.2). Earlier in the chapter we looked at some of the tasks advertising and sales promotion can perform.

9.8 Planning for Advertising

We go on in this chapter to examine the mechanisms by which advertising is actually carried out. But first, it is essential to remind ourselves that this will all be done as part of a carefully planned operation. We shall not start preparing an advertising campaign without first asking questions such as:

- Who are our customers or stakeholders who we wish to influence?
- What are their needs?
- What do we have (or what can we develop) that will meet those needs?
- How important to the various sectors in our target audience are the various elements in the marketing mix and how can we best handle each?
- If promotion is an important element, what promotional mix do we need?
- In particular, is advertising of value in this situation and, if so, what must it communicate (facts, atmosphere, customer benefits) and to whom (customers, dealers, our own salespeople, other stakeholders)? How can we define our 'target audiences'?

In Chapter 6 we looked more closely at the whole business of devising marketing plans. From that, it is clear that advertising decisions must be a part of a whole complex of decisions that together form the total marketing plan.

9.8.1 How Advertising Plans Are Developed

Like so much in marketing, developing a sound plan for advertising is largely a matter of asking the right questions. If, on answering the questions in the previous section, it seems that advertising has a part to play, then we go on to ask the following:

- What is the objective of advertising in this particular situation? It could, for example, involve any of the tasks set out in Section 9.3.1, and there are many others. There may be more than one task (e.g. to make customers more aware of the product and to secure wider retail distribution).
- What is the audience we are communicating with? We must be very clear what/who our 'target audience' is. There may be more than one, in which case can we communicate with them all at once or do we have a number of quite separate communication tasks to do?
- What is the message we have to convey? It may well be different for each audience. Consumers may need to be told of the product's performance, whereas dealers will be more interested in the profit they can make. The public may wish to hear about community relations with the police or about new initiatives from local councils providing 'best value'.

In an industrial context, the factory manager will want to know that a machine will give fewer breakdowns and higher output, and the financial director that it will reduce capital outlay and hence reduce overdraft charges.

- What is the best medium? Is this a job for television, the press, posters or some kind of 'below the line' activity? In other words, how are we best going to reach our target audiences with our chosen messages?
- What is the best timing and frequency? Do we need to advertise now, in three months, in six months, over what period? Is it better to have a short sharp burst or would a larger campaign, 'spread thin', be better?
- How can our message be expressed most effectively?
- How much should we be spending to achieve the above?

9.9 Deciding on Advertising Budgets

The 'How much should we be spending?'question just posed is a crucial one, for how much we have to spend will have a big influence on what kind of advertising we can do. It is not much use thinking of national television if the budget comes out at £1000. Unfortunately, it is a particularly difficult question to answer.

Up to a point we can arrive at the answer by way of the break-even approach (Section 13.3.1). Since our promotional costs are probably an important element in our variable costs, we can plot them against anticipated sales and try to assess at what point further promotional expenditure should show diminishing returns. But, in the first place, there is likely to be a fair amount of guesswork in it (how else can we arrive at the level of 'anticipated sales'?) More important, however, is that we are still dealing in total promotional costs. These may well include the expense of a sales force, sales literature (sometimes very costly indeed in the case of high technology industrial products) and other forms of sales promotion. In a sense adding, say £65,000, to the advertising budget means operating with one less salesperson. What is the correct approach to this difficult question?

Some well-tried approaches exist, the main ones being the following:

1. **Arbitrary methods**. While, clearly, they cannot be recommended, many companies simply pick a figure 'off the ceiling' or on the basis of 'that's what we can afford'.
2. **Percentage of sales – or some other financial parameter, such as profit**. An 'easy' and superficially attractive method is to allocate a proportion of sales revenue to advertising. But which sales revenue? Last year's, this year's, what we anticipate next year? Various companies in various ways use all approaches. The method has the advantage of making calculations easy – if anticipated turnover is £X000, then the advertising budget is Y per cent of £X000. But the underlying assumption is either that the level of advertising expenditure directly determines the level of sales or that advertising is a luxury you buy according to how much profit you are making. A variant of this approach, often used in a fairly predictable market, is to allocate an amount for advertising on a per unit basis, e.g. 5p per case or per dozen of anticipated sales.

3. **What competitors are spending**. Clearly competitive expenditure cannot be ignored, since it may provide, especially for a company entering a new field, a good general guide to the kind of expenditure that may be necessary. But it can be very misleading because:
   (a) It assumes that competitors know what they are doing, when, in fact, their level of expenditure may be hopelessly uneconomic and based on sheer guesswork.
   (b) Companies in the same field have a quite different promotional mix, e.g. in the cosmetics field Avon concentrate on direct selling, Boots rely largely on 'captive' customers in their own retail outlets, and many others spend heavily on advertising in order to get their products on to retailers' shelves.
4. **On a 'task' basis**. If it can be decided what task(s) advertising needs to perform in the particular circumstances, a suitable advertising programme can be worked out and costed to give the budget necessary to achieve the task(s). In principle this must be the correct approach, but unfortunately there are always many ways of achieving the desired result, often with wildly different costs. Nor is it easy to decide what concentration of advertising is necessary to achieve a particular effect.

In order to simplify the above, there are four questions, that are essentially a combination of most of the above approaches, that might be asked:

1. What can the product afford?
2. What is the advertising task?
3. What are competitors spending?
4. What have we learned from previous years?

In an example, the approach might give answers such as the following:

1. £675,000 is all that is allocated in the preliminary budget.
2. £750,000 would achieve the advertising exposures regarded as desirable.
3. £700,000 will buy a share of advertising equal to the product's share of the market.
4. £700,000 was spent last year, but there are indications that brand share is responsive to the amount of advertising support.

Discussions would probably take place around the range of £650,000 to £750,000. Ultimately, the decision will lie in the character of the organization and the confidence it has in its economic forecasts. The conservative will settle at a low figure; the thrusting, expansionist organization will invest in its future.

9.10 Advertising Agencies

The production of advertising material is a complex business. A number of different parties work on it, but principally the parties involved are: the **advertisers** (companies marketing products or services, including manufacturers, service providers, retailers, importers, franchise holders etc.); **advertising agencies** (companies specializing in the development and production of advertising campaigns for a variety of 'clients'); and the **media** (newspaper and magazine publishers, TV and radio programme contractors, cinema owners, transport authorities, poster contractors and the like).

It is perfectly possible for the whole process of advertising to be carried out within the company. Selecting media, designing and writing advertisements, taking photographs, preparing artwork for printing and many other things are then all done within the advertising department. There is a particular tendency for this to happen when the company has a very large number of products, each with a high technical content. The promotional mix will contain a high element of sales literature, exhibition material and so on, all of which must be carefully worked out in close collaboration with technical experts. Even press advertisements may contain a fair amount of technical information, for example in fields such as telecommunications, plastics and building materials.

This is the exception, however. More usually the technical content of advertising materials is small. To produce promotional material for coffee, underwear or furniture, it is rarely necessary to go into the technicalities of how they are produced. Even for products such as electrical appliances, the technical content of the main promotional material is very small (although there may well be some service manuals and other supporting materials that are technical).

In general, then, the people who write and design advertising material do not need to be skilled in the technicalities of the products themselves. Rather, they need to be experts in the advertising business – in communicating. Such people are mainly (though by no means solely) found in advertising agencies, and it is in advertising agencies that most advertising material is produced, for three main reasons:

1. The obvious advantages of bringing together within one organization all the skills that go towards producing good advertising.
2. The fact that an agency can usually afford to employ a much wider range of skilled and experienced people than an individual advertiser.
3. Historically, in the UK (and in many other countries, though not all), advertising agencies received a commission from the media owners (usually 15 per cent) for all space or time bought on behalf of their clients. This means that they could afford to pay writers, designers, media experts and advertising planners to act on their clients' behalf. Clients do not usually obtain these commissions or, if they do, it is likely to be a smaller percentage so that it would cost them more to 'do it themselves'. Increasingly now 'fair trading' laws have abolished the enforced commissions not payable to clients, so this consideration becomes less relevant.

9.11 How Media Decisions are Made

Having arrived at a set of advertising objectives and established a budget, we are then faced with decisions on how to implement them. (It works the other way round, too, of course, for if the budget is set by the 'task' method, we must have some idea early on of how the objectives will be reached in order to work out the approximate cost.)

Nowhere is the choice of methods more varied than in the media aspect of the job. A wide variety of kinds of media are available, including the following:

- Broadcasting (TV and radio).
- The press (newspapers and magazines, both consumer and trade).
- Outdoor (posters – buses, trains).
- Direct mail (sending out letters through the post).
- Exhibitions.
- The Internet.
- Emerging technologies like third generation (3G) communications on mobile telephones.

If we want to reach financial directors of large companies, for example, we can choose between newspapers (such as *The Times* and *Financial Times*), magazines (the accountancy journals, *The Economist* and so on) or direct mail.

Usually the selection must be made in four stages, as follows:

1. What kind of media (from a list including the above)?
2. Which particular medium (which newspaper, which radio stations or whatever)?
3. What size/type of space; how much time; how many posters of what size, what frequency of appearance over what length of time?
4. How much will our budget permit us to buy?

It is not possible here to go into all of these areas in depth[ii] but, as an example of the kind of approach, we can take a short look at the way in which one newspaper or magazine might be selected rather than another. This is done by progressively narrowing down the list of possible publications to find the one that will reach the maximum number of our target audience (though sometimes it may be better to concentrate on only a small section of the target audience, to gain maximum impact). Sometimes, of course, 'maximum number' will conflict with 'lowest cost' and a compromise may have to be decided upon. This is normally a progressive process going through a number of stages, as follows:

1. Select those publications that are likely to reach as many of the target audience as possible.
2. Establish the cost of reaching those readers (usually on a 'cost per thousand readers' basis).
3. Arrive at the best publication in terms of maximum number of readers within the target audience at the lowest cost per thousand.
4. Consider whether any supporting publications are needed (for example, the 'best buy' publication may reach only 65 per cent of the target audience; to use a second would reach a further 25 per cent; a third may only reach a further 5 per cent and may not be justified).

Sometimes other criteria have to be taken into account, for example a particular product may need illustrating in colour (fabrics, paint), whereas the 'best buy' may only carry black and white advertisements.

9.12 The Importance of Concentration

We have just suggested that it is important to select the 'best buy' rather than to advertise in all publications that reach the target audience. This is one example of an important general principle in advertising – that of concentration. It may be very tempting to try to cover all the options but this is never the most effective use of money. In general it is better to: (a) use the one best publication rather than many; (b) publish a small number of large advertisements rather than many small ones; and (c) reach a small part of the total potential market strongly rather than all of it with a feeble message. The aim should always be dominance, if need be in a carefully chosen sector, rather than to be just 'one of the crowd' of advertisers.

9.13 How Creative Decisions are Made

9.13.1 The Communication Process

It is still not known precisely how advertising works, and almost certainly it works rather differently in different situations. There are, however, some 'models' of the process that have stood the test of time, one of them being expressed by the mnemonic AIDA, the initial letters of attention, interest, desire and action. (Some authors add satisfaction, and use the letters AIDAS to summarize this approach.) (See Section 7.5 for a development of this model.)

The supposition here is that advertising helps take the customer through one or more of these stages ('action' may be purchase, or some other specific action such as asking for a test-drive or sending for a leaflet). Some people now feel, however, that this model attempts to assign too specific a role to advertising, and that the purpose of much advertising can be better expressed in terms of increasing 'awareness' of the product. It may encourage 'testing' of the product and it helps to provide 'reinforcement' of the purchasing habit.

This latter approach is perhaps a better description of much of the 'brand-awareness' advertising that appears on television. Rarely is it now expected that an advertisement on TV will convert a purchaser to a product for life. The most important contribution of all made by most advertising is the development or reinforcement of a favourable brand image (see Section 10.22).

9.13.2 The Creative Task

Section 9.8 listed the key questions that determine the outcome of the advertising planning process. The creative stage of producing advertising campaigns is concerned with two of them:

- What is the message we have to convey?
- How can our message be conveyed most effectively?

Advertising a new burst-proof tyre will call for different treatment from reminding customers of the existence of a brand of baked beans or canned soup. But, of course, these questions must be answered in the light of the answers to some of the other questions in Section 9.8, in particular:

- What is the objective of advertising in this particular situation?
- What/who is the audience we are communicating with?

Telling doctors about a new drug is clearly a different proposition from announcing a new pop record or persuading companies to consider leasing vehicles rather than buying them.

The advertising budget and the choice of media will also have a bearing.

9.13.3 Devising Advertising Campaigns

Note the word 'campaigns'. Very rarely should a single advertisement be developed (advertising jobs, specific offers such as sale bargains, or a single directory entry such as in Yellow Pages are clear exceptions). Advertising generally is a long-term strategic activity (see Figure 9.1).

The creative team, therefore, will be faced with the need to develop an advertising campaign, bearing in mind the following:

- The target audience.
- The task advertising is to perform.
- The media being used.
- The amount being spent (which may well influence, for example, the size of space, or whether colour can be used).
- The length and frequency of the campaign (can we rely on a steady build-up or must the story be told all in one go?).

These are not necessarily the only factors (in some situations what competitors' advertising is saying will be very important, for example). Any ideas for the campaign must then be matched against these criteria. They should also have the following attributes.

- Be able to command attention against all competing influences. People do not watch television and read newspapers primarily to see the advertisements.
- Be able to sustain interest. Boring or dull advertising is unlikely to exert much influence.
- Be memorable.

9.14 Controlling Advertising

The British Codes of Advertising and Sales Promotion are written by the Committee of Advertising Practice (CAP).[iii] All the main trade and professional bodies representing advertisers, agencies, service suppliers and media owners are members of CAP. In addition to writing the Codes, they agree to enforce them. But even if your company is not a member of one of the CAP trade bodies, you will be expected to observe the Codes and the rulings of the ASA Council.

The central principles of the Codes are based on common business sense: that advertisements should be legal, decent, honest and truthful, prepared responsibly and in line with the principles of fair competition. CAP has responded to changes in consumer attitudes and devel-

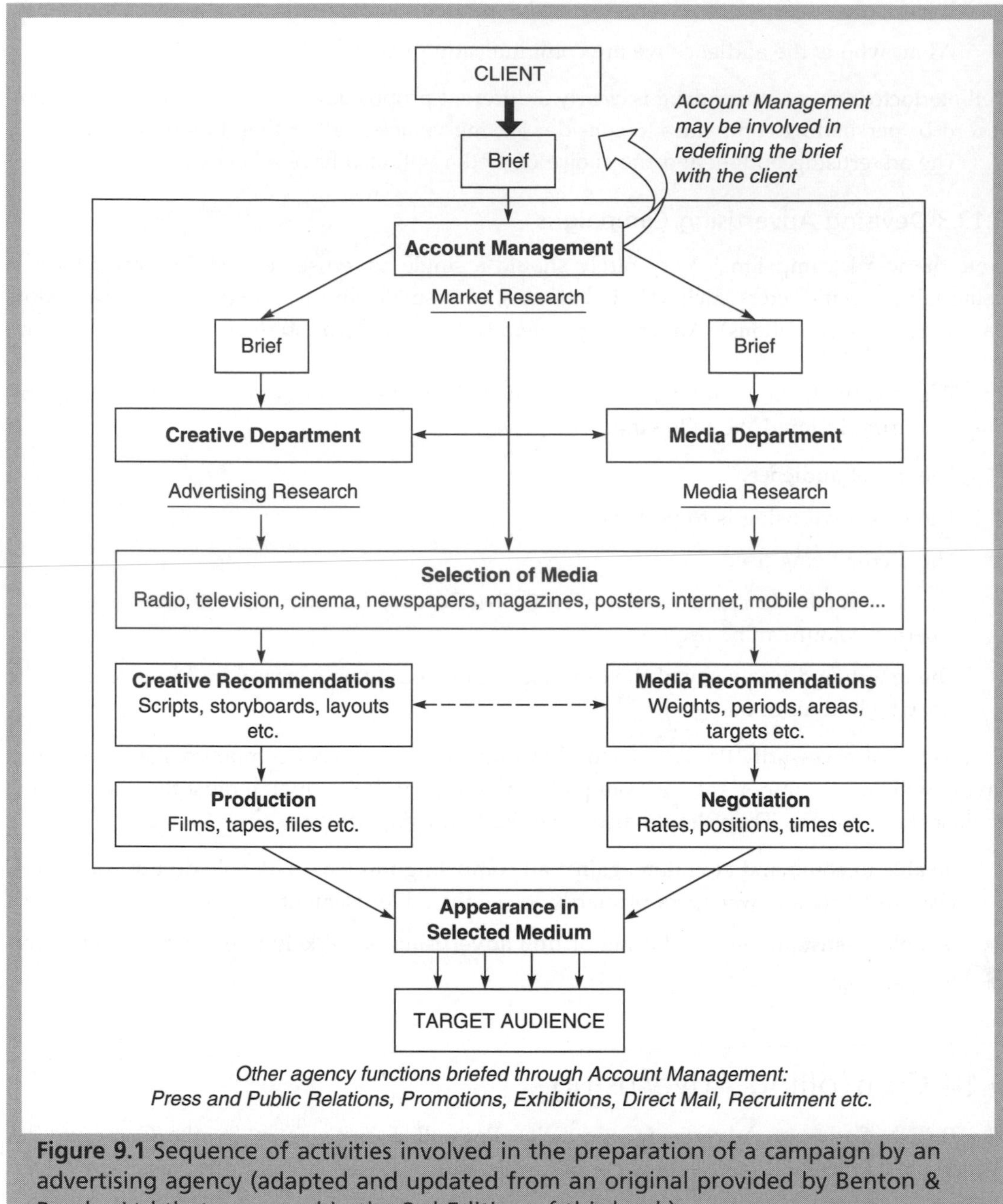

Figure 9.1 Sequence of activities involved in the preparation of a campaign by an advertising agency (adapted and updated from an original provided by Benton & Bowles Ltd that appeared in the 3rd Edition of this book)

opments in marketing and advertising techniques by updating the Codes many times since they were first written. Sales promotion and direct marketing techniques, for example, were in their infancy in the 1960s, and the Internet was used only by scientists. All have been embraced by the Codes as the advertising business has developed.

The ASA and CAP work in four main ways to keep advertising standards high:

1. **Fast, free and confidential advice** – CAP's Copy Advice team are on hand to help advertisers, agencies, publishers and media owners who want to check an advertisement, direct mailing or sales promotion before publication.
2. **Compliance, research and monitoring** – CAP and the ASA spot-check hundreds of advertisements a week and take immediate action to have problem advertisements corrected or withdrawn. Contrary to popular belief, they don't have to wait for a complaint if they identify clear-cut problems under the Codes.
3. **Resolving complaints** – Around 12,500 complaints are made to the ASA each year. It takes only one valid complaint to start an investigation. Complaints that reveal a potential problem under the Codes are formally investigated and the ASA Council's decisions are published weekly on the Authority's website (www.asa.org.uk).
4. **Effective sanctions** – The vast majority of advertisers comply with the Codes because it makes good business sense to do so. If consumers trust advertising, they are more likely to be influenced by it. If that doesn't convince the doubters then the adverse publicity that often results from published ASA decisions usually does. The ASA follows a strict process for formally investigating complaints. This procedure has been tested by the courts and found to be reasonable and fair.

9.14.1 The Complaints Procedure

Assessment and investigation – Complaints are first assessed to see if there is a case to answer under the Codes. The advertiser or agency might be contacted at this stage for a copy of the advertisement if it hasn't been sent in with the complaint. If an investigation is required, a summary of the complaint is sent by the ASA to the advertiser asking for comments or for evidence to back up any challenged claims.

Draft recommendation – After investigation, the ASA Executive drafts a report outlining its findings and recommending either that the complaint be upheld or not upheld. The draft, which is confidential, is sent for comment to those involved in the investigation before it is sent to the ASA Council for their ruling.

ASA Council adjudication and publication – Council members are sent the draft recommendation with a copy of the advertisement. They meet once a month to make their rulings and consider any of the recommendations that might need further discussion. The advertiser, their agency and the complainant will be told about the Council's decision before it is published on the ASA website.

9.15 The Good Advertising Checklist

Balancing the needs of industry and consumers is the purpose behind the Committee of Advertising Practice. If you work in the advertising business you will be bound by the self-imposed rules in the British Codes of Advertising and Sales Promotion drawn up by the

Committee of Advertising Practice. The checklist in Table 9.2 will help you spot the common pitfalls.

Table 9.2 The good advertising checklist

Issue	Comments
Substantiation	Advertisers must hold evidence to support all objective claims. Ask them if they can support claims that seem unlikely, particularly claims for health and beauty products.
Social responsibility/ decency/fear and distress/ safety/antisocial behaviour	Is the ad socially irresponsible, likely to offend its audience or cause fear or distress without good reason? Does it show unsafe or antisocial behaviour? Does it encourage people to break the law?
Advertorials	Check these are clearly marked as advertisements; their content is subject to the Codes.
Alcohol	Ads must not portray alcohol in an irresponsible or unsafe way. Ads for alcoholic drinks must not be directed at or appeal to people under 18 and people shown drinking should be and look over 25.
Comparisons	Check that comparisons are clear and fair.
Distance selling/money off the page	The advertiser's or promoter's full name and address must appear outside the coupon and the delivery time should be stated: usually no more than 30 days.
Employment/business opportunities	Check that ads do not include unrealistic earnings claims. Ads for home-working schemes should give readers a clear description of the work and details of any outlay. It is best to check the content of any follow-up literature.
Free offers	Free offers may be conditional on the purchase of other items so long as the costs are clearly stated. Public rates of postage can be charged but not packaging and handling.
Lucky charms Help Note	Ads must not imply lucky charms and the like can directly affect the user's circumstances. Advertisers may, however, refer to lucky charms acting as a reminder for users to think positively, perhaps improving their confidence and therefore circumstances, so long as the emphasis is on the user's state of mind.
Motoring	Speed and acceleration must not be the predominant message.
Prices and taxes	Unless addressed to the trade, all quoted prices should normally include VAT and other non-optional taxes and duties. Prices must match the products illustrated.
Privacy	The Codes urge advertisers to get permission from individuals featured in ads, except for those in crowd scenes. If they do not have permission, advertisers should not unfairly show people in an offensive or adverse way.

Sales promotions	Check that promoters have stated all significant conditions and limitations. A closing date and preconditions of entry should normally be included prominently. The promoter's full name and address should be stated in a place that can be retained by entrants.
Qualifying claims/small print Help Note	Check that claims are clearly stated or are suitably qualified so that consumers are not misled. Qualifying claims should not contradict anything stated elsewhere in the ad. Small print must be clearly visible to a normally sighted person reading the advertisement once at a normal speed.
Telephone numbers	If the ad includes a telephone number charged higher than the standard national rate this should be stated, e.g. 07712 123123 (mobile), 07000 123123 (above standard national rate).
Travel Help Note	Airport names should normally be stated if more than one serves a city. Prices must include all pre-payable taxes. If the purchase of holiday insurance is compulsory this should be clearly stated, along with the typical cost. Ads must not mislead as to the availability of flights.
Vanity publishing Help Note	Most vanity publishers do not select manuscripts on merit, contribute to production costs or market books effectively; any such claims should be checked. Promises that customers can recoup their costs or gain financially from the sale of their books are unlikely to be true. The content of any follow-up literature should be checked.

9.16 What of the Future?

Like everything else in the new millennium, the advertising business is changing. Will viewers pay for programmes on demand and zap past any advertising clutter, leaving advertising agencies with about as much importance as a 78-rpm phonograph (vinyl record) on the interactive superhighway? In Britain, total advertising expenditure has plateaued and the total advertising agency work force has fallen considerably since its 1989 peak. It is difficult of course to be sure of the long-term significance of such trends. Many industries have suffered similar setbacks during recessions. However, the growth of the 'media independents' and other changes in the way the business operates mean that it is highly unlikely that agencies will ever resume the supremely dominant role they once had.

Another factor that may be leading in a similar direction is the growing strength of retailers' own brands, which makes it increasingly difficult for manufacturers to achieve and sustain a dominant position in the marketplace through massive advertising expenditures. It was suggested that, once the mid-90s recession was over, the media owners would be able to recover and the costs of advertising would soar. While there was pressure on broadcast advertising rates, the other marketing techniques, such as direct response (through press advertising or direct mail perhaps) assumed much greater importance. Already we are seeing the development of more direct links with customers, and interactive TV shopping is underway. Things are very unlikely to look the same in five years' time.

CASE STUDY

What follows is an account of how the UK's first Internet bank, Egg, got the edge over its competitors.[iv]

In the late 1990s, the UK was still dominated by the major banks, converted building societies and a few remaining mutual organizations. In the late 1980s, direct financial institutions like First Direct had appeared, since when the market had seen a continued growth of direct transactions, primarily over the telephone. Deregulation had encouraged new, non-traditional organizations to enter the market and competition had increased.

As the UK's first Internet bank, Egg's initial challenge was to create a new brand that stood out in the market and met the needs of customers. The Egg brand was built around the philosophy of tailoring products and services to individuals. Its brand statement 'Egg is your ground-breaking partner, who is always there for you, offering simple, smart, financial solutions' clearly spelt out its offer.

Egg first used TV advertising exclusively when it was launched in 1998 to build a strong customer base. Its initial campaign, featuring presenter Zoe Ball and former athlete Linford Christie, promoted Egg Savings Accounts and reflected the brand's attitude. The advertising reflected the brand's core values – a brand that was transparent, mutually beneficial, empathetic, modern, fresh and liberating. Egg then went on to use national press advertising extensively to acquire and cross-sell to its customer base, launching a series of motivating offers. As the market became increasingly competitive, Egg had to reinforce its differentiation. Its third campaign, aired in October 2000, relied less heavily on the promotion of products.

Within a week of its first launch, Egg had received 1.75 million Internet 'hits' and nearly 100,000 telephone enquiries. The Egg Card, launched in October 1999, rapidly commanded a 9 per cent market share of all credit cards sold in the UK (source: MORI MFS tracking survey). By June 2000, brand awareness had reached 79 per cent – a similar level to Halifax, First Direct and Virgin Direct. By March 2001, Egg had 1.575 million customers, which was nearly six times more than its nearest stand-alone competitor, and its brand awareness score had grown to 88 per cent – only slightly behind more established names such as Barclays. Meanwhile, Egg.com is currently the third most visited e-commerce site in Europe (source: Jupiter MMXI Europe).

In 2000, Egg launched a WAP (Wireless Application Protocol) service to complement its existing Internet platform. This allowed customers to access their account and other services over their mobile phone. It also created a 'fund supermarket', Egg Invest, which gave customers the opportunity to choose from a wide range of unit trusts and ISAs from several fund managers. Its service offerings were also increased with the launch of a shopping mall – Egg Shop – featuring over 200 retailers. Egg Insure was launched to offer motor, home, life and travel insurance through a panel of insurers. In April 2001, Egg TV went live with its interactive digital television service that allows a broader range of consumers to access Egg via their TV.

At the time Egg was launched, research carried out by the Henley Centre indicated that, in fifteen years' time, two of every three financial service products would be sold by e-commerce. In 2000, 16 per cent of Internet users had purchased financial services products remotely (source: NOP Internet Tracking). The Director of Brand Communications, Tony Williams, stated that: 'The ongoing challenge for Egg is to ensure that the brand stays at the forefront of e-commerce by continuing to innovate in terms of products, customer services and communication. It is our intention to dominate this rapidly growing market.'

Questions

1. At what phase of the product life cycle do you feel the internet banking industry is currently?
2. What implications do your conclusions to question one have on how you would define the advertising strategy that Egg should now follow?

Summary

- Advertising is the term used to describe 'paid-for' messages of all kinds in media owned and controlled by people other than the advertiser.
- Sales promotion activities, on the other hand, use tools and media controlled directly by the advertiser.
- The place of advertising in the marketing mix is determined by: (a) the circumstances, (b) the task, (c) the product and (d) cost-effectiveness.
- The tasks advertising can be usefully employed in include the following: (a) announcing new products and product changes, (b) aiding salespeople, (c) entering new markets and expanding old ones, (d) keeping existing customers 'sold', (e) inviting enquiries, (f) selling direct and (g) creating a brand or company image.
- Sales promotion is normally tactical (whereas advertising is mainly strategic) and concentrated at point of sale.
- Advertising and sales promotion are essential ingredients in the competition between companies, which is an important element in our economic system.
- The unethical use of advertising and sales promotion is restricted both by legal restraints and by a voluntary control system.
- Advertising plans are developed on the basis of: (a) objectives, (b) audience, (c) message, (d) medium and (e) budget.
- Advertising budgets can be worked out by a number of methods, of which the task method is normally regarded as the most significant.
- The business of advertising is done by: (a) advertisers, (b) agencies (and companies supplying ancillary services) and (c) the media.
- Advertising agencies are companies concentrating on the development and production of advertising campaigns on behalf of clients. The main departments are account management, creative, media and production.
- Media selection decisions are made on the basis of coverage (of the target audience), and cost (on, for example, a cost per 1000 readers or viewers basis).

- Concentration of resources is an important principle of advertising.
- Creative decisions are made on the basis of selecting a message that will: (a) command attention, (b) sustain interest and (c) be memorable. The desired message must also be carried in a way that is appropriate to the target audience.

References

i Wilmshurst, J. and Mackay, A. *The Fundamentals of Advertising* (Butterworth-Heinemann, 2nd Edition, 1999)

ii See Wilmshurst, J. and Mackay, A. *The Fundamentals of Advertising* (Butterworth-Heinemann, 2nd Edition, 1999) for a more full treatment of the subject.

iii Information freely available from the *Committee of Advertising Practice* web pages, January 2002.

iv Adapted from a report in *Marketing Business*, September 2001.

Further Reading

Excellence in Advertising. Edited by Leslie Butterfield (Butterworth-Heinemann, 1999).

Wilmshurst, John and Mackay, Adrian. *The Fundamentals of Advertising* (Butterworth-Heinemann, 1985 and 2nd Edition, 1999). A general study of the whole subject at a basic level and contains many up to date facts and figures.

Aitchison, A. *Cutting Edge Advertising* (Pearson Education Imports, 1999). A hip but not trendy guide to the many angles involved in the creation of print ads.

Questions

1. Suggest current advertising or sales promotion campaigns that seem to have as their objectives:

   (a) Announcing new products.
   (b) Inviting enquiries.
   (c) Improving company image.
   (d) Stimulating immediate sales.

2. Why do you think pet foods are so widely advertised on television? Why is insurance more frequently advertised in the press?

3. Imagine that a new pet superstore has invested heavily in their Internet pages. Discuss how you would promote them to defined target audiences.

4. You are the marketing manager of a company about to launch a new rechargeable hand power drill. List the categories of information you would give the advertising agency that is to prepare an advertising campaign for you.

Chapter 10

The practice of sales promotion

Introduction

By the end of this chapter you will:

- Understand what is encompassed by the term 'sales promotion' – and how it differs from advertising.
- Appreciate when sales promotion particularly can have an important role in effective marketing.
- Be aware of the many different tasks that can be performed by sales promotion.
- Know some of the criticisms that are levelled at sales promotion and how they are countered by the industry.
- Be aware of the main types of sales promotion and their uses.
- Know how to evaluate the contribution of sales promotion activities.
- Have an outline understanding of exhibitions, direct mail, public relations, loyalty schemes and sponsorship.

'Sales promotion can be described as the hysterical arm of marketing operations.'

John Winkler. *Winkler on Marketing Planning*

10.1 What Sales Promotion Is

Here we have yet another term that is used by different people to mean different things. The distinction made by a number of authors and one we have followed here (see Chapter 9) is that 'advertising' describes messages carried in media owned and controlled primarily by people other than the advertiser, and 'sales promotion' messages are carried by media controlled by the company itself.

John Winkler,[i] in the quotation at the beginning of the chapter and in the chapter it introduces in his book, is referring particularly to the sometimes frantic efforts to persuade customers to buy one brand rather than another. Grocery products, petrol and confectionery are areas where this kind of activity is common – premium offers, gifts, competitions and 'points' on collection cards are typical manifestations.

Some would say that sales promotion could just as easily be called merchandizing, below the line activity, non-media advertising – and more. Others include in their definition of sales promotion free circulation magazines, special discounts, exhibitions and bribery, including special payments of all kinds to dealers!

'Consumer promotions' might include:

- Special price sales.
- Free sample distribution.
- Premium offers.
- Contests.
- Point-of-sale demonstrations.
- Coupon offers.
- Combination or banded pack product offers.

'Trade promotions' might include the following:

- Provision of display materials.
- Co-operative advertising schemes.
- Contests for sales staff.
- Special discounts.
- Special quantity rate terms.

Clearly there is much scope for argument as to what goes in and what is left out of a definition of sales promotion. In this chapter we include all the above but also, for convenience, sections on direct mail and PR, although they would not necessarily be included under this heading by other writers.

In this way we put direct mail in the sales promotion camp and for convenience we will deal with trade exhibitions under the sales promotion heading. The terms advertising and sales promotion, then, closely corresponded with the 'above and below the line' distinction that is commonly used, in advertising agencies especially. See the companion web page for a description of how these two terms came about.

Most frequently the term 'sales promotion' was used to describe a special campaign, usually fairly short in duration, to boost sales of a particular brand or product.

As we saw in Section 9.2, public relations was treated a little differently and a distinction was made between public relations and advertising.

10.1.1 The Importance of Sales Promotion

Sales promotion has, until fairly recently, been dismissed as a relatively unimportant medium, largely because, in advertising agencies, it came under the catch-all heading of 'below the line'. In any case, relatively little of the expenditure passes through agencies but tends to be spent directly by advertisers or through specialist companies.

As early as 1978 the more rapid growth of below the line promotion compared with that of above the line advertising was being noted. Sales promotion expenditure grew from £545 million in 1974 to £1853 million in 1977. Advertising Association figures showed advertising expenditure through agencies growing from £1000 million to £1630 million over the same period – a growth of only 63 per cent against the 24 per cent increase in sales promotion expenditure. Such figures have been less quoted more recently. The Institute of Sales Promotion contented itself with the claim (quoted by Alan Wolfe in *Marketing*, 21st April 1983) that 'total expenditure below the line now exceeds the money spent on media advertising'.

A recent Advertising Association Marketing Pocket Book quoted a figure of over £1750 million, of which £1250 million was non-price-related (1999 figures), but stresses the difficulty of definition.

The 1993 Annual Report of the WPP group estimated total sales promotional expenditure at 17.4 billion US dollars compared with total media expenditure of 14.4 billion dollars. This seems to confirm the suggestion that above the line expenditure has been overtaken by below the line.

Unfortunately, it is impossible to arrive at an exact figure for the following reasons:

- There is no easy way to collect together expenditures by individual firms on the many 'bits and pieces' that constitute sales promotion.
- And, in any case, the figure depends on what is included under the heading.

10.1.2 The Role of Sales Promotion

In Section 9.2 we drew a distinction between advertising and sales promotion in terms of the media used. We can also make other distinctions, as explained below:

Sales promotion is often tactical. To a large extent, advertising is used strategically, i.e. it is part of the continuing 'attack' on the marketplace, often with long-term objectives in view. To create a brand image, to generate a flow of enquiries, to influence a whole new market favourably towards a product, calls for carefully planned advertising (usually in conjunction with other forms of promotion) over a long period. Even when short-term results are expected, as in direct sales advertising, this response will usually need to be on a frequently repeated basis, so that the advertising must be continuous. Sales promotion, on the other hand, is more often tactical, i.e. it is designed to achieve a short-term and limited objective, possibly in a limited area or through certain outlets. For example, an introductory price cut or premium offer may be made, coupled with special discounts for dealers, in order to encourage dealers to stock and customers to sample a new product. The promotion would continue for a few weeks only. However, this tactical aspect must be kept in perspective because continuing use of sales promotion does have long-term effects (see Section 10.1.4).

Sales promotion is normally concentrated at point of sale. In general, advertising speaks direct from the marketing company to the customer. Sales promotion usually takes place in close association with the dealers who stock the product. Very frequently, the whole thing takes place 'at the point of sale', i.e. at the place where the customer buys the product. You, the customer, get the free beer mugs from the garage when you pay for the petrol that has just been put in your tank, or the entry forms from the supermarket check-out desk for the holiday competition being run by the makers of the jam you have just bought. Some sales promotion activities ('personality promotions', for example) do take place in the street or (as with some forms of sampling) on a door to door basis, but even then there is usually a strong tie-in with local dealers.

10.1.3 Some Typical Sales Promotion Tasks

Sales promotion includes a very wide range of activities, which can be used in all kinds of situations, but some of the most common jobs it is used for are:

- **Encouraging dealers to stock**. Most retail dealers feel they already have far too many different products, and every new one means dropping an old one or having more capital locked up in stock. So they need considerable persuasion to take in a new line. They must be convinced it will be profitable for them, which means they must be convinced that customers will buy it in reasonable volume. Sales promotion activities can be used both to help in this argument and provide direct cash incentives (e.g. by way of cash discounts or deals like the '13 bottles for the price of 12' used in the wines and spirits trade).
- **Encouraging customers to sample**. With food products, confectionery etc., for example, it is often crucial that customers try the new product – they are almost certainly already buying an alternative they find reasonably satisfactory. They must be given an incentive to try something new. A special price offer, a 'two for one', or even an exciting display may tempt them sufficiently to 'take the test'.
- **'Locking in' existing customers**. Some sales promotion techniques such as 'three for the price of two', much used, for example, by film companies such as Kodak, encourage customers to stay loyal rather than to be constantly switching brands. Other devices with this purpose in mind include 'collectables' such as coupons, which can be exchanged for goods from a catalogue. Loyalty programmes would be included under this heading.

- **Combating competition**. A competitive situation, such as someone else introducing a new product, may call for an intensive short-term promotion of an existing product to ensure that not too many present customers are wooed away, and that, if possible, some new ones are gained to fill any gaps in the ranks.
- **Improving distribution**. This is a similar situation to the first point in the list. An existing product may have 'patchy' distribution, and sales promotion techniques can be used to fill in the gaps and gain extra dealers in the poorly represented areas.
- **Adding excitement**. A well-established product may suffer from pure familiarity. Since most people are well aware of it, it can become boring. Sales promotions liven it up again and revive interest in it.

10.1.4 What Sales Promotion is For

In Section 10.1.3 above we listed the kind of tasks sales promotion can perform. They can be summarized by saying that sales promotion techniques are used to give a short-term 'lift' to a product, in order to achieve a tactical objective – such as getting retailers to stock, getting customers to sample, or attempting to raise sales off a plateau.

This contrasts with the long-term advertising objective of building brand recognition or creating the right associations with the product in a consumer's mind. Often a product much advertised over a long period reaches the point where there is nothing novel to be said about it. A competition or give-away reintroduces the desired novelty and excitement. Often the purpose of sales promotion is to relieve the boredom of a well-established product.

Most often sales promotion is closely associated with the point of sale.

Companies have increasingly realized, however, that whilst sales promotion has largely tactical uses it has strategic implications. Thus there have been suggestions that a consistent policy over several years by the major UK petrol companies of competing largely through sales promotion has had unfortunate long-term effects. The earlier 'brand image' advertising of the main petrol brands gave way to price cuts, discounting through trading stamps and a whole variety of gifts and competitions to be obtained or won by collecting vouchers. It may well be that this procedure actually reinforced a growing belief that there is no significant difference between one brand and another since customers were being urged to buy on the basis of the best sales promotional 'deal' rather than the best petrol or the best service. Clearly this is a danger and continuing price cuts in particular may convey a picture of 'cheapness' rather than of the often more desirable impression of 'good value'.

Interestingly, during the late 1980s the major petrol companies increased their 'above the line' activities while continuing with considerable sales promotion expenditure. In 2000 and beyond the major petrol companies have aimed to achieve greater differentiation. Esso, for example, kept their 'price watch' – although they have recently gone back to offering 'collectable' cut-glass wine glasses at a reduced price. Shell have their 'Optima' brand, and BP have 'BP Select', reflecting their 'Green' or environmental approach.

Certainly many of the big users of sales promotion techniques (Kelloggs and Heinz, for example) aim at sales promotion campaigns that reinforce the value of the brand. For example, Kelloggs were promoting a book on 'Fibre in your Diet' as a premium offer with their high-fibre 'All Bran Plus' cereal, rather than simply offering a 'bargain'.

10.2 The Importance of Point of Sale

We looked in Chapter 1 at the sequence through which a buyer goes, from feeling a need, through a search process, to the purchasing decision. Not until that decision is made is the marketing process complete (ignoring for the moment the importance, which was stressed in Chapter 1, of the customer's post-purchase feelings).

The all-important purchasing decision takes place at the point of sale – in the shop or showroom (or, less typically, when the customer fills in the order form surrounded by a collection of catalogues). At this point it is unusual for 'our' product to be the only one on offer. Usually there is a shop full of alternatives, and this is true whether it is a person buying groceries in the supermarket or the business executive buying stationery or spare parts from their supplier's showroom.

It is at the point of sale that the customer finally resolves which of the alternatives will be selected. Often he or she does not decide until this time which of the many alternatives will best meet his or her needs. Even if this decision has been made, it can be changed at point of sale by a well-presented special offer or even by a prominent and attractive display.

Most marketing organizations are well aware of the desirability of achieving special emphasis for their products. Show-cards, window posters and special display material are all part of the struggle to achieve maximum point-of-sale impact.

However, the dealer often finds himself in the situation of being overwhelmed with the amount of display material offered to him by his suppliers. The more sophisticated he is, the more conscious he is that he needs to get maximum turnover and profit from each square metre of shelf space, and the more selective he will be. He is not usually specially concerned with which brand sells best (his own total profit is naturally his main concern) but only with total sales. He therefore needs to be convinced that 'our' display will increase his profits. Using point-of-sale material to feature a national promotion (especially if it is to be heavily advertised) is one way of doing this, but its apt design is crucial if it is to be used and not discarded.

In some cases point-of-sale promotion is used to persuade people to shop at one particular point of sale rather than another. The petrol promotions are intended to encourage people to buy their petrol or oil from one company's site rather than another's. Trading stamps are another way of achieving this. So are the 'loss leaders' which many stores feature, when one or more items are heavily marked down in price and featured in advertising, on windows etc., to tempt people into that shop in preference to a competitor's. Naturally the hope is that, once in, they will buy other items besides the featured 'loss leader'.

Figure 10.1 illustrates how point of sale works. Let us assume that a customer goes out shopping one day with the intention to get a whole variety of products. They may have in their mind products that are 'recommendations' from other sources (point 1). This may be from their family, other people's 'word of mouth' recommendations, or from advertising and so forth. They also may have gone shopping with specific needs (point 2): to replace their usual domestic products in their cupboard, get themselves (or someone else) something specific, or indeed just buy something to cheer themselves up.

Let us suppose that our shopper's general need is to replace their toothpaste. They may have a simple generic need (point 3) for some toothpaste. They may not be particularly brand loyal and will go for whatever is available on their trip round the supermarket. Alternatively,

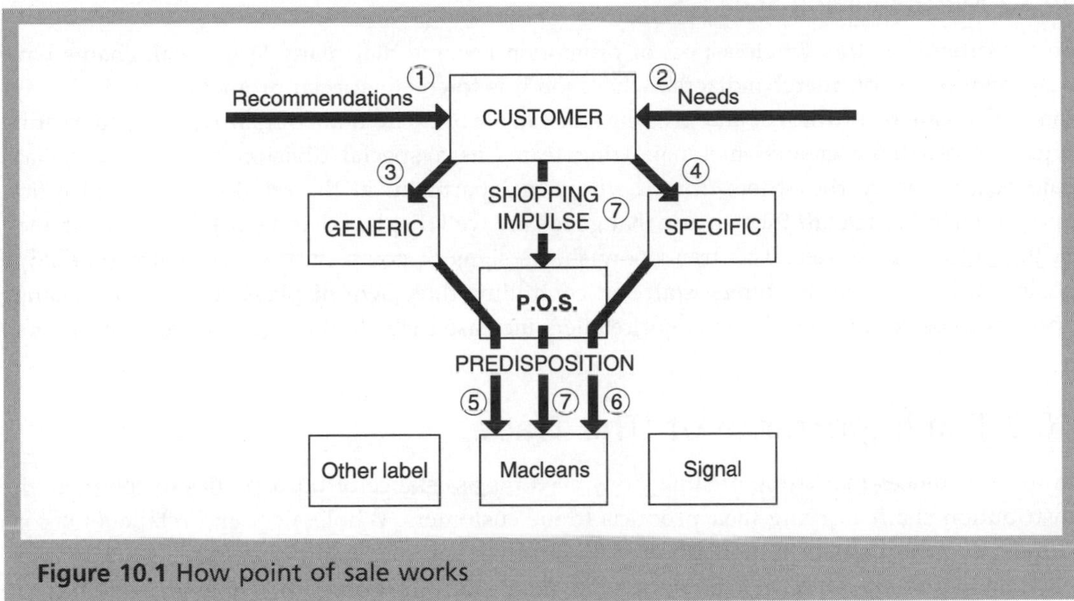

Figure 10.1 How point of sale works

they may be particularly loyal to, say, Signal toothpaste and have that specific brand in mind (point 4).

When they are in the 'toothpaste aisle' in their supermarket, point of sale can have a variety of influences. Let us suppose that, on this particular shopping trip, Macleans toothpaste has a particular display in the store. This might be anything from a '33 per cent extra' on a promotional pack or a promotional offer – like 'buy one get one free' – to a demonstration of the new flavours. There will then be a stronger 'predisposition' at the point of purchase to switch to Macleans. This may be away from the other labels (point 5) – particularly the own label brands – or from the shopper's usual Signal brand (point 6).

Point of sale will also work when the shopper is on their usual trip around the store but without a need in their mind for toothpaste. However, the point of sale promotion may generate an impulse purchase (point 7), where the promotion is such that the shopper drops Macleans into their trolley, happy that they have picked up a bargain.

10.2.1 Packaging

Packaging also has a very important part to play in this area. We have already seen (Section 3.7) that its role is much wider than simply containing and protecting goods during transit. At the point of sale packaging must make the following impact:

- Stand out clearly on the shelf.
- Be clearly identifiable, with the brand name strongly visible.
- Lend itself to building displays (a package that will not stack or is likely to topple or crush gives problems to the retailer's staff).

10.2.2 Merchandizing Staff

So important has this whole aspect of promotion become that many large retail chains have their own teams of 'merchandizers', whose job it is to create special promotions and displays that will create fast turnover and give the store an air of excitement. Similarly, many marketing organizations have created merchandizing teams as a special division of their sales staff. Salespeople secure the orders from the buying department at the retail chain's head office, and merchandizing staff then ensure that goods are well displayed and stock levels maintained in the individual stores. (This trend now shows signs of going into reverse with some large chains excluding manufacturers' staff and controlling their own displays etc., and this change appears to be continuing as the major retailers increase their dominance over their suppliers.)

10.3 The Importance of 'The Trade'

In most instances marketing organizations need the assistance of third parties to complete the distribution chain carrying their products to the customers. Wholesalers and retailers for consumer products, dealers and distributors for industrial products, importers and agents in international marketing, all have to be persuaded: (a) to stock the goods and (b) to promote them to their customers. These intermediaries are collectively referred to by the all-embracing term 'the trade'.

It is customary to speak of 'trade promotions' and 'consumer promotions'. The first type are aimed at encouraging the trade to stock and display the goods, the second at encouraging customers to buy a particular type of product or particular brand rather than an alternative, or at persuading customers to shop at one establishment rather than another. These two types of promotion, therefore, correspond to (a) and (b) above. They both bring in 'the trade', since consumer promotions normally operate through the trade and are dependent on them for their success. Also, of course, consumer promotions are themselves used as an incentive to the trade to stock and display the goods (so that they can be sure of benefiting from the extra sales the promotion is intended to generate). Thus, the two distinct types of promotion are, in fact, very closely linked.

10.3.1 Trade Promotions

Special promotions, particularly those in which some kind of discount is given, are often used to encourage the trade to carry stocks of a product. The discount can be in the form of straight cash or frequently as additional merchandise (thirteen bottles or cans for the normal price of a case of twelve, six cases for the price of five, or something similar). There is a school of thought (less prevalent than it once was) which believes in 'dealer loading' – on the basis that, if the dealer is loaded up with stock, he will have to exert himself to sell it to his customers. Clearly this can rebound on the manufacturer if the dealer in fact finds it difficult to unload the stock he has been induced to take. However, there are situations where, quite genuinely, the dealers need to be persuaded to carry extra stock, e.g. in preparation for a new product launch or a major consumer promotion.

Other types of promotion to the trade include incentives for dealers' staff, for example cash payments, holidays etc., to those responsible for achieving high sales levels. 'Mystery shoppers' may make cash payments to dealers who have the product in stock when they call or to staff who attempt to sell it to them. Window display and similar competitions encourage the display of particular products (but are now much less in evidence as national chains with their own merchandizing policies take over from the independents).

10.3.2 Sales Force Promotions

Just as the trade can be encouraged to stock a particular product or range and to give it display emphasis, so a company may wish to give incentives to its sales staff. Quite apart from various types of commission structure (see companion web pages) sales promotion techniques can be applied in this context. Thus points (or, for example, retail vouchers) can be awarded for meeting targets or quotas, winning competitions etc. Prizes can be goods for the salesman and his family (often selected from a lavish catalogue), or holidays.

10.3.3 Consumer Promotions

These can take a very wide variety of forms and the following list is just a selection of the more popular ones.

- **Premium offers**. The consumer receives a free gift, either with the purchase or by sending in packet tops, coupons or some similar device. Self-liquidating premiums are those where the consumer also sends in money, which covers the marketing organization's cost of providing the gift, though it still represents a bargain to the consumer.
- **Money-off**. A voucher or coupon can be used to obtain a reduction in price when making the next purchase of the same product or another one in the same manufacturer's range. Sometimes there is a money-off offer marked on the pack and relating to the immediate purchase.
- **Banded packs**. Two or more packs taped or wrapped together and offered at a reduced price are a variation on the theme.
- **Sampling**. At point of sale or by door to door delivery, sampling is obviously an attractive way of introducing suitable new products or achieving wider recognition of existing ones.
- **Personality promotions**. 'Resting' actors and actresses in appropriate costume are used as visiting personalities. They travel in decorated vehicles and visit various towns to draw attention to a particular product.
- **Competitions**. These can be used to attract attention, provide a new advertising theme and relieve the boredom associated with a product, referred to earlier. They can be quite complicated to organize, especially as legal restrictions apply to them. Their advantage is that the cost can be known in advance (as against, for example, money-off or premium offers, where the cost depends on the numbers taking up the offer). Attractive prizes can be offered (e.g. holidays), probably at relatively little cost, as the supplier of the prize (e.g. the tour operator) also gains from the publicity and may therefore be prepared to negotiate special deals.
- **Trading stamps or vouchers** (tokens issued with a purchase and redeemable against 'gifts' when enough have been collected). These have the advantage that they are relatively cheap

(and, in any case, represent a fixed outlay), and the whole organization is undertaken by the stamp company. They are particularly attractive to retailers, although some benefit is lost once local competitors issue stamps or cut prices substantially. (Trading stamps in the UK virtually disappeared during the 1980s, probably due to their very success: when most garages or supermarkets offer stamps their competitive value is lost. More recently they have started to re-appear.) Today, they are replaced by collect cards (such as BP Premier Points) where 'tokens' are accumulated onto a plastic card and earn discounts against purchases – in BP's case, from Argos catalogues and stores.

- **Sponsorship**. This means contributing to sporting events, the arts etc., in order to gain 'spin-off'. For example, advertising displays on football stadium fences or on racing cars often get a good showing to wide audiences if the event is televised. Supporting the arts may cause the company to be mentioned in a favourable context in important media.

10.3.4 Industrial Promotions

Sales promotion tends to be associated with consumer products marketing, but similar techniques are used in industrial marketing also. Special discounts and introductory offers are very common, as are competitions with prizes (free holidays are a favourite) for the customer's staff, 'give-aways' such as diaries, calendars, pens and calculators, annual golf or racing parties for customers; and yachts or holiday villas where a customer's staff are entertained. Sponsorship of sporting events will frequently be linked with this kind of activity. Such activities are often more *ad hoc*, less strictly evaluated and less likely to be part of a coherent plan than is the case with consumer promotions.

10.4 Evaluating Sales Promotion

As with all promotional activities, sales promotion is difficult to evaluate, but the attempt must be made. First and foremost, of course, it is, as ever, essential to be clear what the purpose of the particular sales promotion activity being evaluated is. If we cannot be sure what this is, we certainly have no chance of measuring how effective the promotion has been.

It is generally accepted that the effect of any promotional activity is likely to follow an S-curve (Figure 10.2), where increases in promotional expenditure increase the number of buyers. However, beyond a certain point, the returns from additional expenditure start to decrease.

It is rarely possible, however, to relate actual purchases so directly to levels of expenditure and, normally, we need to measure some other dependent variable. There are a number of possible variables that might be evaluated in order to gain a measure of the success of the promotion:

- Number of 'promoted' units taken up.
- Number of new users who repeat purchase.
- Profit per promoted unit and profit for those un-promoted units that can be ascribed to the promotion.

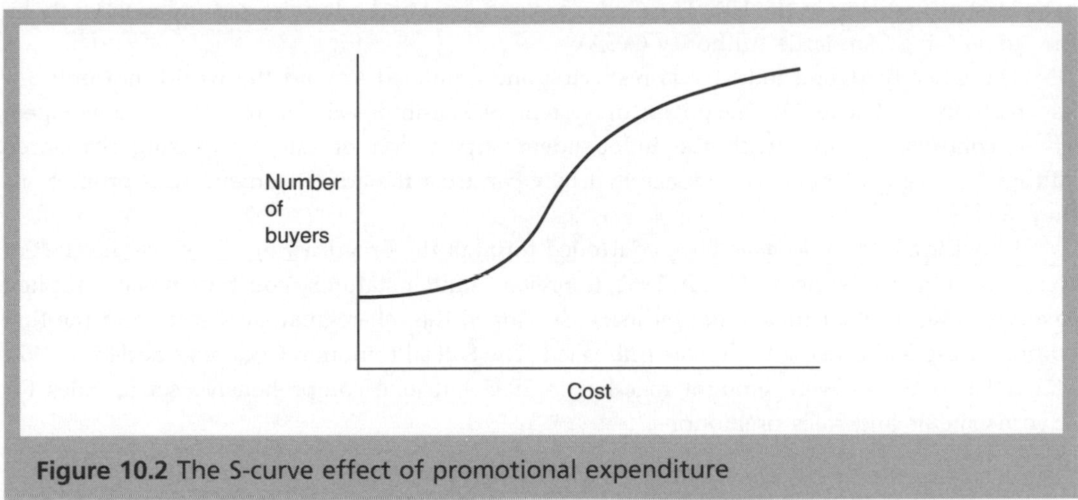

Figure 10.2 The S-curve effect of promotional expenditure

- Attitudes (short- and long-term) towards the brand (product) among actual and potential users.
- Ascribable profit from both new and former users who take up the promotion.
- Ascribable sales and profit against promotional cost.
- Distribution and display increases, increases in impulse buying, and sales, trade and consumer goodwill.

One could elaborate on this list, allocating the labels 'strategic' or 'tactical' to each item, and then examine ways of measuring each. Conducting research to determine the effectiveness of sales promotion is a viable, but difficult, field to work in since the cost of the research may negate the advantage of the promotion in the first place.

It is enough for our purposes to say that, clearly, while the first item on the above list is easy enough to measure, measuring many of the others will necessitate quite sophisticated research techniques. There is a further complication. Sales promotion is rarely carried on completely in a vacuum – other forms of promotion will be happening simultaneously. There is then frequently a synergistic effect, i.e. the collective effect of the various forms of promotion is greater than their individual effects simply added together (2 + 2 = 5, as it has been graphically put). This simply reinforces the difficulty of measurement; it does not mean we should not make the attempt.

10.5 Controlling Promotions[ii]

The Committee of Advertising Practice (CAP) is the industry body that creates, revises and enforces the British Codes of Advertising and Sales Promotion – the rules that apply to nonbroadcast advertising in the UK. The Codes are endorsed and administered independently by the Advertising Standards Authority (ASA).

The UK advertising industry is respected and emulated around the world, not only for its creativity, but also for the powerful system of self-imposed controls it has developed. These controls, together with the independent supervision of the Advertising Standards Authority, give consumers confidence that they can trust the advertisements and promotions they see.

Television and radio have been controlled through the Broadcasting Act since the start of commercial broadcasting in 1955. In 1961, to prevent similar statutory constraints being applied to advertising in other media, the industry developed the self-regulatory system and the first edition of the Advertising Code was published. The Sales Promotion Code was added in 1974 and the two Codes were brought together in 1995 into one comprehensive set of rules for advertisements and sales promotions.

10.6 Loyalty Schemes

Loyalty cards have been one of the marketing stories of the 1990s. In the UK, many retailers and other service companies have developed so-called loyalty cards as part of their marketing mix. In essence, the customer is given a card for free in return for some specific geo-demographic data (see Chapter 3). When that customer makes purchases that qualify for a reward (usually not including tobacco or alcohol products) the reward 'token' is collected on the card's magnetic strip. The issuing company sometimes also keeps a detailed record of the purchases made by the customer on their own systems. This then offers the opportunity for the organization to personalize promotions to the customer in accordance with their known purchasing habits.

It seems that, within the last few years, almost everyone has looked to launch a card scheme. By counting only the supermarket loyalty cards to the end of 2001, 23 million cards had been issued in the last two years alone. Today, according to Mintel, about 63 per cent of adults participate in a loyalty scheme run by one of the leading retailers. However, in the UK more than 40 per cent of us have more than one card in two different competitive retailers. We can shop in a number of competing retailers in the knowledge that we will be rewarded, regardless of how often and how much we purchase.

With so many in circulation, it is necessary to ask how much value retailers add with these cards. Too often, it appears that these loyalty schemes are viewed from a supply perspective only, with the cards representing a way of collecting customer data and enabling more closely targeted marketing programmes to be developed. However, little seems to be done to identify what customers really want from the schemes. Through analysing marketing issues from both the demand and supply perspectives, looking at how consumer, brand and marketplace forces of change work together, it is seen that none of these operate on their own. It is, therefore, important to understand how they come together to be able to develop the best solutions to customer needs. Perhaps loyalty schemes would be more effective if they were taken to the next level, beyond simple point collection and money-off schemes.

10.7 Exhibitions

Trade exhibitions, such as the Motor Show and the Ideal Home Exhibition, are a form of promotional activity that enables marketing organizations to show, and frequently to demonstrate, their products to their ultimate customers without needing retailers or other 'middlemen' to do it for them. Industrial exhibitions such as the Packaging Exhibition and the Plastics Exhibition provide a source of 'captive' potential customers for particular groups of materials or equipment.

However, exhibitions are a very expensive form of promotion. Not only does the cost of building an exhibition stand run into many thousands of pounds at a major exhibition, but there are also other 'hidden costs'. The exhibition will have to be staffed, with consequent loss of normal calls by salesmen; visitors have to be entertained; large quantities of special sales literature must generally be provided; and, for technical shows especially, moving and installing demonstration equipment can be very costly.

This does not mean that exhibitions are not a worthwhile activity, but that some hard-headed questions must be asked as to whether the return will be worth the cost – questions such as the following:

- What kind of people will attend?
- How many visitors do we actually want to our exhibition stand?
- And what do we want them there for? To demonstrate something to them or to gain information from them?
- Are they in a position to buy our products, or just recommend?
- What results do we expect – actual sales or merely an additional opportunity for publicity?
- What kind of follow-up action do we need to take in order to benefit fully?

The last is a particularly important point. It is rare for sales to be concluded at an exhibition; more often it is merely a fairly superficial contact, which must be followed through hard if any business is to result. Because of these considerations, many companies explore other ways of achieving contact with customers – their own 'mini-exhibitions' in a suitable hotel; a travelling caravan, boat or even train; open days at the factory; special seminars and symposia.

Like all forms of publicity, exhibitions must be part of a carefully worked out plan and not embarked upon simply 'because our competitors will be there'. Similarly, great care must be taken to evaluate results (difficult because of the long-term and diffused nature of the outcome) in order to be sure that the money was well spent.

10.8 Direct Mail

By direct mail we mean promotional material sent through the post to selected individuals or companies. It is often confused with mail order – the ordering by post of goods usually advertised in the press or in catalogues. For the full picture, see Chapter 8.

10.9 Public Relations

Much ink (and probably some blood) has been spilt trying to assign public relations its correct position in relation to marketing and promotion. As is so often the case with such arguments, semantics are a large part of the problem. The letters PR are used to mean 'public relations' and also 'press relations', and these two are not the same.

Press relations (more accurately media relations) is the process and technique of providing information to the press and also to radio and television.

Public relations is the much wider activity of communicating with the many groups of people who constitute an organization's public. (The term 'publics' is often used in recognition that each group may need such special treatment that they are best treated separately.) These groups include shareholders, employees, local communities, government departments and many others, as well as suppliers, customers and other 'trading' contacts. An organization or company that has established a good relationship with all its 'publics' will find it much easier to launch new ventures and will have a firmer base from which to deal with any difficulties or disasters.

To communicate effectively with all of these may call for the use of films, house journals, advertising and many other media, as well as the use of press relations activity. The subjects on which communication takes place will also be very broad, so that public relations in this full sense is far more than just an aspect of the marketing activity.

Similarly, press relations can be used in a variety of ways, not simply to supply information about products. However, it is often a vital method of promotion, especially in the case of new products. For car manufacturers it is just as important to get their new model into the motoring sections of the press as it is to launch an advertising campaign. Similarly, technical products rely heavily on being 'written-up' in the technical journals.

New products, especially if they involve new technologies (such as genetic engineering) or achieve things which could not be done before (such as a new drug) are often newsworthy and hence may be featured in the editorial columns of the press or in radio and TV programmes or news broadcasts.

As well as making products widely known (at no direct cost, by contrast with advertising which would often cost a great deal to achieve the same coverage) products featured in this way carry the authority and independent endorsement of the publication or feature writer or the broadcast channel or presenter. It is, of course, possible for this to backfire. The newspaper or TV programme may not like the product or may highlight its less desirable features. But good products offering genuine benefits are more likely to gain than to suffer.

Products that are no longer new may, of course, find it more difficult to be featured in this way. Then we have to look for such things as:

- **Application stories** – new ways in which the product is being used, new problems it is solving ('XYZ adhesive overcomes space shuttle ceramic tiles problem').
- **Orders and expansions** – large overseas contracts, new factories providing employment.
- **Visits** – royalty or other visiting dignitaries seen using the products ('President tries his hand with ABC Bulldozer').
- **Sponsorship** – (see next section).

Like all forms of promotion PR must be conducted on a planned, systematic basis. The following seven-step sequence is a useful approach:

1. **State the problem or aims**. The task could be to launch a new product, inform or remotivate the sales force or encourage a favourable attitude amongst potential customers.
2. **Do the research** to establish the facts about the present situation.
3. **Identify the public**. Decide who you need to talk to and what you need to say to them.
4. **Choose the appropriate media**. This could be anything from TV to newsletters, conferences to films, depending on the objective and the public concerned.
5. **Monitor the effects** to make sure the message is being received and understood in the way intended.
6. **Look to the future** – PR is never 'finished' but always part of a continuing, changing situation.
7. **Maintain financial checks** at all stages to ensure the operation is cost-effective.

The biggest danger with all promotional activity is that it will be conducted on a piecemeal basis. This is a special danger with some of the techniques referred to in this chapter. Yet to treat them as individual events is to risk losing the full return on what is often considerable outlay. We have referred earlier in this chapter to the synergistic effect. A far greater return is likely if personal selling, advertising and all other promotional activities are planned in detail as part of a totally integrated marketing campaign. Then each activity reinforces and is reinforced by all the others: the sales force is trained to seize the openings created by advertising, which is opening the way for them, exhibitions are used to generate 'leads', which are fed to the salespeople – and so on.

10.10 Sponsorship

Increasing sums of money are being invested by organizations of all types and sizes in sponsoring sporting and cultural activities. Thus, something that could once have been regarded perhaps as a minor PR medium is rapidly becoming a distinct and important form of promotion in its own right. The reasons for this perhaps include a desire to contribute to the good of society (and to be recognized as doing so).

Usually, however, there are more specific objectives involved. For example, the advertising of cigarettes on television is forbidden. So, by sponsoring sporting activities such as cricket (e.g. 'the Benson & Hedges Cup'), the manufacturers were able to retain their presence on TV, together with many mentions of their names in a wide range of other media. At the same time, they stood to gain from the association of the brand name with an activity which has healthy connotations, and their contribution to its success is seen by many as a laudable activity. Others, of course, took the view that such contributions amount to a somewhat cynical flaunting of the spirit of the law. This resulted in changes to legislation in the UK by the Labour Government banning the sponsorship of sports by the tobacco companies – save for Formula One motor racing!

Often the link between sponsors and the activity concerned is much more direct, such as oil companies and motor racing or sports wear manufacturers and tennis, and the potential benefits of such an association are obvious.

10.11 Price Promotions

Many people think of price discounts as the obvious way to increase sales. However, as the following straightforward example demonstrates, a simple price cut is not necessarily going to help boost sales sufficiently to retain profit margins.

Let us suppose that a high street chemist buys, say, hair spray at £2.50 a can and usually sells them at £5.00. In any given period they may sell, say, 50 cans. Their gross profit is 50 × £2.50 or £125.00 in the period. Now, if they offered a 10 per cent discount to stimulate sales, how many more cans would they have to sell at the discounted price to make the same gross profit before the 10 per cent price cut? Ten per cent more or maybe 15 per cent?

Let us look at the figures. The new selling price is 10 per cent down on £5.00 – or £4.50. Their profit per can is now £2.00 (since they have still had to buy them at £2.50 per can). So, if they only make £2.00 a can, then they will have to sell 62.5 cans to equal the £125.00 gross profit achieved before the price cut (62.5 × £2.00 = £125.00). Now, 63 cans are 26% more than the 50 the chemist sold at the old price.

Such simple price discounts are easy for the chemist to manage and the customer to understand. Naturally, there are a whole variety of promotions that the shopkeeper might have used to stimulate sales without compromising unit margins quite so much. Alternatively, he (or she) could have created promotions to ensure the necessary volume increases to cover for the lower profit margins.

Where price fits into the marketing mix will be discussed in Chapter 14.

10.11.1 Confusion Marketing

Price discounts have been such as to create an 'everyday low price' culture in Britain. However, when it comes to price structures, many companies appear to have deliberately set out to confuse customers, swamping them with data on pricing, discounts, payment schemes, and so forth, all of which seem to be for the customers' benefit but which, in effect, prevent them from making an informed choice. The aim it seems is to frustrate and confuse, making it impossible for people to accurately compare prices and thereby tempting them to choose on the basis of the brands they know and trust rather than price *per se*.

It seems that some strong brands have a major incentive to confuse customers, as it forces them to make decisions based on brand value, not value for money. In other words, it leads people to buy what they feel comfortable with rather than what might be the most cost-effective. In some areas, there is confusion because the product is complex – like financial services – but in others the complexity is invented purely to stifle out competition.

This practice seems to be most prevalent in sectors where former, incumbent, semi-monopolistic suppliers are now, through deregulation, up against an array of new competitors. Where the new supplier offers lower prices, the incumbent blitzes its customers with an array of price offers that suggest better value for money but which, in reality, make true comparisons hard. This is so-called 'confusion marketing'.

VIGNETTE

Making Things Clearer

Some would say that BT has a deliberate strategy to confuse its customers and has used it to good effect when other telephone companies started to woo them. With up to eight price plans changed roughly every six months, even if the customer is given a chart with all their discount packages, it is likely that few would have the time to work them out. Confusion marketing then creates inertia in the customer base so that they stay with their current brand, and plays on people's laziness over researching rival offers.

Confusion marketing seems to have helped BT and British Gas retain more customers than would have been expected after the arrival of aggressive new competitors. According to a research poll by MORI, after more than ten years of competition, fewer than 12 per cent of residential customers have switched away from BT. Similarly, after three years of competition, British Gas is estimated to have lost fewer then 25 per cent of its customers to rival suppliers.

To be fair, in early 2001, BT simplified its offers under a single discount brand call 'BT Together'. Most of the existing consumer calling packages have been set aside and the new service allows customers to make unlimited local calls in return for a monthly flat fee. As well as simplifying its product range, BT is also counteracting the accusation of confusion by supporting the customer-focused initiatives such as Oftel's telephone price comparison website, www.phonebills.org.uk. The site calculates the cheapest supplier according to the user's typical usage. Apparently, this shows BT performing consistently well compared to its rivals.

Question

1. Consider your – or a colleague's – telephone network suppliers' bill. How clear do you feel the information on their charges is compared with other suppliers, like gas or electricity? Are they better, worse, or the same?

CASE STUDY

Confusion marketing is rife in the current travel market. Some travel brands lure customers with bargains that subsequently prove hard to buy. Going Places, the holiday travel company, offered significant savings on holidays, yet they were very limited offers and only of use to people with extremely flexible holiday arrangements. Ryanair, a low-fare airline, ran into conflict with easyJet and British Airways. In December 2000, Ryanair was taken to court by British Airways who accused the budget airline of 'malicious falsehood' in an advertising campaign in which BA and Ryanair fares were compared. In this instance, Ryanair's fare claims were not found to be misleading, However, in January 2002, Ryanair was reprimanded by the Advertising Standards Authority (ASA) for an advertisement about cheap flights. A newspaper advertisement featured a one-way flight to London Stansted for £19.99, and another to Paris for £29.99. It then stated the offer was for 'every seat on every flight', before adding in small print at the bottom that tickets were subject to conditions and a weekend supplement. Similarly, British Airways' low-cost airline Go was criticized for misleading passengers over the cost of its flights. Again, the ASA was involved and upheld two complaints against the company from rival easyJet. The Luton-based airline objected to an advertisement in which Go promised motor racing fans that its highest fare to Nice for the forthcoming Monaco Grand Prix was more than '40 per cent less than easyJet'. ASA officials said that, from the way the advert was worded, readers were 'unlikely' to realize that the saving only applied when comparing both airlines' top prices. As we can see, the case illustrates that bargain pricing and confusion are never far apart.

Question

1. In what way do you feel that the Advertising Standards Authority have a role in limiting confusion marketing in travel markets?

While some marketers might be using confusion marketing to their advantage, others frequently make fighting complexity the basis of their customer appeal. Virgin has been able to enter complex markets as a self-styled consumers' champion. Virgin moved into the mobile phone market behind a 'simplicity marketing' strategy. Although there seemed to be a comfortable relationship among established companies in the mobile phone market, confusion was rife. Virgin's tariff was much simpler and the company captured 500,000 customers in the first year of trading. They have been able to do the same with their Virgin Direct and VirginOne brands in the notoriously complex financial services sector.

As the 'rip off Britain' phrase and fuel blockades of autumn 2000 show, consumers are increasingly willing to respond if they feel they are not getting a fair deal. Whether that is with energy supplies or high car prices, consumers are becoming more demanding as they become more informed. The Internet allows consumers to be more informed about price comparisons more quickly and easily. Indeed, the Internet is perhaps the biggest factor driving simplicity.

However, while the Internet helps simplify many things, the fact that it is attracting new brands into areas like financial services and travel is contributing to confusion. While this may be as a result of increased choice, sometimes it arises from less innocent motives. Halifax attracted criticism in early 2001 from the launch of its IF (Intelligent Finance) brand. While, on the one hand, it offered attractive interest rates on its current account, it had more significant charges in other areas like overdraft fees.

Another trend in the market that may create new areas of confusion is the so-called 'share of customer' strategy. Brands that have a single product or sector relationship with a large number of customers – such as utilities, banks and supermarkets – are expanding to capture more of a single customer's spend. Tesco moving into financial services, British Gas into telephone services, and Egg (Internet banking) into car insurance are all examples. This share of customer strategy will tempt organizations to put together product packages for their customers in which individual product costs are obscured. New confusion will arise in which it is difficult for customers to understand whether they are getting better value from one package or another.

Perhaps this will give rise to a cyclical swing back to individual product-type providers – expect that to occur around 2010!

10.12 Corporate Hospitality Marketing Trends

Corporate hospitality these days is often much more than an alcohol-fuelled day at a top sporting event. Clients are increasingly looking for something more exciting and adventurous, such as riding the waves on a jet-ski, piloting a four-wheel drive vehicle across a muddy field or parachuting out of an aircraft. They have 'done' Ascot, Wimbledon, Twickenham, the Open golf championship and the test matches, and want to boast about something different when they get back to the office.

The trend now seems to be towards activity and adventure in corporate hospitality and it can be much cheaper than traditional events. Seats for the men's final at Wimbledon, for example, can cost around £2000 each, while giving people the chance to drive a Ferrari for a day comes in at about £200. For a group of clients, the cost can be as little as £35 a head for a full day's activity, although flights and hotel accommodation can push this up to between £500 and £600. Clients relish the challenge of something new, such as test-driving cars on a racetrack, and it seems that such events are enjoyed by both sexes.

However, the experience must be tailored to the client and aligned to the brand so that the company's image is strengthened. An important objective of any hospitality event is to communicate the brand as well as deliver an important event.

Summary

- Advertising is the term used to describe 'paid-for' messages of all kinds in media owned and controlled by people other than the advertiser.
- Sales promotion activities, on the other hand, use tools and media controlled directly by the advertiser.
- Sales promotion is normally tactical (whereas advertising is mainly strategic) and concentrated at point of sale.
- Sales promotion can be used to: (a) encourage dealers to stock, (b) encourage customers to try, (c) combat competition, (d) improve distribution and (e) add excitement.

- Sales promotion has been defined as a 'non-recurring and non-routine sales activity'.
- Although often treated as only an insignificant part of the 'below the line' advertising budget, it can be a very important activity.
- Sales promotion is frequently used to give a short-term boost to sales of a particular product. It is usually concentrated at the point of sale.
- It is much used to gain the support of the trade, either directly through 'trade promotions' or indirectly through 'consumer promotions'.
- Sales promotion techniques can also be used to generate a higher level of sales force activity.
- Evaluating the effectiveness of sales promotion is a vital activity but a difficult one, especially in view of the synergistic effect.
- Exhibitions, direct mail and public relations are important methods of marketing communication.
- All promotional activity must be part of an integrated marketing campaign.
- Sometimes price promotion activity may deliberately confuse customers.

References

i *Winkler on Marketing Planning* (Cassell/Associated Business Programmes, 1972).
ii Information based on freely available web pages of The Committee of Advertising Practice.

Further Reading

Ace, Cathy. *Successful Marketing Communications* (Butterworth-Heinemann, 2001). Ideal for students who need to gain practical insight into promotional planning and implementation.

Wilmshurst, John and Mackay, Adrian. *The Fundamentals of Advertising* (Butterworth-Heinemann, 2nd Edition, 1999). A general study of the whole subject at a basic level and contains many up to date facts and figures.

Questions

1. What types of sales promotion might be appropriate in selling the following products/services?

   (a) Mobile telephones.
   (b) Banking services for university students.
   (c) Do-it-yourself gardening products.

2. What kind of point-of-sale advertising material and displays would you recommend for the following?

   (a) Children's toys such as train sets and electric racing cars.

(b) Motor car accessories.

(c) Expensive cosmetics.

(d) Moderately priced hi-fi equipment.

(e) Office calculators.

3. 'Public relations is an intrinsic part of the marketing mix.' Do you support this statement? What arguments would you use to defend and oppose it? Include in your answer a clear definition of the main areas of public relations.

4. In what ways can sales promotional activities be used to support or encourage the marketing efforts of distributors or dealers? Illustrate your answer with practical examples.

Chapter 11

The practice of direct sales operations

Introduction

By the end of this chapter you will:

- Understand the role and importance of personal selling as a key ingredient in the promotional mix.
- Have a grasp of the nature of the selling process and what it entails.
- Appreciate the qualities needed by a salesperson and the wide range of different selling situations they may encounter.
- Have an insight into the complexities of the selling process.
- Be aware of what is involved in the successful selection, training and motivation of salespeople.

'When all the theorists and planners have had their moment and the production, finance and labour problems have been solved . . . then someone, somewhere has to go out and knock on someone's door and sell.'

L. A. Rogers. *Sales Management*

11.1 The Importance of Personal Selling

We saw in Section 7.4 that, although advertising and related forms of promotion can often communicate with customers far more cheaply, personal selling still (normally) has a more important role. This is mainly for two reasons:

1. Personal selling can deal with the whole of the selling process from making initial contact with a customer to closing the deal and taking the money. Other forms of promotion rarely can.
2. The person to person situation is far more flexible than other forms of promotion. An advertisement can only deliver a standard message to the average customer, but trained salesmen and women can establish each customer's individual needs and frequently can help to shape the product to fit these needs. At worst they can highlight those attributes of an existing product that fit in particularly well with the customer's requirements, and thus score heavily over alternative, impersonal methods of persuasive contact.

We also saw in Section 7.4 that the terms 'selling' and 'salesperson' embrace a very wide range of different situations. At one end of the spectrum is the dairy or bakery delivery person, whose task is primarily to deliver the goods and take the money. At the other end we have the highly qualified salesperson of technical products, who may help to establish the precise need and then join with designers or technicians in developing the product. There will sometimes be a need for 'creative' selling, in order to capture the imagination of customers and show how their needs can be better met in ways not previously considered (for example, by a numerically controlled machine tool or new materials' handling systems that will substantially cut production costs).

In Section 11.3 we consider the qualities called for in selling of this professional and creative kind. But, as stated already, that there is a wide range of selling jobs, and we will come back to this in Section 11.4.

11.1.1 Who Needs Salespeople?

It can be argued that, if the marketing job has been done properly, there is no need for the selling function. If customers' needs have been properly established through marketing research, if technical research and development have produced a product that meets those needs, and if a sound distribution system has been established to make the product readily available to customers, who needs a salesperson?

A supermarket, for example, appears to present a picture from which the salesperson is totally missing. The customers select their own purchases from the shelves without advice or persuasion from anyone except the advertiser. However, selling is still of enormous importance. Salespeople will have worked very hard to ensure that their companies' products are bought in large quantities by the buying departments of the supermarket chains, since many alternative sources of similar products are usually available. Other salespeople (perhaps with a different name, such as 'merchandizers') will have worked with each store manager to get the best position and the most eye-catching display possible for their companies' products. The salespeople are there – even though unseen to the casual observer.

11.1.2 The Role of the Salesperson

There are, in fact, a number of jobs that have to be done, and frequently only the salespeople can do them, even when the marketing task has been thoroughly and carefully carried through and a product that does match the need has been developed. One important reason for this is that very few purchases are made on purely objective criteria. Certainly a product will need to do the task expected of it satisfactorily, but with most consumer products and very many industrial products this is virtually taken for granted. The customer is then choosing from a whole range of products, any one of which will do the job. Other factors then come into the picture.

Thus, visual design, colour and 'appearance' generally have great importance, even with industrial products. Concepts such as reliability are partly a matter of objective assessment, but include such subjective factors as 'Can I trust this company to put it right if anything goes wrong?'.

The role of the salesperson, therefore, includes the following:

- **To understand the customer's subjective (psychological) needs and to demonstrate how their products will satisfy them**. In some cases (such as life assurance) customers may initially have only the vaguest idea what their specific requirements are, and the salesperson will have to work it out for them.
- **To negotiate**. Very often there is a gap between the price being asked for a product and what the customer is willing to pay. The easy way to close the gap is to cut the price, but profit is then sacrificed. The salesperson can solve the problem in another way, which is to enhance the value of the product by demonstrating its particular benefits to the customer and showing how paying a higher price will bring additional value. In some cases (such as cars and certain industrial equipment) the negotiation will frequently necessitate agreeing a 'trade in' price for the customer's present model. In this situation, the salesperson also functions as a buyer.
- **Two-way communication**. The company needs to communicate information to its customers. Often the salesperson is the most effective channel (letters, leaflets and other written communications may never be read, partly because they are likely to be couched in general terms rather than speaking directly to the customer's particular situation). The company also needs feedback from its customers – what pleases them and what annoys them about the service being provided, what are their future plans and what opportunities for profitable sales will these offer?

11.2 The Selling Process

We saw in Section 2.1 that the mechanisms of the buying process are not yet clearly understood, although the section went on to summarize some of the complex factors known to be involved. Similarly, the selling process is not totally understood. Communication is part of it (Sections 7.5 and 9.13.1), as is persuasion directed to the changing of attitudes (Section 2.4).

Much of the literature on the subject suggests that most theories on the selling process are 'experiential', i.e. they are based on experience of what is known to work, rather than any understanding of why and how it works.

One of the 'experiential' theories most commonly used is the AIDAS idea, outlined in Section 9.13.1, which can help to describe the personal selling process as well as the advertising one. However, AIDAS does not explain in any depth how the process works. Another is the 'buying formula' theory, which puts the emphasis on the buyer, who is seen as having a clear understanding of a problem he or she is trying to solve. The salesperson's role is then to help the buyer towards a satisfactory solution, as follows:

Need (problem) ⇒ Solution ⇒ Purchase ⇒ Satisfaction

11.2.1 Organizational Buying Process

A very traditional model has been established that has stood the test of time. It gives clear direction to the marketer of industrial products to ensure that each stage of the process is addressed in order to ensure customer satisfaction. Robinson *et al.*[i] identified eight stages of the industrial buying process and called them 'buy phases' (see Figure 11.1):

1. **Problem recognition** – The process begins when an individual in a company identifies a need that must be met. This may arise from a variety of influences including machine malfunction, lack of productivity and competitive benchmarking, or from salespeople, direct marketing by the supplier organization or perhaps an exhibition. The bottom line is the need for a better product or service, or a lower price.
2. **General needs description** – In order to meet the need identified, the buyer determines the general characteristics and quantity of the needed item. Users and specifiers in the organization are often involved; sometimes influencers who may be external to the organization

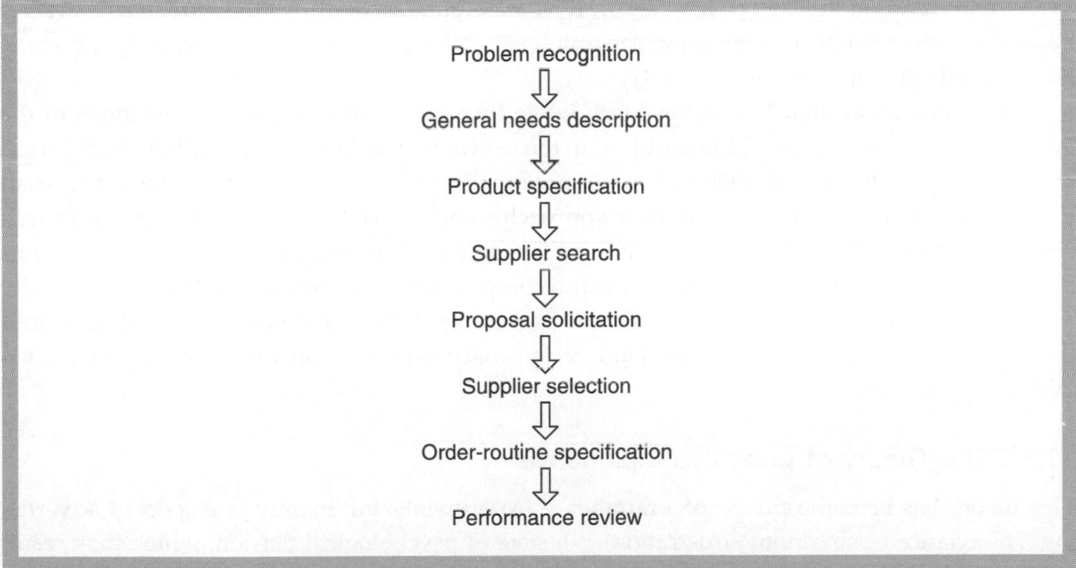

Figure 11.1 Robinson's eight-stage buy phases of organizational buying processes

may also be involved – particularly in technology markets. (See Section 11.5.1 on the decision-making unit or DMU.)

3. **Product specification** – Involves the development of a technical specification for the product, ensuring that it fulfils the need identified and is compatible with the organization. At this stage, the original problem recognition may be modified in the light of further information.
4. **Supplier search** – Involves searching for suppliers that can meet the area of need, from which a short list is developed.
5. **Proposal solicitation** – The buyer will invite short-listed suppliers to submit proposals. This may involve discussion with salespeople and other technical specialists. Again, at this stage, the original problem recognition may be modified in the light of further information. The salespeople have a key role in establishing how their offer differentiates themselves from the competition.
6. **Supplier selection** – This is based on their ability to meet the attributes sought by the decision-making unit of the buyer organization. Factors such as technical capability, product reliability, delivery times, price, support services and reputation may all come into play.
7. **Order-routine specification** – The buyer now writes the final order/contract document with the supplier.
8. **Performance review** – Actual performance is compared with initial specifications. The result of this evaluation becomes feedback for the other stages and will influence future purchase decisions.

The above model may appear simplistic compared to other authors' more complex models developed since. However, this is part of its great strength as it clarifies rather than over-complicates the process. The eight stages represent the typical steps in an industrial purchase; in any real situation more steps may occur. It is, therefore, essential that the industrial marketer researches and models each situation separately. Only in this way can the salespeople become the most effective in their sales activity.

However, all approaches of this kind, while they help one to appreciate the steps in the buying/selling process, give little insight into the psychology of buying and selling. Therefore, a much more complex model (such as that suggested in Section 2.1) is necessary to demonstrate all the factors that may play a part. Simplistic approaches such as AIDAS or the eight-stage approach above have their main value in sales training. They help the salespeople to organize their actions better, without expecting them to grasp the full complexity of why people react the way they do.

A fuller understanding is likely to come eventually through the behavioural sciences and the following two examples of this kind of approach will give an indication of what may eventually emerge.

11.2.2 The Theory of Cognitive Dissonance

This theory has been the subject of a number of experiments, but mainly in respect of advertising. Dissonance (disharmony, frustration) is a state of psychological tension, which may result from purchasing a product, especially if it is an expensive one. People try to keep their 'cognitions' (their set of beliefs about people, products etc.) in a state of harmony. When a choice has been made between several products, the buyer may experience 'cognitive dissonance' through anxiety and doubt as to whether the product will perform as expected and whether the expenditure was wise. An important part of the salesperson's task is to reassure the buyer that their decision was sound and to re-emphasize the benefits the purchase will bring. Car sales staff generally do this instinctively or through experience when, as their customer takes delivery, they make remarks such as: 'This car will give you thousands of miles of happy motoring, Madam; you and your partner are really going to enjoy travelling in it.'

11.2.3 The Buyer–Seller Dyad

Here, the salesperson and the customer are viewed as a 'dyad', that is a social situation involving two persons, and the essence of the selling process is the interaction between the two. An important finding of studies on this theory is that the more alike the salesperson and the prospect are, the greater likelihood of a sale (this is true not only for physical characteristics such as age and height but also for such factors as education, politics, smoker or non-smoker). Particularly interesting is the fact that people who have bought from salesmen or women tend to see them as more like themselves than is in fact the case.

11.3 What Makes a Salesperson?

The sales arena contains many specialists and involves a widely varied set of disciplines, apart from its main task of achieving orders.

As a group, salespeople include the sales administrators who manage the complex business of integrating the activities of what may be a large number of people – particularly in a telesales operation. The people involved may include:

- **Sales trainers.**
- **Sales promotion specialists** – responsible for co-ordination programmes of promotional activities that support the selling function.
- **Sales merchandizing specialists** – who develop support materials to be used by both the direct sales team and also distribution intermediaries where they are used.
- **Invoice control and processing functions** – often including credit control.
- **Order monitoring** – often part of the customer service function.
- **Customer service** – dealing with queries and complaints.

With the development of information technology, many of these activities have been mechanized so that when a customer places an order – as one might online on the Internet – an order confirmation is returned to the customer via e-mail instantly. When the order is despatched via the mail, again a confirmation is generated automatically.

Those who are actually selling (the field sales force) have tasks that vary widely from market to market. Therefore qualifications, abilities and lifestyles differ significantly. There are also considerable differences of work and responsibility within any given sales force, where the hierarchy of general sales manager, regional sales manager, area sales manager and territory manager allows for greater and lesser responsibilities. Major customers may also need to be handled by more experienced managers ('key accounts managers') than the routine smaller customers.

In the light of what we have said so far, is it possible to list the attributes of a good salesperson? Only to some extent; mainly because the attributes required will vary enormously, depending on the kind of selling situation. For example, in many industrial selling jobs a high degree of technical competence will be necessary. Moreover, special qualities will be needed for a man or woman who is expected to seek out his/her own 'prospects', as against one who has merely to call regularly on established buyers of their company's products.

It has been suggested that there are just two vital qualities required of salespeople:

1. **Empathy**. The ability to feel as the customer does.
2. **Ego drive**. A strong personal need to make the sale (not simply for monetary reward).

In many situations the ability to communicate effectively will be important, and in others some strong creative qualities will be necessary, in order to identify ways in which potential customers can benefit from the products available. Occasionally the tough-skinned, 'foot in the door', rather brash type of selling may be called for (perhaps still what comes to the minds of many as 'typical' salesmanship). But this is increasingly rare, as the general level of sophistication of both products and customers rises.

11.4 Types of Selling Situation

We have already touched on the fact that there are many different kinds of selling situation. A variety of different 'positions' have been identified:

- Positions where the salesperson's job is **predominantly to deliver the product**, for example milk, bread or fuel – their selling responsibilities are secondary. Obviously good service and a pleasant manner will enhance customer acceptance and hence lead to more sales. However, few originate many sales.
- Positions where the salesperson is **predominantly an inside order-taker**, for example the salesperson standing behind the counter at the DIY superstore – most customers have already made up their minds what they wish to buy. All this person does is serve them. They may use suggestive selling and upgrade the merchandize being bought, but their opportunities and indeed their motivation to do so are limited.
- Positions where the salesperson is also **predominantly an order-taker but works in the field**, as some web-page design companies have provided the small to medium sized enterprise business community of late. In their contacts with business people, they may even actually be discouraged from applying the hard sell. As with the delivery salesperson, good service and a pleasant personality may enhance their personal acceptance, but they too do little creative selling.
- Positions where the salesperson is **not expected or permitted to take an order** but is called on only to build good will or to educate the actual or potential user. Examples include the

medical representative representing an ethical pharmaceutical company to GPs or hospital doctors.

- Positions where the **major emphasis is placed on technical knowledge**, for example the engineering salesperson who is primarily a consultant to the 'client' companies.
- Positions which demand the **creative sale of tangible products** particularly in the business-to-business technology sectors. Here the salesperson often has a double task: first they must make the prospect dissatisfied with his or her present appliance or situation, and then begin to sell their product.
- Positions requiring the **creative sale of intangibles**, such as insurance, advertising services or education. This type of sales is ordinarily more difficult than selling tangibles, because the product is less readily demonstrated and dramatized. (Intangibles are often more difficult for the prospect to comprehend.)

While there are more complex categorizations of sales position, the fundamental issue is the type and complexity of the buying process, the basis of the exchange transaction, and the type of ongoing customer relationship sought. Today, much of the sales process is being mechanized and automated to gain speed on the one hand and improve scalability to drive down cost on the other. More will be said of the management of the sales function in Chapter 17.

11.5 What a Salesperson Does

It will be clear from what has gone before that the job of a salesperson may include many different tasks and call for many different skills. They will normally have to drive a car and organize their journeys; write reports and keep accurate records. They may need to analyse their territory and pinpoint good prospective customers. They may deliver goods, set up in-store displays, expedite deliveries from the factory and deal with customers' complaints. Certainly, in most instances, they will be responsible for ensuring a continuing happy relationship with customers rather than just conducting a 'once and for all' sale. Increasingly, keyboard and computer skills are needed to enable salespeople to deliver reports and access information 'down the line'.

Even apart from all these peripheral duties, the selling process is a complex one that may include some or all of the following stages:

1. **Creating effective contact at all levels**. In industrial selling particularly, the purchase will be influenced by a number of different people (a decision-making unit or DMU). Design engineer, works manager, buyer and finance director make up one typical DMU (see Section 11.5.1). The salesperson will need to identify and communicate with them all. In other cases, only individuals need be contacted, but they must be found from a wide population. Locating a householder who is currently in the market for a washing machine or a car is not easy. Where do you start?
2. **Establishing effective communication** with all the relevant people and in both directions to and from the seller's organization.
3. **Establishing the customer's needs**, which may include identifying problems the customer is not clearly aware of.

4. **Demonstrating how the company's product can satisfy those needs**, which may necessitate the full range of informative and persuasive techniques.
5. **Getting a profitable order**, which may mean detailed negotiations, arranging credit and bringing carefully calculated pressure to bear on the customer to 'close the sale'.
6. **Ensuring customer satisfaction**, by making certain that the right product is delivered on schedule and performs well, that installation is correctly carried out, and pre- and post-sales service is given (including perhaps such things as training customers or their staff to operate and maintain equipment).
7. **Creating goodwill** and a situation in which future business will develop.

In addition to all this, salespeople must be able to plan their own time and activities so that they are as productive as possible.

11.5.1 Decision-making Units

Identifying who are the members of a decision-making unit, what their precise role is and how they can be influenced is a most important aspect of the sales force task. Although this is especially true in industrial markets, it may well apply in other situations. For example, people selling insurance and double glazing know that it pays to talk to both husband and wife as both play a part in the decision to buy. Even in everyday purchases like breakfast cereals, various members of the household – especially children in this example – have a strong influence and this fact is recognized in the way such products are advertised.

Decision-making units may contain people in some (or even all) of the following categories:

- **Users**. Those who will actually operate the word processor, use the machine, or drive the truck; they may well be consulted by those authorizing the purchase and can certainly have a vital effect on post-purchase satisfaction and hence future sales.
- **Initiators**. The initiation of the decision process may be automatic, such as inventory running low, or it may be initiated by one individual identifying a potential need.
- **Buyers**. The professional purchasing people; their influence tends to be very strong with routine purchases (such as raw materials, standard components etc.) but other voices become more important if a high technical input is necessary or if heavy capital investment is involved.
- **Influencers**. People not obviously involved in the buying process may yet influence it strongly (e.g. doctors are unlikely to prescribe a drug not approved of by specialists and consultants).
- **Deciders**. Decisions may be taken 'down the line' for low-cost or routine purchases but are usually at top level for those where big money is involved; however, there can be surprising departures from this norm.
- **Gatekeepers**. Those who 'get in the way' (buyers who resist the desire of a salesperson to talk to design engineers, secretaries who 'protect the boss' etc.). Advertising, exhibitions and so on can be a way of bypassing them.

- **Specifiers.** Architects specify building materials, design engineers specify components, and it is very difficult to have the specifications altered later, sometimes making selling impossible if one's own product does not 'meet the spec.'. Such situations have to be recognized and the specifier convinced early on that a specification embracing our product will satisfy their requirements.

One person, when buying for themselves or making a simple purchase for an organization, may fulfil all these roles. The more important the purchase, and the more the purchase is of interest to others in the family unit or organization, the more likely it is that the roles will be played by separate individuals. In general terms, the bigger the risk over the purchase (often the cost), the larger the DMU to spread the responsibility over the decision. The marketer or salesperson may, therefore, have to convince a number of people who stand behind the actual individual making the purchase. Moreover, the salesperson may have to bring all these people to the same point in the buying decision at the same time in order for the sale to go through.

11.6 Telesales and Call Centres

Traditionally, call centres have been established as a cost-efficient way of interacting with existing and potential customers over the telephone. Telesales people were employed to make out-bound telephone calls to homes and businesses with the intention of gaining qualified leads to sell products such as double glazing to house owners or stationary to businesses. The aim of the double glazing telesales people was to arrange for a sales consultant to make a call to a prospect to demonstrate their product and make their pitch for business, closing the sale directly. Unfortunately, so many double glazing companies 'got in on the act' that homeowners came to realize that an early evening call at home usually meant that it was another sales call. Even becoming de-listed did little to help, as some companies used random call number generation to ensure they were able to catch everyone in an area!

In-bound call services handled enquiries from customers. Some service organizations developed call centres that were able to handle a variety of incoming calls for different client companies; depending on the number dialled, the operator would respond to a defined script that flashed up on their computer screen as they answered the call. One minute they might be taking an address from a caller enquiring about a company's environmental Green campaign, and the next providing assistance on the AIDS help line! Some companies developed their own dedicated call centre.

In-bound or out-bound, these interactions were seen almost as a necessary evil and, as such, were handled with as little expense as possible. The competitive advantage came from merely having a call centre rather than the quality of service it provided to either the customer or the business. The focus, therefore, was very much on maximizing agent and call centre efficiency at the minimum possible cost.

11.6.1 Call Centre Association[ii]

The Call and Contact Centre industry has experienced huge growth, particularly during the last five years. This gave the potential to change and improve customer services and communications within a wide range of private and public sector organizations.

The Call Centre Association (CCA) is the professional body for the call and contact centre industry in the UK. The organization is independent, has no commercial influences and is funded by member subscriptions. Its key objective is to facilitate knowledge transfer across member organizations with the ultimate aim of measurable standards of operation.

In 2001, the CCA had over 480 members with two-thirds based in England and Wales and the remainder based in Scotland, Ireland and overseas. Members have unique access to the membership database for networking purposes and solution forums. Their database is not released to any other organizations and members are required to comply with this.

For further information on the CCA, see the companion-web page for this book: www.bh.com/companions/075065449X. Within the CCA there are several types of membership available:

- **Corporate membership** is open to companies operating contact centres within their organization and they can become members of the CCA either on single site basis or as a corporate group.
- **Consultation membership** is also open to development organizations across the UK that have an interest in the positive progression of the industry.
- **Public sector membership** is available to public sector organizations that have an interest in, and are currently addressing, the Modernising Government Agenda.
- **Supplier membership** has recently been developed to allow suppliers to the industry to join the CCA.

2001 sees the launch of the CCA Standards: A Framework for Best Practice, which is designed to provide a framework within which expectations of efficiency and customer service can be fulfilled. It is a collection of simple statements designed for the industry by the industry against which it is possible to judge if the focus on customers and staff is being maintained during development or major change. The Framework seeks to identify areas in which activity should be focused, but within that focus it allows complete freedom of commercial decision-making.

Summary

- Personal selling is seen as a crucial part of the selling process from initial contact through to post sales satisfaction.
- The selling process was analysed as an eight stage process that has been used to model organizational buying processes.
- There are many different types of salesperson and types of sales jobs, each requiring different sorts of attitudes and aptitudes.
- The Decision Making Unit (DMU) is composed of a variety of different people, each with a particular role in the buying process.
- Telesales and Call Centres were described as an ever more popular method of accessing customers and providing them with a point of contact with the company.

References

i Robinson, P., Faris, C. and Wind, Y. *Industrial Buying and Creative Marketing* (Allyn & Bacon, 1967).

ii For more information, visit their web page: www.cca.org.uk.

Further Reading

McDonald, M., Rogers, B. and Woodburn, D. *Key Customers* (Butterworth-Heinemann, 2000). Very useful for the business-to-business practitioner.

Smith, Ian. *Meeting Customer Needs* (Butterworth-Heinemann, 2nd Edition, 1997). Looks at the buying process, making it easy for customers to buy, and customer care.

Tack, Alfred. *Sell Your Way to Success* (Panther, 1967). Unfortunately for the present purpose most books on selling are of the experiential kind – 'this is how I did it and see how successful you will be if you follow my example'. Tack's is a very good example.

Cleveland, Brad., Mayben, Julia. *Call Centre Management on Fast Forward*. (Call Centre Press, 1999). A useful, practical guide to managing an inbound call centre in the new millenium.

Questions

1. Would you expect the information aspect or the persuasion aspect to be more important in selling each of the following products? Say why in each case.
   (a) A brand of cigarettes with low-tar rating.
   (b) A computer controlled machine tool.
   (c) Low-fat cheese spread.
   (d) A multigrade engine oil.
2. Sales managers frequently complain that 20 per cent of their sales force make 80 per cent of the sales. How would you account for this phenomenon and what recommendations would you make to a sales manager with this problem?
3. Who might be members of the decision-making unit considering the purchase of the following?
   (a) A fork-lift truck for stacking reels at a paper mill.
   (b) Sheet steel for manufacturing domestic appliances.
   (c) Continuous stationery for the information technology department of a large government agency.
   (d) Vehicle parts for the stores department of the maintenance unit of a large brewery's road tanker fleet.
4. What special qualities might be required in a salesperson for the following?
   (a) Management consultancy.
   (b) Aircraft.
   (c) Books.
   (d) Life assurance.
   (e) Breakfast cereals.

Chapter 12

The practice of e-commerce

Introduction

By the end of this chapter you will:

- Have reviewed the development of the Internet and become familiar with everyday terms.
- Realise that e-commerce enables a regular dialogue with customers over time to build trust.
- Further recognise that with that trust comes 'permission' to help future profitable exchanges.
- Be able to make a reasonable estimate of a practical marketing budget for the Internet.
- Be able to evaluate an Internet marketing programme.
- Develop an appreciation of new marketing initiatives possible through the Internet.

Is mass marketing due for a cataclysmic shake-out? Absolutely. A new form of marketing is changing the landscape, and it will affect interruption marketing as significantly as the automobile affected the makers of buggy whips.

Seth Godin. *Permission Marketing*[i]

12.1 The Development of the Internet

In the last couple of years, a huge number of new sites and services have been launched on the Internet. The digital and Internet revolution is gathering momentum. So, what is the Internet?

The word 'Internet' is a broad term that refers to the fast-expanding network of global computers that can access each other in seconds by phone and satellite links. If you are using a modem on your computer, you too are part of the Internet. The general term Internet encompasses a variety of elements:

- **E-mail** – the sending and receiving of electronic mail and files (such as word processed documents and pictures).
- The **World Wide Web** (the 'Web') – a vast network of websites consisting of individual web pages.
- **Internet chat** – using technology such as Internet relay chat (IRC) or ICQ ('I seek you') to exchange typed messages with other Internet chatters in real time, in a public or private chat room.
- **Newsgroups** – the 80,000-plus newsgroups are collectively referred to as Usenet, and millions of people use them every day. To read and post messages in newsgroups you need some news-reading software, typically Outlook Express or Netscape Messenger. The ever-growing newsgroups have been around much longer than the World Wide Web, and are an endless source of distributed information, gossip, news, entertainment, sex, politics, resources and ideas.
- **Internet mailing lists** – sometimes called e-mailing lists. You can subscribe to these for free, getting the message regularly sent to your e-mail address, and you can post messages for fellow list members to read. There are around 90,000 of these lists covering every topic under the sun.
- **Bulletin board services** (BBS) – a kind of notice-board system for posting messages.
- **Video conferencing** – using software such as Windows NetMeeting to communicate audio-visually with other people in real time.
- **Telnet** – software that allows you to connect across the Internet to a remote computer (e.g. a university department or library). You can then access that computer as if you were on a local terminal linked to that system.
- **File transfer protocol** (FTP) – the method the Internet uses to speed files back and forth between computers. In practice, you don't need to worry about FTP unless you are thinking about creating and publishing your own web pages: then you need some of the freely available FTP software to upload your pages to your web hosting service.

Speaking of the Internet can be compared to the way we speak of 'the printed word' when we mean books, magazines, newspapers, newsletters, catalogues, leaflets, tickets and posters. To most people, 'the Internet' means e-mail and web pages.

People have compared the Internet and digital revolution with the birth of book-printing technology developed by Johann Gutenberg, William Caxton and others in Europe in the 1400s. As we all know, the arrival of book printing had a massive impact on society then, and has done ever since.

The Internet has been around for over thirty years, e-mail some twenty years or more, but the World Wide Web has only been around since 1994, and is still in a very early stage of development. We are witnessing the very beginning of an enormous revolution in global digital communications, one that is likely to have a massive impact on how future generations live and work.

12.1.1 In the Beginning

Do you remember when the Internet was termed 'new media'? Some would say that this is hardly an appropriate term for a media that celebrated its thirtieth birthday during 1999. It is more appropriate to view the Internet as entering the next stage of its evolution – its 'Third Age'. This Third Age will make the Internet radically different from what has gone before and will present a whole new series of challenges and opportunities for marketers.

- **The First Age** – This was the period from the birth of the communications infrastructure in 1969 until the development of the World Wide Web. During this time, the Internet evolved from being a US communications network designed for military purposes to gaining wider use, particularly throughout the academic and scientific community. At that time, the number of users was relatively low.
- **The Second Age** – The next phase of the medium followed the development of the Web and the launch of the Mosaic browser. This enabled the Internet to move towards becoming a mass communications medium. Usage evolved from niche to mass market in leading countries while the applications for which the Internet could be used became widespread.

  During this period the Internet became an important communications channel for marketing people and many companies integrated it into their marketing mix for such uses as online shopping, consumer communications and brand development, as well as internal uses such as company e-mail systems, their intranet, and for supply chain management.
- **The Third Age** – The Internet has just entered its third stage of development. This recognizes the fact that it is an underlying communications infrastructure and not simply PC to PC communications over a network. The technology becomes less important as users don't see the technical hardware but the messages carried. It is the message not the medium. While the PC will remain important, we are experiencing a break-up of communications delivery mechanisms. Consumers will use different devices, not limiting themselves to just one. Each separate device will be appropriate for different messages delivered in different ways. The Web, as we know it, will be just one manifestation of Internet communications.

  The different devices will include the PC, digital TV and the mobile phone. The immediate growth is almost certain to come through mobile phones and hand-held computers. This provides the user with information any time, any place. The next level of delivery devices may be household appliances which will increasingly be sold as 'network-ready'. This will include the smart fridge that re-orders when products are used, but may also be monitored remotely in case of malfunction or products approaching their use-by dates. Smaller devices will include access through the wristwatch, or even, potentially, the networked person.

12.1.2 Some Aspects of the Third Age

So, we don't have time or do we? At last, a breakthrough that could solve one of life's fundamental problems. An aspect of the Third Age of the Internet is that it **addresses the problem of 'not enough time'** to an even greater extent. Information itself is merely a commodity and 'Third Age' companies will recognize that, in order to generate profit, they will have to add value to the information. Time has a key role to play here as the value may be added through the relevance and speed of information.

Information providers will be able to deliver information to the consumer where and when he or she requires it. The type of information required and time when it is needed will determine the medium through which the information is delivered. Information has different time values. For example, the morning newspaper is already out of date as it covers the previous day's news. Important items of news can be delivered direct to the consumer through a mobile phone. Further detail can be found on a website accessed through a PC. However, both these delivery mechanisms do not make it easy to browse, and so there is still a clear role for media such as newspapers for other types of information such as that which is non-time-specific or needs time for reflection. The key for marketing people will be to provide information at the right time for the consumer – when they want it and in a format they want. To do this, marketing people have a problem that will be explored in Section 12.2.

Unlike traditional marketing communications, Internet-based technologies enable marketers to **genuinely address individual consumer needs** through personalization and one to one marketing. This is one of the most significant areas for the future success of marketing. Data gathered through purchasing profiles or anonymously through website browsing can be used to improve the user's experience. Note here that the experience is improved not so much by the content of the web pages but by the ease with which the individual finds the information that they want. The biggest benefit for the customer is that it makes the site easier to use. Moreover, addressing individual consumers strengthens the relationship through a higher level of user satisfaction, which is more likely to lead to greater usage and higher sales.

Internet time is a whole new concept. Not only does it allow the delivery of information to where your customers need it, but the Third Age will also allow pre-empting of consumer requirements through personalized delivery of information. Information services allow the consumer to choose the information they want and how it should be delivered. This can also be personalized further and adjusted over time so that the level of relevance of the information continually rises. While this ought to be possible with direct marketing means, marketers have for so long used a scatter-gun approach that many of the communications become 'clutter'. When a company that you bought your pension from, that knows your age, sends you savings plans designed for an age group twenty years your senior, you have just received 'clutter' through your letter box. (See also Chapter 8 on 'The practice of direct marketing').

Until now, the USA has driven development of the Internet. As it moved through its Second Age it expanded around the world with some countries and regions, notably Scandinavia, recording very high levels of penetration. However, **the Third Age will shift the balance of power to Europe**. The high level of mobile phone penetration and market importance of companies such as Nokia and Ericsson means that Europe will drive developments in this area.

However, the shift in balance of power is not just about the suppliers in the market but will also be consumer-driven. Disposable income has hindered Internet development in some countries through a low level of PC ownership. However, the ability to access the Internet through other means, most notably mobile phones, inevitably opens up this communications network to more people. In some emerging markets such as Central and Eastern Europe, mobile phone connections are growing faster than fixed lines and certainly faster than PC expansion (see Section 12.5, 'Third Generation Telephones').

It is clear that the proliferation of Internet devices will require an in-depth understanding of how the devices are used. Each type of delivery will use the Internet as its communications infrastructure but will deliver information in a different format. Consumers will choose a variety of devices to access varying levels of information at work, at home or on the move, whichever is the most convenient. The format of the message will depend on what it is saying and the intended delivery device.

The Third Age will mean new marketing opportunities. In turn, this means that marketers will have to rethink how they communicate with consumers. The new delivery devices will enable marketers to deliver communications messages that are appropriate for the device. Recognition of the fact that the Internet has become personal and portable will be a key to future success.

Tracking the consumer and the way in which the medium is used will become increasingly important. Companies that develop an in-depth understanding of consumer behaviour and how the different access devices are used will have most to gain from the Third Age.

12.2 The End of Traditional Marketing?

12.2.1 May I Interrupt You?

The problem with traditional marketing approaches is that, the harder you try, the harder things become. Unfortunately, customers have a finite amount of attention. They can't watch everything, remember everything, or do everything. As the amount of 'noise' in your customer's life increases (i.e. communications from you, your competitors and even your non-competitors trying to grab the customer's attention), the percentage of messages from you that get through inevitably decreases. Customers also have a finite amount of money. They can't buy everything, so they have to choose that which is of most value to them. But since their attention is limited, they will be able to choose only from those things they notice.

Unfortunately, the more products offered, the less money there is to go around. Every time someone buys a Burger King meal, they don't buy a McDonalds one. As the number of companies offering products increases, and as the number of products each company offers multiplies, it is inevitable that there will be more losers than winners. So, in order to capture more attention and more money, 'interruption marketers' must increase spending. And, as we saw in Chapter 9 when discussing setting advertising budgets, spending less money than your competitors on advertising in a cluttered environment inevitably leads to decreased sales.

But this increase in marketing exposure costs a lot of money.

'Interruption marketers' have little choice but to spend a bigger and bigger portion of their company's budgets on breaking through the noise. However, as we have seen, spending more and more money in order to get bigger returns leads to ever more noise. There is thus a classic catch-22 situation: the more they spend, the less it works; the less it works, the more they spend.

The only way to overcome this problem is to target your money more concisely than your competitors, which is why direct marketing developed to overcome this problem. However, everyone else is also doing it. And just because a company knows that a given customer has bought a pension from them, what right has that customer given that company to interrupt their leisure time to tell them about a new savings plan? So, 'Please go away and let me read my paper/listen to my radio/watch my television programme/travel to work – in peace!'.

The process of making sure that your customers are ready to listen to you is just like a salesperson making an appointment to speak to a buyer. The buyer has to agree to let the salesperson in to enable conversation to occur – they must give the salesperson permission to take up their time and talk to them. This process, where customers allow you to talk to them, is called **permission marketing**.[ii]

12.2.2 The Dating Game

Permission marketing demands that, in addition to looking downstream and turning customers into loyal customers, marketers now need to look upstream – to the stages long before someone becomes a customer. The challenge facing most companies is that they notice people too late. The process of getting new customers needs to be re-engineered. Prospects go through five steps, as illustrated in Figure 12.1.

Today, so many organizations do not notice, track or interact with people until they indicate that they are customers. Some do not even pay close attention until the consumer becomes a loyal customer. Unfortunately, a few don't notice their customers until they have cause to complain and head off to become disgruntled former customers.

Quoting Seth Godin again: 'It's essential, given the high cost of talking to strangers, that marketers move their focus of attention up the stream. They need to have a process in place that nurtures total strangers from the moment they first indicate an interest.'

And this is why it is a dating game. When a stranger indicates that they are interested, then, at that moment, a whole range of carefully considered messages must begin to be applied.

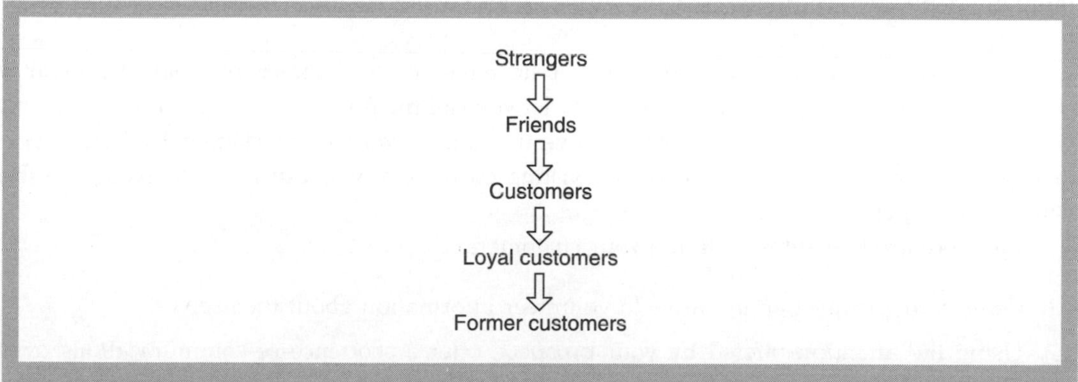

Figure 12.1 The five-step change from prospects through to former customers

Get it wrong, and the 'prospect' will turn away. However, if we listen hard and send out the right messages, then we can inform, cajole and encourage this stranger to become a friend. And once they become a friend, if we apply enough focused communications and exchanges of the right sort, over the right time period, building trust along the way, with willingness by both parties, then a relationship blossoms. And once it is there, we must work hard to nurture and maintain that long-term relationship.

And it is the same in business relationships. When a stranger indicates an interest, a whole suite of marketing messages are applied to turn that stranger into a friend, and that friend into a customer. But do you know how your company does this now? Most marketers have no idea. They rely on a hodgepodge of randomly delivered interruptions and hope that from this primordial soup will rise a fully formed customer. This is where computers and permission marketing can make such a difference, according to Godin.[iii]

"Computers and permission marketing can change that. You can now choose whom you reach. When you reach them. The order of the messages. The benefits offered. You can create dozens or even hundreds of paths for an individual to follow from the first contact until the highest level of permission is granted. If the marketing messages you send are anticipated, relevant, and personal, they will cut through the clutter and increase the prospect's knowledge of the benefits you offer. An organization that is focused on this process early on will always outperform one that isn't."

There is a certain synergy between direct or 'one to one' marketing and permission marketing:

- In **direct marketing**, the marketer works to change the focus from finding as many new customers as possible to extracting the maximum value from each customer.
- The **permission marketer** works to change the focus from finding as many prospects as possible to converting the largest number of prospects into customers. Then they leverage the permission on an ongoing basis.

You can't build a one to one relationship with a 'date' unless the person explicitly agrees to the process. It's the same with customers. Everything from discovering a date of birth to building mutually dependent computer systems with a major vendor requires an overt agreement from both sides.

By measuring the depth of permission you have with each customer (one may allow you to send merchandise 'on approval', another may let you call them when a new product comes in), you can begin to track the benefits of your investment in permission marketing. By focusing on how deep your permission is with your existing customers, you can begin to recognize the value of your permission asset.

So, there are five steps to dating your customers:

1. Offer your prospect an incentive to volunteer information about themselves.
2. Using the attention offered by your prospect, offer a sequence of communications over time, teaching the customer about your product or service. Build trust along the way, bringing them closer all the time.

3. By listening to what the customer finds of value, reinforce the incentive to guarantee that the prospect maintains the permission.
4. To get even more permission from the customer, offer additional incentives.
5. Take your time to ensure that the permission you have gained changes the customer's behaviour towards profits.

Just like any other human alliance, once it is established, we must work hard to nurture and maintain that long-term business exchange relationship. For it is only if both sides profit that the relationship will endure.

12.2.3 Permission Granted

In 'permission marketing' the same simple steps are almost always followed. While each campaign is very different, the concept behind each step remains the same. So, you interrupt customers with a message designed to get them to show they are interested. Thus, they volunteer or say 'yes' to begin a rewarding exchange of information achieved over time. This builds trust that you can leverage into a sales relationship. However, the first step will still be to stop the consumer from doing whatever they are doing and listen to you. That is one reason why there will always be socially acceptable 'interruption marketing' media. We need to get that initial attention.

In order to make the marketing messages you send relevant and personal, you need to get some data about your prospects. But this can only be obtained if you are honest with your prospect: what sort of relationship would be based on tricks, gimmicks or dishonesty? Permission marketers are totally open about their objectives with the consumer. They make it crystal clear what they will be doing with the data they collect and exactly why it's beneficial to the consumer to give the data.

For example, people who visit a website are sometimes asked to give their phone number. But what's in it for them? Without a specific reason for them to behave in a particular way, without a reward or a benefit, the overwhelmed visitor will probably refuse. So, the reward you offer a consumer must be obvious and simple. You could call it bait. No one would argue with the idea that, when you go fishing, you ought to use the most effective, most obvious bait you can find. The same is true when you try to attract consumers.

After you have interrupted your prospect, they have every right to be annoyed, so the bait had better not leave a bitter taste in the mouth. However, once they are engaged in a bargain, and you have exchanged data with the person, you need to teach the prospect more about what you have to offer that will interest them and eventually leverage the permission you have just obtained.

If you are using a medium where frequency is cheap (like the Internet), take your time. Build trust through frequency. Tell your story patiently to each consumer who is willing to participate in the exchange. (Compare this with your experience on the receiving end of some telesales operations. Since the cost of the exchange is more expensive, requiring a one to one dialogue, the salesperson may be impatient – if you will not buy first time, they may be a little short with you and the relationship will be broken for ever.)

When you tell your story, be personal, be relevant, be specific. And always be anticipated. Anticipation, of course, is even better than expectation. Without surprising the consumer, gradually raise the level of permission you extract. Keep that trust – it will all too quickly be broken if you are heavy-handed.

Then, by constantly raising the magnitude of rewards you offer the prospect, you can fight attrition[a] and compression[b] and keep the consumer interested. By continuing the dialogue, you can teach the person, until a stranger becomes a friend and then a friend becomes a customer. Of course, the process doesn't end with the first sale. It just becomes one to one marketing. Using the permission already granted, you then work hard to expand the 'share of wallet'[c] and build a permission asset that is ever deeper and more powerful.

12.2.4 So How Do You Go About It?

As is so often the case, some marketers fail at the first hurdle and miss out on some basic analyses. All too often, there is a rush to produce a website without sufficient thought to what it is going to do – except be a virtual billboard. The result is that the organization focuses on content rather than process, i.e. 'let's get the words and graphics looking right' rather than thinking about how people are going to interact with the site and how the site fits in with other company communications media. Without such thinking, how can the permission be engineered? Here are some key questions that must be answered in order to have a coherent strategy when facing the Web:

- What are we trying to achieve?
- Can it be measured?
- What is the cost of bringing one consumer, just once, to our website?
- What is the cost of getting that consumer to return?
- If this works, can we scale it?

12.3 Working With the Internet

Over the last few years, many people have been proclaiming that the Internet will forever change the world. Yet with Jennicam, spam, chat rooms about lizards, and downloadable photos of Terri Hatcher (the actress best known for playing Lois Lane to 'Superman' on the recent TV series) it's not clear to most marketers what all the fuss is about.

Jeff Bezos, the man behind Amazon.com is on his way to becoming a billionaire – but his 'company' appears to be just a bookstore (although, more recently, a music and other goods store too). This 'bookstore' is now worth more than Barnes & Noble and Borders Books combined. Yahoo! has a market capitalization more than New York Times Corporation, which owns

[a] Attrition is where the customer gets irritated by the relationship.

[b] Compression is the tendency of rewards to become less effective with repetition.

[c] 'Share of wallet' refers to the share of the customer's expenditure on a given range of items. Explore which needs you can satisfy, then use the knowledge you have, and the trust you've built, to make that additional sale. Increase your product offerings to customers. By being customer-focused instead of retail-focused or factory-focused, a manufacturer or merchant can widely increase its offerings, thus increasing this share of wallet.

newspapers and magazines around the USA. Is there really something going on here, or is this another Klondike gold rush?

There is something very big going on, but as you will have seen from the previous comments, it's not what some of the experts believe. The Internet is the greatest direct marketing medium ever invented. It is not TV.

Here are **six of the biggest benefits it offers** to direct marketers:

1. **Stamps are free**. It does not cost any more to e-mail one or one hundred thousand people through the Internet. You just send one message to your service provider – it does the rest.
2. **The speed of testing is one hundred times faster**. Because the interaction is very rapid indeed, and because the cost of contacting a great many people is so small, you can test your approach very quickly.
3. **Response rates are fifteen times higher**. If a customer has to drop what they are doing to talk to you, or if they have to write back by filling in your form, then response rates are going to be much lower than if someone just has to click on a box on their screen.
4. **You can implement 'curriculum marketing' in text and on the Web**. This means that you identify the lifetime value of the relationship with that customer and then develop a 'curriculum' of communications over that lifetime. A salesperson knows that, for some accounts, they cannot expect to make a sale on the first visit. Rather, they will have to build up a relationship over time. It is the same on the Internet. You can keep written communications with the prospect, bringing them ever closer to becoming a friend and then a customer. From that point, the ongoing relationship grows and prospers as the curriculum is developed over time.
5. **Frequency is free**. You can identify and efficiently talk with individuals over and over again. As with the 'free stamps', the low cost of Internet communications means that you can keep the dialogue going much longer than a salesperson could; their visits cost so much that they have to make a sale soon in the 'relationship' or they will be out of a job.
6. **Printing is free**. When a prospect wants to keep a hard copy of the information you send them, it is to their cost, not yours.

12.3.1 Permission Marketing on the Internet

Here are the six simple steps to any permission marketing campaign in the context of the Internet:

1. **As the marketer, give a prospect some incentive for coming forward.** On the Web, you can use banner advertising on other sites and search engines to gently interrupt consumers and offer them an opportunity to say yes to a marketing programme. This is the 'bait' and the only media cost of the entire campaign. It must be very clear right from the outset what people will gain by opting into the programme. In the right context, permission marketers use banners, as they are just about the only ones who can use this medium effectively. A banner is a great way to get momentary attention and possibly opt-in from large numbers of individuals – and cheaply.

You could offer the 'bait' through other media to highly targeted groups by direct means but this could cost more.

2. **Using the attention offered by the consumer, deliver a story over time, teaching the consumer about your product or service.** Once a consumer has bought-in, use e-mail to remind your prospect to go back to the website. More than 80 per cent of Web users list e-mail as the main reason they go online. Because the e-mail box is regularly visited and, for many, constantly open, welcome messages get lots of attention and reaction. Provided that the messages are welcome and give the recipient something of value – every time – then the permission will be maintained and the exchange will continue. Just as with our dating example, if the messages from one party are too frequent or too irrelevant the relationship will go no further. Marketers use e-mail to teach the consumer about the benefits of the product. Moreover, through the exchanges, the marketer can gain personal insights to make the marketing messages ever more personal.
3. **To guarantee that the prospect maintains the permission, reinforce the incentive.** Because e-mail is virtually cost-free via the Internet, the two-way communication allows the marketer to confirm if the consumer is 'listening'. By getting responses, it's easy to see who is involved in the campaign and it is easier still to give bigger rewards to people to maintain their interest. As the prospect moves further along the path from stranger to loyal customer, the rewards can be structured accordingly.
4. **Offer extra incentives to get even more permission from the consumer.** For each viewer, listener or reader a mass-market campaign must be the same. But using computer power, you can make it effectively one to one marketing. So, you can give direct rewards to the customer to keep them involved, and continuing offers and rewards to leverage more permission. Those individuals that need more incentives to stay active can get them without spoiling the whole system.
5. **Over time, leverage the permission and turn it into profits by changing consumer behaviour.** What is a list of people that want to hear from you worth to your organization? What about a completely personalized e-mail list of hundreds of thousands or millions of people, totally loyal, who want and expect to hear from you on a personal and relevant topic, related to purchases? In many cases it may be the most valuable opportunity for the organization.
6. **Continue to show the customer you care and keep the relationship fresh.** A marriage is a contract made in heaven, re-signed every day. Just as with any other human relationship, it will need to be nurtured and will change as the needs of both parties develop. Therefore, continue listening to your customer and prevent them from even thinking about becoming disloyal. Why should they? Only if you let them, will they go.

12.3.2 Setting your Web Budget

Every commercial website should be set up 100 per cent focused on getting strangers to give you permission to market to them. That is all. Your website doesn't have to be expensive or complicated or big or fancy. Instead, this shop window to your business should be obsessed with getting permission.

Once you look at the Web in this way, it all makes sense. For example, you can easily calculate exactly what it costs to earn one more permission. The formula is:

$$\frac{\text{The cost of banner advertising to reach 100 people}}{\text{The number of people who visited your site (of 100 possible)}}$$

This will give you the cost of getting one visitor to your site, once. Multiply this cost by the percentage of punters who visited your pages that decided to take part in your programme and gave their e-mail address and invited you to contact them in some way. (Note, the more obvious what the person is going to gain from the relationship, the more valuable the permission. Just as a salesperson will be shown the door if they tricked a buyer into making an appointment, conning people into giving their e-mail address is a waste of time.)

Once you know the cost of getting that permission, compare it to the lifetime value of one of these permissions, and then you can determine if the investment is worth it.

For example, imagine that you're starting a 'wine of the month' club. The sums might look like this:

- Banners at £100 per thousand.
- 2 per cent of the audience of those banners click on to visit your site (this is the 'click-through rate').
- So, 2 per cent of that 1000 is 20 visitors to your site.
- Thus, £100/20 = £5.00 per visitor.
- Let us suppose there is a 20 per cent opt-in – 4 of the 20 – leading to a cost per permission of (£5.00 × 4) = £20.00.

If, over time, half of the people with whom you engage in a dialogue become customers, it's costing you about £40 to get a customer. If the 'lifetime' value of this customer is £300.00 because they buy, on average, four cases of wine at £75.00 each in just the next year alone, you're way ahead of the game.

It gets even better if your company sells a wide variety of products or if the products are more expensive or complicated. How much does it cost Calvin Klein or Dell Computers or BMW to teach one more consumer all about their new products? Calvin Klein pays huge shelving allowances and salaries just to put one person in front of a prospect to teach her about a new face cleanser. Dell might spend between £100 and £1,500 to teach just one more IT professional about a new workstation.

It costs a car company almost £100 to get someone into the dealership. Using permission marketing, they could start these dialogues for about £5.00 each and take their time, weeks or months, educating consumers about the new Z3 Roadster due for launch in December 2002 and then provide an incentive to visit the dealership.

12.3.3 The Foundations to Your Permission-based Website

Some foundational points for running your permission-based website successfully are discussed below.

Test your offer to make it the right 'bait' – In order to interrupt your prospect and structure a marketing campaign to get 'opt-in' permission, the media cost is heavily weighted at the beginning. You pay for attention now and get it later. If you do not actually ask for any money during your first interaction with the prospective customer, you can expect a much higher response rate than you would with a traditional direct marketing campaign. With other more expensive methods of having a direct dialogue with prospects over time, like the mail or the phone, you probably could not afford to wait for the sale. 'Opt-in' permission will go way up, though, if the media chosen, the banners that are used, and the entire process are tested and optimized.

Of course, if you're already using other media, you can gain from this tremendously by adding a feature that allows the customer to say they are interested. For example, every commercial you run can feature an e-mail address with a tag that reads, 'For free advice on web marketing, write to us at info@daw.co.uk'.

A while ago, no-one put a free-phone 0800 number in an advertisement. Today it is commonplace. An e-mail address is even better. It buys you permission and costs you nothing on the margin.

Let the prospect know exactly what they are going to gain – As with our salesperson, it does not pay to con people into giving you permission. Plan to have a mutually beneficial dialogue, and the more you tell people about what to expect, the greater the anticipation you will be able to create. This is important as you work to leverage it for future changes of behaviour and profits.

Hiding things in the small print will not work. The focus of the promotion or campaign should match the permission you're asking for. Amazon.com, for example, does quite well in using e-mail to remind people to come back and buy more books or compact discs. (It's part of the deal when you sign up with them, and, as they are targeted and relevant, most people expect and enjoy the messages.)

Resist the temptation to automatically rent, sell or trade the permission someone has given you. Also resist the temptation to upgrade the permission granted. As mentioned earlier, this usually upsets people, weakens their trust and fails dramatically online. Suppose you requested a brochure for the BMW Z3 Roadster and the next thing you know you have a salesperson knocking on your door to get you to sign for the credit arrangement on your new car!

The Direct Marketing Association is trying to take the high ground in the privacy debate and has published very specific guidelines that it asks members to follow.[iv]

The single largest reason given by consumers for not shopping online and for not opting into promotions and marketing programmes online is jeopardizing their privacy. While the online shopper knows that there is no privacy in terms of future contacts, the real concern is being inundated with further e-mails. People are becoming aware that, in the wrong hands, one scrap of information about them can lead to an onslaught. As soon as the data are shared, their value decreases. By maintaining the privacy, the marketer enhances the asset.

Making a promise, an overt deal, and keeping it regularly re-enforced is the secret to long-term success in permission marketing – as it is in any relationship!

Send and receive information electronically: do not use people – There are 86,400 seconds in a full 24-hour day. So, if you have 86,000 people in your permission database and it takes your computer one second to handle each one, your system will crash!

Worse, if you are marketing to the public, if just 1 per cent of the people in your permission database require human contact every day, then for each million people on your permission database you will have to handle 10,000 customer service requests a day! One of the huge limits on AOL's earnings growth is that one-third of all their employees are in customer service. Not only is AOL paying a fortune for this, but also the quality of the care isn't nearly as high as it would be if much of it were automated.

When creating an online permission marketing campaign, it is essential that you let your punters know what to expect. If they expect a human to be instantly available to answer their questions, they will ask questions and you should be prepared to answer them.

While it is possible to automate much of the customer contact elements of customer service, people are getting frustrated by not being able to get the answers they want from 'a machine'. Therefore, it is crucial that you make your automated systems as robust and accommodating as possible. Then it is essential that you filter your users and make sure that only the people who actually need human involvement are getting it. And you can achieve this by making it very easy for consumers to escalate an issue when a human is truly needed.

Online customers think they are clever: treat them that way – It is believed that online prospects are twice as likely as the national average to have a qualification beyond secondary school. This is a group of people used to being right, used to understanding how things work, and used to getting them to work quickly. They are knowledgeable and want their computing to give them the answers they need. They use them at work and/or they use them at home for leisure.

If you have done any recent web surfing, you will know what it feels like when you start using the Internet. Your machine crashes, sites are slow to download, and then you need some 'latest' software just to view. Then up pops 'fatal errors' and 'Java script errors' and 'browser errors'. Then you find a 'plug-in' is missing. It seems that at every turn the Net reminds you how stupid you are, how out of date your computer is, and how much of your precious time you have wasted. World Wide Web – or World Wide Wait!

Of course, all this is a great opportunity for your organization: if you can build simple tools that work, and you can make people feel clever for using them, then prospects will flock to you and stay with you. To be really accepted by all, never build anything that isn't fun on a 14.4 modem, or over AOL, or with an old browser.

The reason e-mail is the most significant application is that it is simple and does exactly what people expect it to do; your permission marketing campaign should function exactly the same way.

12.3.4 How to Evaluate a Permission Marketing Programme

As the old saying goes, 'what gets measured, gets done'. So, the fundamentals of any measurement system will be to measure what is important in the marketing programme, as this is what will get done. There are ten questions to ask when evaluating any marketing programme:

1. *Have you developed the best bait you can?*

Consumers are selfish. As consumers, we all are. In our pursuit of satisfactions we are out for what we can get. It may be a direct satisfaction for ourselves or the satisfaction that comes from doing something for someone else. So, for the prospect, is there a clear and obvious benefit being offered, or is there a contest or promotion that offers an even better benefit to a select group of consumers?

There's no room for subtlety or selfish behaviour on the part of the marketer, however. Marketers that offer better bait with a more obvious benefit will always attract more consumers than their competition. The best bait is easy to describe, coveted by a large portion of your target market and economical to deliver. And the bait must be tangible enough that the consumer will give up precious attention and privacy to participate. Choosing the right bait is essential. It must also resonate with the product or service you offer. If there's a high overlap between the bait and the ultimate message, you're far more likely to attract and keep the right people.

For example, compare the two approaches:

(a) Find out about the new BMW Z3 Roadster and you can enter a free competition to win one ...

(b) Find out about the new BMW Z3 Roadster and you could keep the keys ...

Obviously bait doesn't have to be a prize. It could be a coupon, information about an interesting subject, entertainment, or membership to a privileged group.

2. *What does the next permission cost?*

How much does it cost to get one more person to sign up to opt-in? Outside the Internet, this is calculated by dividing the cost of advertising by the number of expected participants. With direct marketing and online on the Internet, it is simply media costs divided by the number of people granting you permission. Note that permission always costs something. Tracking it and calculating its worth is essential if you want to maximize your ROI (return on investment).

3. *When permission is granted, how far can you go?*

This is a fundamental measure. If someone gives you the right to send him or her a brochure, that's all you have been given. Being very clear about exactly what the prospect can expect ensures that there will be no misunderstandings and no cancelled permissions. You will have to earn further permissions to take the prospect onto the next stage.

4. *How much does it cost to send one more marketing message to one more person?*

With direct marketing, this number could be a few pence for a letter or phone call but it could be several pounds if you are sending printed brochures. Online, the cost is nil. Choosing the right frequency, mechanism and media for your audience maximizes your return.

5. *How many respond to which communications?*

Once you have gained permission from your prospects and begun to send out messages, how many people respond and through which medium? Many people search for information on the Internet yet still order over the telephone. How many take action based on which messages? How can you use a feedback loop to prospects to increase the personalization and the relevance of the messages over time?

You can undoubtedly increase this number, often many times over, by testing various approaches.

6. *What are you going to do about compression?*

Some incentives have a tendency to become less effective over time. So do you have a feedback loop and technology in place to increase the bait as its effectiveness begins to tail off? For example, if you were a 'wine of the month' club, you could monitor regular customers and note when their frequency of buying started to taper off – perhaps indicating that they were switching to another supplier. This would be a good opportunity to follow up with some new rewards to recapture the interest and enthusiasm of these consumers.

In our example used earlier, if it costs you £40 to attract a new customer but only £5 in additional 'anti-compression' rewards to keep them, it is pretty obvious what to do.

7. *Are you treating the permission as an asset?*

Virtually all companies measure their assets every day, be that inventory in the warehouse or the amount of money in the bank. Yet what measures do you have of your permission base? Each marketer in your organization should be made acutely aware of exactly how wide and how deep this permission is. Over time, this asset can be leveraged and increased. Both width (the number of prospects) and depth (how far you have got permission to communicate with them) take an investment, but as with all assets, if that investment is measured over time, the ROI can be calculated.

8. *How are you leveraging the permission?*

It is possible to leverage permission once it is built. For example, going back to our salesperson, when you have permission to talk with relevance and personalization to a given buyer, you can come back with new messages to that person and dramatically increase profits. For example, introducing your brand of quality clothing to loyal purchasers of your brand of quality fishing gear is a sensible use of the company's number one asset – your right to talk to well-heeled anglers.

In addition to leveraging new product sales, marketers can try to increase consumption of existing products or partner with other companies to gradually share permission. An airline might do this with hotels, for example. Instead of renting the names of the airline's frequent fliers to a hotel chain, it could feature the hotels in the anticipated monthly mailing to its loyal customer base. If some of those consumers end up at the hotel, the airline can leverage their ability to talk with these individuals.

9. *How are you going to increase the permission level?*

Once a permission pattern has been set, the obligation of the marketer is to increase it. Without proper care, the permission to correspond with an individual will fade. But by focusing on how to earn more and more trust from the prospect, the marketer can increase the permission, making it a more valuable asset over time.

Amazon.com is in the middle of this process. When a customer first buys online, the permission is very fragile. A consumer is happy to be reminded periodically of something of interest at Amazon – for instance, if the customer had bought the fourth Harry Potter novel they would not mind being told that J. K. Rowling had produced a fifth – but the customer is not expecting e-mail from the company. However, by running a promotion with small but fun prizes, Amazon is able to get much more active participation from a portion of its list. It moves consumers up the permission ladder and makes its mailings anticipated. The next step would be to get more personal and relevant. Once Amazon knows that you like Harry Potter, it can sign you up for an automatic review of the fifth book. Or it could cross-sell to CDs by offering you the Harry Potter soundtrack. Or perhaps a special discount programme on a book chosen every month based on your interest – like a new print of *Lord of the Rings*.

The next level will be to sign people up for a book or music club and then get their permission to select a book or CD and send it on approval in exchange for a discount or some other benefit.

10. *What is the lifetime value of a single permission?*

If permission is short-lived – as it is, say, at a tourist attraction – then the amount the marketer would be willing to invest should be less than it would be when the permission can last a very long time. Marketers win when they can convert what many see to be a short-term permission cycle to one that lasts for a much longer period of time. Cinemas, for example, could aim to turn the one-off film trip into a loyalty programme that can last for months or even years. UGI Cinemas are doing this in the UK. For a fixed monthly subscription, you can see as many films a month as you like. By spreading the cost of acquiring a new customer and keeping them over a longer period of time, a cinema can dramatically outpace its competition.

12.4 A New Vocabulary

With e-commerce has come a whole new vocabulary, yet it is one that is changing rapidly. However, the changes are such that it will not be possible in a text of this nature to keep up with the latest offerings from the rapidly changing world of information technology. That said, there follows a selection of new approaches of interest to the marketer of the future that will support the fundamentals of the future of e-commerce.

12.4.1 iTV Marketing

According to recent research from industry consultants Strategy Analytics, 625 million people around the world will have access to online services on their TV sets by 2005, including online shopping, banking, games, information and interactive entertainment services. Currently, the most advanced market in the world is the UK, where 40 per cent of homes were estimated to have interactive digital television by the end of 2001. All the UK's major digital platforms, satellite, cable and terrestrial, offer a wide range of interactive services such as interactive sports coverage, t-commerce (television commerce, as opposed to e- or electronic commerce), games, e-mail and so-called walled garden Internet – where there are restricted sites available.

As the Web and TV merge, the opportunities to interact with consumers increase. Consumers are increasingly using interactive advertisements to find out more about products, make purchases and communicate through e-mail. The opportunities seem endless.

12.4.2 WAP Marketing

Wireless Application Protocol (WAP) was the first step on the road to a mobile Internet when it was launched. While its arrival was promoted by the mobile operators as the 'Internet on your phone', the reality of simple black text hyperlinks and a lack of graphics and movement was a disappointment for many of those who took up the service.

However, despite the slower functioning and relatively poor interface of the WAP system, uptake is on the increase, and by 2002, the vast majority of new mobile phones produced come with WAP as standard. Similarly, the number of services available has multiplied. In addition to news and entertainment information, users can get directions, play games, check train times, and much more.

Until the 'third generation' (3G – see Section 12.5) licences and the technology reach the market, WAP is predicted to grow in use and popularity. WAP sites are not right for every business, but if appropriate can be a useful route particularly to the teenage market.

12.4.3 Short Message Service (SMS) Marketing

More commonly known as 'text messaging', SMS has grown beyond everyone's expectations. In December 2000, an estimated 20 billion text messages were sent worldwide – a seven-fold increase in a year. It is massively popular with young people, but recently all generations have started to use it. Properly used, it is a marketer's dream, because it is virtually impossible not to read a text message you receive. And, of course, there are hundreds of SMS services that mobile owners can subscribe to, including news and information services, sport scores and clubbing guides, all sent by text.

Advertising opportunities are already on the increase, and SMS, in a similar way to e-mail, allows a two-way communication with individual consumers. SMS is now a fully accessible marketing tool, and its use is set to grow. Already, location-based services are emerging, such as the ZagMe service at Lakeside shopping centre on the M25 to the east of London. Visitors are invited on arriving at the shopping centre to send a text message to a number and, in return, they receive special offers from shops in Lakeside as they shop. The effect was to create mini-stampedes around the store as shoppers rushed for bargains.

12.4.4 Viral Marketing

Viral marketing is not just about sending games around the Net on e-mail, although games can be a good viral tool. It is about creating word of mouth in everything you do on the Net. In essence, viral marketing creates an incentive for others to communicate your marketing message through the Internet or e-mail, via methods such as attachments or sign-up forms. Attachments enable you to add a degree of personality to your brand and encourage consumers to interact, as well as to find out more about you and your product or service.

Just like their more dangerous cousins (viruses), viral marketing campaigns can spread across the entire Internet in a matter of days. No other method of marketing has been found that can generate such massive 'recommendation' marketing status with such a relatively small outlay.

Viral marketing is an extremely effective Internet marketing strategy and is a system of promotion that allows your marketing message to spread from one person to another.

The simplest and most effective form of viral marketing is the creation of e-books. These are free books created on a specific subject that visitors can download. As the books contain useful information, those who download the book can offer the same information free on their own sites as a bonus to their own visitors. This process continues and can result in a lot of traffic for the original creator of the book, who will have their website address displayed in the book.

12.4.5 E-zine Marketing and How To Do It

While surfing the Net is becoming a national pastime, most Internet users only *return* to their favourite five to ten websites. So, how do you get them to return to yours? One option is via e-mail using **mailing list software**.

Mailing list management programs (sometimes called 'listserves' after the original of this type of program) automate subscriptions and unsubscriptions, as well as the process of mailing to each of the subscribers. Mailing list software has two major uses:

1. **Discussion groups** – These are discussions carried on via e-mail, in which each person's e-mailed comments are echoed to every other subscriber. In moderated lists, the moderator filters out all the annoying 'unsubscribe me' requests, and only passes on the more important, on-track contributions. To keep the number of daily messages from the list under control, people often subscribe to a digest version of the discussion, which may be sent once per day.
2. **Newsletters** – In the typical public newsletter, anyone may subscribe freely, though only the moderator or list owner sends mailings to people on the list. In a private newsletter, the moderator controls both subscriptions and mailings.

Discussion groups can be powerful, with great potential for education and community building. Some manufacturers set up a 'user group' of people who are familiar with their products. Company representatives, as well as more experienced laymen, share information with the less experienced. Groups can build customer loyalty and provide significant customer support. In addition, the individual or company which sponsors or moderates the discussion can build an excellent reputation – and significant business – from discussion group members, who often number in the thousands.

In addition to hosting discussion groups, as stated above, companies can use mailing lists to power e-mail newsletters, which:

- **Remind** former visitors with brief information about new articles, products and features on their website.
- **Inform** with a regular newsletter containing helpful information along with material about one's business. Often such newsletters are also archived on a website, creating an increasingly valuable information resource (examples being *Web Marketing Today* and *Web Digest for Marketers*).
- **Enhance a reputation** through occasional articles of interest. A weekly or monthly publishing cycle is not crucial.
- **Nurture potential customers** during the gestation period until you have engineered 'permission' to the point where they are ready to purchase or sign a contract.
- **Support existing customers** with ongoing information.
- **Solicit paid subscriptions** for newsletters with proprietary information not readily available elsewhere.
- **Earn revenue** from paid sponsors of the newsletter.

One of the best ways to obtain subscribers is to ask visitors to sign up when they first enter your website. Offer incentives to 'register' – find the best bait! Then, in the registration form ask if they would like to receive updated information, notice of new articles or products etc. Make it easy for a visitor to receive a 'free subscription' by asking for the prospect's e-mail address in a box and pressing the subscribe me button. But be very careful. Don't contribute to the glut of unwanted e-mail. And *don't* add someone's name to your mailing list without his or her explicit permission – even if you graciously offer to unsubscribe them. People will resent it!

12.4.6 Pros and Cons of E-zine Marketing and How to Get Started

When you compare the cost of distributing information via e-mail as against printed fliers and postage, e-mail wins hands down as it is essentially free.

Content, however, is of prime importance. If you offer information people value, your newsletter will gain subscribers. View the time researching and preparing for a newsletter as marketing time needed to maintain and develop a business.

There are limitations, of course. An e-mail newsletter excels in sending information in words but not graphics. Moreover, list maintenance will be just as important as with any database marketing initiative (see Chapter 8). E-mail addresses are always becoming obsolete, and not all mailing list software will automatically unsubscribe such addresses.

Here is a simple guide for people wanting to get started with e-zine marketing – once they have taken on board the 'permission marketing' philosophy explained in Section 12.2, of course!

- Ask your Internet Service Provider (ISP) how much they would charge for set-up and monthly charges for a major mailing list, and budget accordingly.
- Decide how access to the newsletter will leverage permission from your prospects.
- Brainstorm with staff and colleagues concerning how you can offer a value-added newsletter to your customers and potential customers.
- Set up a method by which website visitors can subscribe.
- Tell people how to subscribe (and unsubscribe) in every issue
- Create an archive of past issues on your website. It makes your website increasingly valuable.

12.4.7 Affiliate Marketing

Affiliate marketing is a simple concept, allowing you to offer a commission to other site owners for recommending your product or service. Recent surveys have shown affiliate marketing to be one of the most effective forms of long-term online advertising, and it has the additional benefit of being performance based. Affiliate marketing consists of entering into a partnership with an 'affiliated' site. This site then places a link on its page, whether it is a banner, text, button etc. and directs the consumer to the vendor's site. It is a win-win situation as it provides e-commerce-enabled sites (known as merchants or advertisers) the ability to receive highly targeted quality traffic and therefore sales, and your organization (one of the affiliates) with revenue for each sale, lead or click-through from your website.

There are two main routes of entering into an affiliate relationship. Either you can enter an existing scheme, in which case you need to identify the best-fit scheme for you, or you can start your own. If you decide on the latter, you may need help to identify and recruit potential affiliate partners.

Here in the UK the arrival of top UK affiliate networks such as Tradedoubler, Affiliate Window and UK Affiliates has made affiliate marketing accessible to both the novice hobby site and the expert 'superaffiliate'. Banners, logos or text links are supplied by the merchant in the form of simple 'cut and paste' Hyper Text Meta Link (HTML) code which includes all relevant affiliate tracking codes (these are needed so that the affiliate can gain commission; they are of course unique to each affiliate). It is then up to the affiliate to place these links strategically and in context on their website in order to generate revenue. Merchants will pay varying commission levels depending on the type of action that is made – a click-through to their site, or a lead for a registration or a sale on one of their products or services. The affiliate's only task is to gently persuade the visitor to click on these links (known as pre-selling) and drive traffic to the merchant site. By using effective banners and/or running competitions, merchants can encourage click-through. However, it is then up to the merchant to convert the traffic the affiliate is kindly giving them into sales and then take care of customer orders, credit card processing, customer service, inventory and shipping.

12.4.8 Newsgroup Marketing

Newsgroups are a touchy subject, given their non-commercial nature and strict anti-spamming rules. E-mail allows you to join discussion groups where like-minded people swap news, gossip, discuss new developments, ask each other questions and send information and advice. This is done by sending a message to the group's e-mail address and this gets passed on to everyone else in the group and you get everyone else's messages in return. You can be part of a group for as long or as short a time as you like. You can be entirely passive and just read the messages that come in or you can take an active part by forwarding messages.

Internet service companies have devised methods of carefully monitoring over 60,000 newsgroups to keep clients informed with what the public really thinks. It is, therefore, possible to keep track of opinions on your company, your products and services, and even your competitors. Keeping your finger on the pulse of newsgroup discussions allows you to respond quickly to damaging or slanderous commentary that could affect your reputation, answer customer queries and respond to opportunities identified on your behalf.

12.4.9 E-mail Marketing

Done badly, it is the worst *faux pas* on the net: spam! Done correctly, it is the marketing 'killer application' that allows you to communicate directly with consumers, one on one, when you want, for next to nothing. You can rent e-mail lists, grow your own, and get support to plan e-mail marketing campaigns and track effectiveness.

Many companies have shied away from e-mail marketing because of the bad reputation it gained through spam or unsolicited e-mail. However, renting or sponsoring quality 'opt-in' lists can provide highly targeted marketing results. Having agreed the target demographics, research the optimum lists, negotiate and buy the space, and either write or get help with the e-mail message. Over time, through development of your own lists, you can build closer relationships with your consumers through e-CRM (electronic customer relationship marketing – see Chapter 18).

E-mail is by far the cheapest and quickest way to communicate regularly with your consumers. Highly specific targeting can be undertaken and a real understanding of your client base is built over time.

12.4.10 Online Advertising

Banners – small space advertisements that appear on another site – are getting a bad press at the moment, but should they really be canned for their ever-decreasing click-through rates?[a] Or are we asking the wrong questions and getting the wrong answers?

Click-through rates in 2002 are reputed to average 0.4 per cent for animated gif banners, with averages slightly higher for moving DHTML displays and other creative executions such as pop-ups and superstitials. Understandably, advertisers are beginning to question the value of online advertising, having seen these averages drop from as high as 5 per cent only a few years ago. Banners are unique in that they are one of the few advertising tools that have an accurate measure of response, but is this measure the right measure? Advertising is not simply about soliciting a direct reaction, it is also about raising awareness and brand building. The industry obsession with click-through rates ignores the capacity of banners to fulfil these other objectives.

For the right product, and the right marketing objectives, banners can still be one of the most effective online marketing tools. The Internet allows for precision placement of advertisements and also for highly creative 'interruption' marketing techniques to be deployed. Try not noticing the next time a DHTML banner floats across your browser window!

12.4.11 Online Promotions

If you have only a short time period to launch a product online, don't try to bring the people to you, take your product to the people. Some agencies regularly organize competitions promoting their clients' products on large third party websites and get massive exposure at low cost. It is a scientific process of identifying the best target sites in terms of demographic fit and traffic levels, and then negotiating the best deal. Competitions run from a week to a month, and there have been excellent results with partner sites such as GMTV, AOL, Sky Sports and CITV.

In addition to the exposure this gets for your product, you can often increase your e-mail marketing database by negotiating a share of data capture with the third party sites. At the same time, you can get your press release in front of the web editors for additional free exposure.

12.4.12 E-mail Stationery

You brand your stationery, your business cards, your communications and your website ... so what about your e-mails?

E-mail has become the main tool of communication for the modern business, yet most companies still send black text on white background for their day to day e-mail communications. Modern businesses send thousands of e-mails each week, and every message is a missed opportunity to reinforce your brand.

What most companies fail to realize is that you can now add branding to your e-mails and turn them into a dynamic communication tool. E-mail stationery can be stamped onto your outgoing e-mails allowing you to add colour, your logo and your company news onto every e-mail sent. Because you can hyperlink the images in your stationery, you can use it to drive

---

[a] The 'click-through rate' refers to the number of people that click on a banner advertisement to go to the advertised site.

traffic to your website too. Recipients simply click on the links in your e-mail stationery to launch their browser and go directly to the page on your website that you want them to visit. E-mail stationery can result in massive increases in site traffic and business.

12.5 Third Generation Telephones

As we saw in Section 8.6.2, the mobile communications industry has evolved in three stages:

[Analogue] → [Digital] → [Multimedia]

Three generations of mobile phones have emerged so far, each successive generation more reliable and flexible than the last:

- **Analogue**: You could only easily use analogue cellular phones to make voice calls, and typically only in any one country.
- **Digital** mobile phone systems added fax, data and messaging capabilities as well as voice telephone services in many countries.
- **Multimedia** services add high-speed data transfer to mobile devices, allowing new video, audio and other applications through mobile phones – now music, television and the Internet can be accessed through a mobile terminal.

With each new generation of technology, the services that can be deployed on them become more and more wide ranging and truly limited only by imagination. We are reaching that stage with 3G. During the first and second generations different regions of the world pursued different mobile phone standards, but are now converging to a common standard for mobile multimedia called third generation (3G) which is based on a single technology. Europe and North America both pursued their own separate standards for analogue communications and different standards for digital; 3G will bring these incompatible standards together.

The third generation of mobile communications systems will soon be implemented. Following on the heels of analogue and digital technology, the third generation will be digital mobile multimedia offering broadband mobile communications, with voice, video, graphics,

Table 12.1 The transition of mobile phone technology to third generation

Generation	Type	Time	Description
First	Analogue	1980s	Voice centric, multiple standards (NMT, TACS etc.)
Second	Digital	1990s	Voice centric, multiple standards (GSM, CDMA, TDMA)
2.5	Higher rate data	Late 1990s	Introduction of new higher speed data services to bridge the gap between the second and third generation, including services such as General Packet Radio Service (GPRS) and Enhanced Data Rates for Global Evolution (EDGE)
Third	Digital multimedia	2010s	Voice and data centric, single standard with multiple modes

audio and other information. This transition is shown in Table 12.1. For more information on this fascinating new area, go online to www.bh.com/companions/075065449X.

Summary

- The Internet has grown very rapidly and is only roughly thirty years old.
- We are all so 'busy' that we don't have time and don't want to be interrupted all the time, which has given rise to the idea of 'permission marketing'.
- It is essential to track people through a five-step metamorphosis, taking them from strangers into friends into customers into loyal customers – and then stop them becoming former customers.
- There are six key benefits of the Web: 1, Stamps are free; 2, Testing is fast; 3, Responses are high; 4, Curriculum marketing is possible; 5, Frequency is free; 6, Printing is free.
- There are six steps involved in organizing effective permission marketing on the Internet: 1, Give them a 'bait'; 2, Tell them a story over time; 3, Reinforce the incentive; 4, More incentives = more permission; 5, Leverage permission into profits; 6, Invest in the relationship.
- There are financial checks that you can give to evaluate your Web marketing.
- There is a whole new vocabulary entering into the language for e-commerce and marketing in the new media.
- Find out more online at www.bh.com/blahblahblah.

References

i Godin, S. *Permission Marketing* (Simon & Schuster, 1999).
ii See Stephen Godin's excellent text on the subject for a full discussion on permission marketing.
iii Godin, S. ibid.
iv See the Direct Marketing Association Code of Practice online: www/bh.com/blahblahblah.

Further Reading

Godin, S. *Permission Marketing* (Simon & Schuster, 1999). An excellent text on the subject for a full discussion of permission marketing. A 'must read'.

McDonald, M. and Wilson, H. *New Marketing* (Butterworth-Heinemann, 2002). Built around the leading concept of a value exchange with customers; an essential guide on how to harness the latest technology.

Smith, P. R. and Chaffey, D. *eMarketing eXcellence* (Butterworth-Heinemann, 2001). A highly structured and accessible introduction to the subject.

Bickerton, P., Bickerton, M. and Simpson-Holley, K. *Cyberstrategy* (Butterworth-Heinemann, 1998). For senior people with no technical background, this text discusses business strategy for Extranets, Intranets and the Internet.

Questions

1. What do you think would be appropriate 'bait' for a permission marketing programme for the following?

   (a) Pet products.

   (b) Gardening products.

   (c) Marketing consultancy and training.

2. Evaluate your organization on how early in the process of 'dating its customers' it notices people.

3. Considering your City or County Council where you live, what sort of things would you be interested in finding out about how they are spending their money? Would the Internet be a good medium for these communications? Explain your reasoning.

4. It has been suggested that third generation telephones offer a new medium for all marketers. Discuss this statement from the point of view of marketers of:

   (a) Home entertainment products.

   (b) Industrial products.

   (c) Financial services.

Chapter 13

The practice of pricing

Introduction

By the end of this chapter you will:

- Understand that price is a complex issue and that deciding what is the 'right' price is not an easy matter.
- Be aware of the key aspects that have a bearing on what the price of a product should be.
- Understand the influences on pricing professional services.
- Appreciate that setting the level of price is one ingredient in the strategy for marketing a product (or range of products) successfully.
- Be familiar with a logical process for setting prices.

'But if you have a good product, don't spoil it by trying to sell it too cheaply. In other words, give the consumer the price which he wants and remember that it is not necessarily the cheapest price which will give him the greatest satisfaction.'

A. Gabor. *Pricing in Theory and Practice*

13.1 What is Price?

Price means something quite different to those on one side of the deal and those on the other. Price tells the supplier, manufacturer, service provider or retailer if their accounting methods are good enough and how much profit they will make; and it tells the purchaser what the cost will be to them, though cost is not necessarily evaluated purely in terms of immediate cash payment.

A large proportion of individuals, when they buy a high value item like a car or house, do so through a hire-purchase or mortgage agreement. The important factor then becomes the size of the weekly or monthly payment. An industrial purchaser may actually be expecting to save costs by installing a particular piece of equipment. In both cases, the purchaser may well be comparing the value or benefit they will get from this purchase with that from spending the same money in some other way.

In Kotler's 'four Cs' (see Section 5.7), cost is the equivalent from the customer's point of view to price from the seller's. It is the cost of ownership that often goes beyond the consideration of initial price paid. For example, while a given car may have a similar specification to another make, and be at pretty much the same market price in the showroom, the cost of ownership of each make may differ in the potential owner's eyes. Such issues as the cost of spares, cost of servicing, availability of a dealership network countrywide, as well as second hand value, all add up to the 'cost of ownership' from the driver's point of view.

Both personal and industrial buyers see price to some extent as a signal of quality. A. Gabor, in the article quoted from at the head of this chapter,[i] gives some examples of products that failed to sell because they were priced too low. In one case, oil with an unusual specification could not be sold at a low price, but when re-offered as a special formulation at a high price, it sold very well. In the early part of the new millennium, the lager Stella Artois was positioned in its advertising as being 'reassuringly expensive'. Dropping its price in order to capture a greater volume share of the market could undermine its multi-million pound brand position. Anderson Consulting or KPMG could not provide low-cost consultancy without undermining their credibility in the market. People expect to pay premium rates for premium products or services.

It is easy to test that this is a commonplace reaction. Ask any group of, say, a dozen people what they would expect to pay for a normal household appliance such as a refrigerator of a certain size and appearance. While they may be fairly vague about the price, after a little discussion most will agree on it falling within a band, such as £175 to £225. Only a small number would be willing to pay more, and they would expect to obtain better quality in return. Usually no one would be willing to pay a price below the agreed range because of the danger of receiving a product of unacceptable quality. Thus prices are a signal to the buyer of both cost and quality.

13.1.1 The Plateau Effect

For many products there is a top limit on price, above which few people are prepared to go for a given level of quality. Traditionally, the haberdashery and drapery trades always priced items at one farthing below the shilling unit price (e.g. 1s 11¾d or one shilling, eleven pence and three farthings). While 2 shillings may have been simpler, it may have represented the upper limit of the generally accepted price of a given item, and the cost of a small packet of pins was a farthing, making a simple additional sale possible.

The lack of small fractions of currency units and a high rate of inflation obscure to some extent the fact that this approach to pricing is still commonly applied. However, a look in most shoe shops, for example, will still show footwear at prices such as £39.95 (or even £39.99), and many other examples can readily be found.

It is well established that when buying gifts people have a sum of money in mind. They go shopping for something costing 'about a couple of pounds' or 'somewhere around a fiver'. Sometimes it is important that a present is known by the receiver of the gift to have cost a lot of money. Some perfumes, jewellery, and certain brands of chocolates illustrate the point. Offering these products at a lower price might well make them less, not more, attractive to the buyers.

Companies selling items intended to be given as gifts produce them at prices that fit into one of the categories in which customers themselves rank gifts. Thus, one company produced a range of birthday cards incorporating a game or a 'cut-out' to meet the need of mothers whose children have been invited to a school friend's party; an ordinary birthday card costing, say, 80p would be 'too little', and a gift costing, say, £5 'too much', but a card also serving as a small gift and costing perhaps £1.50 is 'just right'.

Thus the purchaser does not see the price of a product simply in terms of 'what is the cheapest'. Rather, price is one element in the total 'bundle of satisfactions' which, as we saw in Chapter 3, is what really constitutes a product in the customer's eyes.

But this is a very subjective approach. Let us now examine some of the other factors that enter into pricing decisions.

13.2 The Economist's View of Price – Market Pricing

In classical economics, as we find it in the basic textbooks, the view of price stems from the theory of supply and demand. Simply put, this states that:

- Demand will fall as price increases.
- Supply will rise as price increases.

This is logical and in agreement with common sense to a large degree. It is obvious that, all things being equal, the rise in price of a product will cause fewer people to want to buy it, and the demand will fall off ('demand' in economics means the quantity that will be bought at a particular price). It is equally obvious that, if manufacturers are supplying a limited quantity of goods at a given price, then the unsatisfied demand will tend to force up the price and, as the price rises, more manufacturers will be inclined to produce similar goods, so that the supply will increase.

In economic theory a measure called **elasticity** is used to indicate how much demand changes in response to an increase or decrease in price. This can be calculated as follows:

$$\text{Price elasticity of demand} = \%\ \text{Change in quantity demanded} \ / \ \%\ \text{Change in price}$$

Thus, if elasticity is less than 1, a change in price gives a less than proportionate change in demand – the demand is relatively inelastic. If elasticity is more than 1, then a change in price gives a more than proportionate change in demand, and the demand is relatively elastic. In a situation where demand is high and supplies low, manufacturers may be able to price very high or 'charge what the market will bear', as it is often expressed.

Economists are accustomed to indicating these relations graphically, as in Figures 13.1 and 13.2. When these two graphs are superimposed we get the position of a point of equilibrium at E (Figure 13.3), where the quantity supplied, Q, is equal to the amount demanded at price P.

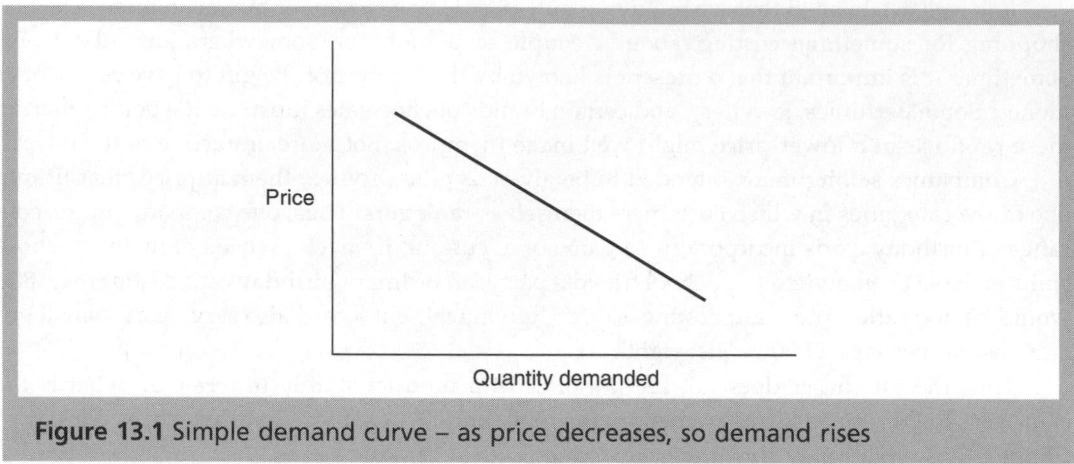

Figure 13.1 Simple demand curve – as price decreases, so demand rises

Now, while it is true that in real life there will be a tendency for things to reach equilibrium in this way, in practice it is not usually quite so simple. The reason lies in the phrase 'all things being equal'. In real life all things are not equal.

For 'laws' of supply and demand to be true, economists have to assume a state of **perfect competition**, i.e. a market in which all suppliers and buyers are fully aware of the prices at which goods are available, and where each type of goods is homogeneous. This is true in certain markets, such as primary commodities (e.g. metals, grain, cotton), currencies and stocks and shares. But in most markets in real life buyers and sellers do not have complete knowledge of the prices at which goods are on offer. And, much more important, goods are certainly not homogeneous, but widely differing in performance, quality and many other respects. Indeed, in a competitive economy, the seller's aim will normally be to bring about a situation where his product or service is clearly different from other people's – to establish, as we saw in Section 1.6, a 'competitive differential advantage'.

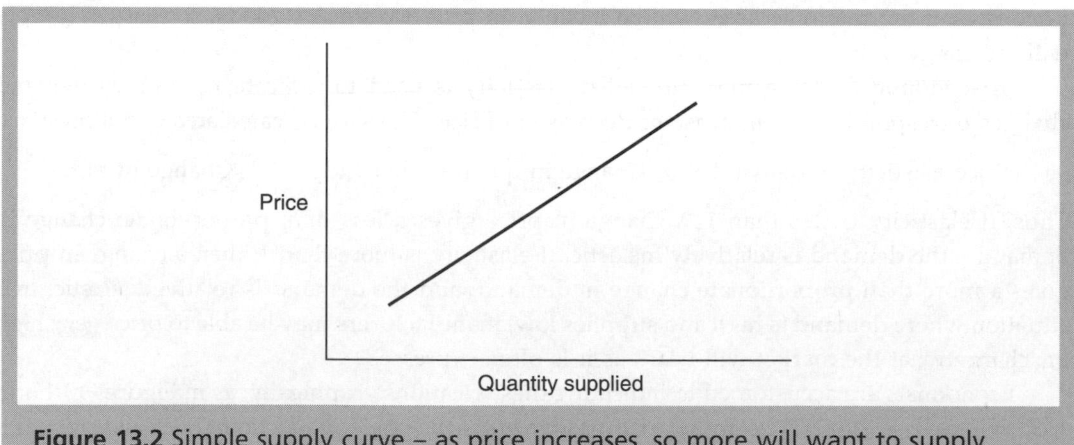

Figure 13.2 Simple supply curve – as price increases, so more will want to supply

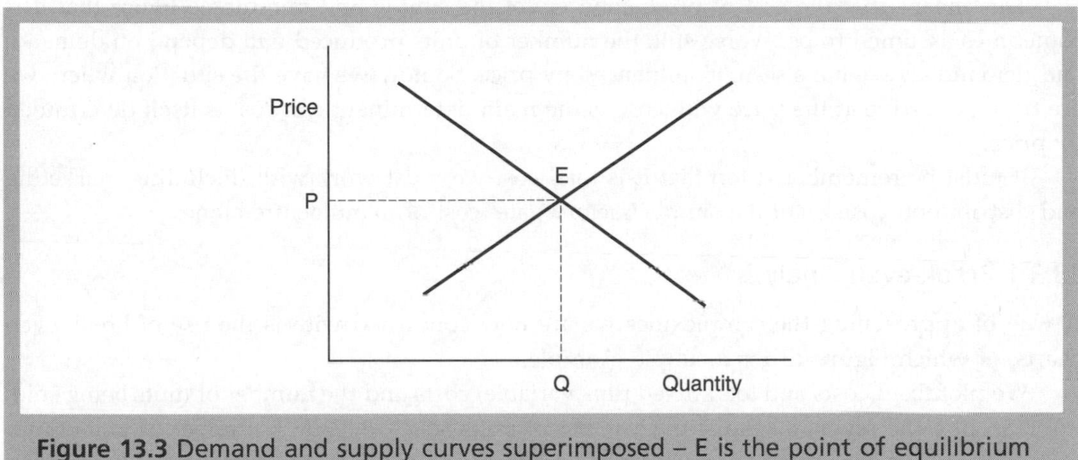

Figure 13.3 Demand and supply curves superimposed – E is the point of equilibrium

Thus, although total demand for a particular category of goods is an important factor in determining the price people will pay, it is by no means the only factor and is frequently not even the most important factor. For example, the total demand for confectionery may well have virtually no bearing on the price that can be obtained by a manufacturer of very expensive, high quality liqueur chocolates mainly bought as Christmas gifts. What then are the other factors affecting pricing decisions?

13.3 The Importance of Manufacturing Costs – Cost-plus Pricing

Most people, whether beginners in the study of marketing or senior businessmen, when asked how prices are arrived at, will start from the cost of manufacture. The most common approach is 'cost-plus', or calculating the basic production cost and adding on a margin for profit.

While the preceding sections will have indicated that cost and profit margin may not be the sole keys to arriving at the 'right' price, clearly they are important elements. At worst, if costs are not recovered, the firm cannot survive. Similarly, if a 'reasonable' profit is not obtained, again the firm cannot survive in the long run.

The cost-plus approach, therefore, contains some all-important elements and also has the merit, in principle, of simplicity. In practice, however, things are not so simple, because we need to know: (a) what the cost is and (b) what a reasonable profit is.

The problem with determining the cost is that usually the cost per unit depends on the quantity being produced. This is because there are certain fixed costs – rent, rates, capital charges or rental on machinery and equipment, certain wages and salaries – that are incurred whatever the level of production. As the quantity produced increases, the fixed cost per unit decreases. In addition, there are variable costs incurred as each unit is produced, for raw materials, power, and some other wages. It is the total of fixed costs and variable costs divided by the number of units produced that gives us the total cost per unit.

This means that the cost of production is not the simple and immutable figure that it is sometimes assumed to be. Worse still, the number of units produced will depend on demand, and demand, as we have seen, is influenced by price. So now we have the situation where we are trying to arrive at the price with cost as the main determinant, yet cost is itself determined by price.

It must be remembered too that it is total cost we must work with (including marketing and distribution costs), not the simple 'factory gate' cost of manufacture alone.

13.3.1 Break-even Analysis

A way of approaching the complexities we are now concerned with is the use of break-even charts, of which Figure 13.4 is a simple example.

We plot fixed costs and total (fixed plus variable) costs and the number of units being sold. We then plot the revenue against the number of units sold (revenue = number of units times price per unit). Where total revenue equals total cost we have the break-even point, but only at that price.

We can go on to plot a series of break-even charts at different prices, to establish how many units we would need to sell in order to break-even at each price in turn. At the same time we can do a similar series of calculations (or they might have to be 'intelligent guesses') to find what the level of demand is likely to be at each price. We can then say, 'At price level X, demand is likely to be Y units and at Y units we do or do not break-even'.

The **'break-even volume'** can be calculated, using the formula:

$$\text{Break-even volume (BEV)} = \text{Fixed costs} \ / \ \text{Price per unit} - \text{Variable cost per unit}$$

Thus, if a firm has fixed costs of £100,000, a selling price of £6 per unit and variable costs of £4 per unit, the break-even quantity (the quantity that must be sold before any profit is achieved) is 50,000 units. That is:

$$\text{BEV} = £100,000 \ / \ £6 - £4 = 50,000$$

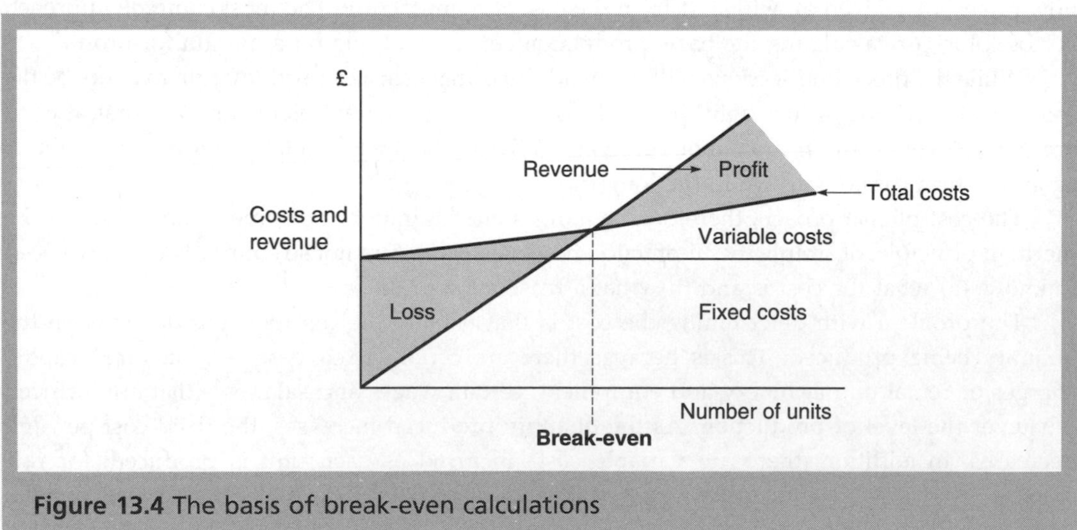

Figure 13.4 The basis of break-even calculations

The figure arrived at when variable cost per unit is deducted from selling price is known as the **contribution**. In the example above, the contribution will be £2.00 per unit.

We see, then, that the cost per unit changes as the number of units changes. Generally speaking, the cost per unit decreases as the total number of units increases. However, it is possible to reach a situation, as depicted in Figure 13.5, where, beyond a certain point (C in the figure here), overtime rates or shift-work, coupled with fully utilized equipment (where further volume can only be achieved by subcontracting the production to another supplier), lead to a sharp increase in cost per unit.

Thus, to fix a price based on cost plus profit, we have to decide first at what level of production the cost is to be calculated. If in fact that level is not reached, profit may be much less than anticipated or there could even be a loss. Even greatly exceeding the anticipated level of production may bring higher costs in some cases – with the same result.

In any case, our price must be related to what customers expect to pay. Cost represents the level below which the price cannot go. In situations where manufacture is on a contract basis – in civil engineering for example – the level of output is exactly known in advance. The desired margin of profit can be added to produce a price that is then either above or below the competition's, and acceptable to the customer or not acceptable. But in the majority of situations, where cost per unit depends on the (as yet unknown) quantity to be produced, other factors have to be taken into account. (See Sections 13.4, 13.5, 13.8 and 13.9.)

13.3.2 Standard Cost Pricing

A development of the cost-plus approach to setting prices is to use cost 'standards' based on management accounting systems. Variable costs of production (materials, labour, bought-in components etc.) are added up and divided by the number of units intended to be produced, to give a variable cost per unit. Similarly, running costs of the organization (rent, rates, energy, maintenance etc., together with management and administrative costs) are totalled and divided

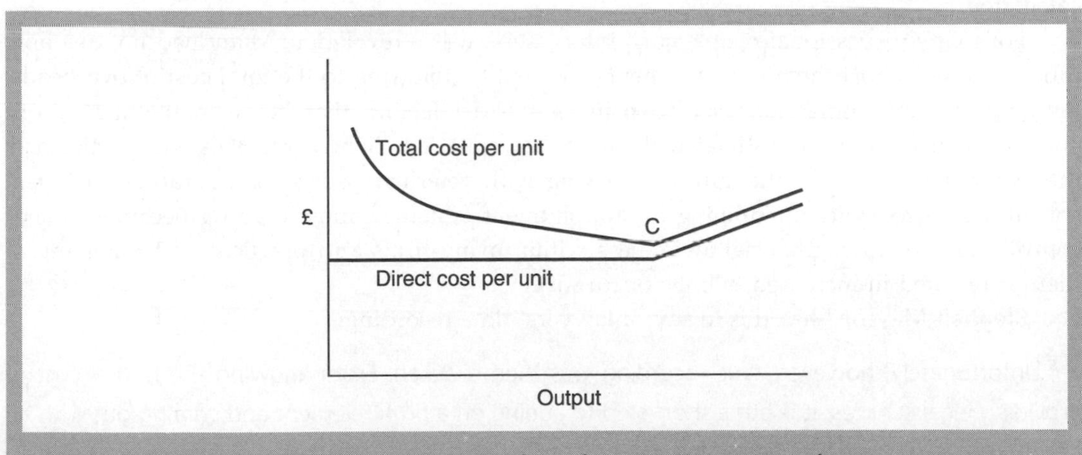

Figure 13.5 How cost per unit can sometimes increase as output rises

by the number of units to be sold, to provide the fixed cost per unit. Finally the profit required is added in on a per unit basis.

Adding together the variable cost, fixed cost and profit per unit gives the selling price. This approach is much used by companies producing a large range of products because it allows a complex situation to be subjected to disciplined control using standard accounting methods.

While nothing could be simpler, it turns out that this is not the most successful method of setting prices. The first problem is that it assumes that costs are the thing that causes people to buy. But customers are not the least bit interested in costs. They are interested in getting what they want at a price that reflects the value of the product or service to them.

Using a standard cost system, full cost accounting, full cost pricing, call it what you will, if your fixed costs are treated on a percentage basis, then if you manage to get your fixed costs down, your selling prices go down too. This is not the best way to drive profit up! So, as your selling price goes down, so will your actual profit per unit (but not your magic percentage profit). There was one agency chairman who placed a notice in his account manager's office: '17.5 per cent of nothing is still nothing!' alluding to the fact that charging a fixed commission on a small fee results in an even smaller figure. (See Section 13.8 for variations on pricing structures.)

In other words, using costs as a basis for calculating prices needs tempering by consideration of what customers want and what they are prepared to pay if maximum profit is to be achieved (and sometimes if the company is even to be perceived as a high-quality supplier – See Section 13.1).

13.4 Pricing of Professional Services

Time recording was originally 'sold' to the legal profession (and then the other professional service firms such as accounting and consulting) as a way of measuring the cost of providing legal services. By comparing the hours spent on various aspects of client work with the overhead costs of running the business, the hourly cost rate (or expense of time) can be calculated.

For many professional people such information was a revelation. Many had no idea how much it actually cost them to serve clients – except by referring to the total cost of overheads. Before then, many professional service firms only had a 'feeling' that they were making a profit and they constantly underestimated the time they spent on client work. This was particularly the experience of one of the authors working with veterinary surgeons operating an 'open' consulting period without running an appointment system. Time recording became a major contributor to greater financial awareness within many firms and practices and for many of them it resulted in increased billings or turnover.

Stephen Mayson[ii] has this to say of lawyers' time recording:

> "Unfortunately, however, time recording was then hijacked. From knowing the hourly cost of providing legal services, it is but a short step to adding on a profit element and coming out with an hourly charge-out rate – a charge that can be used for calculating fees based on the amount of time spent on a client's matter."

At first glance, this appears a reasonable way of charging clients for legal advice (certainly better than the traditional approach of weighing the file and guessing at what the client can afford). However, the ability to record time shows nothing more than the ability to record time. If a lawyer charges a client by the hour, what incentive is there for them to work quickly and efficiently? Simply put, the longer a lawyer works on a matter, the more the client will have to pay. To quote Stephen Mayson again: 'Such a system has no intrinsic merit. It overlooks the value of a matter (and of the advice given), bears no necessary relation to the expertise brought to bear by the lawyer involved ...'

For lawyers, there exists an Order that guides them on the evaluation of their costs:[iii]

'3. A solicitor's costs shall be such a sum as may be fair and reasonable to both solicitor and entitled person (this means a client or an entitled third party), having regard to all the circumstances of the case and in particular to:

(a) the complexity of the matter or the difficulty or novelty of the questions raised;

(b) the skill, labour, specialised knowledge and responsibility involved;

(c) the time spent on the business;

(d) the number and importance of the documents prepared or perused, without regard to length;

(e) the place where and the circumstances in which the business or any part thereof is transacted;

(f) the amount or value of any money or property involved;

(g) whether any land involved is registered land;

(h) the importance of the matter to the client; and

(i) the approval (express or implied) of the entitled person or the express approval of the testator to:

  (i) the solicitor undertaking all or any part of the work giving rise to the costs or

  (ii) the amount of the costs.'

In a market economy, the price of economic resources is a function of supply and demand. In this sense, the professional service provider's fees may well reflect the industry life cycle and the services life cycle (see Chapter 3); they will also depend on what clients perceive their providers to be selling. However, it would be a rare occurrence for any jurisdiction to leave the marketplace entirely to its own devices to determine the level of all professionals' fees. There is, in fact, usually a continuum from strictly regulated fees to unregulated.[iv]

13.5 Pricing to Achieve Target Profits

The assumption made in simple economics theory is that in a situation of imperfect competition companies will be 'profit maximizers', that is, they will aim to make the highest profit the situation allows. A simple approach to achieving this is to charge 'what the market will bear' – the highest price that customers are prepared to pay (although once again we have the difficulty that in many situations price will affect the quantity sold). In practice, however, most companies seem rather to aim at a satisfactory level of profit – in economics language they are 'satisficers'.[v] But this brings us back to the question introduced at the beginning of Section 13.3 – what is a satisfactory level of profit?

Clearly it is not enough to aim purely at the greatest amount of total profit, regardless of all other considerations. For example, suppose a business with £100,000 invested in it earns profits of £20,000 – or 20%. Then suppose that profits could be increased by a further £2000 per annum – or 2% – but only by using further capital of £100,000. Clearly, this would not be a good use (and risk) of the additional £100,000, which would earn more in the bank, even if the base rates were low (as they were in early 2002).

We have to look then at maximization of the percentage of profit in relation to the capital used in the business (usually referred to as 'return on capital employed' or 'ROCE'). There is a slight complication, since capital employed can be calculated in a number of different ways, but only the principle need concern us here.

A company can set as its objective a return of 10 per cent, 20 per cent or whatever on the capital employed in the business. The break-even approach can be used to establish whether a given project is likely to achieve this result and, only if it is, will the project be taken up.

13.4.1 Market Pricing

In Section 13.4 we referred to charging 'what the market will bear'. An alternative, more useful, term is market pricing. This is where the only sensible price to charge is what the customers perceive the product to be worth. Obvious examples are things sold by auction – in the art market, for instance. The price is what the highest bidder is 'prepared to go to'. Similar conditions apply to a large degree in the used housing market, where the vendors can ask whatever price they like but what they get ultimately depends on negotiating the best price a buyer is willing to pay. An important consideration in many situations, however, is the buyers' perception of the product they are being offered. When the products are unique and/or appeal to a select group of people, this can be the overriding consideration.

13.5 Marginal Cost Pricing

In a highly competitive situation companies may have the opportunity to gain business if they can offer a sufficiently low price. This is especially the case where individual contracts are negotiated such as for large construction projects, but is also increasingly evident in markets such as electrical appliances, where discount houses and other large retail chains are often in a position to 'shop around' for the best bulk discounts.

The question may then arise, 'What is the lowest level at which it makes sense to take the business?'. One approach to this is to carry out a marginal costing calculation. In economics, marginal cost is the cost of producing one more unit. Usually in practice this means that fixed costs are already being recovered by a sufficient level of sales of units priced as discussed in the previous sections. The cost of producing extra units then affects the variable costs only, so that even if a very small profit per unit can be added, the business is worth taking.

We can go on from there and argue that even at no profit the business would be worth taking, because it may use resources (including people) that would otherwise stand idle. The danger here is that success in selling at these price levels may lead to additional orders and perhaps the situation indicated towards the end of Section 13.3.1, where additional business actually eats into existing profits. For this reason many do not regard marginal costing as a method of pricing but 'purely as a way of deciding whether certain orders should be accepted or not'.

13.6 Competitors and Pricing

Clearly, what competitors are doing cannot be ignored when setting prices. For example, a company with a small share of the market will probably find the general price level already set for him. This does not of course rule out the possibility of finding a differential advantage, which will enable a price well above the general level to be charged, especially if only a small segment of the market is being attacked. (See also Chapter 6 on marketing planning; Figure 6.8.) For example, the fact that ballpoint pens are widely available for a few pence does not prevent Parker's doing good business with very expensive (and top quality) pens for the gift market.

Very often it will be wise to accept competitive prices as the starting point for any development of a marketing strategy. This does assume, however, and possibly wrongly, that competitors have got their sums right. Against this, in an established market consumers will probably have come to accept this level as the 'going rate', and will need a lot of convincing if they are to accept something different. Traditionally the concept of the 'just price' has been talked of in some quarters. This was supposed to be the price acceptable to both buyers and sellers. Normally, of course, this will be the price level that has been obtained in the market over recent times – in other words, what the major competitors in the field are currently charging.

Where the 'going rate' is set in this way by competitors, it is often useful to do backward costing, i.e. start with the price at which the product must be sold and then work backwards to the price at which it has to be produced if profit targets are to be met.

The term **competitive pricing** is sometimes used to describe a price-setting policy where the 'going rate' set by competitors is used as a reference point. A price may be set 'in line with' the competitor's price or 'higher than' or 'lower than' the competitor's price, perhaps on the basis that we wish our product to be perceived as 'better than' or 'cheaper than' the already established competitive product. (See also Chapter 2.)

13.7 Pricing Strategies

We have already indicated that, rather than a single price that is right for a particular product, it is more likely that buyers will be thinking in terms of an acceptable price range. This will be with a 'ceiling' price above which demand might be expected to fall off significantly and a 'floor' price below which costs would not be recovered. It is even possible, by changing the attributes of the product (e.g. by giving it additional features or promoting its exclusive qualities), to gain acceptance for a price well above the normal range.

Even within the generally acceptable price range, however, the company must make a decision about where in that range to pitch its prices. In making such decisions there is often a strategic element, depending partly on what the company's objectives are. There are five common price objectives:

1. Achieve target return on investment or net sales.
2. Stabilize prices.
3. Maintain or improve target share of market.
4. Match or undercut competition.
5. Maximize profits.

In a situation where the aim is to stabilize prices, i.e. avoid price cutting, price wars and consequent lowering of profits, then clearly a follow-my-leader pricing policy is likely to be adopted. There are, however, a whole range of pricing strategies that may be adopted, and here we focus attention on the two extremes, normally referred to as 'skim-the-cream' and 'penetration pricing'.

13.7.1 Skim-the-cream Pricing

This means setting a price high in the acceptable range of prices, sometimes for a short period only, often for longer. It is largely, though not exclusively, associated with new products, for the following reasons:

- In the early stages of a product's life (because there are few direct alternatives) demand is likely to be less elastic, i.e. less price-sensitive.
- A high price may segment the market. Exclusivity can be used to appeal to certain income groups. At a later stage lowering the price can widen the appeal.
- If a mistake is made, it is easier to lower the price subsequently than to raise it.
- High initial prices can be used to recoup heavy research and development expenditure (a reason why this policy is commonly followed by the home electronics industry among others).
- Since production capacity may well be limited initially, a relatively low level of demand can be an advantage.

Typical of products where a 'skim-the-cream' policy is applied are newly discovered ethical pharmaceuticals. Here there is high investment on research and development to be recovered, a market virtually closed to competition by patent protection – at least in the short run – and a probable high demand if the new drug cures a disease previously hard to treat.

It is also often used for all kinds of high-technology products. Cellnet telephones when introduced in the late 1980s cost several hundred pounds, but by 1994 could be had for under £50 and came lighter in weight and with better performance. Now mobile telephones are often free when linked to particular tariffs and customers are encouraged to change their phone to 'suit their moods'.

13.7.2 Penetration Pricing

Here a relatively low price is set in order to gain maximum penetration of the market as quickly as possible. This has obvious advantages where large economies of scale can be gained from higher levels of production, and it also makes the market less attractive to competitors. A necessary condition of successfully applying this approach is, of course, that reducing the price will substantially increase the demand, i.e. the demand must be elastic.

Once a company has gained dominance of the market by penetration pricing, it can be very difficult for a competitor to enter successfully. The classic and often quoted example was the introduction of the small Japanese motorcycle in the early 1960s, pioneered by Honda. Apart from being low priced, they were also very reliable. Once they had established the brand and a network of dealerships, and had begun to win competitive motorcycle events, they then moved up to the larger capacity machines. This had the effect of nearly decimating the UK motorcycle manufacturers' market and it was not until the late 1990s that the Triumph brand once more became a serious competitor in the more prestigious superbike sector.

The Internet opened the door for popular music artists to market their own music rather than sign a contract with a major record label. Offering their own music at less than the price of the CD in a retail shop allows them to carve a niche in the market. Since the cost of selling extra units of music – downloaded tracks – is so small, even a small profit per unit can be such as to make the whole enterprise profitable. In this way, artists can penetrate the market and achieve a significant share of the listening public's attention without losing out to the record label. By 2002, such practice was reputed to have cost the music industry several billion in lost revenue.

13.8 Price Structures

So far we have talked of 'a price' or 'the price'. In practice, a whole structure of related prices has to be devised.

Only when the manufacturer sells direct to the user is there a simple one-price arrangement. Usually we need to ask 'The price to whom?'. Where the goods pass through a distribution chain, such as manufacturer to wholesaler to retailer to customer, there may be a whole series of prices appropriate to each stage of the process. Wholesalers and retailers each need revenue to cover their own operating costs and profit. Traditionally this was often achieved by the manufacturer fixing the end price to the ultimate customer and allowing a discount to the retailer and a further discount to the wholesaler.

The price structure would then look something like this:

Retail price	£5.00
Less retailer's discount 20 per cent	£1.00
Price to retailer	£4.00
Less wholesaler's discount 10 per cent	£0.40
Price to wholesaler	£3.60

The abolition of resale price maintenance meant that manufacturers could not enforce a fixed retail price. So, in the UK at least, the alternative system is now much more common. The producer starts at the other end with a price **'ex factory'** (i.e., for goods bought direct from the manufacturer) and dealers at each stage add their own **'mark-up'** to cover costs and profit, as follows:

Ex-factory price	£3.60
Wholesale mark-up 10 per cent	£0.36
Price to retailer	£3.96
Retail mark-up 25 per cent	£1.00
Retail price	£4.96

The difference between mark-up and discount is sometimes confused, and it is important to get the distinction clear. A 20 per cent discount is the same as a 25 per cent mark-up. (For example, if a retailer bought from a manufacturer at £80 and sold for £100 he would be adding a 25 per cent mark-up. If, however, the manufacturer sets a 'recommended retail price' of £100 but sells to the retailer at £80 he is giving a 20 per cent discount off the higher price.)

Frequently used in pricing are 'quantity discounts'. Here the price will vary according to the quantity bought (on the basis that transport costs, administration and so on will be proportionately higher on small deliveries than on large ones). Some manufacturers rely exclusively on quantity discounts and do not have separate wholesale or retail price lists. Anyone can buy direct and the price is determined solely by the quantity bought.

A further source of price differences is '**differential pricing**'. Different price levels may be set, for example, for delivery to different parts of the country (to reflect transport costs). Rail fares are commonly cheaper at times when fewer people travel (in an attempt to divert pressure from the overloaded trains to those with free capacity). Hotel rates are cheaper in the 'off-season' or at weekends for the same kind of reason.

Clearly, in all the calculations in Sections 13.3 to 13.8, close liaison with the accountants within the company is vital. They will need to supply many of the figures, and in return they will need to be advised of any pricing proposals, so that they can study the implications.

See Sections 10.1.4 and 10.11.1 for observations on price promotions and the confusion that has often been developed to limit price comparisons between competitors by customers.

13.8.1 The Importance of Negotiation

In many business-to-business marketing situations, the price structure worked out by the marketing organization will often be merely a starting point for discussion. Large retail chains, industrial organizations and public authorities (such as county supplies departments or regional hospital authorities) normally place very large contracts. This gives them enormous buying power and makes their business highly desirable. So a dialogue has to take place between buyer and seller and this demands negotiating skill on both sides in order to arrive at the most advantageous 'deal'. Often the negotiations with large buyers will be handled by specialist salesmen often called key accounts executives or national accounts executives (see Section 16.2).

13.9 Price Changes

There can be a number of situations that cause companies to consider changing their prices:

1. Substantial changes in cost.
2. Hold-ups in output (e.g. strikes, raw material or component shortages).

3. Sharp increase in demand.
4. Change in competitors' behaviour (e.g. price increases, changes in output).
5. Changing economic situation including changing currency exchange rates.
6. Legislation or other pressures from government.
7. Changing price as a deliberate marketing strategy.

13.9.1 Price Cutting

Firms can be 'pushed' into deliberate price cutting because, for example: (a) they must have immediate cash; (b) sales must be increased urgently or (c) management feel the need to do something.

Alternatively, price cutting may be used as a deliberate 'pull' strategy in order to, for example: (a) drive out marginal producers; (b) achieve lower costs by expanding sales or (c) improve distributors' turnover and hence encourage their support. In the early years of the new millennium a 'soft' market (due to the global slow-down in the world economy and the events of 11th September 2001 in New York) meant that in many markets price could not be strictly maintained. Hotels, for example, would offer very attractive prices for rooms or conferences when faced by a knowledgeable customer determined to get a discount. Airlines were offering more and more attractive discounts in their desperate need to keep the decrease in sales volume and/or market share as low as possible. Many operators brought in the receivers. In the UK, the tourist industry faced many additional problems caused by a foot-and-mouth outbreak that closed much of the British countryside.

13.9.2 Competitors and Price Changes

Before deciding on price changes it is necessary to consider what is likely to be our competitors' response. This may be to:

- Match our new price.
- Cut the price still further (assuming our new price is lower).
- Offer alternative benefits (e.g. product quality, service, advertising or other forms of promotion).
- Offer better back-up to resellers.
- Attempt to persuade the price-cutter to come back into line (by persuasion and/or threat of retaliation).

(NB When faced with price cuts by a competitor some action must be taken or the company's own volume will probably suffer.)

A company's attitude to price changing should be influenced by its relative positions in a particular market. Thus a brand leader can probably also be a 'price leader', whereas a company with a small market share may have to fix its prices very much in the light of the lead given by its larger competitors.

13.9.3 How Customers React to Price Changes

Customers may see a price change as meaning, for example, that:

- The quality of the product has changed.
- The product is about to be superseded.
- The change will be followed by further changes in the same direction.
- The seller is in financial difficulty.

A large increase in price for an item that represents an important purchase may affect customers in the following ways:

- Alters their financial resources and so changes their pattern of spending on other things.
- Makes it necessary for them to borrow.
- Increases their monthly repayments.

The effect of price cutting on customers will vary, depending on:

- Frequency of purchase.
- Timing of the price cut.
- Whether the product can be stored.

As with competitors, the likely reaction of customers to any price change must be very carefully considered before any action is taken, and should be continuously monitored.

13.9.4 Distributors and Price Changes

Account must also be taken of the likely reaction of distributors who may be carrying stocks purchased at the old price. Consideration may have to be given to compensating them if the new price is lower. See also Chapter 16, Section 16.2, dealing with account management.

13.10 The Price-setting Process

Figure 13.6 illustrates the complexity of the price-setting process. The person or group with the task of setting a price has first to deal with a mass of information and arrive at an acceptable price range based on an assessment of:

- The market, including PEST factors (see Section 1.7).
- Cost – see earlier sections of this chapter.
- Customer expectations.
- Competitive strategies.
- The economic situation etc.

But this will seldom lead to a clear-cut, one and only 'right' price. The company's own policies and goals will have an influence. Typically (though oversimplifying the situation), sales people tend to argue for a lower price to make their task easier; production people would prefer not to

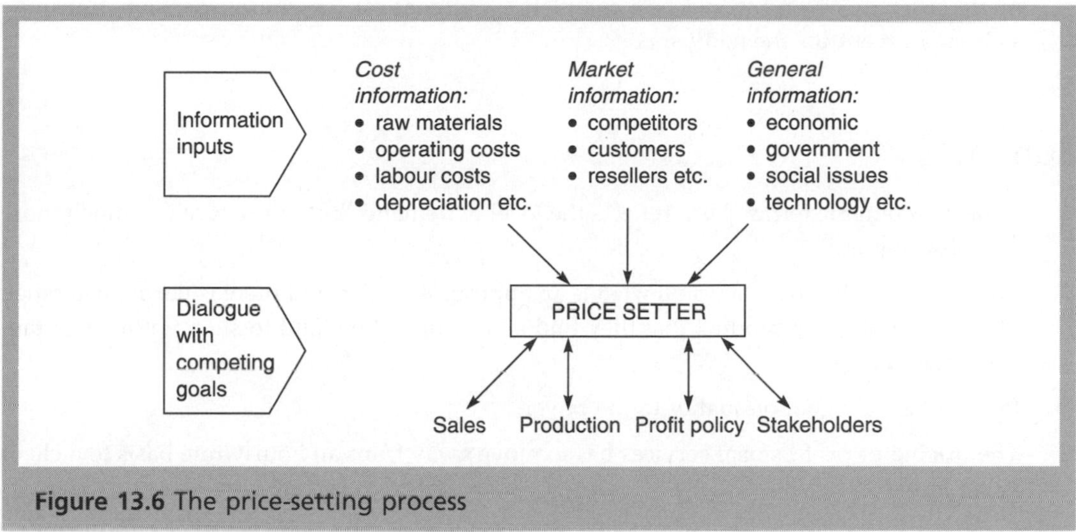

Figure 13.6 The price-setting process

be too restricted in their choice of production methods, materials etc. and so tend to argue for a higher price; and finance and general management will 'take a view' on the profit level that is desirable or essential.

The following is a suggested sequence to be followed in the price-setting task:

1. Identify end customers and distribution channels. Establish any views and feelings they have about price.
2. Define the level of service, sales support etc. that will be necessary.
3. Consider competitors' pricing policies and evaluate them in terms of:
   (a) relative power in the marketplace (e.g. are they in a position to dictate price levels? – see Section 13.6);
   (b) what their reaction is likely to be to any pricing moves we make;
   (c) how loyal are their customers and ours (how much would a lower price encourage customers to switch suppliers)?
4. Estimate likely sales levels and then calculate costs of manufacture, distribution etc. (see Section 13.3).
5. Establish the 'floor' price and 'ceiling' price and decide on pricing strategy (see Section 13.8).
6. Establish prices of individual products within the range. This is sometimes referred to as '**team pricing**', i.e. prices are established not one at a time but considering the collective effect of the prices of the whole product range. For example, one particular marque of car may have an 'entry level' or 'economy' model at a very attractive price (enabling advertising to claim 'The new Sorcerer from only £7995'). However, other models with more accessories, better performance etc. are priced differently. The top of the range Sorcerer

might cost £15,995 and would be a completely different car (engine, suspension, transmission etc.) except for the body shell.

Summary

- In basic economic terms, price reflects the level of demand, but in practice is a much more complex matter.
- Buyers have subjective views on what is an appropriate price and there is normally a range of prices for a given product that they find acceptable. They tend to shop within a certain price bracket.
- Price is also a signal of quality to the buyer.
- The pricing of professional services has to move away from an hourly rate basis to a client value basis.
- From the seller's point of view, cost is only one element in fixing the price. Cost is in any case not simple to arrive at, because cost per unit normally varies with output, which is itself influenced by the price.
- Break-even analysis enables cost per unit to be calculated at various levels of demand and on different price assumptions.
- Companies may be profit maximizers but are more likely to see their objectives in terms of reaching an acceptable profit target when they behave as 'satisficers'.
- Competitors' pricing policies are an important factor, and may influence choice of pricing strategy between the two extremes of skim-the-cream and penetration pricing.
- A company's price structure will probably take account of wholesale and retail profit margins. In addition, or as an alternative, it may include quantity discounts. In some situations a differential pricing policy may be adopted.
- On different occasions prices have to be adjusted and the impact of this on consumers and distributors will need to be accurately predicted, as well as the likely reaction of competitors.

References

i A 'classic statement' in *Management Decision* (Summer 1967); included in *Modern Marketing Management* (Penguin, 1971).

ii Mayson, S. *Making Sense of Law Firms* (Blackstone Press, 1997).

iii Solicitors' (Non-contentious Business) Renumeration Order 1994, from Annex 14D, *The Guide to The Professional Conduct of Solicitors* (The Law Society, 3rd Edition, 1999).

iv See also Skordaki, E. and Walker, D. *Regulating and Changing for Legal Services: An International Comparison*, Research Study No. 12 (The Law Society, 1994).

v From Chambers Dictionary, this means 'to aim for or achieve that which will satisfy or suffice, rather than a potential maximum.'

Further Reading

Baker, Michael, J. *The Marketing Book* (Butterworth-Heinemann, 5th Edition, 2002). A useful general text but with a valuable chapter on pricing strategies.

Questions

1. How much account should be taken of competitors' prices in fixing the price of your own product?
2. Under what circumstances does marginal costing become a sensible business policy?
3. Name three products that seem to you to have an elastic demand, and three that have an inelastic demand.
4. In setting an original price on a product, the marketing manager needs to consider more than manufacturing costs. What are some of the major marketing considerations in this type of pricing decision?

Chapter 14

Integrated marketing planning

Introduction

By the end of this chapter you will:

- Understand the need to integrate your marketing communications so that customers do not receive conflicting messages from your organization.
- Recognize that the integration of global promotions is more difficult because countries differ on what techniques are permitted in each area.
- Have reviewed a ten-point checklist on positioning for brand promotions.
- Have seen integration in action through a review of a recent case study.

'... if we are discussing a single brand, then everything associated with that brand must be fully integrated in support of the brand's positioning and personality.'

Tom Brannan. *A Practical Guide to Integrated Marketing Communications*

14.1 The Situation Today

The cost of using the media is continually rising, and we saw in Chapter 8 how direct marketing is taking over from broadcast advertising. We then saw in Chapter 12 how we should engineer 'permission' from our prospects so that we can market to them most effectively. Competition intensifies by the day and this, plus media cost rises, make it increasingly tough to ensure that your message cuts effectively through the 'clutter' to 'interrupt' and reach your target customer. However, as product differences continue to get less and more organizations fight for your customers' 'share-of-wallet', communication – meaningful, effective communication – plays an increasingly important role in business success.

Indeed, in many areas, there are only two differences between competing brands: power of communication and speed of response – and this applies in both consumer and business markets. Section 3.5 showed that service life cycles are changing to meet clients' needs for speed and efficiency. Genuinely superior products are relatively rare. The nature of modern business has driven poor brands and products out of the market; those that are left are pretty much worthy competitors.

Even if you have a competitive differential – is it sustainable? It will not be long before you have some copycat at work, jumping on your particular bandwagon. We have to work still harder at the 'innovation cube' to improve our competitive edge (see Section 3.10).

Successful companies and brands share a number of common factors. Other authors have detailed many of them, from TQM and the drive for zero defects, to 'fifth generation' management and 'employee empowerment'. However, one of the most fundamental needs so rarely written about is the need to ensure that the organization speaks with one voice about the products and services on offer. It is hard enough to be heard above the 'clutter' without having your messages confused all the time.

Consider BMW, Virgin, Coca-Cola, Tango, Sony, Toshiba, or J. Sainsbury. These cover markets from fast-moving consumer goods (fmcg), through consumer durables to business-to-business (B2B). They cover the full range of customer value and lifetime usage. But they are very similar in their commitment to consistency in their communication. Because of this, they have a very consistent message in terms of their brand offering and perception in the minds of the consumer. We know what we'll get from these brands – they deliver something beyond the tangible product or service. The market has a relationship with these brands that makes it harder for competitors to dislodge them and to create preference for their own products.

14.2 So Why Integrate your Message?

There are two main benefits of adopting such an integrated approach. The first is perhaps best illustrated by analogy.

Suppose we met one of our acquaintances on three successive occasions. The first time they were in usual business attire discussing marketing plans at a CIM Conference; the second they were dressed like a dispatch rider and walked into your organization's mail room; and the next they were sitting in a cardboard box on the street, begging for loose change.

So, what would you make of them? All three characters are perfectly common these days. If you saw any one of them it might not be too remarkable. However, if you saw them on three separate occasions you might be pretty confused, to say the least.

Now, since our prospects get 'interrupted' by our offering on only a few occasions – unless you have a massive budget – if, each time they do interact the brand is 'dressed' differently or speaks in a new accent this will confuse them. Unless we are setting out to deliberately confuse the prospect, it makes sound business sense to get the messages consistent – every time.

We made the case in Chapter 12 that we need to build a relationship with our prospects and develop trust. And to do that, we need to be consistent. However, mere consistency is not enough. Consistently being ignored will not do the relationship any good! We need to establish a differential and maximize the number of contacts we have with our prospect if we are to be truly successful.

We all have finite budgets to deal with, and being consistent will cost less than ever-changing campaigns. Consistent images and design lead to savings in production. However, the biggest benefit is that our consistent messages build up over time, each subsequent 'hit' reinforcing and refocusing our message. Our budgets go further. Thus, a combination of marketing communication techniques and a consistent message gives more opportunity to increase the number of times we 'meet' our customer. This cumulative effect of saying the same thing through different media and techniques improves the efficiency of our communications.

14.2.1 Who Does It?

Quite simply: you do. If you are a communication specialist in your organization – or an agent for one – the most important part of your job is to work to integrate the messages through all the various media that impact your prospects and customers.

For those that have them, brand protection is frequently left to the advertising agency. Marketers may be more mobile in their jobs and need to resist the temptation to make unnecessary changes in the brand communications, unless conclusively supported by the appropriate facts. Agencies will often hold the corporate template and have some consistency to ensure continuity of tenure of the brand. However, the direction on this should come from within the company itself.

If an organization is using more than one outside supplier for their marketing communications support, they need to be particularly careful that the agency has the brand's best interests at heart and are objective about brand communication. Since the client company should be in control, the head of communication cannot and should not try to delegate true integration.

14.3 Integrated Campaigns

As discussed in Chapter 7, it is important that the ingredients used in the marketing mix and the promotional mix, whatever they are, make a coherent whole. Each activity, each piece of promotional material (advertisement, leaflet, display stand or whatever) must be part of a well-conceived plan. This is why the term 'integrated campaign' is used to describe this carefully worked-out scheme, where all the individual pieces fit together and support each other. If this is not done, a conflicting effect can result, with poor response from customers – who are confused rather than motivated by the varying messages they receive. An integrated campaign, on the other hand, can have a synergistic effect — that is, the total effect can be greater than the sum of the various individual activities.

In order to have a positive effect on the customer's buying behaviour it is worth reflecting on the internal influences on them.

14.3.1 Internal Influences on Behaviour

The first internal influence we will consider is **perception**. This refers to how we personally select, organize and interpret information to create a meaningful picture of our environment.

We automatically screen out what we consider to be irrelevant. This has obvious implications for marketers. For example, where an advertisement is competing with many others for our attention, the promoter will often introduce novelty and contrast to attract our attention. By the same logic, repetition of the same advertisement may simply 'switch us off' – we have adapted our perception. As we grow older and experience life, we learn that certain stimuli mean certain things, and begin to expect that they will continue to mean these things. All stimuli are thus interpreted by comparing them with past stimuli and experiences.

In using stimuli that attract our attention, advertisers sometimes convey the wrong message. For example, a female model draped over a new car at the Motor Show may attract more attention than the car she is meant to promote; a strong storyline in a commercial may be remembered, but not the brand being advertised. The aim of most marketers is to ensure that it is their product that 'jumps out' from the shelf and dominates the other cans or cartons.

A product can be seen as a selection of stimuli that communicate meaning. For example, price signifies a certain level of quality, and the design or shape of the packaging may say more about the product benefits than the actual sales message. Consumers will notice a well-known set of stimuli much faster than an unknown set; thus a well-known brand image or label will stand out on a shelf compared to less-known competitors. If a manager does not understand the meaning of the stimuli or symbolism being used in a product or promotional message, then it is likely that consumers will not understand, or will misinterpret, the intended meaning. This is clearly a problem with exported products, when a message or product must cross cultural or social boundaries.

VIGNETTE

Same Product, Different Perceptions

Elida Gibbs produce a body spray called 'Impulse' that is sold throughout the world. Although the product is essentially the same from market to market, consumers use it for different purposes. In the UK it is bought as an antiperspirant, that is, for its sweat-reducing properties. In other parts of Europe it is bought as a lightly perfumed deodorant which will stop body odour. This example illustrates how a simple product like a body spray is perceived and used in distinctly different ways according to the social and cultural background of particular markets.

Attitudes constitute another strong internal influence. Attitudes are feelings for or against something. We are predisposed to feel favourably or unfavourably. This is sometimes expressed as liking or not liking a particular object. Theorists, however, cannot agree how an attitude should be defined, and this has resulted in heated debate in the literature as to how attitudes are best measured.

Marketers frequently wish to develop more favourable attitudes among consumers towards their products. This is often done by giving positive information, promoting positive feelings by the careful use of imagery or symbolism, or encouraging positive intentions by showing the suitability of products for certain situations.

However, the question, 'Do we always hold an attitude?' arises. If you are asked to fill in an attitude questionnaire consisting of a five-point scale from 'like' to 'dislike' about a new product, you may not always be able to do it – you may not know enough about the product or care enough about it to bother. The product or behaviour involved in its use has to be important to us before an attitude matters. I may be able to tell you that I like or dislike certain features of a car, but never actually consider these features when buying a car. If I have very low knowledge, then my attitude will be very simple and very easy to change. Conversely, if I have a lot of knowledge, then the attitude will have many dimensions and be more difficult to change. The more knowledge we hold, the more interconnected and integrated it will be with other attitudes.

So, what is the link between **attitudes and behaviour**? We have focused on attitudes because of our belief that they relate strongly to behaviour. If we know positive things about a product, if we have positive feelings about a product, then logic would lead us to believe that our behaviour is likely to be consistent and we are likely to buy the product. To increase sales, the argument goes, marketers should increase the number of people who hold favourable attitudes, or increase the degree of positive knowledge and feelings. This will cause favourable behaviour.

It is quite possible for us to hold one attitude and do something completely different. We do not endlessly repeat the same behaviour until a change of attitude takes place – other factors also affect us. We may like beef curry but equally like other meals, and thus switch between alternative meals or offerings. The particular attitude may not be relevant to our behaviour, or other attitudes may be of more importance.

The measurement of our attitude towards a brand or other object may also be misleading if our attitude to the use of that brand within a certain situation is not also measured. It is wrong to ask what we think about an object (for example Rolls-Royce cars) without also asking what we think about the situation of buying and using a Rolls-Royce. We may have very positive feelings towards Rolls-Royce cars, but would never consider buying one – we cannot afford it, our garages are too small, and our friends might disapprove!

14.4 Global Promotions and Integration

Globalizing promotions can be extremely difficult or impossible depending on the particular type of promotion planned. This creates its own problems for maintaining an integrated campaign – especially when an initiative in one region is not permitted in another. Table 14.1 gives an outline of some national differences in what is allowed by law in particular countries. Moreover, one would need to consider the cultural differences between countries, as what may be acceptable in one country, say, the UK, may not be as acceptable in another.

However, as discussed in Chapter 10, sales promotion can assist in the achievement of a number of different objectives. It can:

- Increase the rate of repeat purchases.
- Motivate resellers and their staff.
- Build customer loyalty by influencing their regular buying habits for the brand.
- Encourage new product trial.

Table 14.1 The range of promotional methods permitted in some European territories[a]

Promotion	UK	Austria	Belgium	Germany	Luxembourg	Norway	Switzerland
Price discount	✓	✓	✓	✓	✓	✓	✓
Free product	✓	✓	?	✓	✓	✓	✓
Discounted product	✓	✓	✓	✓	×	✓	×
Competition	✓	?	✓	?	?	?	✓
Discount voucher	✓	?	✓	×	?	×	×
Cash back	✓	?	✓	?	×	?	×
Extra product	✓	?	?	?	✓	?	?
On-pack premium	✓	?	✓	?	×	×	×
Collectables	✓	×	?	?	×	×	×
Free draw	✓	×	×	×	×	×	×

[a] Adapted from Wilmshurst, J. *Below the Line Promotions*, Butterworth-Heinemann, 1992.

While Table 14.1 may be the picture for some territories in Europe, broaden your horizons further and the picture becomes still more confused. So, how do we protect a brand across international boundaries with global communications media becoming more usual to our target audiences?

14.4.1 Advertising Association Hits Out at EU

In January 2002, the Advertising Association was reported to have criticized the European Union over its decision to stall a proposal that would remove national restrictions on sales promotions across the EU. The Advertising Association backed proposal would see the removal of a number of country-specific restrictions on sales promotions. It would also allow procedures and services that were legally recognized in one Member State to provide sales promotions within any of the other fourteen countries.

However, the industry body claims the proposal's passage through the European Parliament has been halted by a European Union Council of Ministers' Working Group who have, according to the Association, 'bulldozed through a measure' designed to delay proceedings.

The regulation, which has taken nearly four years to prepare, was approved by the European Commission in October 2001. To become law, however, the regulation has to be discussed and agreed upon by committees from both the European Parliament and the Council of Ministers.

It appears that harmonization throughout the European Union may take some time yet.

14.5 The Integration of Communications

14.5.1 A Single, Enduring Message

Our aim is to create a single, central message that leads to one core creative idea that is implemented across everything we do. This integrated communication is maintained over time, when the developments and enhancements of the campaign can be seen to have evolved from the central idea rather than to be departures from it.

VIGNETTE

Consistent Approaches

Avis car rental – 'We try harder' – has shown a consistent approach that has been deliberately controlled in tone and message for many years. Equally 'Intel Inside' has been a recent exponent of integration from advertising, through direct marketing, to point of sale. Heineken lager used the 'Refreshes the parts other beers cannot reach' brand image for over a decade, and this 'refreshing' approach has been maintained through a successful campaign into 2002 with 'How refreshing, how Heineken' copy. So, even though there is a new generation of lager drinkers since the first campaign was used, the image still endures.

Delivering a clearly defined message to an identified target audience in an effective manner will form the fundamental purpose of any marketing communication activity. To do that for any company or brand, it is important to understand the hierarchy of communication, as outlined in Figure 14.1. Essentially, the positioning is the **'What** do you want the audience to feel about the brand?' while the personality is the **'How** do you want the audience to feel about the brand?' and the proposition is the **'How** to achieve the other two'.

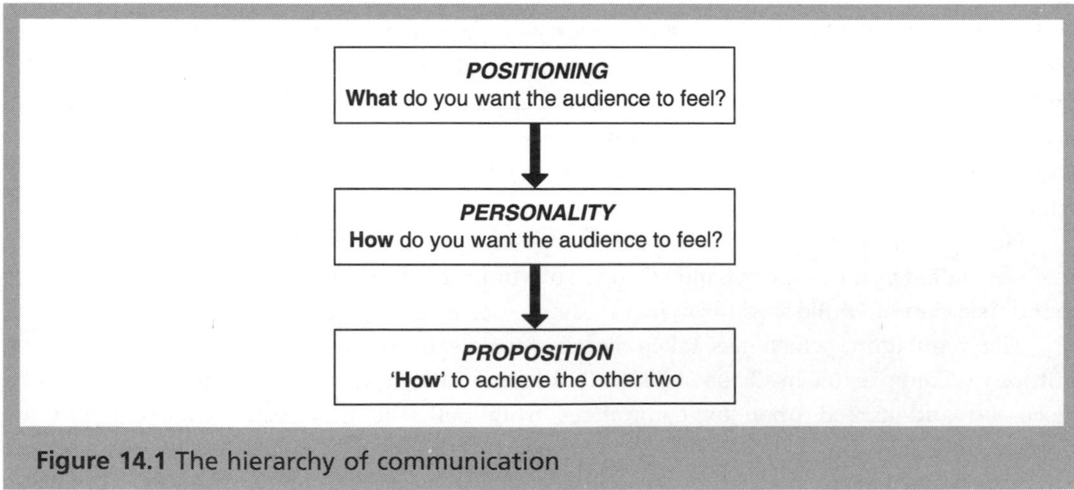

Figure 14.1 The hierarchy of communication

The key attributes of a good customer proposition are as follows:

- Simple – don't expect customers to work hard to understand you.
- Concise – deliver your message in as few words as possible.
- Clear – deliver a single message that doesn't confuse.
- Consistent – make sure everyone in your team delivers the same message.
- Customer-facing – above all, focus on benefits not features.

In integrating any campaign, **positioning** and **personality** are our two watch-words; everything we do, every campaign we run, every message we send must be referred back to this model.

The first test: We need to be confident that every message fits the descriptions we have established for each of these stages. Only then can we move on to the second test.

The second test: We need to check the physical elements of the proposed transmissions (in whichever forms we intend to use) to ensure that they look and feel like the brand.

Both tests must be applied to every part of a communications campaign. Many modest organizations make the mistake of running these checks through themselves, yet do not make the savings they suspect. Only the prospective buyers are capable of saying whether a proposed activity is true to the nature of the brand. This is where even a relatively small proportion of our funds used to test the prospects perceptions will pay dividends if we are not led up the wrong path.

If you have decided to segment your market, try to use a slightly different proposition for each of your target groups. This helps increase the effectiveness of your message. But you should be careful to ensure that the different propositions you use are consistent and don't contradict one another. In general, the best way to proceed is to devise an overall proposition and to fine-tune this for different target audiences.

14.5.2 Integration Planning

Any effective communication is the outcome of structured thinking combined with research into the needs, wants and desires – as well as attitudes – of the target customer. Without these, integration is academic because our communication is more than likely to be off-target. In Section 14.2.1, the point was made that, when planning such activities, you may need to ensure that two or more creative suppliers (designers, agencies, PR companies etc.) are also co-ordinated so that their activities are integrated.

14.5.3 How We Develop a Positioning

Through our activities and corporate behaviour our products, services, brands – and indeed our organization – will develop an image in the minds of our prospects and customers. This is the same whether we are talking about a fast-moving consumer product or a local government body – they all have an image developed, sometimes almost by serendipity. We have two choices: either maintain or alter that image. If we do neither, at best we fail to reach our potential, at worst we leave ourselves highly vulnerable to sharper competitors and lose our competitive differential advantage.

That competitive differential advantage is what positioning is all about. Positioning can be described as a definition of the core characteristic of the brand that we believe will differentiate it in its market and that will motivate people to select it in preference to competing brands. For local governments and county councils, the establishment of an enduring, clear brand position is used to help people feel good about their community and to feel that they are getting 'best value' from their local services. It is the sum total of what we want our audience to think, feel and believe about the brand. It is a fundamental starting point to integrated communication since it provides the single focus around which every aspect of our messages will be built. Without a clear positioning, there can be no true integration.

For example, Häagen Dazs was launched as a premium ice-cream product. It achieved a strong adult following and had many imitators. It moved to being somewhat avant-garde 'sex in a tub', a highly sensual eating experience illustrated by the 'beautiful people' in its advertising and other communications.

Repositioning can also save failing brands, as in the case of Lucozade that moved from a revitalizing drink for the infirm to a modern sports drink.

So, in order to develop a position for your brand, there are a number of key elements that must be in place to ensure that the position endures in the marketplace.

- **Strategic positioning**. Go for the long-term, not just a quick fix for the sake of advertising. Moreover, is your positioning sustainable and not easily copied?
- **Focused**. Remember that you have to overcome all that 'clutter' in the market, so there is no point confusing your prospects. However, see Section 10.11.1 for observations on price promotions and the confusion that has often been purposefully developed to limit price comparisons between competitors by customers.
- **Market-oriented**. Being customer-led applies particularly in business markets and hi-tech products. Marketers are frequently enthralled by the technologies that surround them while, often, the market is not. Chapter 3 dealt with the issue of technology driving a market rather than customer demand.

In the early days of most technical markets, the innovators (see Section 3.12.5) lap up the technical messages. However, as the market expands, competition enters and the price declines, and the rest of the market comes on board. That was the case with many household appliances and especially in home entertainment. It would seem to be risky today to position such products purely around technical features although, as we saw in Section 5.2, some computer manufacturers still offer a range of features in their advertising even though many potential buyers would have no idea what all the details meant.

The common error in industrial markets is to position company brands entirely around the products, thus ignoring the real influence of emotional issues in business buying. The key is to ensure that the positioning is developed from a market-oriented view. (See Section 14.3.1 where we explored the internal influences on behaviour.)

Here are some more pointers for positioning your product or brand:

- **Does it 'deliver'?** We need to be able to justify the product rationally (or 'near rationally') before it will be acceptable to the market. Thus the positioning must come from the strength of the business. Audi claim 'Vorsprung durch Technik', which would fall down if their cars broke down easily or if they lacked the technical refinement of competitive models. Avis claim 'We try harder', which would be nonsense if their staff did not really try to make a difference. However, the reality is often not quite so clear-cut.

Did all cowboys smoke Marlboro cigarettes for all those years? Hardly, yet the cigarettes are such that we could imagine cowboys smoking them – and that unconscious willingness to accept the positioning is the key to their success. Thus, we really need to understand our customers.

- **Broad-shouldered**. This is the point where a multi-product or a company brand is significantly different from that for a single product or service. Such an umbrella brand must, by definition, be capable of covering a wider range of activities. Although the analysis process doesn't change as a result, in many respects it becomes more difficult.

  Note the differences between Ford and BMW. Ford promote the brand of each model, the Ka, Focus, Puma, Cougar and Mondeo, where 'Ford' is subordinate, yet BMW promote 'the ultimate driving machine' where individual models are just a series – 3, 5, 7 – even the Roadster is a Z3.
- **High ground**. As with all of these points, what are the motivators in the market? Any brand positioning needs to be capable of capturing the hearts and mind. It must, therefore, capture at least some area of the available 'high ground'.

  The main motivator in the shower gel market may well be the ability to wash ourselves clean. However, it is doubtful that a brand positioned merely as 'getting bodies clean' would make much of a dent in competitors' shares.
- **Distinctive**. Obviously, to develop competitive differential, we need to be different from our competitors. There is little point in investing in being the same – we would risk doing our competitors a favour. Would you launch a lager on the basis that it is 'refreshing' or a car that is 'the ultimate driving machine'? So, know your competition.
- **Sustainable**. Competitive differentials need to be sustainable over time – otherwise you will have to reposition them constantly. 'Time' is not, however, an absolute commodity in marketing. What is the product life cycle or the service life cycle? It is rare to have a brand that is only in the market for a year or so. Therefore, think strategic and go for the long-term rather than be reinventing your brand all the time.
- **Motivating**. We need to ensure, above anything else, that our prospects prefer our offering over any competitive offering. Motives have been described as a driving force within people that impels them to act. The two components are:

  1. An aroused state, or drive, which pushes a person into action.
  2. A goal that gives a reward designed to reduce that drive.

  Thus, the likelihood of a person striving towards a certain goal, such as status through the ownership of a BMW Z3 Roadster, depends on the perceived value of the goal object (status) and the expectancy that the behaviour (ownership of a BMW Z3 Roadster) will help the individual attain that goal. The amount of tension felt through having unsatisfied needs will depend upon a number of internal and external factors.

We all have many needs, both physical and psychological, but are not always in a frantic race to satisfy them. Some we may decide never to satisfy – others to satisfy only intermittently. The gratification of needs depends upon past learning as to which behaviour will be successful in achieving satisfaction, and our attitude towards such gratification. Thus: motives arise from needs, motives activate and direct behaviour, and motives select goals.

The selection of a goal depends on the success in satisfying needs on previous occasions. A goal can be positive, such as improving status, or negative, such as avoiding an undesired state. Toothpaste may be used to avoid bad breath and tooth decay, while also achieving social acceptance by producing clean white teeth. Marketing communications can, therefore, stress the connection between the purchase of a product (action) and the resultant benefits (goal). Stressing the relevance and importance can also increase the value of the goal (e.g. clean, white teeth) and social acceptance.

We must, therefore, develop positioning that is based on our factual discoveries of the market (research) rather than hunches or guesswork.

- **Catalytic**. Clearly, none of the above will be of much value if it did not enable us to be creative about the type of communications and the methods that we use to reach our target market.

Use Figure 14.2 as a checklist to eliminate the obvious failures and to narrow your focus down to one or two strong candidates. If the issue is not resolved at this point, it may be necessary to develop several written statements, summarizing variants of each option, then take these back to the market.

Even if a clear leader seems to have emerged, the process will be valuable to positively exclude other ideas; it may also be of use as a basis for further research back with the market to establish the most appropriate positioning before committing funds to a campaign.

	Option 1	Option 2	Option 3	Option 4	Option 5
Strategic					
Focused					
Market-oriented					
Deliverable					
Broad-shouldered					
High ground					
Distinctive					
Sustainable					
Motivating					
Catalytic					

Figure 14.2 Checklist for positioning a brand or product (adapted from Brannan, T. *A Practical Guide to Integrated Marketing Communications*, 1995)

CASE STUDY

Stuart Little – A Case Study on Integrated Marketing

The following information was obtained from Hester Woodliffe and appears courtesy of Columbia Tristar Home Entertainment (CTHE).

The Film

'Stuart Little' was recognized by the British Video Association Awards in 2001 in the Retail Marketing Initiative for the Films category. Based on the classic book by E. B. White, 'Stuart Little' is the story of a mouse raised by a human family, the Littles. The stars were Hugh Laurie (formerly in '101 Dalmatians'), Geena Davies (Academy Award winner, 'Thelma and Louise'), Jonathan Lipnicki ('Jerry Maguire') and Michael J. Fox as the voice of Stuart Little. The film was significant in that it featured some amazing special effects as the central character interacted with both humans and animals, achieving groundbreaking Academy Award nominated effects, which were not possible two years before. Director Rob Minkoff, co-director of the Lion King, brought the story to life.

The film was first screened in UK cinemas in June 2000, achieving an amazing £17.8m box office income. This was the fifth highest grossing movie of 2000. It was released on retail VHS and DVD on 27th November 2000.

Campaign Objectives

There were some clear campaign objectives written for the film's video and DVD release into the retail market:

- To be in the top five retail VHSs of 2000.
- To generate awareness of the groundbreaking DVD features.
- To ensure 'Stuart Little' was 'front of mind' as the perfect Christmas gift.
- To create an 'event status' and totally integrated marketing campaign 'below the line' and 'above the line'.

- To sell 800,000 VHSs by Christmas.
- To sell 122,000 DVDs by Christmas.

Advertising Campaign

The advertising objective was clear: to 'own' the weekend pre-release and week of release to generate high awareness very quickly among the target audience, boosted by a sustaining campaign in the key retail weeks before Christmas.

National TV Advertising

The budget for the advertising was £685,000 which included solus advertising – for 'Stuart Little' alone – and £270,000 for 'co-op' advertising – where 'Stuart Little' was advertised by a particular retailer. The 'co-op' press advertising, budgeted at £100,000, was to be featured in both national newspapers and women's magazines. The strategy for the advertising was heavy pre-release and during the first week to raise awareness quickly; this was achieved as follows:

1. 100 TVRs[ii] over the weekend before (this was called 'Stuart Weekend').
2. Followed by a further 100 TVRs during the week of release.
3. Reminder ads in weekends in run-up to Christmas.

The channels chosen were ITV, GMTV, CITV, C4, C5 and satellite, providing 65 per cent coverage and a cumulative total of 260 TVRs.

Outdoor

There was also a £350,000 high street poster campaign used as a reminder medium. There were 1400 sites chosen in London, Birmingham and Manchester over a two-week campaign from 4th to 17th December. This was important in the crucial run-up to Christmas and to act as a sustaining medium.

Below the Line Activity

Third Party Promotions

Objective: secure additional promotion for 'Stuart Little' in the high street in non-traditional outlets.

Rather than leave the communications to just advertising and promotions in the usual outlets selling video films, the advertising was supported by a series of third party promotions in non-traditional outlets. This was to broaden the awareness of the campaign and three key avenues were chosen. Given that Christmas was a time for 'office parties', photo-processing shops and dry cleaners were chosen as both were felt to have particular consumer traffic at this time. Moreover, as television shops were also very busy at Christmas, Boxclever (ex Radio Rentals stores) were also engaged in a third party promotion.

Thus two significant promotions were run with Supasnaps, Sketchleys and Boxclever stores:

1. Stuart Little point-of-sale promotions appeared in 625 Sketchleys and Supasnaps high street stores. The material included window stickers, standees, mobiles and 'A' frames (see later for a description of each item). There were also branded photo wallets available in Supasnaps and branded hanging tags in Sketchleys.
2. Granada Home Technology and Radio Rentals amounted to 900 stores in the UK. They featured 'peel and reveal' instant win scratchcards (with a chance to win a home cinema system) and a competition to 'win your height' in DVDs – this helped emphasize the smallness of 'Stuart'. In each store there were 'Stuart' themed windows and a 'Stuart Little' area in-store.

Publicity Campaign

This was engineered to focus on the DVDs. *Chat* magazine (with a UK circulation of 425,000) ran a full page crossword promotion, with additional copy on the DVD extra features and DVD prizes. At the same time, *DVD Monthly* (with a UK circulation of 30,000) ran a 'Stuart' CD-ROM cover-mount. There were also exclusive interviews with Director Rob Minkoff and the special effects co-ordinators in the DVD press.

Other Activity

In addition to the main promotions, there were several significant activities all using the same visual elements as the rest of the campaign:

- Hamleys (the London toy store) ran a 'Stuart weekend' promotion on the 3rd and 4th of December.
- £80 Stuart 'goody bags' competitions were run across all media, reaching millions of kids and parents.
- Multimedia reviews, competitions and features.

Retail Point-of-sale Material

There was a wide range of exceptional Christmas display materials to create an 'in-store theatre'. The range included:

- Free-standing display units – Standing some five feet high, these reinforced card units stood in-store, featured 'Stuart' and held VHS videos showing nine video box-facings for customer self-selection.
- Standees – These were approximately four feet high card cut-outs of 'Stuart' floor standing in-store, designed to catch children's attention – particularly pre-release to generate early awareness.
- Hanging banners – A3-sized posters designed to be suspended from the store ceiling.

- Mobiles – A5-sized cards designed to hang from string in the store, able to turn in air movements.
- Counter stand – Designed to hold eight videos, the counter stand would normally be placed at or near the cash desk.
- Wobblers – Small posters suspended on plastic arms, the 'wobblers' are often used attached to shelves or other fixed points in the store.
- Bunting – A row of 'Stuart Little' flags, in three different designs, to be tied across inside or outside the store.
- Posters – Four different designs were offered.

Retailer Promotions

A number of different stores ran their own promotion. Some were 'self-liquidating' in that the cost of the promotional item was covered by the offer price.

- Woolworth: lunchbox + beaker for £2.99.
- Tesco: baseball cap and T-shirt for £2.99.
- W. H. Smith: rucksack + jigsaw + crayons + colour cards for £2.99, free beanie pre-order, and 'deal of the week'.
- Asda: consumer café promotion.
- HMV: bookmark, gift wrapping paper and 'deal of the week'.

'Stuart Little' Website

The original website created to support the cinema release was redesigned to promote the availability of the video and DVD through the usual retail stores.

Budget Breakdown

The budget breakdown was as follows:

Media	44 per cent
Retail promotions/co-op	34 per cent
Point of sale	16 per cent
Third party promos	2 per cent
Publicity	2 per cent
Other	2 per cent

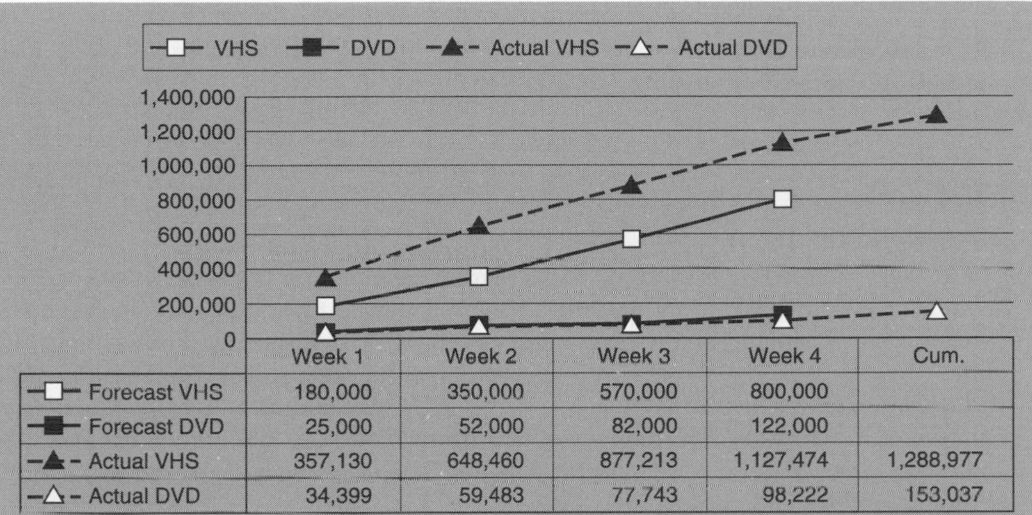

	Week 1	Week 2	Week 3	Week 4	Cum.
Forecast VHS	180,000	350,000	570,000	800,000	
Forecast DVD	25,000	52,000	82,000	122,000	
Actual VHS	357,130	648,460	877,213	1,127,474	1,288,977
Actual DVD	34,399	59,483	77,743	98,222	153,037

Results of the 'Stuart Little' campaign (*source: CTHE's Objectives and the Official UK Charts Company*)

Results of the 'Stuart Little' Campaign

The marketing campaign was extensive, fully integrated and found to be highly effective in all areas: advertising, third party links, in-store offers, POS, publicity, and in terms of added value with the various stores. The VHS video exceeded all expectations, as it became the fifth biggest selling VHS of 2000. It sold the most VHS units in any one month, ever (beating 'Men in Black').

The DVD performed very well despite the genre – it is essentially a children's film – and it continues to sell.

'Stuart Little' also performed well on rental – with 950,000 transactions to date.

It appears that 'Stuart Little' is now an extremely well-known 'brand' which means that the market is 'all set and ready' for 'Stuart Little 2' which is planned for release in the summer of 2002.

Watch this space. . . !

Summary

- If we met someone three times and each time they were a different persona, we would be confused. Not integrating marketing communication has the same effect.
- Responsibility for brand protection must lie with the brand owner and continuity needs to be maintained across personnel changes.
- How customers perceive the brand is fundamental to our understanding of the market.

- The integration of a global campaign is more challenging yet still achievable.
- There are a wide variety of criteria that a proposition should be compared to so that a sustainable competitive advantage is achieved.

References

i From the retail marketing website http://www.mad.co.uk, January 2002.

ii TVR (Television Rating). A 'rating' is the percentage of sets in homes that *can* receive commercial TV (which means virtually all homes in effect) that *are* in fact switched on to a commercial TV channel at any given time. So, an advertisement spot that went out at a time when 20 per cent of homes are switched on would achieve 20 TVRs. These would be added up to give a cumulative total, so that 400 TVRs would mean that *on average* each household has received the commercial four times. (For more information on TV advertising, see Wilmshurst, J. and Mackay, A. *The Fundamentals of Advertising*, 2nd Edition, 1999.)

Further Reading

Clow, Kenneth and Baack, Donald. *Integrated Advertising, Promotion and Marketing Communication* (Prentice Hall, 2001). Gives students an integrated learning experience by incorporating Internet exercises and a 'Building an IMC Campaign' project.

Yeshin, Tony. *Integrated Marketing Communications* (Butterworth-Heinemann, 1999). A book specifically tailored for students undertaking the Integrated Marketing Communications module of the CIM Diploma.

Picton, David and Broderick, Amanda. *Integrated Marketing Communications* (FT/Prentice Hall, 2000). A European-based text covering all elements of marketing communications; a comprehensive and cohesive textbook.

Shimp, A. *Advertising, Promotion and Supplemental Aspects of Integrated Marketing Communications* (Prentice Hall, 5th Edition, 1999). Fully integrates all aspects of marketing communication, providing a complete treatment of sales promotion, point-of-purchase communications and advertising media selection.

Wilmshurst, J. and Mackay, A. *The Fundamentals of Advertising* (Butterworth-Heinemann, 2nd Edition, 1999).

Questions

1. Consider the Stuart Little case study and evaluate the campaign on the twelve criteria of positioning. Give your reasons for each criterion.
2. BMW have used the 'ultimate driving machine' proposition for their cars. Explain why you feel this brand position is appropriate for both their top of the range 7-Series motor car as well as the smaller vehicles in their range.
3. Consider a TV advertisement for a deodorant or antiperspirant and try to distinguish the social and cultural images being used to promote the product.

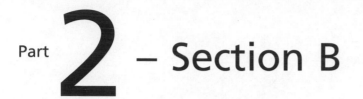

Part 2 – Section B

The Practice of Marketing – *Delivery*

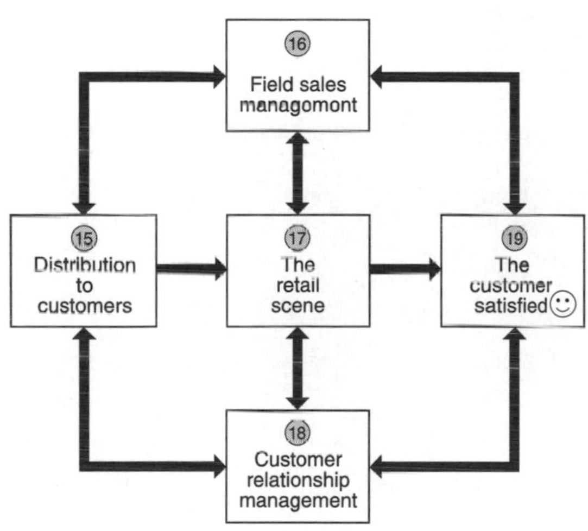

Chapter 15

Getting the goods to the customers

Introduction

By the end of this chapter you will:

- Understand why it is crucial to make products easily available in the marketplace – in the 'right place'.
- Appreciate the wide range of possible ways of distributing products.
- Be aware of the factors in making decisions about the best way to distribute our products.
- Realize the general importance of being readily accessible to customers.

'Stocks of a commodity piled high in a factory warehouse are about as useful to the customer or user as milk down on the farm is to a householder living in the middle of London or Manchester.'

Leslie W. Rodger. *Marketing in a Competitive Economy*

15.1 The Importance of Place

Place was one of the all-important 'four Ps' listed in Chapter 5 as elements in the marketing mix. Only when all four are right and correctly balanced with each other will the customer receive in full measure the satisfaction they are seeking. As we saw in Chapter 5, to take the customer's view, we should not be looking at distribution *per se* but the convenience of accessibility to the product or service.

So far we have considered in detail how the 'right' products are produced (Chapter 3) and how the 'right' price (Chapter 13) is arrived at. Now we need to consider how products can be brought to the 'right' place – where the customer wants them to be in order to be *convenient*.

In some very simple situations there is no problem about this. The village baker baking his bread on the premises, with his customers all around him, simply made the goods available and his customers came a few hundred yards to him or he took his wares a few hundred yards to their homes. But there are not many such village bakers left, in the UK at any rate, nor many similar situations. The more usual case is that manufacture on a large scale is carried out at one location, and customers live in very many other widely separated locations, hundreds or even thousands of miles away. Often at these separate locations, the service elements in the product distribution occur at 'consumption'.

Generally speaking, customers are in no position to go to the manufacturer and, in any case, they want the goods or services to be provided where they are. Somehow the manufacturer must make it so.

Someone buying a car does not want to have to travel more than, say, 20 miles to view and test it, and certainly not to have it serviced. People living in towns do not want to have to travel to the country for their milk or their fruit. Having their wants provided for at the place of their choosing is part of the convenience that customers pay for when they buy a product.

It is sometimes feasible or even essential for the manufacturer to deal direct with his customer. The civil engineering contractor building a power station and the bespoke tailor making a suit will certainly need to. The manufacturer of chocolate bars, canned soups or refrigerators does not need to. So a company offering products or services has two basic decisions to make in this area:

1. Is there any vital need to deal direct with the customer?
2. If not, what is the best method of providing the product or service at the place where it is convenient to the customer?

15.2 The Channels of Distribution

A producer has the choice of dealing direct or of passing their goods through other organizations, including wholesalers and/or retailers, sometimes collectively referred to as resellers. The routes followed by the products (or at least their ownership) as they travel to the ultimate customers by way of these other organizations are usually called the channels of distribution. There are a number of choices available, as illustrated in Figure 15.1.

The figure shows the five main variations that are possible. Avon Cosmetics and Encyclopaedia Britannica were classic examples of companies selling direct to the consumer, but the Internet has opened up a channel for many more companies to sell direct to consumers. Many goods and services, from heavy machinery and raw materials to nuts and bolts and stationery, are also sold direct to industrial users. But consumers still purchase a high proportion of goods such as groceries and services (such as travel) from resellers.

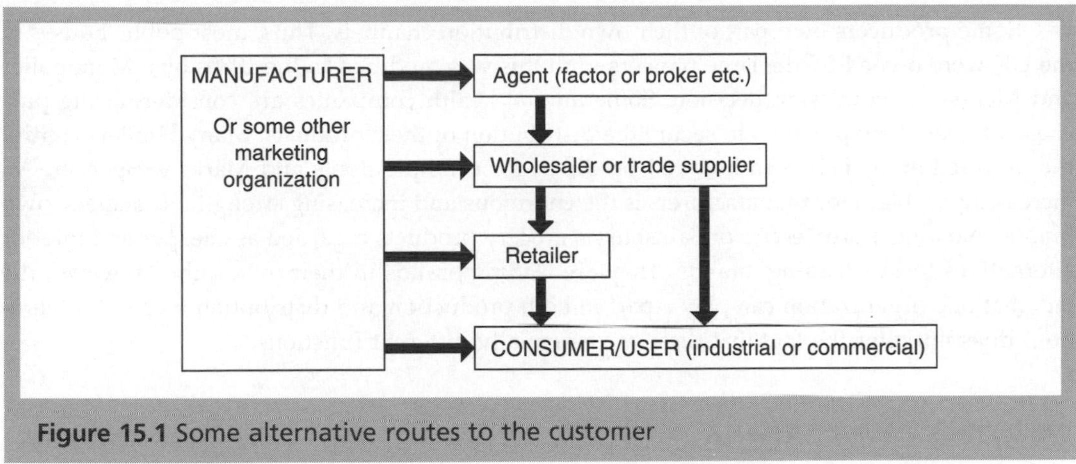

Figure 15.1 Some alternative routes to the customer

15.2.1 The 'Intermediaries' Function

Operating the channels of distribution are the 'intermediaries', sometimes called 'middlemen' – independent businesses standing between the producer and the household consumer or industrial user.

The first group – brokers, factors or agents – differ from the others in that they normally arrange sales transactions but do not take title to the goods. But there is widely differing usage of the various terms.

Retailers are people whose main business is to sell direct to the ultimate private user. In some cases (e.g. cars, TVs, domestic appliances) they may also carry out servicing and maintenance after the sale, although increasingly with electrical goods this is a quite separate function.

Wholesalers are concerned with selling to others (mainly retailers) who are buying in order to resell or to those who are buying for business use (i.e. not for personal consumption).

There is some overlap of function. Some retailers may sell on occasions a large quantity (at discount) to a company for business use – the wholesale function. Wholesalers may also do some retailing. It was at one time usual, for example, for British builders' merchants to have a 'trade' (for purchase by builders and decorators) and a 'retail' counter (for purchases by individuals for their personal use). More recently many of them have become 'cash and carry' suppliers to the trade and do-it-yourself shops for householders (see Section 15.3).

The intermediaries' function is that of 'concentration, equalization and dispersion'. Frequently the quantity and assortment of goods produced by a firm are out of balance with the variety and amounts wanted by consumers or industrial users. A business needs paper, pencils, computers and desks. A homeowner with a garden wants grass seed, topsoil, fertilizer, a rake and a roller, and eventually they hope to need a lawnmower! No single firm produces all the items either of these users wants and no producer will sell any of them in the small quantity the users desire.

The job to be done involves: (1) collecting or concentrating the output of various producers, (2) subdividing these quantities into the amounts desired by the customers and (3) dispersing this assortment to consumers or industrial buyers.

Some producers own part of their own distribution channels. Thus, most public houses in the UK were owned by the large brewers until this was modified in the 1980s by a Monopolies and Mergers Commission decision. Some animal health companies are considering the purchase of veterinary practices to secure the distribution of their products. Many retailers control the production of their own branded products, for example Boots and Marks & Spencer. An increasing problem for manufacturers is the enormous and increasing strength of retailers' own brands. No longer are Tesco's or Sainsbury's grocery products regarded as cheaper and inferior alternatives to the 'leading' brands. They are leading brands in their own right. However, the fact that one organization can play a part in both production and distribution (vertical integration) does not alter the fact that these are essentially different functions.

15.3 The Retail Scene

To understand fully the reasons behind the way in which distribution channel decisions are made it is important to be clear how the retail section of the marketing system is made up. This is described in more detail in Chapter 17. For the present, it is sufficient to be aware of the wide variety of routes to customers, which include:

- Direct marketing – including door to door direct selling, 'party plan', mail order through catalogues, selling 'off the page' through advertising direct to consumers, and one's own retail outlets.
- Independent shops.
- Chain stores – 'the multiples'.
- Department stores.
- Co-operative societies.
- Discount stores.
- Franchises.
- Supermarkets, hypermarkets and superstores.
- Cash and carry and voluntary chains.

15.4 Selecting Distribution Channels

'Intermediaries' have a number of very important functions, which may be summarized as follows:

1. **Assembling products at the place most convenient to the purchasers**, in the 'mix' and variety they desire. People like to buy their cigarettes at the same time as their newspaper, and house owners their wallpaper, fertilizer and barbeques all at once. Manufacturers of electronic equipment may want to buy a wide range of components from one source.
2. Making it easy for **potential customers to see and examine products and to compare alternatives**. Electrical appliances and furniture are good examples.

3. **Offering a range of pre-sale and post-sale services,** such as technical advice (e.g. what power an electric heater should have for a particular size of room); delivery and/or installation and fitting (e.g. carpets) and after-sales service (e.g. for central heating, cars and business machines).
4. Making it **easy for customers to buy in the quantity they need**. The butcher can supply one or two kilos of beef, but the farmer is not geared up to do so; the grocer will supply one small can of baked beans, but the Heinz factory despatches them by the truck-load.

All these functions could in theory be carried out by the producer, and sometimes they are – many farmers have a wayside stall selling seasonal fruits such as strawberries and many will supply meat ready for the home freezer. Any producer has to decide who will carry out these functions – themselves, a middleman or a series of intermediaries. A number of factors influence the decision; they are related to the kind of market, the kind of product and the kind of company concerned, as follows:

1. **The market**. Industrial products will need different channels from consumer ones. A market with very many potential customers will more likely need intermediaries to service it than one with only few customers. Conversely, a compact market is easier to serve direct than one that is widely dispersed. Products bought frequently in small quantities at low cost are more likely to need intermediaries than high-cost items bought infrequently.
2. **The product**. Generally speaking, items of low unit value are likely to have larger chains of distribution. Heavy and bulky items are likely to be delivered direct from producer to user (even if an intermediary carries out the selling). Perishable goods need special channels of distribution, equipped either with appropriate storage facilities or geared for a quick turnaround. The range of products may have a bearing – for example, electrical retailers are reluctant to deal with too many suppliers, and a producer with only one or two products might have to deal through wholesalers. Products whose customers are not clearly aware of their need (such as life assurance) or which are custom-built (e.g. civil engineering projects or tailored suits) are more likely to be sold direct.
3. **The company**. Dealing direct with customers and providing all the facilities that go with this (storage depots, delivery vans, servicing arrangements etc.) can be very expensive. So smaller or under-capitalized companies tend to have to use intermediaries. Companies entering a market of which they are unfamiliar may also need the expertise of intermediaries accustomed to dealing in that market.

The factors discussed above influence mainly whether or not intermediaries will be used, but another decision has also to be made. Which channels of distribution are appropriate? This decision will be influenced in the main by:

1. **Customer contact** – which channels are best in touch with the target market for the product concerned?
2. **Facilities** – which channels have the facilities for display, servicing, special storage, or whatever the particular product might need?

3. **Control and motivation** – whether the producer will be able to exercise control over the way the wholesalers/retailers handle his product. Will he or she be in a strong or weak bargaining position? Is the product likely to be of sufficient interest for the dealer to give it active support?

As an example of the kind of question arising here, a small manufacturer might, from some points of view, be glad to sell his entire output to Marks & Spencer's or Halford's, for it would relieve him of many problems. However, it would also leave the manufacturer with very little room for manoeuvre, and make them vulnerable. A producer whose product represents only a small profit potential for their retailers will find it difficult to get them to give it the strong promotional support it might need.

15.4.1 Overlapping and Split Channels of Distribution

We have spoken so far as though a producer needs to choose one single channel of distribution. In fact, very frequently a multiplicity of channels will be used. Mars bars and cigarettes are not only sold in CTN (confectionery, tobacconist and newsagent) outlets, but also in supermarkets, on garage forecourts and in pubs.

Often different channels are used to reach different segments of the market. Engine oil is sold when garages use it in carrying out oil changes for customers. But around half of all car owners put in their own oil, which they buy mainly from such other outlets as accessory shops (Halford), supermarkets (Tesco), and chain stores (Woolworth).

Even something with a clear-cut and obvious distribution channel of its own will have other subsidiary ones as well. Greengrocers were the traditional channel for fresh fruit and vegetables, but these could also be bought from general stores, supermarkets and garden centres. Increasingly, supermarkets have taken over as the main distributors of fruit and vegetables to householders, often charging significantly higher prices than the 'traditional outlets' but offering added value through better presentation, packaging and highly controlled quality.

Distribution patterns are constantly changing, with new types of retailers developing and old ones disappearing. The old-style drapers have gone, boutiques have taken some of the traditional business from department stores, and do-it-yourself stores have blossomed everywhere. And how many people under 80 have even heard of an oil chandler or a haberdasher?

15.4.2 A Dynamic Situation

One could compare the pattern of distribution to the hour hand of a clock. It is actually moving all the time, although at a given moment it looks static. Producers must, therefore, always keep their distribution channels under review to ensure that they are not relying on obsolescent ones, while their competitors' products are flowing towards outlets that are in a phase of rapid growth.

One final point. The 'obvious' channels are not always the most effective. For example, garages look like the best outlets for replacement car tyres, yet a whole new business has developed in stocking and fitting tyres. The reason? Customers only buy a replacement tyre when they must. Then they want quick 'while-you-wait' service with the right tyre in stock. Traditionally, each garage fitted just a few – it was a slow-moving business and skilled fitters were taken off a repair job to (grudgingly) fit tyres. The profit margins were high to reflect the high stock value, low turnover and cost of fitting. The specialist companies get high turnover, have lower costs and so can 'give away' part of the profit margin in lower prices. The sale of paperback books shot up when they ceased to be sold only in bookshops and became available as 'impulse buys' for people at airports, railway stations, in hotels and shops, or just walking along the street.

15.5 Distribution Channel Decisions

The decision as to the distribution channels that a marketing organization is to use is a vitally important one for two key reasons:

1. The decision affects all other aspects of the marketing operation. For example, the pricing structure will depend on the number and types of intermediaries being used. The sales force structure and management will vary enormously if the choice is between direct sales to the user and using dealers as intermediaries.
2. It normally presages long-term commitments. For example, manufacturers of cars, farm machinery or earth-moving equipment need outlets to sell and service their products. Setting up a channel of dealers to carry out these tasks means they are investing in stocks and equipment. Consequently, these arrangements do not easily lend themselves to short-term changes.

15.5.1 Some Key Aspects of Distribution Channel Decisions

There are several aspects to be considered when deciding on the distribution arrangements for any particular marketing operation. These include:

- The types of intermediaries to be used and the number of stages, e.g. retailers or retailers/wholesalers (see Section 15.4).
- The number of each type of intermediary to be used.
- The tasks and responsibilities to be carried out: (a) by the marketing organization and (b) by the organizations forming the distribution chain.

15.5.2 Decisions on Numbers of Intermediaries

The second of the above aspects is often an especially important one, and is closely linked with other crucial decisions concerning market share, sales volume and profitability targets. It is customary to distinguish three levels of 'market exposure', as follows:

1. Intensive distribution, where efforts are made to get every possible suitable outlet to stock the product (e.g. torch batteries or ice cream).
2. Exclusive distribution, where the number of outlets is deliberately limited (e.g. top quality fashion goods). Some of the objectives that might lead to this approach are:

   (a) Enhancing the 'image' of the product and hence achieving higher mark-ups.

(b) Encouraging dealers to support the product more strongly and sell it more aggressively – because it limits their competition and offers them high profit opportunities.

3. In between these extremes come varying degrees of selective distribution. Here, the marketing organization seeks to find the optimum number of outlets. On the one hand, they want adequate coverage of the market, but on the other, they do not want to have the expense of dealing with large numbers of outlets yielding only small sales volume (examples include domestic appliances, microcomputers, tyres and car batteries.)

15.5.3 The Dangers of 'Thinking Big' for Small Brands

There seems to be an assumption among most large companies that any successful niche brand can be grown into a national, even international, power brand if placed in the hands of a large, sophisticated brand marketing company. However, this assumption is the root of many unsuccessful mergers and acquisitions.

There are fundamental differences in mindset and strategic thinking between people who create niche brands and those who have spent their careers with market leader brands. These differences are cultural to each brand, and the incompatibilities can seldom be overcome. So, the thinking of the acquirer dominates, the strategies that made the smaller brand successful are abandoned, and a profitable brand at three per cent market share becomes an unprofitable brand with six per cent share. One such difference is that of distribution. Niche brands often are created with limited, protected distribution.

VIGNETTE

Destroying Niche Brands

Yardley's of London was a highly respected cosmetics line sold for many decades only in the company's elegant retail store in London, department stores and a few premium chemist stores. Subsequently, the company underwent several acquisitions, and after each one its distribution was expanded. In a few years, Yardley's was in every chain chemist and discount store. A brand that once enjoyed an impeccable image and high margins became a 'low-end football' kicked all over the retail map. The London store was closed, and the brand has vanished from upper-end retailers.

Snapple is a more recent example of a highly successful niche brand that, after acquisition by Quaker Oats, was decimated.

The fundamental misunderstanding by both the Yardley's and the Snapple acquirers was that, in both cases, the brand's limited distribution was one reason for its success.

Question

1. Can you name any other products that have a niche distribution that might risk being undervalued by 'over distribution'?

The problem begins when the acquirer pays too much for the smaller brand. To recoup its overpayment, the acquirer must increase sales quickly. Expanding distribution is the fastest way. So, there's an immediate sales spike, as pipelines of new outlets are filled. When the brand starts appearing everywhere, consumers perceive that the brand has lost its caché, and they lose interest. As the brand gathers dust on retail shelves, heavy promotional activity and deep discounting follow as nails in the coffin.

Distribution is only one factor. Other strategic differences between acquirer and acquiree include advertising and pricing policies, publicity, packaging, sales representation, and every other promotional tactic.

Entrepreneurs, who operate in ways almost opposite to brand leaders, create successful niche brands. Revlon and Coca-Cola blossomed, Yardley's and Snapple shrivelled and died.

It seems to be a basic principle of competing against a brand leader. It is unrealistic to believe that marketers of brand leaders can change their stripes to those of a niche player. And, in most cases, it seems they are too arrogant to allow the smaller brand's people to continue exercising their own ideas.

It will be interesting to watch Gatorade now that PepsiCo owns it.

15.5.4 The All-important Cost and Profitability Factors

This brings us on to what in essence is the crux of all decisions regarding distribution channels. The aim must always be to choose the distribution pattern that will, in the long term, yield the desired sales volume at the lowest cost.

While it may often be very difficult to do in practice (although that does not mean it should not be attempted), in theory it is possible to compare alternative distribution channels by means of the following simple calculation:

$$\text{Rate of return} = \frac{(\text{Estimated sales revenue}) - (\text{Cost of channel})}{\text{Cost of channel}}$$

Then that channel (or set of channels) which gives the highest rate of return will be chosen.

15.6 Physical Distribution

As well as deciding through which channels goods will move or selling will proceed, one must consider another whole aspect of distribution. This is the business of physically moving products from factory to customer – the logistics.

Until fairly recently this was often taken for granted, and frequently allowed to happen rather haphazardly. But with rising costs of transport, labour and buildings, transport and storage can become a very significant part of the total end cost of the product.

The practice of physical distribution management (PDM) has developed to deal with this part of the business in the most cost-effective manner. Essentially, this deals with every aspect of getting goods from the end of the production line safely and economically to the user. It means approaching the whole business on a 'system' basis, not as a series of separate fragments. Some of the many elements making up the system are transportation, warehousing (including location decisions), stock control, packing and materials handling, and order processing. The costs of each of these cannot be viewed in isolation, nor can their efficiency in terms of ultimate satisfaction to the customer.

For example, looking purely at warehousing, it might appear that reducing the number of area depots from fifteen to twelve could save money. However, some customers would then be farther from a delivery point and transport costs could well rise to an extent greater than the savings achieved by cutting out some depots.

Reducing stock levels would save interest on the capital tied up (or enable it to be employed more profitably elsewhere). However, at the same time, the risk of being out of stock would increase (unless other steps, also with costs attached, were taken to offset the risks), with the consequent chance of delays in delivery and ultimately loss of business through poor service to customers.

To decide between centralized stocks as against regional storage depots, one would have to balance the saving on building or renting of depots, coupled with double-handling and transport (factory to depot, depot to customer), against the cost of longer journeys (factory direct to customer) with half-empty vehicles and probably the need for a more expensive vehicle fleet. Similarly, using expensive forms of transport (such as airfreight to overseas markets) may enable urgent delivery requests to be met at a lower total cost than holding stock at numerous points around the world and thus being able to cut distribution costs.

Other considerations include the relative costs of owning and operating a transport fleet as against hiring transport services from a specialist contractor such as British Road Services or BOC, who will often operate with vehicles in the liveries of their large regular customers.

15.7 Revised Customer Relationships

A further development of this recognition of the need to consider the overall 'logistics' rather than tackling things piecemeal is the increasing emphasis being given to the 'just in time' (JIT) approach. This originated in Japan, where it is known as 'kanban'. It is part of a much wider approach, which regards suppliers as partners rather than adversaries. To achieve high quality at low cost, the Japanese manufacturers rely on long-term partnerships with a small number of suppliers. By working closely with them to develop tight delivery schedules, they eliminate the need for large – and therefore costly – stocks of parts and materials. Whatever is needed is delivered precisely when it is needed and not before – just in time.

See the companion web page on international marketing where there is a section on marketing in China.

This viewing of the whole situation as a totality is the other side of the coin discussed in Section 15.6. Both for supplier and as a buyer, it is the efficiency of the total system that matters, not just how the individual parts work. The successful operation of the JIT approach is, of course, dependent on a very efficient information system. It really comes into its own when it is part of a whole package of measures, including total quality management (see Section 5.6) and the full recognition that everyone at all stages of a project must deliver what their 'customers' (which will include colleagues within their own company as well as those in partner organizations) need in order to carry out their responsibilities effectively.

15.8 Distribution for Industrial Markets

While we have talked mainly of consumer markets, the same kind of factors will apply in distribution for industrial markets. Industrial consumables may indeed follow a virtually identical pattern. Thus, stationery and similar goods are frequently sold through retail shops stocking a wide range of such materials, as well as direct to big users.

Only when we come to the heavier, less frequently bought, items do we find a totally different pattern. Here, problems of weight, size, installation and servicing force the use of special techniques and tend to favour a direct sales approach, with delivery direct from factory to user. We then see a tendency to use specialists for some aspects of distribution – for example, transporting wide loads, packing for shipment by air or sea, or the making up of container loads.

15.9 International Distribution

All the factors discussed in connection with channel selection and physical distribution management become more complex if we are dealing with an international, not merely a national, situation and this aspect will be explored in the companion web page. The basic concepts remain the same, however.

15.10 The Wider Aspects of Place – Accessibility

The 'physical' aspects of the place element of the marketing mix are fundamentally concerned with making the product or service as easily accessible to customers as possible. The definition of marketing as 'Making it easy for customers to buy' has a point. Sometimes as customers we have the feeling that some organizations try to make it as difficult for their customers to buy from them as they possibly can. Inadequate telephone systems, uninformed staff, complex and barely comprehensible order forms are all examples. If we are to achieve Kotler's aim of having 'delighted customers', we need to remove all these barriers and annoyances. These are the wider aspects of the 'place' element in the marketing mix and why Kotler proposed that 'place' in the marketing mix should be replaced with 'convenience', as this is the key element from the customer's perspective.

There are a number of ways in which this can be done which we explore in the following section.

15.11 Changing Your Channels

A recession brings an opportunity to prioritize your selling strategies.[i] In the current economic climate, few industries can say that their sales aren't suffering. Blame it on the economy, blame it on 11th September – whatever the case, changing your selling strategy is in order. The first place to start? Deciding which channels are working for you. Follow the steps described below to determine a profitable strategy in 2002.

1. Prioritize customers and products – Sales executives should be asking themselves which customers and products are going to bring in the most profit during the next year, and then drop the ones that aren't at the top of the list. It sounds easier than it is, because most sales people want to hang on to any client who's bringing them commission.
   Tim Furey, CEO of Marketbridge, a sales consulting firm in Bethesda, Maryland, says that many companies evaluating their three tiers of customers (Tier I being large-business clients and Tier III small-business accounts) are finding that they can't cover their small-business accounts with field sales people anymore. 'I'm working with two Fortune 500 telecommunications and high-tech companies right now that are taking all their field sales people out of Tier III,' he says. 'They're covering this group with third-party distributors or using more call centre coverage instead.'
   Such strategies will help these companies come out relatively unscathed when the economy rebounds. It forces sales people to put an extra service focus on their biggest, most stable clients, who will still exist when there's a brighter economic outlook.
   But for other companies, prioritizing customers has meant abandoning the call centre altogether. Tim Lybrook, president and CEO of Teletron, a company in Bloomington, Indiana, that helps businesses analyse and control their telecommunications information, recently closed his call centre in favour of face to face selling. 'Today it's no longer about just cutting costs for customers,' Lybrook says. 'You have to solve their problems and we learned that we are more effective in doing so when we're in front of the customer.'

2. Integrate multi-channel coverage – Just because a company decides to make one channel a priority over another doesn't mean certain customers don't still need to be serviced by more than one of your sales entities. Amid a weak economy it's paramount that sales people cater to the wishes of their most prized accounts, according to Furey: 'Major clients want coverage by their salesperson, supported by telesales and Web applications, too,' he says. 'Customers want to alter their coverage – they don't want to have to pick a channel.'
   It's dangerous to get caught in single-channel mode. That's why Scott Koerner, executive vice president and chief operating officer of Zones Inc., a computer products reseller, in Renton, Washington, has established channels based on the size and need of his business clients. He's found that the small-business group responds well to call centre service, while the mid-size and bigger businesses want more. 'The small-business group is more consumer-like, but our core business wants to use the Web for much of its interaction with us, and also wants personal attention from their rep,' he says. 'That frees up our account executives to call on new customers and work to service everybody better.'

3. Abandon what isn't working – Partnerships and alliances are the key to increasing your customer base in these trying times, but that doesn't mean every partner is worth keeping. Now is the time to cut some of these partner channels loose, before they drain your business of time and resources. 'Everybody needs to do some pretty significant rationalization of partner channels,' Furey says. 'I recommend cutting the bottom 20 per cent of partners out.'

What to look for in those you're keeping? Koerner says he can't go wrong with his alliance with Compaq and IBM. 'We work together to service our top two levels of customers – the competition from Dell is fierce, so partnering achieves a service level that can surpass what Dell can do,' he says. 'IBM keeps satisfied customers and we build the relationships with them.'

Summary

- Producers have a wide range of distribution channels open to them when deciding how to sell and physically move their products from the factory to the customer.
- Intermediaries (agents/factors, wholesalers and retailers) exist to provide customers, at the point most convenient to them, with the desired choice of goods, to make goods available in convenient quantities and to offer the necessary pre-sale and post-sale supporting services.
- The distribution system is complex and constantly changing. Producers must keep it under regular review. The present and 'obvious' channels are not necessarily the ones that will be most effective in the future.
- The choice of channels is determined by the size and characteristics of the market, the type of product and the capabilities of the producer, as well as by the nature of the distribution channels available.
- Very often a multiplicity of channels will be used, not just a single type of outlet. Systematic approaches such as JIT are also important considerations.
- Physical distribution management is becoming increasingly important as the relative costs of transport handling and storage continue to increase.
- Distribution to industrial concerns and to customers in other countries involves an extension of the same principles.

Reference

i Lead article, *Journal of Sales and Marketing Management*, January 2002.

Further Reading

Burton, Graham. *Effective Marketing Logistics* (Macmillan, 1975). A comprehensive view of the physical distribution aspect.

Christopher, Martin and Peck, Helen. *Marketing Logistics: Customer Service and Supply Chain Strategy* (Butterworth-Heinemann, 2002). Looks at value creation through marketing processes and how it is delivered through the supply chain.

Friedman, Lawrence and Furey, Tim. *The Channel Advantage* (Butterworth-Heinemann, 1999). Deals systematically with how to develop high-performance 'go-to-market' systems. Shows how different channels can be utilized and integrated.

Mercer, David in *Marketing* (Blackwell, 1992). Has a very comprehensive chapter on these aspects.

Questions

1. Suggest suitable channels of distribution for:

   (a) Paper plates and cups.

   (b) Handmade chocolates.

   (c) Folding garden chairs.

   (d) Automobile components.

2. Describe in detail the distribution functions carried out by:

   (a) A cash and carry grocery wholesaler.

   (b) A garden centre.

   (c) A franchised supplier of domestic heating oil.

   (d) A travel agent.

3. Franchising is becoming more and more popular as a method of marketing. What do you consider to be the advantages and disadvantages of this method of trading?

4. In what ways could a 'traditional' high street retailer of electrical goods react to competition from an out of town discount house recently opened a few miles away?

Chapter 16

How selling is managed

Introduction

By the end of this chapter you will:

- Appreciate what makes a successful sales organization.
- Know what is involved in effective sales management.
- Understand the need for computerized reporting and control/monitoring systems.

'A sales organization, like any organization, is a group of individuals striving jointly to reach certain common goals ...'

Richard R. Still and Edward W. Cundiff. *Sales Management*

16.1 The Task of the Sales Force

The kind of sales force a company needs and the way it organizes it will depend on its marketing objectives. These in turn will be influenced by the kind of markets it is operating in, and its position in those markets.

The sales approach will be very much affected by the company's present position. If it is in control of the majority of the business in an area or in its particular field, it will concentrate on regular service calls to retain existing business. At the other extreme, where competitors dominate the scene, the emphasis will be on pioneering – developing a sales approach appropriate to each major potential customer (account management) and backing it with senior management staff (appropriate to the decision-making level within the customer's company) and a full technical team if necessary. The typical situation may call for a mixture of these two approaches.

Clearly, however, the type of people needed and the organization and back-up required to support them could vary considerably.

Other factors will similarly influence the type and size of sales organization employed. A company aiming at rapid growth will want a large sales force geared to winning new accounts. A marketing strategy designed to 'pull' products through retail outlets by massive advertising aimed at consumers will lead to a quite different sales organization than a strategy which emphasizes the 'push' techniques of offering retailers big cash and other incentives to carry stock and then encouraging them to display and sell the goods to consumers.

A company very concerned with creating a long-term build-up of strong customer relations (relationship selling) will have a different sales force from one aiming principally at quick short-term profits. A company whose marketing strategy is to sell direct to end-users will need a different sales force from one dealing through a multi-layer distribution chain.

Sections 7.4 and 11.4 outlined the many different types of selling, and which of these the company is concerned with is strongly relevant. The concentration of customers in many markets into a small number of very large customers calls for special sales treatment (see below).

16.2 Key Accounts

Increasingly a high proportion of a company's revenue may come from a small number of large companies. These 'key accounts' need special treatment, partly because of the mere fact of the importance of their business and partly because the way they place contracts may be quite different from the way a small company buys.

Special cases are the large national organizations such as banks, supermarkets etc. where local managers have some autonomy but where head office exerts a greater or lesser degree of control over buying policy and may want to place large national contracts on favourable terms.

Sometimes the local manager can only place orders for products that are 'listed' by head office. It is then a major sales task to achieve this listing – normally the job of the 'national accounts' (another term for key accounts) sales force. Only when they have succeeded can the rest of the sales force achieve success.

The integration of the activity of key accounts into the corporate plan is often overlooked. The flow diagram in Figure 16.1 aims to demonstrate the flow of plans that ensure that what a salesperson is saying to a customer (the micro level) is consistent with and supportive of where the company wants to head (the macro level).

16.2.1 The Account Profile

Planning the business by key account – especially if we want to add value or differentiate our offering – requires that a certain amount of information on these accounts be obtained. Rather than collect a whole gamut of 'would be nice to knows' a more disciplined approach is preferred.

Fundamental information needed about an account is likely to include:

- Basic contact details, address, phone, web address etc.

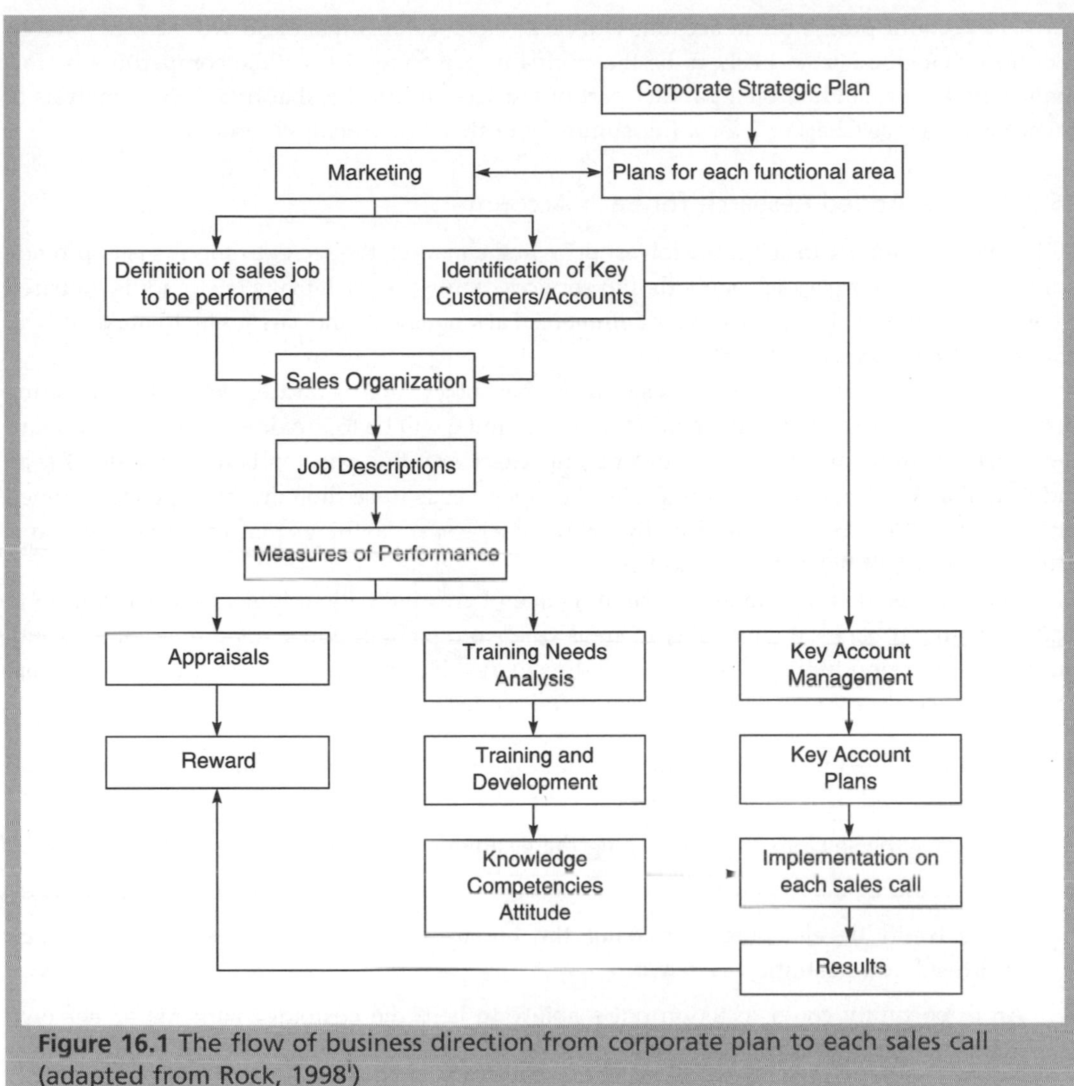

Figure 16.1 The flow of business direction from corporate plan to each sales call (adapted from Rock, 1998[1])

- Details of the corporate identity.
- The people, an organization chart, key influencers and decision-makers – and what sort of people they are.
- Their operation – what they do, how they do it, what they use.
- Their marketplace, their customers, their competitors and issues on their business.
- How they do business, contractual arrangements, tender systems, purchasing procedures.

Naturally, the sort of information collected will be dependent on the type of business; essentially, one needs to decide what it is that you need to know to manage your business.

The account profile on an account will be a reference document and will be fairly stable; the most dynamic part is likely to be the company personnel. Issues like competitive performance are better handled on a parallel part of the account profile: that of a SWOT analysis of each business. See Chapter 2 for a full summary of the SWOT analysis process.

16.2.2 Value Added Research for Each Account

Unless you are aiming to sell at the lowest price in the market, the secret to success is to provide added value to your package of goods and services. It must be such that a customer is prepared to reflect this extra value in the type of commercial arrangements they are going to make. It is all about creating positive differentiation.

There should be a marketing position on this subject that is addressed in the marketing plans (see Chapter 6). Part of the marketing programme will be to provide ways of differentiating ourselves in the marketplace. However, the exact way this position is implemented for an individual account may well be unique, and as such needs to be thought through and planned on an account by account basis. Equally, there may be specific things that we can do with one account that might not apply to another.

The process of 'value added research' is one of creatively identifying what we can do to add value to our package, preferably in areas where our competition is not doing it and cannot match it. Most opportunities to do this will directly revolve around products and services. Here are some ideas, but this is by no means a definitive list:

- Apart from the product itself, there is the way that it is packaged, transported, stored and delivered, and in what quantities.
- There may be some aspects of helping the customer get the best performance out of it.
- There could be the minimization of risk through technical support and quality guarantees.
- There could be elements of making the buying and selling process easier through improved administration systems.
- An opportunity could focus on one's ability to help the customer with his or her own quality programmes.
- There might be financial issues of cash flow, inventory costs or contribution to profit.
- It might involve one's experience in marketing to help customers achieve their marketing and sales objectives.
- In distributive businesses, opportunities could be in the form of one's ability to help customers define market opportunities and then to provide assistance through training and promotion, or even physical help in selling the product out to their own customers.

There are also opportunities to do things outside the normal avenues of activity and discussion. For example:

- ICI Group had its own plant engineers carry out an energy audit of a customer's plant, saving them thousands of pounds a year in energy bills.

- Union Carbide Australia, which had had its share of industrial trouble, was able to give some good advice to a customer facing similar challenges.

Issues of safety, ecology and the environment, communications, marketing, management systems, quality programmes, legal interpretations and computing are all areas where suppliers can contribute to a customer's business by sharing experience.

In order to identify the opportunities that exist to add value to a customer's business, there needs to be an audit providing a thorough knowledge of the customer, how they operate and what their objectives are. If a supplier can demonstrate that they can make a contribution to a customer's business, the customer is more likely to identify more opportunities. The more times the account management cycle is successfully rotated, the more the customer is going to respond, and the better the whole process operates.

The invention, or innovation cube described in Chapter 3 is a good place to start your search.

16.2.3 Computers in Account Management

The information technology market moves so fast that whatever gets written down seems to be out of date within weeks! While that may be the case, the issue of obtaining information in the format that the account manager can use is still valid, and computers have taken the march in information handling. The computer better handles most of the steps in account management. It is neater, safer, has easier access to a wider variety of people, and is easier to manage and to cross-reference. It also means that the account managers can take all the information with them on their laptops, taking the office with them on the move. And with Internet linkage, updating and sharing information is faster than ever.

Account profiles are the first and most obvious items to store on computer. Account SWOT analysis and value added searches are also useful to have to hand, although some would say that since these are intellectual exercises, they should not be added to 'on the hoof' as they risk being a form-filling exercise for the accounts people. It is important for the accounts team to think about the account, about the business relationship, and about their business there. Having to enter everything on a computer can impede this process, as it can be a mechanical interruption of thought.

It is probably better that the account SWOT and the value added search be done 'manually'. However, the outcomes from each of these exercises should be recorded on the computer as part of the second page of the full account plan in 'Items from the preparation', as 'Action items from the SWOT' and 'Priorities from value added search'.

The account plan should be on the computer. Not only is it easier to manage and for others to have access too, but it also makes it easier to review action items in different ways. For example, if the salesperson were following the logical flow from an objective to strategies and down to the action items, it is easier for them to write them in that form. But the way people carry out actions is to look at what needs to be done in chronological order. The salesperson would need to know what they have to do in total with a given account in the next month. The computer allows the salesperson to review the actions in subject order and in sequence order. They can then be transferred to diary format. The computer then becomes a contact record, also measuring the number of visits made compared to the plan. Comments can be written instead of writing a visit report. The account manager then has virtually the whole customer planning, implementation and reporting needs together in one format, instantly ready to share throughout the organization as required.

16.3 The Organization of the Sales Force

The company's situation will determine the kind of job a sales force needs to do and the kind of people best fitted to do it. Other factors come into play when we start to consider how many salespeople we shall need. For example, how many points need to be called on, and how frequently? How many effective calls can be made in the average working day?

In Section 6.5 we saw how the marketing department could be organized in various ways, including possible subdivision by region, product and market. Clearly, the sales force organization would fit into this same pattern.

The Concise Oxford Dictionary's definition of the word 'organize' includes 'make into living being . . . form into an organic whole . . . give orderly structure to, frame and put into working order'. But by its nature the selling task tends to be fragmented and unorganized. Sales people are apt to be individuals, whose work takes place away from direct supervision; necessarily, they operate very largely 'under their own steam'. Hence, there is a very strong need for an overriding framework that will 'give orderly structure' to the work. But, because the salesperson's own personal contribution is so vital, the organization must not be a dead set of boxes and lines on a piece of paper; it must 'make into living beings' the various people and facilities that it brings together and whose activities it exists to guide and direct.

This organization will include not only the salespeople calling on customers but many other people as well. In most cases a considerable clerical staff or well-designed computer-based information system is needed to process orders fed in by salespeople. Orders must be recorded and a follow-up system operated to see that they are delivered when due, instructions must be passed to production and/or despatch departments, and sometimes quotations must be prepared or special delivery arrangements made. Thus, behind the salespeople in the field, there will usually be a considerable number of supporting staff, as well as the sales manager and his or her immediate aides, whose duties include supervising and directing the field sales force.

At the end of the day, the whole of the sales organization, like every other part of the company, must be concerned with producing maximum profit at minimum cost. Anything that contributes to this goes into the organization, and anything that does not comes out.

Having warned of the danger of organization charts becoming dead things rather than the 'living being' we need, we may nonetheless show how a typical sales organization might look by attempting to put it down on paper (see Figure 16.2). Depending on the size and nature of the operation, the field sales organization itself might become quite complex, along the lines shown in Figure 16.3. The 'divisions' could, of course, follow any of the patterns suggested in Section 6.5.

In management theory terms, most of the people in the various levels in these organizations have a 'line' relation to each other. The commanding officer of an army regiment is able to exercise authority down through the organization, so that his or her orders eventually result in

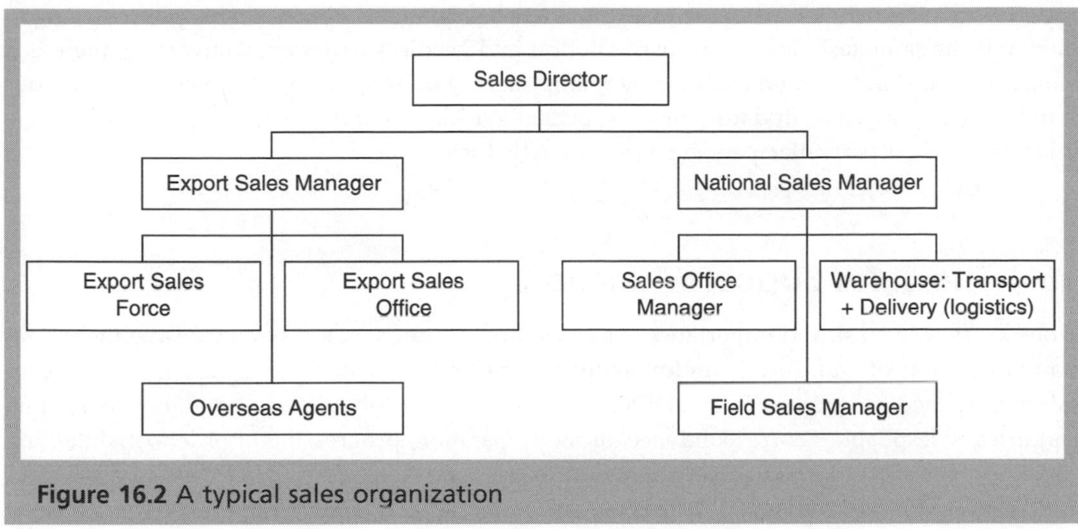

Figure 16.2 A typical sales organization

actions being taken by the privates at section level. At each level the officers and NCOs have 'command' over those beneath them in the organization. This is known as a 'line' relation. By contrast, staff officers, intelligence units and the like have the task of providing information and giving advice, so that theirs is a 'staff relation'. Marketing research is often one of the marketing functions of the 'staff' rather than 'line' category.

The sales director and everyone in his or her organization is very much concerned with causing things to happen, not merely planning and advising. That is, therefore, a line relation.

An important aspect of a good organization is the avoidance of conflict. Every member of the team must be clearly aware of what his or her job is and have a fair idea what he or she can

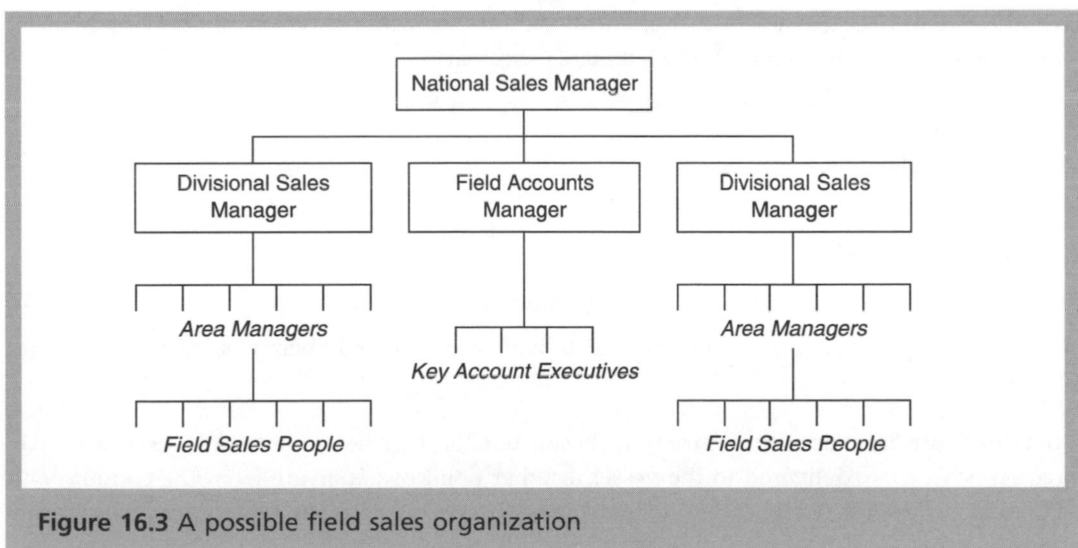

Figure 16.3 A possible field sales organization

expect from others. If this is not the case, there will be situations where two people are trying to carry out the same task, leading to wasted effort and needless irritation. Conversely, there is a danger of 'gaps' in the organization, where important tasks (e.g. seeing that a customer's order is properly processed or updating the salesperson's stock of literature) do not get done because it is not clearly a particular person's task to see that it is done.

16.4 The Sales Support Function

If one looks at the task and importance of a sales support function, it is often true that there is no standardization of duties, but undoubtedly the majority of work performed is in servicing salespeople and customers. Such activities will include customer correspondence, telephone enquiries, salespeople's correspondence, order preparation, progressing of orders, maintaining customer records on the database, stock records, statistical records and returns, credit control and possibly market research, advertising, sales training and sales promotion. With much of this work now being done by call centres, the sales office is rapidly becoming a thing of the past (see Section 11.6).

From the above list of duties of the sales support function, one would need to distinguish strictly routine, day-to-day matters from specialist functions. In a consumer goods company that is highly oriented to the consumer market, advertising may form a major part of its sales activities and, as such, would not be classified as a routine daily operation. In a company manufacturing, say, packings and packaging for industry, advertising may be a very minute part of its sales operations and be relegated to a routine consideration. The activities which can be regarded as routine or as specialist will thus depend on the type and size of the company.

16.4.1 Export Sales Office

Exporting comprises a whole series of additional office functions, which can be very burdensome. They include arranging the following as necessary:

- Shipping and despatch.
- Customs clearance.
- Insurance of goods and perhaps of credit.
- Initiating and progressing all necessary documentation.
- Routine contact with overseas customers and agents.
- Calculating quotations and prices (which may entail detailed awareness of exchange rates etc.).

Quotations can be made on a variety of bases, but the two most commonly used are f.o.b. (free on board), i.e. delivered to the vessel or other point of departure from the country, and c.i.f. (cost, insurance, freight), i.e. delivered to the port of entry in the country buying the goods.

16.4.2 Inside Sales Staff

We have perhaps so far given the impression that the real selling task is done face to face with customers out 'in the field', and that the tasks of people in the sales office are supporting ones. But this is often not the case. Many companies (printers and art studios, for example) have 'inside sales staff', who carry out a great deal of the day-to-day liaison with customers, leaving the 'outside' people free to seek out new business or spend more time with especially important customers.

Where the sales task is of the 'order-taking' type, especially when this is repetitive, virtually the whole selling job can be done on the telephone. A number of companies supplying retailers with a standard consumer item (for example, canned or frozen food, or confectionery) make a regular 'out-bound' telephone call to ask the retailer for their restocking requirements. The field salesperson can then concentrate on opening new outlets, introducing new products, and merchandizing.

In the media field, the television companies do a great deal of their selling of advertising 'spots' or air-time on the telephone. In classified advertising particularly, newspapers are well aware of the cost-effectiveness of this approach (many owe a high proportion of their revenue to their highly trained 'tele-ad' staff).

Where these inside selling functions are taking place, they will still further complicate the organizational structure. A constant task of sales management is to review the methods being used in the light of their costs and the profit they generate. Since relative costs are constantly changing and market situations are very fluid, the sales organization in all its aspects must respond to the changes.

16.5 The Management of the Sales Team

Management has been defined as 'getting things done through other people'. Except in the most unusual circumstances, or when the scale of operation is very small indeed, no one person can carry out alone the sales task for his or her company. The sales manager is, therefore, faced with having to achieve certain aims with the help of many other people. It is his or her function to direct their efforts so that those aims are achieved. The job will include the following responsibilities:

1. Defining the tasks to be done.
2. Selecting the best people to do them.
3. Setting them individual tasks and objectives.
4. Guiding, instructing and training these people as necessary in the performance of their tasks.
5. Making them accountable, i.e. setting up ways of ensuring that the appointed tasks are carried out or that any shortcomings are noted and corrected.
6. Devising the best form of organization within which all the members of the team can work.

Some of these responsibilities we have already dealt with, but 3 and 5 are given further consideration in Sections 16.6 and 16.7.

16.6 Allocating Sales Territories

We have just indicated that an important aspect of sales management is to define the individual tasks each member of the team is to carry out, and make sure that each of them is accountable. So far as the field sales force is concerned, an important aspect of this is the allocation of sales territories. The starting point, as ever, is the company's marketing objective. If a particular market is to be tackled, how can it be best done? With a typical consumer product, are sales to be direct or through distribution channels, and which distribution channels? If certain types of retail outlets are required, how many are there, how are they spread geographically, and how often will they need to be visited?

With a sophisticated industrial product, such as telecommunications equipment, the market may well be the whole world. But which countries represent the main potential? How do they buy? Is it better to negotiate directly or through agents? Either way, how many salespeople, with what characteristics, will be required, and how many buying points in how many countries can each handle?

From these kinds of question we can begin to develop an idea of the kinds of task each person has to perform and over what area. The amount of support they can be given will further influence the answers. Perhaps this will be by follow-up phone calls from head office, by merchandizing teams or by technical demonstration teams. (Some companies have a 'travelling circus', often in a caravan or even a boat or train, to demonstrate their products and answer technical queries.)

Once the load, in terms of number of customers and their size and complexity, which each person can carry has been arrived at we can start splitting the total market into 'territories' or 'areas'. Depending on the nature of the market and the product, an area could be a continent (in the case of a technical product with few potential users) or a small part of, say, London or Frankfurt (in the case of a consumer product needing widespread retailer stocking).

A basic dilemma in the allocation of sales territories is whether to divide the total market into areas of equal sales potential or areas of equal workload. The difficulty arises from the fact that a compact territory with a small number of large users is much easier to work than a much larger territory with smaller users scattered about in it. Many factors go to determine the effective length of a salesperson's working day, including driving time, waiting time, administration time (writing reports etc.), non-selling activities (e.g. investigating complaints), breaks and selling time. The compactness or 'diffuseness' of the territory will influence the vital selling time. Thus, salespeople's performance will be much affected by the nature of their territory.

The shape of a territory may also have a bearing on the efficiency with which it can be covered. A salesperson that is based at one end of the territory will spend more time travelling than one sited in the middle. A territory designed around the transport system can be more efficient than one that ignores it.

16.7 Evaluating Sales Performance

Because of the point made at the end of the previous section, it is not possible to judge a salesperson's performance purely by the total volume of turnover he or she is able to achieve.

Turnover will depend very much on the factors just referred to, as well as on the salesperson's own efforts and capability.

Yet an important part of sales management is to ensure that people perform as well as they can. This in turn means setting targets that can be achieved. A further important part of the sales manager's task, therefore, is to devise effective ways of evaluating performance. This can become a very complex affair, especially as the task is rarely simply to increase total sales in the short term, but is likely to include such other matters as:

- Gaining new customers.
- Keeping numbers of lost customers at a low level.
- Introducing new products effectively.
- Carrying out or monitoring merchandizing plans.

Thus, any comprehensive evaluation scheme must take account of these and other relevant factors. Actual sales performance will probably be evaluated against a quota, based on what the salesperson is judged to be capable of achieving in the light of the particular circumstances of the territory, the tasks to be performed etc.

Total evaluation will then be under a series of headings, such as: (a) performance against quota, (b) new customers gained and (c) customers lost. A short-term assessment of performance could be made on the basis of: (a) number of calls made, (b) ratio of orders to calls, (c) average size of order etc.

16.8 Sales Force Communications

It is obvious from the previous section that a well-organized system of communication is an important aspect of sales management. Most salespeople are required to compile regular reports, usually on a daily and/or weekly basis. This reporting provides the sales manager (or the regional sales manager acting on his or her behalf) with the vital control information needed to assess whether things are going according to plan. The need for information and its value when received must, of course, be balanced against the loss of effective selling time it may represent (although salespeople are often required to complete their records 'out of hours').

Regular communication is a two-way necessity. Salespeople need a reaction to their reports, both for guidance on how to use their efforts most effectively and also as a boost for morale (nothing is more soul destroying than spending hours completing detailed reports that no one seems to read). They also need a regular supply of information from head office: information about the state of the market, competitors' activities, their own company's forward plans, advertising activities, how best to present their products and overcome objections, and (depending on circumstances) a whole host of other aspects. Increasingly, of course, equipping salespeople with portable terminals from laptops so that they can key straight into a sales office computer network, often including an e-mail facility, provides this rapid two-way information system. WAP phones are also becoming increasingly popular (see Chapter 12).

The sales conference is another important method of imparting information and, at the same time, developing a sense of team spirit and company loyalty, which is otherwise made difficult by the 'lone operator' nature of the salesperson's job. Cost pressures may sometimes operate against the large 'set piece' sales conference, and smaller regular conferences with less 'ballyhoo' may take their place. In any case, small regional conferences can be held on a more regular basis.

Newsletters are also an important method of keeping salespeople updated. There is a danger, however, that they may either usurp or duplicate the vital regular person to person communication (face to face, by phone or by letter) from the salesperson's immediate superior (such as the area manager or district manager). In other words, effective public relations is essential (see Section 10.9).

Wherever possible, the salesperson should be provided with a full range of sales aids. These can perform the dual function of reinforcing the salesperson's own words and ensuring that the company's message reaches the customer exactly as it left head office. Sales literature, sales manuals and visual aids all have a part to play.

Summary

- The nature of the sales task will derive from the company's marketing objectives.
- Because of the nature of the selling task, effective organization is vital.
- Organization must be viewed in a flexible way, with changes being readily made in reaction to the fluid situation in the marketplace.
- The field sales force must be complemented and supported by a suitable sales office team. In some cases a large part, or even the whole, of the selling task will be carried out by 'inside' staff, rather than by a 'field' sales force.
- In some situations telephone selling assumes special importance.
- In export selling, documentation and administration put additional burdens on the sales organization.
- The management of the sales organization entails the vital job of translating general objectives into individual tasks and targets.
- The allocation of sales territories, setting up targets, quotas and the evaluation of performance in relation to them are further crucial aspects of the management task.
- Effective management is dependent on a good system of two-way communications.

References

i. Rock, J. *Key Account Management* (Business & Professional Publishing, 2nd Edition, 1998).

Further Reading

Kotler, P. *Marketing Management* (Prentice Hall, 1993). Chapter 19 on 'Sales Force Decisions' gives clear insight into the key decision areas.

Baker, Michael, J. *The Marketing Book* (Butterworth-Heinemann, 5th Edition, 2002). Includes a useful section on the sales function.

Rock, J. *Key Account Management* (Business & Professional Publishing, 2nd Edition, 1998). An Australian text that provides a good foundation in the subject.

McDonald, M., Rogers, B. and Woodburn, D. *Key Customers* (Butterworth-Heinemann, 2000). State-of-the-art strategies for B2B relationships are defined clearly.

Questions

1. What characteristics and competencies would you look for in a regional sales manager in the following situations?

   (a) In charge of the Midlands region in the UK for a grocery products company.

   (b) Responsible for Central and South America for a telecommunications manufacturer.

2. Suggest three different situations in which telephone selling could be a suitable sales method.

3. What are the key factors to be taken into account when allocating sales territories?

4. What sales aids would you recommend for a sales force selling a range of agricultural machinery?

5. Different sales forces have different roles. What are the main factors that determine the role of a sales force?

Chapter 17

The retail scene

Introduction

By the end of this chapter you will:

- Have an appreciation of the variety of types of outlets in the retail market.
- Understand how retailers are aiming to increase loyalty to their stores in the face of competition.
- Recognize why retailers are after more than market share *per se*; they are aiming to increase their 'share of wallet'.
- Have reviewed some recent examples of innovations in the retail market.
- Explored the role of in-store advertising.
- Seen how advances in information technology have changed the functions in retailing.

'The shop owner should also make it continually easier for the purchaser to get the goods and continually more convenient for the user to use them. Every little improvement of whatever character should be noted . . . and people will come to think that all your articles are improved. So also all new lines should be advertised, and people will come to think that all your lines are new.'

Philip Smith. *Successful Advertising* (1878)

17.1 The Retail Scene

The best and possibly only way to obtain an understanding of the retail scene is by observation and personal experience, whether in marketing or simply as a retail purchaser. Using the UK as an example, what follows is meant to point out some landmarks and provides definitions of the more common expressions used in describing the retail scene. It should always be remembered in this context that distributors' marketing interests will not always precisely coincide with manufacturers' distributive objectives, and that a bargaining situation exists always between the two parties, in which each will endeavour to secure the best possible terms of trading for itself. This partly explains the emergence of multiple groups and voluntary chains that are able to exert immense buying power in dealing with the bigger manufacturers.

17.1.1 Direct Marketing

Producers carry this out in the following ways:

- **Door to door direct selling** by companies like Avon Cosmetics. Salespeople of industrial products calling on company buyers are also 'direct selling' of course.
- **'Party plan'** by Tupperware containers, 'WeekEnders' clothing and others. Both these categories use part-time representatives selling on commission to people in their homes.
- **Mail order through catalogues** (e.g. Cotton Traders, Land's End etc.). Here, there is no face to face contact and the whole transaction is carried out through the post. Although 'agents' sometimes hold a catalogue and earn a commission on any orders they take for their friends and relatives, it tends to be passive rather than active selling.
- **Selling 'off the page' through advertising direct to consumers** (e.g. World Books, Damart thermal underwear – Damart also use catalogues). The Internet has taken the place of catalogues for many.
- **Own retail outlets**, such as Boots and Marks & Spencer.

As we saw in Chapter 8, increasingly, use of computerized mailing lists (which enable potential customers to be categorized and then informed of products of particular interest to them) has led to the term 'database marketing' being used to describe this kind of activity.

17.1.2 The Range of Retail Outlets

- **Independent shops**. 'The independents' account for the majority of shops but only a minority of the turnover, since they are smaller and have less capital and expertise than the multiples. They are losing ground to the multiples as a result.
- **Chain stores**. 'The multiples', as they are called, are groups of retail stores (such as Next, Woolworth, Sainsbury) with common ownership and varying (but usually high) degrees of central direction and control. They normally have a common 'image' (range of goods, promotion, decor and so on) and may specialize in a particular type of merchandise (e.g. Tie Rack, Sock Shop). On the other hand, the 'variety chains' such as Woolworth, Marks & Spencer and British Home Stores (BHS) carry a diversity of goods.
- **Department stores**. These act as a collection of 'shops' or departments all under one roof, each with its own buyer and range of goods. There is central ownership of the whole operation, although sometimes parts of the store are rented out (e.g. to manufacturers of a branded range of cosmetics or clothing), when they are known as 'shops within a shop'.

- **Co-operative societies**. In many ways 'co-ops' resemble chain stores but traditionally were owned by their 'members' who, when they shopped regularly, were paid a 'dividend' out of the trading surplus – this dividend taking the place of profits to shareholders. Owing largely to their democratic structure, they suffered a little from poor management and have lost part of their share in the market. But they still account for a very substantial proportion of all retail sales, especially in the North of England. In more recent times, in order to counter the growing strength of the supermarket chains, they have largely substituted cut-priced goods and trading stamps for the old-style dividend. Some have gone 'upmarket' and offer comparable quality and prices to the leading chains, such as Sainsbury or Asda. Others offer a distinctive advantage by being neighbourhood 'open all hours' or '24–7' shops.

- **Discount stores**. These are large 'warehouse' type shops, saving on costs by: (a) out of town locations (hence lower rents etc.), (b) minimum service and displays and (c) bulk purchase. Hence they are able to offer goods at substantially lower prices than conventional retailers are. They are especially common in the electrical goods and furniture fields (partly because of the traditionally high profit margins), where their large range of goods in stock is an added attraction.

- **Franchising**. Combining the advantages of centralized management expertise with the vigour and flexibility of the independent, the franchiser supplies a name and 'image', plus products, services and general knowhow, including advice on locations, loan capital facilities and methods of operation and control. The franchisee supplies all or a large part of the capital and agrees to purchase supplies from the franchiser. This is particularly common in the catering field (e.g. Wimpy Bars, Burger King) but also in many other fields (e.g. Dyno-rod drain cleaning service, the Body Shop and a number of 'quick print' shops). Coca-Cola operates a franchise system, with area distributors buying special syrup from the company, diluting and bottling, then distributing in their area.

- **Supermarkets, hypermarkets and superstores**. Usually operated by multiples, though not always, supermarkets are self-service shops with a sales area of over 4000 square feet. They are especially common in the grocery field, but are spreading, particularly into hardware. Originally in town centres, more recently many have been sited out of town to ease customers' traffic and parking problems – and incidentally to take advantage of lower rent, rates etc., and easier unloading for delivery vans.
  Hypermarkets are defined as self-service shops on one floor with at least 25,000 square feet of selling area. Usually they are out of town and have very large free parking areas. They normally carry a wide range of merchandize, and in a sense are self-service department stores all on one floor, although there is a much lower degree of self-sufficiency for each department. They offer customers the full advantage of 'one-stop shopping' at attractive prices. 'Superstores' are a variant on these and this term is becoming more commonly used. Many of the grocery 'supermarkets' like Tesco and Sainsbury have broadened their product range to increase their 'share of wallet' from their customers and have moved into financial services. They also offer shopping online with home delivery.

- **'Cash and carry' and voluntary chains**. When grocery distribution was transformed by the rapid growth of supermarkets, wholesalers lost a great deal of their traditional business because many of their retailer customers lost business or closed. Some wholesalers themselves closed. Many of the remainder had to change their methods.

One outcome of this is 'cash and carry' where, instead of a regular call from the wholesaler to take orders from the retailers, followed by delivery of the goods ordered, retailers now frequently go to the wholesaler's warehouse and collect their own goods – on a self-service basis – and pay cash. This reduces the wholesaler's costs very considerably. Booker 'cash and carry' supplies, among others, hotels and restaurateurs.

The term cash and carry is also used to describe a kind of retailing, especially in grocery, where private consumers have access to a similar kind of warehouse and can buy foods etc. 'by the case' at bulk prices.

A further development is that some wholesalers have led their retail customers into the formation of voluntary chains (Mace, Spar and Londis are examples). This enables the 'independents' to stay independently owned but to gain some of the advantages enjoyed by the multiples – a common image, a central pool of management expertise, better access to capital, joint promotions and some degree of bulk purchasing.

17.2 Loyalty Cards

Loyalty cards have certainly lost their sparkle over past years, but some retailers are persisting with reward schemes to great effect. (See also Section 19.3.1, p. 361.)

The concept of the humble Green Shield Stamp – once derided by marketing people – has come a long way. In the past Green Shield Stamps were a key factor in retaining customer loyalty, a science that brands and retailers are desperate to crack. Electronic schemes may have replaced paper stamps but the basic idea still remains the same, albeit with the added benefit of new technology enabling retailers to record customers' behaviour for future use.

The push to capture new customers is widely quoted as costing six times more than the effort to retain existing ones – so theoretically it is cost-effective to pump money into loyalty schemes. Retailers have managed to keep customers with price cuts, reward schemes or product quality. However, the retail research group Verdict[i] found that 70 per cent of customer defections to rival stores in 2000 were the result of dissatisfaction with the shopping experience, rather than price or products.

However, loyalty is different in different sectors; shoppers are most loyal in personal care and least in clothing. Pharmacies such as Boots the Chemist and Superdrug have seen returning custom because, according to Verdict, 'these are shops that involve your trust'. Shoppers may return to the same chemist, for example, because of individual and expert service for personal ailments. Verdict's research shows that, outside the personal care sector, customer loyalty continues to decline. Greater choice also seems to be encouraging shoppers to hunt for bargains.

17.2.1 Price not Loyalty

Such obsession with price has led to a game of one-upmanship between the UK's largest supermarket chains. In September 2001, Tesco and subsequently Sainsbury announced price cuts totalling £100 million. Safeway sends leaflets to more than nine million homes each week, advertising between fifty and sixty discounted price deals, while Asda's marketing has long been focused on low prices. However, this approach has its problems. First, it allows customer loyalty to be dictated by one issue, price. Second, price cutting may mean that consumers infer cutbacks elsewhere, such as in product quality, service or even profit margins (see Section 13.9).

Loyalty cards were once seen as a panacea for keeping customers dedicated to a particular store or brand, and shoppers initially seemed wooed by the power of plastic. After the boom of the late 1990s, however, loyalty cards are now on the decline. They now appear to be a 'blunt instrument' as a means of attracting new customers.

In May 2000, Safeway withdrew from its ABC loyalty card scheme. Research revealed that Safeway customers were confused about the advantages of the scheme and that using the card did not change their views on the store. Safeway concluded that loyalty is earned, rather than something that can be manipulated through a loyalty card scheme; they replaced the scheme with £80 million worth of price cuts.

17.2.2 Revitalization of Schemes

Rather than dumping loyalty card schemes, other retailers have chosen to rebrand or reposition them. In August, Tesco redesigned its Club Card with a 10 million-strong mailout, sending a 'personalized' card including the name of the card user. This gave the chain a chance to clear out its database and emphasize its new offers.

VIGNETTE

Card for Customers to Treat Themselves

Boots' Advantage card is not primarily designed to offer savings, but to encourage shoppers to treat themselves with further Boots products. Thirteen million people have signed up to use the card, and the four points to every pound the card offers is an inflation on rivals' schemes. Experience shows that points add up quickly and can give a tangible gift. Therefore, customers see Boots as offering value with its loyalty card and they appear to like using it as a chance to give themselves a treat, such as a lipstick or fragrance.

Question

Given the loyalty cards from most of the major supermarkets, why is it that they still do not appear to generate significant loyalty and price cutting is still so rife in the sector?

Equally, loyalty schemes can be about giving customers benefits through vouchers and not cash savings.

VIGNETTE

Petrol Points

M&S is one retailer to have linked up with petrol retailer Total Fina Elf to take part in its reward scheme, which offers points for petrol that convert to vouchers for various retailers. Since Total Fina Elf wants to encourage large users of petrol to shop with it, it has also developed a loyalty scheme where points win prizes. They want to create 'points junkies', with drivers looking for their next 'fix of points' and passing over other petrol stations to shop with Total Fina Elf. This increases sales and gets people into forecourt shops.

Question

Compare and contrast this scheme with the Esso 'price watch' scheme. Which do you think encourages loyalty and sells more petrol?

17.2.3 What Retailers Get From Loyalty Cards and What Customers Want From Retailers

For retailers one of the most appealing aspects of loyalty cards is the way they can be used **to collect data**. This includes age, income and shopping habits, creating a way of tracking customers and targeting them directly. This approach is perfect for Boots, which has a customer base comprising 80 per cent women. Their customers are aware that they have the information to tailor stores in the right way to give them offers and promotions.

There is a school of thought, though, that there is no secret to customer loyalty other than offering good service. The adjacent vignette describes how Morrisons is taking this approach to good effect. Safeway is following suit with better offers and availability, more fresh food and improved customer service. Again, the strategy appears to be working and engendering loyalty in their customers.

VIGNETTE

No Frills – and No Loyalty Cards

A report last year put Bradford-based supermarket chain Morrisons top for customer loyalty. The research, by the Verdict Group and Forum Europe, said 54 per cent of shoppers were advocates of Morrisons' 'whole shopping experience'. The chain, which has 113 stores across England and Wales, believes that a traditional no-frills approach to retailing is key – and that means neither loyalty cards nor a strong Internet presence.

'Our total offer works: value for money, good old-fashioned customer service, a one-to-one personal service and exemplary standards of shopkeeping,' says a spokeswoman.

Morrisons has a 'market street', with fresh food counters and specialized staff, such as fishmongers and butchers, to advise customers on preparing meat and fish. 'Shoppers like a specialized advice area,' the spokeswoman adds. And the proof is in the statistics: last year customer numbers at Morrisons rose to 7.5 million and turnover increased by 7.6 per cent compared with 2000.

Question

Would you advise Morrisons to offer a loyalty card to reward loyalty? Give your reasons.

17.2.4 Share of Wallet

Diversifying is another method retailers are using to keep their customers coming back. Sainsbury and Tesco have moved into banking, while Safeway has teamed up with the Abbey National in some stores.

VIGNETTE

Combining Services

Boots Advantage card users are now being offered a donor card, Advantage card and credit card (in combination with online financial service provider Egg), all on one strip of plastic. Boots also gives its top three million Advantage card users a health and beauty magazine four times a year. Boots Advantage kiosk points have a touch-screen TV and voucher dispensary, offering card users competitions, product information and double points promotions. Opticians, dentists and health and beauty services ensure that the brand stretches across all areas of personal care. There is even a wellbeing centre with a gym and swimming pool in Westway Cross, Middlesex. The Advantage card penetrates all these areas, with customers able to redeem points for the health and beauty services.

Question

Discuss how you feel that the Boots loyalty card develops opportunities to increase a customer's 'share of wallet'.

Consumers are sufficiently well informed to suspect a breakdown in quality due to overzealous price cutting. They also know that price cutting can often be followed by price rises.

But, at the same time, they get 'a kick' from being rewarded for loyalty. The trick is for retailers to make shoppers trust them enough to return through incentives that do not impact on the pleasure or price of their shopping experience.

The issue of loyalty schemes will be picked up again in the companion web page, which can be found on the BH Website: www.bh.com/companions/075065449X.

17.3 Examples of Innovation in the Retail Scene

CASE STUDY 1:

Sainsbury's Loyalty Card Data Helps P-O-P Design[ii]

Two new Sainsbury stores, in Camberley and Crawley in the UK, are employing point-of-purchase (P-O-P) material designed using information gathered from the chain's Reward card data. The new insights have given them a better understanding of customer segments, which is now enabling them to flex product ranges, promotions and store layout in different areas and to improve their overall customer offer. The Sainsbury Central store in Camberley, Surrey, has proved popular among a target audience of young professionals with high disposable incomes. Its in-store design uses digital signage. The concept was to make topical offers since plasma screens don't cost that much anymore and it is easy to swap information around fast.

A 'hello' video wall at the store entrance shows videos at different times of the day. The morning loop depicts coffee, croissants and brioche, while lunchtime footage features chopped fresh vegetables steaming in a wok cooked on site by specialist Indian and Chinese chefs. The products featured on the display are restocked at set times during the day to ensure availability. Both stores are relatively small, measuring 13,000 square feet and had not been refurbished in recent years.

Three more stores were scheduled to open in 2002 using the same format.

Question

Given that some supermarkets are open 24 hours, what would be appropriate digital signage for early evening from 6 to 8 p.m. and for very early morning 4 to 6 a.m.?

CASE STUDY 2:

BP Petrol Stations Join the Information Superhighway[iii]

BP is refitting its petrol stations to offer motorists a host of new facilities, including free Internet access. BP Connect stations are being designed to provide travellers with more time-saving services. These include a facility which allows customers in a hurry to pay for petrol while at the pump, and an online service through which visitors can check the latest travel, weather and news updates from BBC News Online. The first stations to go online are at Hammersmith and Southgate in London. A roll-out to a further eighty UK sites is planned through 2002, and 300 are scheduled to open worldwide. Each refit costs £1 million.

The BP Connect stations are open 24 hours a day and each will have two e-kiosks. One offers free use of BBC News Online or the option to pay and surf the Net. The other is dedicated to buying products online.

AA 'Roadwatch' is providing online traffic updates. Since the situation on UK roads is getting worse with the rise in traffic volume because of problems with the trains and unusually wet weather conditions, any means to give motorists more information and arm them with alternative routes is likely to be welcomed.

Question

What Internet sites could benefit from advertising at the workstations in the BP Connect stations?

CASE STUDY 3:

UK Retail Chains Brew-Up Big Business for Coffee Nation[iv]

Drinks machine firm Coffee Nation is planning to install up to 1000 self-serve coffee machines over the next few years at outlets including Focus/Do It All, Texaco petrol stations, Welcome Break service stations and Megabowl bowling alleys. Focus/Do It All and Megabowl are currently testing the machines, and Coffee Nation is talking to several other large retailers. Texaco plan to roll-out the initiative after getting positive feedback from customers and average sales of 600 cups a day.

The outlets pay nothing for the machines but must carry out simple maintenance. A minimum level of sales is agreed, with the outlet taking a share of profits above that.

Coffee Nation has worked to develop the new self-serve machines, designed to deliver espresso-based coffee from fresh beans and milk, in an easy-to-use format.

After testing at four sites, the design group interviewed customers at different stages of making a purchase. There were forty in use at the beginning of 2001, mainly located along major motorways in Texaco and Welcome Break service stations, and they plan to develop the 1000 machines mentioned above over the next two to three years.

Each coffee machine contains a computer to notify suppliers when stock levels are low or repairs are needed. The company is also setting up a helpline for users. Current machines produce a ticket and customers pay at the till. New machines will be coin operated.

Question

How do you feel coffee outlets like 'Pret', Starbucks, or 'Costa' might respond to this initiative from Coffee Nation?

17.4 Successful Retailers are Like Dogs

The above statement comes from the tendency of successful retailers to hunt in packs and bark loud!

The Huskies who survive are the ones who cluster into a furry wad to share body heat when the temperature drops to 40 below zero. The most successful retailers are the ones who cluster their stores by market to share management, distribution and advertising costs.

McDonald's, Wendy's and Burger King use this strategy. It is also the favourite of video and music stores. Smaller retailers start with a couple of outlets. Sales peak in the first year but seldom increase, because one or two stores in a major market simply cannot spend enough to get an adequate share of the retail consumer's ear. Customer counts cannot be increased. Average store sales never achieve a respectable fraction of sales per store in clustered markets.

A fundamental of retailing is the ability to spend enough on the brand to be able to buy an adequate share of the retail category's 'promotional voice' to the consumers in the market. This is because 'share of voice' has always led proportionately to share of consumer awareness, which leads directly to market share.

Many brands that are successful in some markets with ten, fifteen or twenty-five stores still try to move into new markets with one or two. They seldom succeed. McDonald's spends millions of pounds locally on advertising, not including the millions more spent on TV ads that penetrate a region. A brand with a handful of local burger shops is in deep trouble competing with this level of spending.

If McDonald's opens one new store in a given region this year, that one new hamburger stand will open on day one with the benefit of millions of pounds worth of advertising. In addition, that store will benefit from the best possible purchasing agreements with vendors, employee training, management supervision, commercial property research, lowest sign costs, legal help etc.

The UK is one of the more successful franchise markets for Blockbuster Video stores because the local franchisee built up the market early with adequate stores to promote. As a result, a lot of smaller video rental stores have been forced to close. And make no mistake, in the case of the McDonald's, Blockbusters and others, they don't want to compete with their competition. They want their competition out of business. Yet many major areas have only one or two Blockbusters, and their owners make no money on substantial investments.

Retail chains succeed best and continue to expand existing markets where the economies of shared advertising, distribution and management are greatest.

Yet owning the territory with a massive presence isn't just a retail rule. It applies to packaged product brands as well. In 1995 Anheuser-Busch introduced Busch Bavarian Beer in the US. It was one of the first brands in America whose geographic distribution selection was based on television markets not state lines. This meant that every market that had Busch on the shelves had a Busch promotion, and so not one Busch promotional dollar fell on one ear without a Busch Beer available nearby.

Put this way, it is all very fundamental – clustering is essential. And then, like the Eskimo sled dogs, you need to put out some 'heat', too. In other words, investment into a market is crucial to get that share of voice!

17.5 The Role of In-store Advertising

To see chocolate brands launching ice-cream products is nothing new and the concept of a ketchup brand appearing on a packet of crisps has been covered, too. Now Tango, known for its fizzy drinks and wacky advertising, is moving into food products.[v] The product, the latest in a long-term trend of brand diversification across many industry sectors, is to be sold in mainstream grocery outlets and convenience stores.

One of the things this will mean is innovative in-store advertising. Tango is a brand that appeals to the young, and as such its new product has to compete with all manner of confectionery, soft drinks and mobile phone cards to succeed. With such impulse-driven purchases the store itself becomes the automatic choice of marketing communications focus, especially for a new launch. A brand built up on advertising that created playground cults can afford to be nothing less than innovative when it chooses to expand.

How far a brand can be stretched is a point that will always generate discussion, with one example always raised eventually. Virgin Megastores are destination outlets for music lovers. But will the same shoppers later be interested in buying their wedding dress from Virgin Bride? And flying to their honeymoon on Virgin Airlines, while drinking Virgin Cola? Will they then turn to Richard Branson for their pensions? Quite possibly, it seems. (See the Virgin Direct case study on the companion web page: www.bh.com/companions/075065449X.

So, how far can the Tango brand stretch? Its move into the wider world of non-drink FMCG products will no doubt be carefully planned. It has dipped its toe in brand extensions before, by launching a still version of its drinks. This resulted in a relatively short-lived product that could be seen as a cautionary tale. The cheeky Tango brand has the potential to really shine in-store given the right treatment – and the potential to earn scorn from fickle young consumers if it gets things wrong.

17.6 Information Technology in Retailing

Computing in retailing has developed significantly in the last ten years to a point that some would consider being overkill.

17.6.1 Warehouse Withdrawal Data

For years, account managers used warehouse withdrawal data to show:

- Where they were missing out and where the supermarket had been missing out.

- That home brands are overexposed and performing badly.
- How good one supplier is and how poor another is.
- Why one product should be taken off the shelf and another placed on the shelf.

The masses of data were used as a very powerful weapon in the hands of individuals who extracted information from it, analysed it and presented it as part of a sales argument.

However, warehouse withdrawals were just a start. They only told you what had been taken out of the central warehouse and there was a time lag between the warehouse and the store. Therefore, the specific effects of promotions and price cuts were harder to assess and the results were generalized across a number of stores with possibly quite different demographics.

17.6.2 Electronic Point of Sale

Bar coding and scanning was the next breakthrough. It allowed, in principle, the identification of sales and changes on a store by store basis, over periods as short as a few hours. Electronic point of sale (EPOS) measured exactly how much of which product in a given time was sold, because it measured what went through the till.

In principle this allowed the identification of which products sold better in which stores and the effects of:

- Promotions.
- Point-of-sale merchandizing.
- Different pricing.
- Changing an item's position on the shelf.
- Increasing or decreasing facings on the shelf.
- Company block versus product block.

The answers to many merchandizing questions were finally within everyone's grasp. Each store could stock the products which really worked for that particular store, rather than having a fixed 'planogram' for every store.

Specific shelf-management software programs encouraged this. Using such software, a shelf layout can be changed without having to see what fits and what does not. By making certain assumptions about the effect on sales by making shelf changes, you can enter margins and calculate expected changes in contribution to profit for different shelf layouts. Sadly, the assumptions were just that – untested ideas about how the customers would actually behave in store.

17.6.3 Scan Data

With scan data it became possible to carry out a few experiments to test whether assumptions made concerning merchandizing were, in fact, correct. **Direct product profitability** (DPP) was a further refinement. Product performance on the basis of only gross margin 'on the shelf' gave a biased view as it did not take account of profit allocations elsewhere in the supply chain (see Section 13.8). In the past there had been plenty of other costs that had been lumped together as overheads because they could not be separated and allocated. These included the costs of receiving goods, transporting them round the central warehouse, taking them out of the warehouse, delivering them to the store, putting them in the stock area, keeping them there, putting them on the shelf and, finally, packing them in a plastic bag at the checkout.

If you consider two products with the same margin, for example a two-litre soft drink and a toothbrush, it is clear that the costs of performing the above activities must be much higher for the two-litre bottle than the toothbrush, because of its weight and size.

Direct product profitability provides a method for measuring the costs associated with the above activities, so that they can be attributed directly to the product rather than just lumped together as overheads.

There is a prescribed method developed by the FMC (Food Marketing Corporation) in the USA for measuring the direct product costs. While it is a costly and lengthy procedure, it should allow retailers to have a much better idea where and how they make their profit. Unfortunately, the cost of developing a meaningful 'planogram' of each store negated the advantage offered by the calculation of DPP, particularly as there has been a trend towards more centralization rather than less, no doubt driven by the need to drive operating costs down.

Scan data, when linked to loyalty schemes, do give the retailer significant leverage through being able to track each individual's shopping habits, products bought, frequency of visit, transaction value etc. Unfortunately, as is so often the case with these things, more and more data do not always improve management decision-making!

In January 2002 it was announced that pub-style **'happy hour' price cuts** were being planned in leading supermarkets including Tesco and Sainsbury. This is made possible by new **electronic shelf-pricing** that allows store chiefs to reduce grocery prices at quieter times of the day. The electronic pricing can be programmed to progressively reduce prices of perishable food items such as dairy foods, bread and fruit. The system involves an electronic display on shelves that can show an item's full price, its cost per weight and the 'happy hour' price. It uses a radio transmission system to inform store managers of items that are selling well and those that are nearing their sell-by date. It can be 'interactive' with shoppers, displaying nutritional information such as salt content, calories or allergy details.

While this system has been available for several years, and is widespread in France, Germany, Holland and America, it is only now beginning to be taken seriously in the UK as techniques have improved and costs have come down.

It is expected that some consumer groups may be against variable pricing as it could lead to confusion among shoppers and make price comparisons between shops difficult. Nonetheless, it appears to be something that competitive pressure from retailers will force into stores. The appearance of the stores is unlikely to change beyond changes to shelf design and the way that products are merchandized at different times of the day.

Summary

- There is a wide variety of customer-facing approaches in the retail scene, each available to suit different customer choices and distribution aims.
- Loyalty cards have proven very useful for some retailers yet others have withdrawn them in favour of price promotions.

- Innovations in the retail sector have been many and varied.
- Successful retailers are like dogs – they hunt in packs and bark loudly!
- In-store advertising at the point of purchase is considered to be the key to success for many new products.
- New technologies at the point of purchase have led to some significant changes of late, and new innovations are just around the corner.

References

i Reported in *Retail Marketing*, January 2002.
ii Reported in *In-Store Marketing*, News section, January 2002.
iii Reported in *In-Store Marketing*, News section, March 2001.
iv Reported in *In-Store Marketing*, News section, June 2001.
v Reported in *In-Store Marketing*, News section, January 2002.

Further Reading

Friedman, Lawrence and Furey, Tim. *The Channel Advantage* (Butterworth-Heinemann, 1999). Deals systematically with how to develop high-performance 'go-to-market' systems. Shows how different channels can be utilized and integrated.

Friedman, Lawrence. *Go to Market Strategy* (Butterworth Heinemann, 2002). A useful text to review the use of new technologies and new channels, involving all the available routes to market.

Questions

1. Consider the range of types of retail approaches and explain which you feel would be most appropriate for:
   (a) Spare parts for World Superbike motorcycles.
   (b) Paper clips.
   (c) A range of soft furnishings for boats and caravans.
   (d) Canadian muffins.
2. Developing loyalty is becoming important for many retailers. Outline how you feel the following oraganizations might improve their customer loyalty:
   (a) Solicitor firms.
   (b) Railways.
   (c) The Blood Transfusion Service.
   (d) The British Legion.

3. Chocolate bars to ice-cream, soft drinks to foods, and the Virgin brand were examples of brand diversification and proliferation. Discuss other popular brands where such diversification and proliferation might prove to be profitable, justifying your examples.

4. Electronic point of sale (EPOS) has advanced in recent years to the point where supermarkets are planning to reduce the price of certain foods as their 'best before dates' shorten. Discuss how you feel that the elderly on finite weekly budgets will receive this and describe what supermarkets can do to simplify things for this group of customers.

Chapter 18

Customer relationship marketing

Introduction

By the end of this chapter you will:

- Have an understanding of the importance of maintaining good relationships with customers.
- Know how customer relationship management (CRM) has developed to date.
- Recognize the importance, and limitations, of the call centre within CRM.

'True leaders will be those that don't just optimize within an industry, but that actually reshape and redefine their industry.'

Michael Porter. *Rethinking The Future*[i]

18.1 What is Customer Relationship Management?

Companies that are thinking about implementing CRM need to be aware that it is a business process enabled by technology, not a technology itself. It can be easy to believe, when talking to companies that sell information technology, that IT can solve all of the customer relationship problems a business has. However, without clear, measurable goals and a detailed understanding of how every customer will be treated, any CRM project will fail – and fail expensively.

The most critical part of CRM is the integration of business processes and the technologies that support them. The ultimate aim should be to provide a single view of the individual customer across the organization, and to provide that view to anyone who needs it. Customers are becoming more demanding, competition is growing, and the number of ways that customers will want to interact – the customer channels – will continue to multiply. The ability to service an individual customer cost-effectively, with quality and consistency – no matter what the channel – will be one of the key success factors for any business.

One definition of customer relationship management is as follows: 'CRM is a collection of technology-enabled business processes aimed at winning, knowing and keeping profitable customers.' Compare this definition to that of marketing given in Chapter 1 and you will see some similarities. Moreover, as we saw in Chapter 8, where we explored direct marketing and database marketing, and the role of the 'call centre', there have been strong moves to treating customers as individuals. Today, with the ever-increasing speed of transactions and interactions, it is becoming recognized that the cost of getting a customer far outweighs the cost of retaining one. With new communications enabled by the Internet and the telephone, the ease with which organizations can build lasting relationships with customers is becoming fundamental to building a secure future for the organization.

To many, this will simply seem to be best business practice. And, at the highest level, that is exactly what it is. However, it is when we consider the 'how' rather than the 'what' of CRM that the shift in thinking becomes apparent.

Despite CRM being, of necessity, an enterprise-wide issue, we will now turn to explore exactly how the call centre will be affected by the overall move towards customer relationship management.

18.2 Call Centre Management[ii]

18.2.1 In the Beginning

It was the turn of the century and the dawn of a new age in communication. The telephone had been invented a few decades earlier, in 1876, and the telephone service was growing rapidly. The public was beginning to depend on, and even expect, reliable service.

As the subscriber base grew, telephone companies were having to deal with new resource planning problems. Automated central offices hadn't been invented yet, so human operators were required to establish connections for callers. One big question was how many telephone operators were necessary? Too few and service would be unacceptable to callers. But too many would be inefficient for telephone companies and would drive up costs for subscribers. Further complicating the issue was the fact that calls arrived randomly, driven by the myriad of motivations callers had for placing their calls.

In the years that followed, many bright people would grapple with these resource management challenges. One of the first was A. K. Erlang, an engineer with the Copenhagen Telephone Company who, in 1917, developed the queuing formula Erlang C. The formula is still widely used today in incoming call centres for calculating staffing requirements. Others who followed Erlang focused on developing disciplined forecasting techniques, scheduling methodologies and system reporting parameters. The advances continued.

Things have come a long way since the early 1900s. Today, there is no need for operators to connect calls since the process has been automated. But if you manage a modern call centre, there is at least a ring of familiarity to the challenges the early telephone pioneer faced. Forecasting calls accurately, staffing appropriately and getting the right people and other resources in the right places at the right times continue to be key objectives.

18.2.2 A Definition for Incoming Call Centre Management

The Incoming Calls Management Institute has developed a working definition of incoming call centre management that, over recent years, has been published numerous times. It is as follows: *Incoming call centre management is the art of having the right number of skilled people and supporting resources in place at the right times to handle an accurately forecasted workload, at service level and with quality.*

This definition can be boiled down to two major objectives: 1, to get the right resources in the right places at the right times; and 2, to do the right things. Or, more succinctly, to provide service level with quality.

The ability for call centres to accomplish these objectives didn't happen overnight. The call centre industry has evolved through three major stages:

1. **'Seat of the pants' management** – very little consideration of service level in planning.
2. **Service level awareness** – an effort to maintain service level as calls arrive, but only a vague correlation to service level in planning.
3. **Correlating service level to the organization's mission** – choose an appropriate service level and tie resources to achieving it.

Many individual organizations have evolved through the same general stages, and most have now linked service level to quality and their overall mission. But to do so, a systematic planning and management process is required, which can be summarized in nine steps:

1. **Choose a service level objective.** Service level, which takes the form of 'X per cent of calls answered in Y seconds', should be understood, taken seriously and adequately funded. It should be appropriate for the services being provided and the expectations of the callers using those services.
2. **Collect data.** The ACD and computer systems are important sources of planning data, telling you how many calls you're getting, how long they last, what the patterns are, and how the call mix is changing. But you also need information on what marketing and other departments are doing, changes in legislation, competitor activities, and changes in customer needs and perceptions.
3. **Forecast call load.** Call load includes three components: average talk time, average after-call work (wrap-up) and volume. A good forecast predicts all three components accurately for future time periods, usually down to the half-hour. But forecasting in today's call centre must go beyond incoming calls. It must also reflect the other choices that customers have for interacting with the organization, such as e-mail, faxes, video transactions and Web-integrated transactions.

4. **Calculate base staff.** Most call centre managers use Erlang C to calculate staffing requirements. Erlang C is the formula used in virtually all workforce management software systems. But new capabilities, such as skill-based routing and complex network environments, are presenting new challenges. And computer simulation programs are holding promise for providing answers.
5. **Calculate trunks (and related system resources).** Staffing and trunking issues are inextricably associated and must be calculated together.
6. **Calculate rostered staff factor.** Rostered staff factor, also referred to as shrink factor or shrinkage, adds realism to staffing requirements by accounting for breaks, absenteeism, training and non-phone work.
7. **Organize schedules.** Schedules are essentially forecasts of who needs to be where and when. They should lead to getting the right people in the right places at the right times.
8. **Calculate costs.** This step projects costs for the resources required to meet service and quality objectives.
9. **Repeat for a higher and a lower level of service.** Preparing three budgets around three different service levels provides an understanding of cost trade-offs, which is invaluable in budgeting decisions.

The best-managed call centres do a good job of resource planning and management. They have a process that is systematic, collaborative and accurate. But the call centre world is changing ...

18.2.3 New Opportunities, New Challenges

Today, we are creating enormous opportunities for interacting with customers. New services built around the World Wide Web, video capabilities and other multimedia technologies are notable examples. Many call centre managers are justifiably wondering where the changes are taking them.

In fact, the term 'incoming call centre' is being doggedly challenged by many, just as it is becoming a household term. What is it? A centre that handles calls? Hardly. *Calls* are just one type of transaction. Further, the word *centre* doesn't accurately depict the many multi-site environments, nor the growing number of organizations that have tele-working programmes. 'Call centre' has evolved into an umbrella term that can refer to reservations centres, help desks, information lines or customer service centres, regardless of how they are organized or what types of transactions they handle.

So, what about call centre planning and management? Have the rules changed? Should the planning process change?

One perspective is ... yes and no. Consider integrated Web services. Assume that customers and potential customers browsing a website can click a button, be connected to the call centre and receive immediate live assistance. To plan for and manage this environment, first choose an appropriate service level for these transactions (Step 1). Then establish processes for collecting data related to these transactions (Step 2). Next, forecast the load (Step 3), and calculate on-phone staff and system resources required (Steps 4 and 5). After that, utilize rostered staff factor to add realism to scheduling requirements (Step 6), and organize schedules for the agents who will handle these transactions (Step 7). Finally, analyse costs and compare them to other service levels (Steps 8 and 9).

How about video calls? Again, begin by choosing an appropriate service level objective. Then collect data, forecast the video call load, calculate the base level of agents required, plan for system resources etc. The objectives would be to get the right number of video-equipped agents and necessary technology resources in the right places at the right times, doing the right things. The fundamental resource planning challenge faced by young telephone companies almost a century ago continues to be important: get the right people and supporting resources in the right places at the right times. This will be true into the foreseeable future.

So, how will call centre management be different than in the past? Perhaps most notably, there will be more types of transactions to manage and those transactions will be increasingly complex, as technology automates simple and routine tasks, leaving reps to manage interactions that require the human touch. Customer expectations will continue to climb, and callers will be unforgiving of organizations that do not provide the choices and services they demand. Reps will need good writing and customer service skills, just as they did before call centres arrived, and finding the right mix of technology and human capital will be an ongoing effort.

Widely published business consultant Charles Handy says, *'The past is important. We need a sense of history.'* But he also warns, *'You can't walk into the future looking over your shoulder. You can't stumble backwards into the future.'*[iii] We are at an interesting point in call centre history. We can learn from the past, but we are at the begining of a new era and have the chance to shape it. As we saw from the quote at the beginning of this chapter, leaders will reshape their industry rather than just optimize their position in it. The stakes are high. The challenges are real. And the opportunities are invigorating. Call it 'call centre management on fast forward'.

18.2.4 From the Back Room to the Boardroom

Recent studies are clear. In many sectors of the economy, call centres have become a major factor in customer retention, competitiveness and agility to adapt to changing markets. Senior executives are increasingly aware of that and are supporting initiatives to attract the best people possible to their call centres. As call centres play an ever-increasing role in regional, national and international economies, governments are rolling out the red carpet to attract new call centre businesses and capable people to run them.

The call centre management profession – once in the category of 'mystical arts' or a back room function – is at long last getting the attention it deserves. An important step to meeting the challenges ahead is to recognize that it is a legitimate, bona fide profession. That means staying in tune with the growing body of industry knowledge. It means continual personal growth and development. It means keeping abreast of evolving technologies and developing a network of other professionals and resources you can count on. In short, it means that you have to pay the price in time and effort.

Some call centre managers view the future with apprehension. They are concerned about the impact and uncertainties new technologies will bring, the ever-smarter competition and the increasingly diverse transactions their call centre will have to handle. They wonder how they are going to compete in an environment that is on fast forward. While there will be changes and challenges ahead, the very things that are bringing uncertainties are also bringing opportunities. Therefore, organizations need incoming call centre professionals who can help them sort through the changes and make the transition into the next era.

In short, the opportunities are immense. Some would say what a great time to be involved with incoming call centres.

18.3 How Will CRM Affect the Call Centre?

Customer relationship management (CRM) has come from nowhere to be the 'hot new thing' in business theory. But what of the business practice?

18.3.1 The Role of the Call Centre

As we saw earlier in Chapter 11, call centres were about providing customer contact points as efficiently as possible and at least cost. Although cost is still an issue (especially in service-only call centres), the situation today is far removed from this picture of a low-cost, 'pack 'em in' philosophy. More and more companies have established call centres and therefore the competitive advantage they provided, derived from their status as a cheap method of customer interaction, was eroded. At the same time, companies increasingly began to understand the potential for call centres to provide both quality service and valuable information (both for themselves and their customers). These changes have led to, and will continue to cause, a sea change in the way call centres are operated.

18.3.2 The Importance of Good Customer Relationships

By organizing all available information on customers in such a way that it can be presented coherently, in a timely fashion, and by leveraging the myriad of opportunities provided by customer contact, growth-oriented businesses are investing to increase the real value provided by the call centre. In addition, companies are realizing the importance of good customer relationships, in terms of increasing customer retention, increasing customer value and attracting new customers. The quality of customer service therefore becomes paramount, as it has a strong impact on the bottom line.

The focus of the call centre is shifting from cost reduction to profit maximization through improved service and increased availability and use of information. This is illustrated by the pressures perceived by call centre managers. In a recent Datamonitor survey of 300 European call centre managers,[iv] options such as 'increasing customer satisfaction and loyalty' were rated the highest, far above the more traditional view of decreasing costs. This drive towards adding to the company's bottom line is paramount: over half of the respondents from financial services, telecoms and retail industries saw themselves as profit/revenue generators. These business sectors also tend to be the leaders in customer relationship management: coincidence?

So what does this mean for the call centre? The key aspect of CRM, which will really affect the call centre, is the increase in customer contact channels that must be serviced to the same high quality as the call centre. Of the new channels – live Internet, mobile phone, interactive TV, e-mail, kiosk – the most important in the short term is e-mail.

18.3.3 Dealing with E-mail and Other Internet Contact

The general increase in e-mail availability and Internet access has important repercussions for the call centre. In fact, the integration of these channels with more traditional telephone interactions causes the call centre to become a multimedia environment, which could be more accurately described as a contact centre.

Already, 94 per cent of survey respondents' companies have a website, and 69 per cent of those without said that they would have one by the end of 2001. And although the telephone will remain the most important contact method, the proportion of contacts received by e-mail is predicted to increase by 15 percentage points by 2003 (see below), far outpacing the website call-me button, fax and letters.

The primary driver for this increased 'web-enablement' comes from customer requirements, rather than cost issues (reduction of marketing, phone and agent costs all scored averages considerably less than demand from customers). Such a customer focus is true evidence that CRM is affecting the attitude of those who decide what the call centre is there for. The advance of the Internet is good news for call centres, since web-enablement is seen to decrease costs as well as increasing service levels in well over half of cases. E-mail volumes in real terms will grow by well over 1000 per cent in the typical call centre by 2003. In many cases, some form of e-mail management software will be required within the next twelve to eighteen months, and agents will need to be trained to handle high e-mail volumes as well as telephone calls. Early anecdotal indications show that multimedia blending (e-mail, Internet contact and telephone) increases agent job satisfaction without necessarily increasing salaries. It can also be used as part of a career progression.

It is also true that the way in which success in the contact centre is measured will have to be changed. Even among the early adopters of multimedia contact, e-mail response **service level agreements** (SLAs) are in place in only around half of operations. Every call centre worth the name has tightly defined and measured telephony SLAs and expect to see this with e-mail before long.

Quite apart from e-mail, contact centres can expect to be deluged by other Internet contacts. With almost $1.5 billion lost in Europe in 2000 through lack of online customer service (and this is set to rise to $60 billion by 2004 if things continue as they are), the ability for companies to service their customers and prospects in a satisfactory way across any or all channels should be the paramount concern for anyone managing a customer contact centre.

The Internet has lit a fire under shoddy customer service: it has never been so easy for a prospect to find a company to do business with and, conversely, it has never been so easy to go elsewhere. In addition to e-mail, companies can expect to be dealing with text chat (an online text conversation), web page collaboration (helping a customer around a website, or filling in a form with them), providing online self-service, and answering website-initiated requests for call-back (via a Web 'call-me' button).

18.3.4 Supporting the Front Office

Most of the discussion on how CRM will affect the call centre is necessarily focused on the front office, and how the customers interact with the contact centre. However, in order for agents to cross-sell, up-sell and be provided with the superior level of accurate customer information that they need, there must also be a supporting architecture.

Whilst much of the change in the middle and back office is of less immediate relevance to the call centre, there are business processes that will be initiated in the depths of the company which will only generate true value in the hands of the agent. Apart from the actual customer interaction aspect, the other key technological areas of CRM are:

- **Analytical CRM**: Through the use of data warehouses and analytical tools, this will collate, analyse and provide customer profiling and predictions to be used in marketing campaigns and live customer–agent interactions (e.g. 'this type of customer has a good chance of buying product X at this point in the conversation').
- **Integrated channel management**: The key to CRM – the right information to the right channel at the right time; providing the customer with the same high-quality service while maintaining information in the enterprise which is up to date and accurate.

18.3.5 What Happens Next?

Most true CRM implementations cost in excess of £3 million, require multiple solution providers and a very high level of visible support from senior people within the company. The call centre is, therefore, very unlikely to be the prime mover in any CRM implementation. However, the call centre and the Internet are usually the first channels to be integrated, so the call centre management team is likely to be a strong influencer in deciding which solutions to use and which business processes to change.

It is impossible to list all the major players in the CRM arena. What should be noted is that no-one can provide total CRM technology, not least because CRM comes as much from within the business – through its change in processes – as it does from without – from its change in technology.

18.4 The Customer Contact Centre: The Face of CRM[v]

'The reports of my death are greatly exaggerated.'

Mark Twain, cable from London to the Associated Press (1897)

Twain's famous response to his premature obituary is an appropriate starting point to discuss the notion that the call centre is dead. His humorous response can equally be applied to recent suggestions that the call centre's time has also passed.

Leading companies have in fact experienced great success by more effectively managing their relationships with customers and implementing formal customer relationship management (CRM) solutions – and it is the call centre that has emerged as a vital element in these solutions.

By successfully implementing CRM solutions, companies like Gateway 2000 have gained a substantial share of the PC market. They have done this by customizing the PCs they build according to each customer's demands, a process that would otherwise have been impossible. Amazon.com has managed to build a loyal community of customers who regularly return to purchase books, videos and CDs, and Continental Airlines has established itself as a premier airline for business travellers, regularly winning awards for its superior customer service.

18.4.1 Building Loyal Customers Through the Telephone, E-mail and the Web

The success of CRM in these companies is due, in part, to their skilful use of the call centre – or more appropriately the **'customer contact centre'**. The customer contact centre is an effective channel of communication between customer and company. The customer contact centre is, therefore, the face of CRM. Below we look at some vital qualities of a customer contact centre.

The customer contact centre is somewhat different to the traditional call centre we are familiar with. One difference is that the customer contact centre system **can manage communications through a variety of media** – it handles customer e-mail and Web interaction as well as telephone communication. Amazon.com, for example, maintains both e-mail and telephone contact with its customers, although eBay, the leading online auctioneer, handles more than 60,000 customer e-mails per week though its customer contact system and almost no telephone calls. The point here is that, in an effective CRM solution, the customer contact system must be able to manage communication with a customer through a variety of media.

A second requirement for a successful customer contact solution is the ability to effectively integrate inbound and outbound communications – customer contact centres **need to listen and speak**. Unlike two separate call centres – one inbound and one outbound – that are isolated from each other, an effective customer contact system must be able to manage both outbound and inbound communication in an integrated fashion.

VIGNETTE

An Integrated Customer Contact System

Continental Airlines is currently implementing a customer contact system for its 'OnePass' frequent flyer programme. This system not only allows the airline to handle incoming requests from its members about their accounts and flight information quickly, but also enables the company to proactively contact members to inform them of schedule changes or additions to the airline's routes that may be of interest. This integrated customer contact system, handling both inbound and outbound communications, eliminates the problem of two separate facilities, neither of which would know what the other was doing. By using such a system, Continental Airlines is able to maximize both the value of each customer contact and the productivity of their agents.

Question

What other service providers could gain from this approach?

A third requirement for an effective customer contact centre is that it is closely integrated into the overall CRM solution – **the customer contact centre and CRM need to be connected**. As the primary point of communication between the customer and the company, the customer contact system must effectively capture all relevant information received and report it to the CRM system. For example, managers need to know which products are selling quickly – and to which customers – and which products are being passed over and why. They need to ascertain which campaigns are confusing or alienating to customers and which elicit positive responses (e.g. which products are generating the most after-sales calls, and why).

The customer contact system must also be effective at receiving and using the information derived from a comprehensive CRM solution. Outbound campaign agent scripts, for example, must incorporate the latest data from the CRM so that agents can effectively deliver the right information to the customer. The customer contact centre 'face' must be connected to the CRM system 'brain'.

MobileComm, a large North American paging service provider, gives us a useful example of this. By connecting its CRM system to the customer contact centre, MobileComm can pull data from its CRM that indicate that a customer has recently signed up for the service, but not yet used it. With these data, the customer contact centre can provide a script to an agent, instructing the agent to ask the customer if he has experienced any problems with the service – or the agent can offer the customer additional training on how to use it. Alternatively, if the data within the CRM show the customer to be a regular user of the service, the customer contact centre can provide another script instructing the agent to ask if the customer would like to purchase a second battery or perhaps upgrade to a higher usage plan.

18.4.2 From Call Centre to Customer Contact Centre: Keys to Success

The message here is that the call centre is far from dead. It has instead evolved into a customer contact centre. This new customer contact system must provide certain key elements in order to be successful:

1. It must handle e-mail and web communications as well as telephone calls.
2. It must provide integrated inbound, outbound and blended capabilities.
3. It must be integrated effectively into the overall CRM system.

Customer contact systems such as Ensemble from Davox deliver just these capabilities, and forward-thinking customers like Continental are implementing them with great success. This more powerful customer contact system is, in fact, a vital element of CRM. It is the face of CRM – the primary means by which companies communicate with their customers.

Summary

- Customer relationship marketing is a collection of technology-enabled business processes aimed at winning, knowing and keeping profitable customers.

- Incoming call centre management is the art of having the right number of skilled people and supporting resources in place at the right times to handle an accurately forecasted workload, at service level and with quality.
- In customer relationship marketing it is important to correlate service levels with the organization's mission.
- By organizing all available information on customers in such a way that it can be presented coherently and in a timely fashion, and by leveraging the myriad of opportunities provided by customer contact, growth-oriented businesses are investing to increase the real value provided by the call centre.
- The customer contact centre is an effective channel of communication between customer and company. The customer contact centre is, therefore, the face of CRM.

References

i Porter, Michael E. *Rethinking the Future* (Rowan Gibson, Ed., Nicholas Brealey Publishing, 1997), p. 51.

ii This section is based on an excerpt from the book *Call Centre Management on Fast Forward: Succeeding in Today's Dynamic Inbound Environment*, by Brad Cleveland and Julia Mayben. Brad Cleveland is President of Incoming Calls Management Institute, and is a sought after speaker and consultant. Julia Mayben is a researcher and award-winning writer.

iii Handy, Charles. *Rethinking the Future* (Rowan Gibson, Ed., Nicholas Brealey Publishing, 1997), p. 32.

iv Courtesy of Steve Morrell, Global Programme Monitor, Next Generation Contact Technologies, Datamonitor plc, tel: 020 7675 7358.

v Based on information from Vic Hallows, Davox (Europe) Ltd.

Further Reading

Christopher, M., Payne, A. and Ballantyne, D. *Relationship Marketing* (Butterworth-Heinemann, 2002). A valuable text that looks at how to create long-term profitable relationships with targeted customers.

Gummesson, E. *Total Relationship Marketing* (Butterworth-Heinemann, 2nd Edition, 2002). CRM is the focus of this text, with updates for Internet, e-business and one-to-one marketing.

Payne, A., Christopher, M., Clark, M. and Peck, H. *Relationship Marketing for Competitive Advantage* (Butterworth-Heinemann, 1998). Contains a selection of contributions from experts around the world linked by editors to cover the breadth of the subject.

Questions

1. Within your own organization, evaluate the current customer relationship management systems you have. How would you improve the type of information being collected and disseminated to increase their sophistication in handling the customer relationship?

2. Consider the customer relationship management systems of the following types of organization and compare their needs:
   a) A local cinema.
   b) A Premier League rugby club.
   c) A Web-based pet superstore.
   d) A low-cost fares airline.
3. If you were asked to advise a firm on developing a customer relationship management system, what steps would you recommend and what factors should be considered?
4. Compare and contrast your experience of the customer relationship management offered by your bank or building society with that of your colleagues.

Chapter 19

The customer satisfied, today and tomorrow

Introduction

By the end of this chapter you will:

- Appreciate the impact that customer satisfaction can have on customer retention.
- Recognize that customer service goes beyond the product offer but through to the management of an ongoing relationship.
- Understand the place of loyalty cards as a way of collecting data.
- See the place that the human face has in securing customers' business.
- Explore how one might manage customer service in professional service firms.

'I'm just trying to keep my customer satisfied ...'

Paul Simon

19.1 Happy Customers = Happy Stakeholders

Whoever your organization's stakeholders are (see Section 1.4), be they staff, the public, or the City, keeping them 'happy' is fundamental to organizational success. And, quite obviously, keeping your existing 'customers' – those people whose needs, wants and desires the organization aims to fulfil – happy will help your business prosper. Thus, managing and developing your existing customer base is integral to growing your business.

Often 20 per cent of customers will deliver 80 per cent of a company's revenues. While it is acceptable to focus time and resources on these key customers, care must be taken that smaller customers are not ignored. It is five to six times more expensive to attract a new customer than it is to keep a current one, so managing a customer base means one needs to focus on customer retention as well as acquisition.

Once a customer is acquired, there is always the opportunity to sell them additional products (cross-selling), or a more expensive version of their original purchase (up-selling). Since there is already a relationship with the customer, these activities are easier and more profitable for an organization than finding and winning new customers.

In his book *Keeping Customers For Life*, Richard F. Gershon breaks down the reasons why companies lose customers:

- 68 per cent are upset with the treatment they have received.
- 14 per cent are dissatisfied with the product or service.
- 9 per cent begin doing business with the competition.
- 5 per cent seek alternatives or develop other business relationships.
- 3 per cent move away.
- 1 per cent die.

The fact that a massive 68 per cent of customers move away following disappointment in the way they have been treated is significant.

19.1.1 Customer service

Maintaining a high level of customer service goes beyond simply offering a high quality product. It also applies to the way the relationship is handled on an ongoing basis and how much value is added at each stage.

Organizations need to be:

- Credible – so that customers believe in the offering.
- Accessible – so that customers can talk to the organization.
- Reliable – so that customers know what to expect from the organization.
- Excellent – in everything the organization does.

This attitude should permeate the whole organization and be apparent in everything undertaken, from answering the phone and solving complaints to keeping clients informed about new developments. Customers also appreciate more formal service initiatives, such as:

- Rewarding frequent purchasers.
- Bringing in incentivized referral programmes.
- Distributing regular newsletters.
- Organizing customer-based events, like site visits and corporate hospitality.

To achieve consistent results, organizations need to establish and monitor all staff's standards of service. This will mean that targets for internal as well as customer-facing procedures are established. These might take the form of anything from putting a limit on the number of times the phone can ring before it's answered, to devising service level agreements specifying what a client has a right to expect. Employees need to be rewarded by offering incentives for adhering to – or surpassing – prescribed service levels.

Most importantly, organizations must never become complacent – they must always work towards continuous improvement. Customers will be impressed that the organization is striving for higher and higher standards and will want to 'stick around' to take advantage of the benefits.

19.2 The Power of the Consumer

Consumers are having a bigger say in the way markets develop so 'brand owners beware!'.

As has previously been mentioned (Section 1.4) 'consumer advocacy' is seen as an emerging social value. However, only recently in the debacle over genetically engineered foods, has its potential strength for the future been seen. If there is one overriding lesson from the GM foods story, it is that the application and implementation of new technologies needs to be properly managed and communicated to the consumer.

In 1990, there were no GM crops in commercial cultivation in the western world. The first food products started to appear in 1992. Tomato and soya-based products were launched in 1996. The area planted with GM crops jumped from two to twenty-eight million hectares worldwide. Consumer disquiet was gently simmering when Monsanto began its information campaign to explain the science behind GM foods in April of that year. The point of escalation came in 1998 and the issue was quickly picked up on a global basis. There is now renewed debate between all parties over various assessment procedures for genetically engineered foods, exacerbating consumer confusion.

There are some strong influences underlying increased consumer advocacy. We will consider some of these on the following pages.

A desire for integrity. Consumers will look more closely at companies and their brands. They will look at the integrity of production and at other elements of the value chain. The debate is less about quality but rather more about the sanctity and integrity of the processes used to get products to market. The entire supply chain will be included in this. The desire for integrity is expected to increase because of the renewed focus on environmental issues.

The collapse of trust and respect for traditional authority. Another driver shaping consumer advocacy is the collapse of consumer trust and, increasingly, a lack of trust in traditional forms of authority such as governments, many companies and other well-worn, formerly respected figures.

According to the *Economist*, European governments 'have a distressingly bad record of suppressing "inconvenient" scientific data and, when that does not work, of simply lying about food safety'. The role of authority is important as it represents a potential source of reassurance for consumers. However, consumers are becoming increasingly sceptical of information presented by figures of authority since 'experts' have a habit of presenting differing and, sometimes, opposing views. Consumers are realizing that they have the power to shape markets.

The need for transparency. The need for transparency is a natural consequence of the breakdown of trust and authority. Being genuinely transparent about new technologies and providing honest marketing messages will become increasingly important. A lack of transparency causes suspicion and confusion.

The speed of information transfer and global impact. Consumers seem to be able to communicate information faster than many companies. The sum of this communication flow is the result of them making individual choices. A message can be posted to a newsgroup in a nano-second; a consumer recommendation that used to reach a handful of friends in days now reaches millions worldwide in minutes. On Sunday evening, 14th January 2002, BBC2 aired a programme on cloning stem cells: 'How to Build a Human Being'. Within seconds of the programme announcing that it had an Internet chat room dedicated to the subject, there was a worldwide debate on the issues.

Call to action. The old debate about consumer environmental concern was that it rarely led to action. This has been finally laid to rest. Powerful lobbying groups can facilitate consumer action. In the case of genetically engineered foods, the call to action has been seen in the increased sales of organic foods. (Although this shift has also been complicated by various food scares in Europe.)

Retailers as a pressure group. Among other parties, retailers seem to have been the most vociferous and responsive to consumer advocacy, even potentially adding fuel to the flames and becoming a pressure group in their own right. This should also be seen in the context of the observation that retailers seem to have been able to hold on to their perception of trust.

Across Europe, Greenpeace has now logged twenty-five major retailers including Delhaize Le Lion, Auchan, Carrefour, Edeka, Esselunga, Migros, Asda, Iceland and Marks & Spencer who are taking/have taken action to eliminate genetically engineered products. One retailer to react was Aldi, announcing in October 1999 that it would not use genetic engineering in its own label products. Iceland in the UK has almost succeeded in hijacking a range of consumer issues by prompt action.

A number of factors need to be taken into account when looking at the potential power of consumer advocacy in the future. Companies need to examine carefully how the desire for integrity and trust, and a need for transparency could impact their brands and their products. The overall objective should be to enhance the trust construct in their brands.

There is a clear need to manage the communications process for new technologies. The expectation should be that consumers have the ability to vote with their feet. The growth in organic food has been a case in point, as a protest against genetically engineered foods. Managing communications channels is a prerequisite. Public relations should play an increased role in the mix of communications.

19.3 What Right to Customer Loyalty?

As stated in Chapter 1: 'While any organization that is legal has a right to exist, no organization has a right to the support that is required if it is to exist.' So, how are organizations earning their customers' loyalty?

We saw in Chapter 17 that loyalty cards were one of the marketing stories of the 1990s, with many retailers and other service companies developing loyalty cards as part of their marketing mix. Many firms have one and around two-thirds of adults participate in a scheme run by one of the leading retailers. However, more than 40 per cent of us have more than one card from two different competitive retailers, allowing us to shop with competing retailers knowing that we will be rewarded, regardless of how often and how much we purchase.

19.3.1 Limited Usage of Loyalty Cards

Most retailers offer vouchers, discounts or money-off coupons through their loyalty cards. Giving special discounts or vouchers certainly helps customers to stay and reap the rewards, but this does not necessarily make them loyal or, even better, an advocate of the retail chain or brand. Retailers have to develop a long-term strategy in order to gain genuine loyalty from their customers. This extends far beyond just lower prices. Discount vouchers tend to be a short-term strategy, not providing added value for the customer. The net result is that every retailer offers, more or less, the same scheme. This involves collecting data but not giving anything discernible back to the customer except money-off coupons. From the consumer perspective, would it not be easier to simply lower the prices in the store? Unless the loyalty card is able to give consumers some kind of added advantage, there is a danger that they will become increasingly cynical about the marketer's motives. This is especially true if they are giving the retailer valuable marketing data and the opportunity to contact them directly. We reviewed database marketing in Chapter 8 and 'permission marketing' in Chapter 12.

Interestingly, card operators report large numbers of unredeemed points. Customers may be collecting the points but they are not using them. Does this indicate that the level required for a reward is too high or that there is simply a lack of interest?

The main role of the loyalty cards should be to act as the basis of building a relationship with individual customers. By using the customer knowledge acquired through usage of the cards, retailers have a huge potential to focus on communicating better and learning how to add value to the individual customer relationship. This is key to moving loyalty schemes forward and exploiting the potential offered.

19.3.2 Gaining Customer Loyalty

Retailers should use the cards to understand the real reasons for the customers to be loyal. There are some basic rules to gaining loyalty:

- Provide consumers with enough knowledge about the brand.
- Understand the relationship consumers have with the brand and the promise that it offers.
- Exchange information about products and services.
- Provide a pleasurable shopping experience.
- Deliver honesty, i.e. no promise that cannot be kept.
- Respect privacy.
- Simplify matters for consumers: for example, by reducing the deluge of promotions and coupons, and reducing mail and special offers on 'anything for anybody'.
- Stock products and services that customers value the most.

Here we can see how retailers can use their customer data to ensure that only appropriate promotional material is sent to consumers. However, this is still looking from the supply perspective, possibly building a two-way flow of information, but hardly what we would call a relationship or engagement.

Through the loyalty card, retailers have access to information on individual habits and preferences. They know that some customers go shopping twice a week or more in their store but may spend not much more than £20 each time. How do you encourage them to spend more? Others shop once a month and spend an average of £250 each time. Would you like to increase their visit frequency? Others are shopping regularly in rush hours. Could the retailers offer them a discount advantage to shop at another time of the day, during a less busy period? Furthermore, it appears that retailers have tended to frequently offer added value to those who may not be their best customers, such as opening quick check-out lanes for those with small amounts of shopping. So the less profitable customers are rewarded while the ones you value most are waiting in long queues.

By analysing the database, retailers can identify shoppers who spend a lot of money on wine, for example. Value can be added through the identification of these consumers and inviting them to a wine tasting evening at the store. This not only helps to build a relationship but it also offers the opportunity for the retailer to encourage consumers to trade-up to more expensive or more profitable wines. If marketers can identify those who frequently purchase organic food, they can arrange lectures by an organic food specialist and show new products in this category. For the best customers, for example with children, surely it is possible to encourage them to use a home delivery option, without a delivery charge, or at least have bulky products delivered direct to the home.

One successful example of moving forward is Boots the Chemist with its Advantage card. Analysis of the database enabled the company to organize a special Almay beauty evening that was well attended by existing customers. Sales grew remarkably in the following weeks. There are opportunities for retailer-manufacturer partnerships here.

One problem facing retailers is the huge diversity of their customer base. It seems difficult to develop a one-to-one relationship with each of them. However, most retailers know that, for example, 25 per cent of their customers account for 75 per cent of revenue. These customers are worth special treatment or greater attention. This is where loyalty needs to be encouraged. FMCG marketers can learn from business-to-business disciplines. Genuine loyalty must be won and maintained. It is not about simply offering money off. The retailer is looking for consumers to provide data about themselves. From a customer perspective, there should be some tangible return for these data and money-off coupons do not offer this.

19.3.3 Understand the Consumer to Provide Better Service

Above all, it is important to remember that customer loyalty is not generated by loyalty cards but is a function of all aspects of a company's marketing, e.g. pricing, convenience, quality of service etc. Loyalty cards should, therefore, be viewed as part of the wider offer and not an end in themselves. Possibly, companies sometimes expect too much from loyalty cards, viewing them as essential to their business rather than one element of it. Consequently, they are not used to their best advantage and there is no tangible consumer benefit offered. Even within the company, there has to be a clear strategy about how the data collected are used before the loyalty card is launched. There is little to be gained from merely collecting and storing data. Note that Do It All dropped its scheme in March 1998 and Asda has not extended its ClubCard beyond a handful of stores.

Loyalty cards are a great marketing tool that should help marketers to learn more about and provide a better service for their customers. They have the opportunity to help generate a relationship with the consumer but, in order to achieve this, they have to understand what is required in a relationship. They should look for the tangible benefits from the customer's perspective that can only be achieved through an understanding of buying habits. More recent developments include Safeway's tiered rewards that are dependent on the value of shopping using the ABC card. This recognizes that different consumers should be rewarded in different ways according to their usage of the store. However, does it really offer the consumer anything more than a price reduction?

A different route is to combine the loyalty card with a payment card. The Easychip consortium in the Netherlands uses this approach. This ensures that loyalty points are 'earned' whenever the card is used. There is no issue of having to carry an extra card. Nevertheless, this still does not address the customer satisfaction question and will work more by default rather than providing anything extra. However, look out for the merging of payment cards and loyalty cards.

19.4 Customer Service Gets a Higher Profile[i]

The IVANS 2001 Web Site Survey of 110 property and casualty insurance companies in the US found that insurance companies are developing websites that improve customer service by providing increased functionality twenty-four hours a day, seven days a week. The survey has been conducted semi-annually since 1999 to underscore the increasing importance of the Internet to the $420 billion insurance industry.

The insurance industry is often criticized for lagging behind other financial service industries in using the Internet to sell directly to consumers, but such transactions are still incredibly complex. The industry sees the Internet as a tool for their agents and customers, not a sales vehicle.

Online insurance sales comprised less than 1 per cent of sales in the US in 2000, and by 2004 online insurance sales will make up a $10 to $15 billion market – a mere 2–5 per cent of all insurance sales, according to analysts. It appears that technology in the insurance industry is taking giant leaps in investments and sophistication, given the rise of special programming, the need to integrate legacy systems and the proliferation of customer-focused websites.

The dominant trend among insurers, the IVANS 2001 Web Site Survey found, was a rise in the variety of self-service features at insurance company websites, from agent locators to online claims reporting, making insurance a 24–7 operation for consumers.

19.4.1 The Agent-Consumer Link

Agents are playing a prominent role in insurers' Web strategies. More and more websites are steering consumers to agents through locators that list an agent closest to the consumer. Of the insurance websites recently reviewed, 71 per cent had agent locators. If a customer wants to receive a quote or purchase a policy, most websites direct them to agents. The role of the agent appears to be bigger than ever, as websites direct customers to agents to obtain more information and buy policies. The Internet, initially thought to bypass agents, has in fact enhanced their role – by steering business to them.

19.4.2 Self-service on the Internet

In addition to supporting customer-agent relations, the Internet enhances service by providing tools to facilitate meeting customers' needs. Of the websites reviewed, more than 85 per cent provided customer service information, 16 per cent allowed customers to check a payment, 16 per cent allowed policy updates and changes, and 20 per cent offered online claims reporting.

In addition, insurers are recognizing that the Internet has put consumers in command and enabled them to be more educated when making purchasing decisions. Some 64 per cent of the sites provide access to industry information such as research, and another 34 per cent include links to industry websites.

Only 18 per cent of carrier sites offer online quoting, and only 5 per cent of the websites are selling directly to the consumer.

But, at the end of the day, it is the human interface that can best serve the customer's needs. The Internet appears to be seen as an information resource that prospective customers will use in their search for knowledge – but will then contact a human for the final decision. This seems to be the case with many sectors – from the retail car market, through dealerships to financial markets.

19.5 Client Care Programmes in Business-to-Business Markets

Having happy clients seems to be a simple matter of common sense. But research in the early 1990s by Arthur Andersen showed that there is no direct relationship between customer satisfaction and profitability. Even companies with a massive management focus on customer service aren't necessarily successful at it. However, the research did show that those organizations that enjoy high customer satisfaction and strong profitability had certain common characteristics; they were doing broadly similar things whatever business sector they were active in. So, what good practice should a business demonstrate if it is to deliver high client satisfaction profitably? It would include:

- **A thorough, even intimate appreciation of each customer and its business**. What drives it; what are the service attributes it most values; what are its expectations of service providers in general and of your organization in particular?
- **A senior management focus on** and palpable commitment to raising and sustaining high levels of customer satisfaction throughout the organization.
- **Internal consensus and action** throughout the organization in support of a thorough-going customer service ethic.
- **A readiness to adapt service delivery** to the specific needs of each customer, both through 'front office' and 'back office' functions.

More detail follows on what constitutes good practice under each of these headings for professional service firms. As you read on, consider how well-placed your organization is for these attributes of good service. Some of the precepts apply to all organizations, not just know-how businesses like accountancy or law firms.

19.5.1 Understanding our Clients and their Business

Too often reality is far from good practice, with conditions such as:

- Only one partner 'owning' the key contact, and not sharing the relationship or relevant information; or perhaps no individual having responsibility for the contact.
- The relationship being transaction-driven, so the line goes dead when there's no work in view.

Most firms are organized along service or functional lines, and there is often far less cross-department communication than clients have a right to expect. Partners may take a sales (rather than a service) approach to developing client business. Planning meetings may focus on how to introduce new services or new partners rather than pooling research and discussing what the team can do to help create better business for the client.

Good practice involves:

- **Assigning responsibility for client understanding**. Someone or some defined group must be in charge of the firm's knowledge about a client, and be responsible for ensuring that it is current and relevant. The knowledge manager may be someone other than the principal client relationship manager, especially with very large clients where several professionals are involved.
- **Devolving responsibility for client service quality**. Although client care initiatives usually start at the top of a firm, successful programmes quickly become the responsibility of the divisions and departments, as partners adopt the process themselves. Sharing examples of good practice and publicly praising effective role models might encourage this.
- **Obtaining the client's perspective on what service is appropriate and what standards should apply**. Firms have developed various ways of collecting this information, but face to face is best: there is then direct contact with the client and one can explore what really matters to them. A banker growing his loan book aggressively found that his lead law firm made a huge contribution by routinely turning around documents overnight, so that he could arrange more loans and spread his risk more than he had expected. The law firm had been unaware that responsiveness was quite so critical to the client.
- **Ensuring that the client knows what service standards the firm treats as par**. For instance, one health care insurance provider sends all its clients a list of the performance standards its service teams should meet. If they fail to do so, they automatically fine themselves and send the client a cheque for compensation. It doesn't happen very often!

19.5.2 Senior Management Commitment

If managers are to create a new, overt focus throughout the firm on something that many will already treat as routine or deferrable, they must nail their colours to the mast. In some firms, service standards are among the core strategic measures of corporate direction and success, and are constantly emphasized by senior management on every internal platform.

Management must know and be known by at least all major clients. Good practice would also include:

- **Setting performance standards for the 'significant few' clients, and introducing a suitable system of measurement**. Which factors best drive success? One study showed recently that companies reporting greater satisfaction with their advisers put it down mainly to receiving more partner attention. One firm stood out as weak on partner availability and accessibility, which suggested an area where specific targets could be set and service performance improved.
- **A measurement device consisting of a checklist of key service attributes, which is scored by the client**. Which attributes pertinent to your sector are worth measuring? There is no one standard battery of characteristics for professional services, but experience and client research can suggest an appropriate set of values under headings such as: business and client understanding; service team quality; service responsiveness and delivery; deliverables; quality and value; and overall service value.
- **Not shying away from quantification**, as partners will understand the value of having a total service score, client by client, for benchmarking and measuring progress over time. However, some are suspicious of aggregated results by partner or department, thinking that these could be used as sticks to beat them with, rather than as an aid to practice management and partner development. Management must treat such anxieties sensitively and carefully.
- **Building client service standards into partner appraisal routines**, on the basis that what gets measured gets done, and what forms part of partner performance assessment gets partner attention. This is a delicate but important area.
- **Rapid and diligent management action** to follow up weak performance indicators, and to capitalize on strong performance results.

19.5.3 Internal Consensus and Action on the Service Ethic

A strong client focus needs to permeate the whole firm. It can be stillborn if, as too often happens, partners feel the issue is trivial and hardly worth serious effort. They should lead other fee-earners by example, in small detail as well as large.

Good practice will involve:

- **Fee-earners actively contributing to client service teams**, which will probably be cross-functional and which will share client understanding through their account management meetings and plans.
- **All staff feeling included in client service initiatives**. This might be achieved by training and encouraging all members of staff in client problem-solving and team working. For example, one firm's prize-winning switchboard operation earns fees in its own right by training and coaching clients' switchboard operators.

- **Senior management and department heads fostering behaviour that delivers client satisfaction throughout the organization**. For example, individual and team performance reviews incorporating client feedback; recognizing and rewarding good client service behaviour; and linking fee-earner performance measures to client satisfaction indices.

19.5.4 Adapting Service Delivery

Good practice here builds into the service process an initial discussion with the client, which pointedly draws out his expectations of the engagement, and identifies how he will value the service provider's contribution. This initial discussion simply makes clear what the client wants, something which is too often taken for granted. The engagement partner conducts this discussion face to face. Some might prefer the service parameters to remain imprecise, but it is better to have a clear benchmark if you want to aim at delivering more.

Having established an expectations/value benchmark, the engagement team must check back with the client and review their performance during and at the end of the engagement.

Other good practice would be to:

- **Establish cross-functional teams to serve specific clients**, from both front and back office. The latter, for example, might handle all the billing and receivables management for a particular group of clients, so that continuity and effective relationships are established and maintained.
- **Analyse the client's business and processes from time to time**, and review the established ways in which the firm delivers its service. The client should be involved so that he can consider the service provider as an extension of his own resource, and to this end he might be linked into a team network, for example via e-mail.
- **Consider offering an outsourced capability to the client** as a means of simplifying some of the client's processes and to strengthen the long-term business relationship. Recent examples of this include the comprehensive conveyancing service offered by a consortium of law firms to Britain's largest house agents, and BP Exploration's outsourcing of tax and accounting services to a Big 6 firm.

The acid test appears to be whether you really understand what your clients want, whether you are committed to seeing that they get it, and whether you can obtain enthusiastic acceptance of what follows from everyone within the organization. Put this way, it doesn't seem an unattainable ideal. Some firms are clearly making the effort to move in this direction.

CASE STUDY

Service Disney Style[ii] – A Case Study on Keeping Customers Satisfied

When it comes to customer service, Disney in the US is perceived to be one of the best. Organizations that are looking for ways to strengthen this aspect of their business should consider some of Disney's strategies. At Disney, the definition of quality service is 'attention to detail and exceeding guest expectations'.

One Disney saying – 'Our front line is our bottom line' – is especially applicable to companies, for it's those front-line staffers ('cast members') who are largely responsible for Disney's reputation for friendliness and attention to guests. It is calculated that cast members have around sixty chances to interact with guests during the day – chances to enhance or detract from their experience.

Similarly, at any organization, it is those employees who first interact with customers and potential customers – receptionists and front-line people – who are crucial in forming a customer's first impressions of an organization. Thus, it's important to keep that front-line service as polished as possible.

Extra Steps

At Disney, great service means that every aspect of every detail the guest comes into contact with is right. Disney insiders have a term for such attention to detail, 'bump the lamp', which refers to a scene in the movie 'Who Framed Roger Rabbit?'. In the scene, actor Bob Hoskins bumps into a lamp, which sways and casts a shadow on the cartoon character Roger Rabbit. The movie could have been done without the change of shade on the animated character. Maybe nobody in the audience would have noticed, but Disney film makers decided that it was important to take that extra step.

Taking that extra step with customers is a policy enforced by every level of cast member at Disney. Members of the janitorial staff, while working at any of the theme parks, are trained to approach visitors fumbling with maps and ask, 'How can I help you?'. Housekeepers at a Disney resort will creatively arrange any toys or stuffed animals on a guest's bed. In fact, all cast members are empowered to make on-the-spot decisions to enhance a guest's experience. Key to this empowerment is training in Disney's four basic service priorities:

- Safety
- Courtesy
- Show
- Efficiency.

Safety is the top priority, which helps clarify the decision-making process. For example, what should staffers do if an elderly man with a walking stick is preparing to enter the Haunted Mansion, which has a precariously moving walkway? While there are several options, only one possibility emerges after remembering the 'safety first' dictum. The cast member will stop the ride while a recorded announcement plays, saying, 'Ladies and gentlemen, the ghosts and goblins have taken over for a minute'. Then the guest is helped onto the walkway.

These service standards become a tool kit for every cast member, working two-fold – to empower them and to help us measure Disney's effectiveness in terms of guest satisfaction.

Companies can create their own 'tool kit' of service standards for their organization. Of course, they'll have to differ from the Disney standards; when clients deal with an organization, safety is rarely an issue (except when customers are on-site or if they use particular products). So, with safety a lower issue, what would be the most important customer service priorities? Perhaps courtesy would be number one since, while you can be the most efficient person in the world, if you come across as rude, you lose the sale.

The second most important priority for a front-line person might be the ability to listen to what people are actually saying, and not make snap judgements about what they want. Then efficiency might be the next important priority.

Remembering – and enforcing – these priorities can help people make decisions at the point of sale. If they learn that courtesy should not be sacrificed for efficiency, they'll take the extra step of being friendly instead of, perhaps, just printing receipts and moving clients out of the door with the barest minimum of personal attention.

Disney, in combining the priorities of 'show' (read: entertainment) and 'efficiency', entertains guests who are waiting in theme park queues with live performances as well as video monitors, making waiting in line another fun part of the whole experience. (Although it was the author's experience that, with two young children, queuing for several hours in a day was hardly 'fun'!)

Wait Time

Organizations, learning from this example, might determine if there's a better way to handle customers' 'wait time'. Many companies use special tapes for clients who are waiting on the phone, some with recorded announcements promoting products being pushed by the organization! Most consider a message that's more entertaining, such as a music or comedy tape with a related theme.

For clients in a shop (or other public facility) waiting to be served, organizations use a variety of initiatives from offering a coffee or engaging the waiting customer in small talk with a free staff member, to having an organization-related video to watch.

At Disney, the 'Crackerjack' customer service is also the result of hard work and lots of processes in place – delivery operating systems that support and back up the performance of cast members. After discovering that a major problem for many guests exiting the theme parks was the inability to remember where they'd parked, the company experimented with different systems and came up with one that's simple but efficient. After being asked what time they arrived at the park, puzzled guests are told the row in which their car is parked. The key to the system? Specific rows are filled up systematically at different times. Cast members in the parking area are given a list of rows, indexed according to the time when cars were parked. By using this simple system, cast members become heroes to visitors. Agents can follow this example to determine the most common problems clients have when dealing with their agency, and what systems can be instituted for the smooth handling of those problems.

What Does the Customer Really Want?

At Disney, 'a guest is always a guest, and recovery must allow them to be wrong with dignity'. For example, when guests can't find their car or have locked their keys in their car, staff react in a positive way, even though they know that whatever has happened is the guest's responsibility. They soften it by making the guest feel okay.

Disney's system even includes body language. In the 'Disney point', cast members use a full palm or two fingers to direct guests. The one-fingered point is avoided because it's rude.

Staffers are further trained to adapt their style of interaction with guests as the day progresses. Cast members are perky and upbeat in the morning, when guests are excited about their visit and have the most energy. At the end of the day, however, when guests are tired, non-essential conversation is kept to a minimum; cast members will limit their comments to 'Hope you had a good time. Monorails are there, buses are over here', since at that point all guests really want to know is, 'How do I get out of here?'.

Another key to providing customer service is being able to anticipate, articulate and then fulfil the sometimes hidden needs of guests. At Disney attractions, what they perceive people really need is to see Mickey Mouse – and escape from reality. Once Disney discovered that, they decided not to sell newspapers in their theme parks, since when people come in, they just want to be like a kid and play.

All organizations should ask customers what they really need from them: they could be surprised. When members of the health care industry surveyed their patients they discovered that patients' needs were different from what they had assumed. They thought that their patients' primary need when being admitted to a hospital was to get better or get well; but what patients said they needed was to have somebody with them to provide reassurance through their stay.

At one travel agency, they brainstormed the ways they could provide extra service that the client would not normally expect. A database was developed to keep track of clients' special occasions, such as birthdays and anniversaries. They resolved to start mailing cards on a regular basis, along with suggestions for a possible trip to celebrate the occasion. They also started keeping records of when clients' passports expire, so that they could send renewal reminders a year to nine months before, recommending that clients stop by the agency to expedite the process.

Another idea was to provide clients travelling abroad with a list of automatic teller machines (ATMs – or cash dispensers) in the destinations they would be visiting. As for the actual trip, they had a fax waiting for them when they arrived onboard their ship or at their hotel, asking them how things went and saying that, if they had a problem, they should contact the agency.

Such ideas are a good way to make a travel agency stand out from the crowd – an excellent move in an industry where consumers 'can get the product anywhere'. So, when it comes to service businesses, why would customers choose one over another? It comes down to the way they are treated.

Question

Which organizations have you had recent experience of that could gain from an understanding of the Disney experience?

Summary

- The fact that 68 per cent of customers move away from a company following disappointment in the way they have been treated is significant.
- Customer service goes beyond simply offering a high quality product. It also applies to the way the relationship is handled on an ongoing basis and how much value is added at each stage.
- Consumers are having a bigger say in the way markets develop and 'consumer advocacy' is seen as an emerging social value, with action over genetically engineered foods being an example.
- The issuing of loyalty cards is prevalent, but their use in collecting data is only of value in the long run if the customer gains from the process.
- Even with emerging technologies that speed up information sharing, it is still the human face that is pivotal in securing customers' business.
- Four key areas for successful client care in professional service firms are: (a) a thorough, even intimate appreciation of each client and its business; (b) a senior management focus and commitment to raising and sustaining high levels of client satisfaction throughout the firm; (c) internal consensus and action towards a strong client service ethic; and (d) a readiness to adapt service delivery to the specific needs of each client.
- At Disney, the definition of quality service is 'attention to detail and exceeding guest expectations'. This permeates everything they do for 'guests', recognizing that their 'front line is their bottom line'.

References

i Reported in *Business Wire*, 6th February issue, 2001, Greenwich, Connecticut.
ii Material adapted from *Business Wire*, 6th February issue, 2001, Greenwich, Connecticut.

Further Reading

Hooley, G. H., Saunders, J. and Piercy, N. *Marketing Strategy and Competitive Positioning* (Prentice Hall, 2nd Edition, 1998). Chapter 8 is a useful summary of the issues relating to alliances and relationships.

Newell, F. *Loyalty.com* (McGraw-Hill, 2000). An accessible book with US examples of the principle of loyalty.

Christopher, M., Payne, A. and Ballantyne, D. *Relationship Marketing* (Butterworth-Heinemann, 2002). A valuable text that looks at how to create long-term profitable relationships with targeted customers.

Questions

1. Excellent client service was once described as follows: 'delight your customers again and again, and if you fail, recover brilliantly.' Firstly, discuss how you feel the following organizations might delight their customers: (a) a supermarket; (b) a bank or building society; (c) an Internet bookshop. Secondly, assuming that a communication from each of them was misdirected, how do you feel they could 'recover brilliantly'?
2. A corner shop near to where you live asked you for advice on how to increase their customer loyalty now that a new superstore had opened up nearby. What would you advise them to do to retain their share of customers?
3. Discuss the variety of ways that you might evaluate customer satisfaction. Describe the possible uses you could put the information you obtained to.
4. Having read the Disney case study, what would you do to improve the way that customers are treated by your organization?

Index

Marketing titles from BH

Student List

Creating Powerful Brands (second edition), Leslie de Chernatony and Malcolm McDonald
Direct Marketing in Practice, Brian Thomas and Matthew Housden
eMarketing eXcellence, P R Smith and Dave Chaffey
Fashion Marketing, Margaret Bruce and Tony Hines
Innovation in Marketing, Peter Doyle and Susan Bridgewater
Internal Marketing, Pervaiz Ahmed and Mohammed Rafiq
International Marketing (third edition), Stanley J Paliwoda and Michael J Thomas
Integrated Marketing Communications, Tony Yeshin
Key Customers, Malcolm McDonald, Beth Rogers and Diana Woodburn
Marketing Briefs, Sally Dibb and Lyndon Simkin
Marketing in Travel and Tourism (third edition), Victor T C Middleton with Jackie R Clarke
Marketing Plans (fifth edition), Malcolm McDonald
Marketing: the One Semester Introduction, Geoff Lancaster and Paul Reynolds
Market-Led Strategic Change (third edition), Nigel Piercy
Relationship Marketing for Competitive Advantage, Adrian Payne, Martin Christopher, Moira Clark and Helen Peck
Relationship Marketing: Strategy & Implementation, Helen Peck, Adrian Payne, Martin Christopher and Moira Clark
Strategic Marketing Management (second edition), Richard M S Wilson and Colin Gilligan
Strategic Marketing: Planning and Control (second edition), Graeme Drummond and John Ensor
Successful Marketing Communications, Cathy Ace
Tales from the Market Place, Nigel Piercy
The CIM Handbook of Export Marketing, Chris Noonan
The Fundamentals of Advertising (second edition), John Wilmshurst and Adrian Mackay

Forthcoming

Marketing Logistics (second edition), Martin Christopher and Helen Peck
Marketing Research for Managers (third edition), Sunny Crouch and Matthew Housden
Marketing Strategy (third edition), Paul Fifield
New Marketing, Malcolm McDonald and Hugh Wilson
Political Marketing, Phil Harris and Dominic Wring
Relationship Marketing (second edition), Martin Christopher, Adrian Payne and David Ballantyne
The Fundamentals and Practice of Marketing (fourth edition), John Wilmshurst and Adrian Mackay
The Marketing Book (fifth edition), Michael J Baker (ed.)
Total Relationship Marketing (second edition), Evert Gummesson

Professional list

Cause Related Marketing, Sue Adkins
Creating Value, Shiv S Mathur and Alfred Kenyon
Cybermarketing (second edition), Pauline Bickerton and Matthew Bickerton
Cyberstrategy, Pauline Bickerton, Matthew Bickerton and Kate Simpson-Holley
Direct Marketing in Practice, Brian Thomas and Matthew Housden
e-Business, J A Matthewson
Effective Promotional Practice for eBusiness, Cathy Ace
Excellence in Advertising (second edition), Leslie Butterfield
Fashion Marketing, Margaret Bruce and Tony Hines
Financial Services and the Multimedia Revolution, Paul Lucas, Rachel Kinniburgh, Donna Terp
From Brand Vision to Brand Evaluation, Leslie de Chernatony
Internal Marketing, Pervaiz Ahmed and Mohammed Rafiq
Marketing Made Simple, Geoff Lancaster and Paul Reynolds
Marketing Professional Services, Michael Roe
Marketing Strategy (second edition), Paul Fifield
Market-Led Strategic Change (third edition), Nigel Piercy
The Channel Advantage, Lawrence Friedman and Tim Furey
The CIM Handbook of Export Marketing, Chris Noonan
The Committed Enterprise, Hugh Davidson
The Fundamentals of Corporate Communications, Richard Dolphin
The Marketing Plan in Colour, Malcolm McDonald and Peter Morris

Forthcoming

Essential Law for Marketers, Ardi Kolah
Go to Market Strategy, Lawrence Friedman
Marketing Logistics (second edition), Martin Christopher and Helen Peck
Marketing Research for Managers (third edition), Sunny Crouch and Matthew Housden
Marketing Strategy (third edition), Paul Fifield
New Marketing, Malcolm McDonald and Hugh Wilson
Political Marketing, Phil Harris and Dominic Wring